Frontispiece: The Corliss Engine at the Centennial Exhibition, 1876
This vast steam engine, designed without any concessions to contemporary notions of ornament and decoration, was the dominant feature of the exhibits in Machinery Hall. This picture, never before reproduced, is taken from a chromo-lithograph published in *Treasures of Art, Industry and Manufacture Represented in the American Centennial Exhibition at Philadelphia, 1876,* Buffalo, New York, 1877.

JOHN A. KOUWENHOVEN

Made in America

THE ARTS IN MODERN CIVILIZATION

INTRODUCTION BY MARK VAN DOREN

Doubleday & Company, Inc., 1948

GARDEN CITY, NEW YORK

The extracts from *The Journals of Ralph Waldo Emerson,*
edited by E. W. Emerson and W. E. Forbes,
and from *The New Epoch,* by George S. Morrison,
are reprinted by permission of Houghton Mifflin Company.

The extracts from *Nathaniel Hawthorne's English Notebooks,*
edited by Randall Stewart, are reprinted
by permission of The Modern Language Association of America.

The extract from *Perhaps Women,* by Sherwood Anderson,
is reprinted by permission of Liveright Publishing Corporation.

Made in America

Books by John A. Kouwenhoven

MADE IN AMERICA
ADVENTURES OF AMERICA, 1857–1900

For Ann and Gerrit,
Someday;
With Their Father's and Mother's
Love and High Hopes

Preface

This is a book about America. It assumes that the elements of creative vitality in American civilization matter a great deal, not only to Americans but to other peoples as well. It was written in the conviction that we cannot understand either the limitations or the achievements of that civilization if we continue to think of it solely as the product of western European culture, modified by the geography and climate of the New World.

In order to make my point effectively I have deliberately concentrated upon aspects of our cultural tradition which have been neglected in much of the best modern historical and critical writing. This has meant that I have had to rely heavily upon original research among primary sources in many different fields—each one of which is properly the domain of a specialist. The risks in such an undertaking are enormous, and I am not so sanguine as to believe that I have eluded all of them even with eight years of labor and the generous help of many friends.

The idea for the book took shape in 1939 and 1940 while I was teaching at Bennington College, and I remember with pleasure my indebtedness to certain of my colleagues on the faculty there, including Karl Polanyi, Edwin A. Park, Austen Purves, and Thomas Perry. My first attempt to outline this approach to our cultural history was the essay, "Arts in America," which in August 1941 was awarded the thousand-dollar prize offered jointly by the American Institute of Architects and the *Atlantic Monthly*.

It is impossible to name here all those who have helped me with the book since then. Bernard De Voto, Oliver E. Allen, Sherman S. Hayden, Frederick Lewis Allen, Russell Lynes, George R. Leighton, Eric Larrabee, Agnes Rogers Allen, and Lawrance Thompson all read chapters of the manuscript at one stage or another and offered suggestions which I hope I have been able to make good use of. My colleagues on the editorial staff of *Harper's Magazine* bore with me patiently for five years and at a crucial time made it possible for me to have a leave of absence in which to work intensively on the manuscript. At Columbia University Professors Ralph L. Rusk, Allan Nevins, Talbot Hamlin, and Mark Van Doren gave me encouragement and help over a period of years, at the same time warning me of many pitfalls which I may not have succeeded in avoiding. To them, and to Professor Meyer Schapiro, as well as to Walter I. Bradbury of Doubleday and Co., I am grateful for suggested changes and excisions which materially improved the text. And finally, my thanks go to Eleanor Hayden Kouwenhoven, my wife, who prefers that we simply let it go at that.

JOHN A. KOUWENHOVEN

Rupert, Vermont

Contents

Illustrations

xi

Introduction

Made in America forces attention as few books have done upon the main question which American art has long been putting to itself. What is its relation to American life? Or what ought to be its relation? The second question is not quite the same as the first, but under the illusion that it is, it has been asked with even greater anxiety, not to say vehemence. Not to say, also, conviction that the answer is easily known.

John Kouwenhoven makes it brilliantly clear to one reader that the answer is within reach. Mr. Kouwenhoven has his own answer, and everybody who is interested in American art should note it—indeed, will note it, for I cannot imagine that *Made in America* will fail to be widely discussed. But I should like to pay the book a still more serious tribute. It deserves to be deeply discussed. For its answer is of less weight at last than the care, the intelligent and responsible care, with which it frames the question. It is more important that we should think well about American life and art than that we should agree with Mr. Kouwenhoven. I often disagree with him. But never until I read his book had I seen the whole matter in the perspective it now occupies for me. This is what I call "making a contribution."

American art for Mr. Kouwenhoven is of course but a local phase of something much vaster in extent. His broadest view takes in all of Western civilization since the day when democracy and machinery got married and set up their modern house. It even foresees the universal triumph of this force, and I suppose there is no reason to doubt that even now such a triumph is taking place. The "vernacular" is on the march. Yet Mr. Kouwenhoven finds most of his instances in America, and sometimes his horizon is entirely bounded by our two oceans. That is why his book will touch us first of all. But there is no living mind to which it has not much to say, and there is no artist—painter, musician, architect, writer, sculptor, bridge builder, toolmaker, movie director, or house furnisher—to whom its author does not speak.

Europe has always been repudiating its past, but it was our distinction—if distinction—to cut ourselves off so completely from that past as not to know at last what we had repudiated. We did not criticize the immemorial ideas. We forgot them. And Mr. Kouwenhoven is happier about this than I am. His story is of how the arts in America have seldom known how to make themselves at home in an empty house. And certainly it is not often that they have had the air of being at home anywhere.

Toward the end of his book Mr. Kouwenhoven remarks that foreign movies have often been better than our own in spite of the fact that we invented the cinematic art. This might be for the simple reason that the rest of the world has not forgotten, as we have, how to feel and think tragedy and comedy. No idea, even an old one, ought to be alien to any man. Art in America seems to be stuck at some point between the past and now. Neither extreme is sacred in itself. The free artist is the one who can run the whole course, backward and forward, without stopping or stumbling.

The emphasis of Mr. Kouwenhoven is on the latter end of time. He is justified by the fact that so much American art has been old-fashioned. Not timeless, but out of date. It is true that we have not mastered our vernacular. That task remains to be done, and Mr. Kouwenhoven's book, more than any book I know, will assist the process. But what will the vernacular say when it has learned to talk? Something not too different, I suspect, from what great art has always said. Something more humane, certainly, than what America is saying for itself today.

I am not at all suggesting that Mr. Kouwenhoven has overlooked the point I made. Nor am I claiming that I have an answer which could be substituted for his. I have not even said in so many words what his answer is. The reader will find that out, and take delight in doing so. Better yet, he will thoroughly understand the problem before he is finished, either in his own terms or in those the author uses. For again it is Mr. Kouwenhoven's distinction that he has opened the question to its very heart.

MARK VAN DOREN

1

Art in America

To many Americans the arts have always seemed to have little connection with our everyday life. Architecture, painting, literature, and the other arts have been regarded as rather remote subjects, no direct concern of ours. As a people we have been proud of American civilization and of its political and social institutions, but we have been less confident about our performance in the arts. There have been many respected American architects, painters, and poets, to be sure, but their total achievement, regarded from the conventional critical and historical points of view, has appeared to be only a somewhat crude dispersal of the western European tradition. There are, for example, still relatively few institutions in our educational system where American art and literature are not regarded as mere appendages to other—and, on the whole, weightier—matters.

Most historical and critical studies of the development of the arts in America have been based on some variant of John Fiske's theory of "the transit of civilization." Culture, the theory goes, is brought here from Europe by "carriers"— artists, writers, and musicians who migrate to this country from the Old World or natives who return after studying abroad. Thus American culture is regarded as an extension of western European culture, subject only to certain influences —usually thought of as more or less regrettable—inherent in the American environment.

The principal cramping or limiting influences to which culture has been subjected in America, according to this theory, have been the lack of leisure among a people engaged in conquering the wilderness, the gross materialism fostered by the frontier and by industrial capitalism, and the reputed anti-aesthetic bias of our Puritan intellectual inheritance. What is more, all three of these influences have been pictured as interacting with one another in a diabolic circle: Puritanism encouraging (if it did not actually breed) materialism, the frontier strengthening both, and everything conspiring to make leisure impossible.

Yet if we accept the view that American art is an integral part of a western European tradition which, in spite of national variants, is essentially a unity, we inevitably encounter a problem. On the one hand we find that although all the trends and movements and fashions of European art may be traced in work done by Americans, there is nevertheless a quality in the total sum of our painting, our architecture, our music, or our literature which is distinct from the comparative unity of tradition among the arts in the various countries of Europe. As Henry James noted, without enthusiasm, in the book which sums up the impressions he received during a visit to the United States after living abroad for almost a quarter of a century, the way things were done in America was "more different from all other native ways, taking country with country, than any of these latter are different from each other."

On the other hand, however, it is frequently said that in spite of this distinctively American element the arts have been inadequately representative of our national character. In one way or another almost everyone, native or foreign, who has commented on our artistic history has borne witness to the disparity between our achievements in the arts and in the realms of politics, economics, and social organization. That is what Jay B. Hubbell meant when he said that our literature "has always been less American than our history"—an observation that might be applied with equal force to any of our fine arts. For, as Stuart Sherman once summed the matter up, the national genius has never expressed itself "as adequately, as nobly, in music, painting, and literature, as it has, on the whole, in the great political crises." And thus the theory of a transplanted culture leads us at last to the paradoxical conclusion that though art in America is American it is singularly less so than the acts and institutions which embody our history. Fruitful as the study of the interrelationship between American and European art can be, therefore, it clearly must abandon the theory that one is merely a maimed offshoot of the other. There is obviously something left out of our concept of the arts if they are unrepresentative of the civilization which produced them.

What has been left out is a tradition which was developed by people "who didn't know anything about art" but who had to deal with the materials of a new and unprecedented environment—a tradition which not only modified and obstructed the traditions carried over from western Europe but which contributed directly, as we shall see, to the evolution of new forms of artistic expression.

Men everywhere and at all times instinctively seek to

arrange the elements of their environment in patterns of sounds, shapes, colors, and ideas which are aesthetically satisfying, and it is this instinct which underlies the creation of techniques and forms in which the creative imagination of the artist finds expression. In a given culture, such as that of western Europe, certain of these techniques and forms are more relevant than others to the life of the people, and from time to time these become institutionalized as schools of painting and sculpture, orders or styles of architecture, and types of music and literature. As long, therefore, as we are discussing a single, comparatively unified culture like that of western Europe from the Middle Ages to the Industrial Revolution, it is the tradition composed of these dominant techniques and forms which we have in mind when we talk about the arts. But in another culture, in a different kind of civilization, quite different forms and techniques might be in the ascendancy, and some of the arts which were most highly developed in western Europe might be relatively unimportant. The criteria of historical and critical judgments appropriate to the products of the western European tradition would not be adequate to the understanding or appreciation of an art produced in a different tradition. The capacity to enjoy and understand the music of Beethoven or Mozart, for example, is rooted in attitudes and sensibilities which provide little or no basis for an understanding or appreciation of the music of southern Asia.

So much is pretty obvious. Yet for a hundred and fifty years the historians and critics of American culture have, in effect, been applying the established western European criteria of value to the products of a civilization which has had less and less in common with that which produced the forms and techniques from which those criteria were deduced. To the cultural achievements, and specifically to the arts, of a civilization whose dynamics originate in technology and science, they have sought to apply the standards which were appropriate to those of civilizations founded upon agriculture or handicraft commerce.

The civilization which took form in the United States during the first century after the Declaration of Independence was, more than that of any European nation, the unalloyed product of those forces which throughout the world were creating what Charles Beard calls "technological civilization": that is, a civilization founded on power-driven machinery which indefinitely multiplies the capacity for producing goods, and upheld and served by science in all its branches. At most this civilization is two hundred years old, and there has never before been any order comparable to it.

Many people, including a good many historians, like to think of the United States as having been a nation of farmers and handicrafters, relatively untouched by the so-called Industrial Revolution, during a great part of its formative period. And it is, of course, true that until about the time of the Civil War the nation's economy was predominantly based upon agriculture. But it is easy to overestimate the agrarian aspects of our early history, and it is well to be reminded that in significant respects our civilization has from the beginning been dependent upon technology.

The least mechanized of all aspects of our society—the lives of men and women on the advancing frontier—depended upon the machine-made rifles and revolvers which enabled the pioneers to kill game and outfight the Indians, upon the steamboats and railroads which opened up new country for settlement, and upon the telegraph which made rapid inter-

communication possible. It was technological civilization
which made it possible for our people to conquer the wilderness and which ultimately built all our continental diversities
into what the Civil War made clear was an indisseverable
union. And as this civilization spread westward across the
New World it was free, in a way that it could not have been
free in any European country, to develop with relatively little
interference from the habits of mind and social conventions
which had been developed in earlier civilizations, and which,
like the artistic monuments they had created, persisted in
Europe.

It is this fact which gives special significance to the
study of American arts. As this book will try to make clear,
it is not primarily because they are American that they are
worth our notice—though the author does not happen to be
one of those who think it a mark of superior intelligence to
be less interested in the work of their countrymen than in that
of their fellow human beings beyond the seas. Their importance lies in the fact that because they are American, and because America is—for a number of fortuitous reasons—the
only major world power to have taken form as a cultural unit
in the period when technological civilization was spreading
throughout the world—because of both these facts the arts in
America reveal, more clearly on the whole than the arts of any
other people, the nature and the meaning of modern civilization.

As a matter of fact, with the Declaration of Independ-
ence there had been an abrupt and rapid orientation of the
American environment away from the cultural heritage of
Europe. As democratic political ideals evolved in practice and

as technological civilization developed, the social environment became increasingly unlike that which had produced the
western European patterns. The need for appropriate new patterns became greater and greater.

Many Americans were aware of the need for new forms
—for what they called a national literature, or art, or architecture. At first they tended to think in nationalist terms for
the obvious reason that nationalism stood foremost in the consciousness of a people who had just fought a war for political
independence. The answer to our needs seemed to many to be
simply that we produce American versions of Shakespeare
and paint pictures the way the European masters did—but of
American subjects. Many of our early writers, on the other
hand, began with a youthful determination to "forget Europe
wholly," as James Russell Lowell urged in *A Fable for
Critics*, and to write of native matters only, shaping their
literature to the scale of the vast new continent, just as many
painters like Bierstadt tried to develop an appropriate American art by simply increasing the size of their canvases. But
they soon discovered that they could not forget Europe, and
most of them found that they really didn't want to. The comfortable thing to do, then, was to relax into something approximating Longfellow's ultimate assumption that since
Americans were really only "English under another sky" our
literature needn't be expected to differ much from theirs. Of
course, he added, the English stock in America was being
mixed with other nationalities, and our English thoughts and
feelings would therefore be tempered by German "tender-
ness," Spanish "passion," and French "vivacity." But he
obviously assumed that we would remain essentially English,
and that all that the writer and artist need do was carry on the

old traditions. After all, he concluded, "all literature, as well as all art, is the result of culture and intellectual refinement."

Lowell stuck with the problem more tenaciously than that. "It is all idle to say that we are Englishmen," he wrote in 1854, because "we only possess their history through our minds, and not by life-long association with a spot and an idea we call England. History without the soil it grew in is more instructive than inspiring." But in everything that concerned art it seemed to Lowell that the Europeans had us at an immense disadvantage, for they were able to absorb cultural influences through their pores, as it were, from the whole atmosphere that surrounded them, while it required "weary years" for Americans to acquire these things from books and art galleries. The only good which might come of all this, he added rather lamely, was that, having been "thrown back wholly on nature," our literature might ultimately have a fresh flavor.

The nearest Lowell ever came to an answer which would prove fruitful to other writers and to himself was in his *Bigelow Papers*. Defending his use of dialect in these humorous poems and sketches of Yankee character, he declared in the preface to the second series (1867) that the first postulate of an original literature is that a people should use their language "as if it were a living part of their growth and personality, not as the mere torpid boon of education or inheritance." And in these dialect pieces Lowell did manage to capture some of the life and vigor and originality of native speech. But his formal poetry and essays were not much affected by this excursion into the vernacular; as far as style and manner are concerned, they could as well have been written in Cambridge, England, as in Cambridge, Massachusetts, and one feels that this, after all, was really the goal which Lowell wanted to achieve after the original nationalistic fervor wore off.

The quest for a national tradition in this spurious sense ended inevitably in failure. But all during the early years of the Republic we, and our European critics as well, debated the question of American art as if the problem were one of cultural independence. We argued stoutly that we could achieve it; most of the Europeans who came over here to inspect the strange new Republic argued that we could not. Yet both, by implication at least, recognized that beneath the surface manifestations of our society there were the elements of an indigenous culture—something singularly and essentially non-European expressed in our everyday life.

Many of the hundreds of books about America which issued so profusely from the pens of European visitors during the nineteenth century penetrated the truly American character of our life with surprising keenness. But their authors frequently disliked it. It was alien to them and came as a point-blank challenge to the culture which had shaped their own lives. There were, of course, numbers of visitors who—like Harriet Martineau and Alexander Mackay—liked much of what they found here; and a good deal of debate was carried on throughout the nineteenth century between our champions and our detractors. But those who had a vested interest in the survival of the ideals and customs of the older culture were frankly apprehensive about the growing influence of American ways. Here too, however, it was in terms of politics that the conflict was expressed. Captain Marryat, the popular English novelist whose *Diary in America* created a storm of protest among the Americans when it appeared in 1839, frankly announced that it had been his object "to do injury to democracy." And Mrs. Trollope, who emigrated from England to Cincinnati, where she kept a shop in frontier days, professed that her chief purpose in writing the *Domestic Manners of the Americans* (1832) had been to encourage the English people "to hold fast by a constitution that insures all the blessings which flow from established habits and solid principles," and to save them from the tumult and degradation incident to "the wild scheme of placing all the power in the hands of the populace."

Both these writers were keen observers of men and affairs, and their books are a vivid record of what they saw and how they felt about it. They saw men living under democratic institutions without the restraints imposed by an established social order, and they detested it. What little they found to praise was mostly confined to the longer-settled regions along the Eastern seaboard, where English manners and customs had retained the greatest influence and where the American phenomena were most effectively diluted.

American people, still acutely aware of the newness of their nation, were eager to read what anyone wrote about them; hundreds of thousands of copies of books similar to Captain Marryat's and Mrs. Trollope's were sold and read in this country. Like other people, Americans don't enjoy being disliked; so the reaction to such attacks was immediate. Those whose cultural environment was least like that of Europe and who had therefore little emotional attachment to the manners and customs which the visitors were defending, turned bitterly against them, scorning their lack of understanding and their injustice, and were confirmed in distrust of the culture which such critics represented. It was this attitude, for example, which in 1835 led James Hall, the Cincinnati editor, to praise James K. Paulding on the grounds that his novels were "free from the blight of foreign influence."

Those, on the other hand, who still cherished in their homes furniture brought from the old country, whose education was patterned as closely as possible on that of their English cousins, or whose business or profession kept them in close contact with European society, tended often to react more with shame, or at worst with the anger which springs from shame. To them the long series of European attacks was a stimulus to mend their manners, to ape the ways of the older culture, and to adopt its externals so studiously that in the future they would appear less gross. Here was one of the sources of that development of conflicting traditions within American culture which this book will trace.

Both types of response to the travelers' criticisms were unfortunate. Both hastened the already widening split between two divergent streams of national life. As we look at various aspects of our civilization we shall discover, over and over again, tragic evidence of how much it cost those who turned their backs on Europe to lose fruitful contact with the essential humanity embodied in the living masterpieces of Western culture; and just as vividly we shall become conscious of the enervation and sterility which resulted from rootless imitation in this country of alien modes and surfaces. But it may also become clear that what seemed superficially to be a conflict between Europe and America was in reality quite another thing; that it was in essence only a more clear-cut and high-lighted version of a conflict which also existed within European culture itself.

It was easy, indeed almost inevitable, in nineteenth-century America to assume that art had little relation to the affairs of everyday life. Anyone familiar with American history will recall how remote Edgar Allan Poe and Henry James found themselves from the predominant concerns of their fellow Americans. But one need not assume—as some people do—that the things which interested Poe and James were of more aesthetic importance or of greater human value than those which preoccupied their countrymen. The world from which they were remote was, after all, the world of Abraham Lincoln.

Actually the chasm between art and everyday life may well prove to have been merely one manifestation of the catastrophic split which cut right through the whole of nineteenth-century society, both here and abroad. The conflict between the new science and the traditional religion produced an apparently unbridgeable gap between what man knew and what he believed. The development of industrial capitalism tended to divorce the production and distribution of goods from the political system, thus forcing men as unregulated economic beings to commit barbarous injustices which as political beings they had to cope with in terms of an inadequate traditional system. And finally, the tradition of western European art, like that of the Church, seemed to be seriously at odds with the social forces emerging chaotically from the Industrial Revolution.

So irreconcilable have art and technology seemed that many who believe in the creative discipline of form still cut themselves off deliberately from important areas of contemporary experience. One of the most influential modern critics holds that such willful isolation is imperative for the artist. Scientific knowledge, according to Mr. I. A. Richards, has made it impossible for us to believe countless poetic statements about God, the universe, and human nature. Furthermore, scientific knowledge, he maintains, is not of a kind upon which we can base an organization of the mind as "fine" (to use his own exceedingly vague term) as that which is based on prescientific thought. The solution which he offers—and which some of our most talented artists and writers have tried to accept—is that we must cut poetic and literary statements "free from belief, and yet retain them in this released state as the main instruments by which we order our attitudes to one another and to the world."[1]

For all its pseudo-scientific trappings, this is Victorian sentimentality in modern dress. So long as men persist in ordering their attitudes toward life in harmony with concepts which they merely wish were true, they will face life with emotional insecurity and dread. Only when men reckon with one another and the world in terms which take courageous account of what they *know* can they face life or death without fear.

Such wistful and perilous withdrawal from reality is evidence of a split between art and everyday life which, to many people, has seemed more complete in our generation than in any other in history. Actually that split, as has already

[1]One of the bluntest expressions of this point of view, in this instance with Marxist overtones, was contained in Kenneth Burke's demand, in *Counter-Statement* (1931), "that the aesthetic ally itself with a Program which might be defined roughly as a modernized version of the earlier bourgeois-Bohemian conflict." That program, designed to combat the "practical" values which the economic system imposes upon our society, should foster the following qualities: "inefficiency, indolence, dissipation, vacillation, mockery, distrust, 'hypochondria', nonconformity, bad sportsmanship." Mr. Burke did not defend these qualities as either admirable or "good" in themselves, but he urged adoption of the total attitude they reflect "because it could never triumph."

been suggested, and as succeeding chapters will try to make clear, is illusory. What we really have to reckon with is a conflict between two civilizations—one maturing, the other powerless to die. If in the United States for a century and a half the arts have seemed more strikingly unrepresentative of national life than in the countries of Europe, that is because here the art forms inherited from the older culture have had to cope with the new civilization in its most uninhibited aspects. What we have overlooked is the concomitant fact that in the United States—for that same reason—the new civilization has been freest to evolve its own artistic expression.

It is time we considered the frequently crude but vigorous forms in which the untutored creative instinct sought to pattern the new environment. It is in this unpretentious material that we may find the clearest expression of the vital impulses upon which the future of modern civilization depends.

2

What Is Vernacular?

The forms we have so long neglected are in reality the products of a unique kind of folk art, created under conditions which had never before existed. They represent the unself-conscious efforts of common people to create satisfying patterns out of the elements of their environment; but this patternmaking is something altogether different from the folk arts which in recent years have been collected and studied with such enthusiasm. It has nothing in common with the balladry of the Kentucky mountaineers or the decorative crafts of the Pennsylvania Dutch. Unlike these, it is the art of sovereign, even if uncultivated, people rather than of groups cut off from the main currents of contemporary life. The patterns it evolved were not those which are inspired by ancient traditions of race or class; on the contrary, they were imposed by the driving energies of an unprecedented social structure. *In their purest form these patterns comprise the folk arts of the first people in history who, disinherited of a great cultural tradition, found themselves living under democratic institutions in an expanding machine economy.*

It is this unique factor of a democratic-technological vernacular which has been overlooked in our estimates of art in the United States. The development of folk-art forms is always hard to trace. No one bothers to note the patterns of colors, shapes, sounds, and ideas which plain people produce —at least no detailed record is kept until long after the patterns have crystallized and have become habitual. It is especially difficult to trace the emergence of this vernacular, for the patterns through which it evolved were not designed to be kept in frames on the wall, or cherished behind glass doors. These patterns formed tools, machines, buildings, and other objects for use in the routine of daily life. It was into the design of useful things that these people inevitably turned the universal creative instinct. Repressed artistic impulses found release in uncounted rudimentary and personal expressions.

The purest form of this vernacular, the form in which its characteristics are most clearly revealed and can be most readily defined, is represented by technological design. Here craft tradition had least influence and the characteristic impulses of the new civilization were freest to display their energy in patterns available to all the people, cultivated and uncultivated alike.

The men and women who built a civilization in the American wilderness had to relearn a truth which many of their European contemporaries had been able to get along without: the truth of function. They had to become familiar with the nature of materials and the use of tools. The frontier country was strange indeed to those who had been accustomed to the ways of the older culture. James Hall, writing in the *Illinois Monthly Magazine* for June 1831, warned the Western emigrant that he must abandon his predilections, prejudices, and local attachments. "Instead of bringing *society* with him," Hall wrote, "he should cultivate the intimacy of the inhabitants, and by imbibing their feelings and sentiments learn to relish *their* society." And like his predilections and prejudices, his customary tools also had ultimately to be abandoned.

The United States won its independence from Britain with the aid of a tool which had been developed, though not invented, on the frontier. When Washington took command of the Continental Army at Boston he brought with him fourteen hundred frontier riflemen from western Pennsylvania. The Massachusetts troops who watched these leather-jacketed irregulars assemble on Cambridge Common jeered at the incredibly long-barreled guns which the strangers carried; there was something absurd about the length of such weapons in comparison with the stubby, smooth-bore firelock muskets which both the English and Massachusetts men were using. But Washington had been in western Pennsylvania some years before and had seen what those ungainly men could do with their ungainly weapons; and that afternoon on Cambridge Common the Massachusetts men saw too. The lanky Westerners drove seven-inch target posts into the ground and then strode off to take firing position: fifty yards, a hundred yards (at that distance a man with a smooth-bore musket could have hit such a small target only by sheer luck), a hundred and fifty yards, two hundred yards, *two hundred and fifty yards*. There they stopped, lined up in ragged order, and fired; and they hit the posts.

Here was a weapon which revolutionized fighting techniques. Men armed with these rifles didn't have to stand in line, like the British at Bunker Hill, firing volleys at short range and hoping some of the bullets hit someone. This was the Pennsylvania version of the German rifle-barreled gun, developed during the 1730s and 1740s by patient experiment among the gunsmiths around Lancaster, a hunting tool which could pick off a 'coon or a rabbit at long range in the lonely forests. And these rifles played a significant part in America's victory; for so greatly did the enemy dread their effectiveness that, as Roger Burlingame tells the story, Washington later asked other troops to wear the costume of the men who used them, even though there were nowhere near enough of the rifles to go around.

The tools whose design first showed the influence of the American environment were, as one would expect, those which were most widely used in getting food, clearing the land, and making it fertile. The men who came over from Europe brought with them axes, spades, hayforks, manure forks, and plows, and used them as long as they lasted. But when these tools wore out it was difficult to import others, and local blacksmiths hammered out new ones for their neighbors.

Changes in design under such circumstances are made only very gradually; it was quite a while before there was a noticeable difference between the tools used in America and those still used in Europe. But changes nevertheless occur, as old habits give way to new requirements. Fenimore Cooper observed in 1828 that American plows were more "graceful and convenient" and American axes more admirable "for form, for neatness, and precision of weight" than their English equivalents, and by the middle of the nineteenth century, when the Great Exhibition at the Crystal Palace in London provided the first general opportunity for comparative study of the products of all nations, differences were strikingly apparent.

Twenty-five years later the reports of European observers at the United States Centennial Exhibition, held in 1876 at Philadelphia, were filled with detailed descriptions of characteristic American designs. Among the reports of the British Commission, for example, there is a comparison of British and American tools. Commissioner David McHardy noted that the English ax was bulky, while the American was thinned considerably below the eye—a shape which "enables it to be more easily drawn out after the blow is given, and the body of the axe, being much firmer, is not liable to twist in working." Again, in his report on agricultural and laborers' tools, he expressed surprise that the great improvements which had been made in the United States had not been introduced into Europe many years before. The old-style hayfork, for example, with its iron ferrule and strong ash handle, was "a very cumbrous tool"; the manure fork, with its three prongs —usually flat and about an inch broad, but occasionally made in the more efficient V shape—was doubly so. "No accurate judgment," he wrote, "can be formed of the many advantages which have been conferred on the laborer by the introduction of the American steel spade, shovel, manure- and hay-forks." An iron spade quickly became caked with dirt, an iron fork blunted its points easily; but the surfaces of the American steel tools remained clean, and the edges and points remained sharp. Furthermore, the new tools were much lighter; the difference of weight between the old-style and the new steel spades was from three to four pounds in favor of steel.

If, then, we are to judge from McHardy's report, European tools in 1876 had not yet adopted improvements which had been made in America at least sixty or seventy years earlier. For we have record that "long before" 1814 a member of the American Institute "left off the use of common iron spades and hoes," and employed a good workman to make his spade and hoe of trowel stuff, as he called it, "so hard that no stone could injure its edge, and so thin that the spade was driven by hand instead of foot, up to the hub, polished as a razor." With such spades, he testified, he could dig more in a day than two men with iron spades, "and dance in the evening."

Not all foreign observers admired the functional simplicity of American products at the Centennial. A member of the German delegation objected, for instance, that "certain objects of daily use which ought to be richly decorated, like grandfather clocks, show the sad state of American taste by the complete absence of ornamentation." At London's Crystal Palace a similar criticism had been implied in the official commentary on the American exhibits. "The expenditure of months or years of labour upon a single article, not to increase its intrinsic value, but solely to augment its cost or its estimation as an object of *virtu,* is not common in the United States," the exhibition catalogue had announced. On the contrary, both manual and mechanical labor were applied with direct reference to increasing the quantity of those articles which were suited to the wants of a whole people—with the result that the products of American industry seemed to the exhibition's officials to have "a character distinct from that of other countries."

It has frequently been said that Europe surpassed the United States in the mechanical sciences during the first half of the nineteenth century, and it is undoubtedly true that both England and Germany were far ahead of us in metallurgy and in the perfection and elaborateness of their heavy machinery. But to some extent, at least, the notion of European mechanical superiority in this period derives from the fact that technological history has been written chiefly by Europeans who were unfamiliar with American developments. There is ample evidence, however, that even in the first half of the century mechanical progress in America was in a number of important respects less inhibited than that in the Old World. In the development of machine tools, for instance, and of the precision gauges and accurate jigs and fixtures which made possible the mechanical duplication of metal parts for rifles, clocks, and a hundred other objects, the gunsmiths and mechanics of New England were far in advance of the Europeans. When Samuel Colt set up a factory in England in the early 1850s to supply the foreign market with mass-produced rifles and muskets and the famous Colt revolvers which he had been making in Hartford since 1848, he reluctantly discovered that he had to import from America both the machines and the men to operate them. English machines, as he told an investigating committee of the House of Commons, were not sufficiently precise, and skilled English workmen seemed to be unable to operate the machines made in America. Recognition of the superiority of American machine tools for precision work was given by the British government itself when it established the Royal Small Arms factory at Enfield Lock in 1853. It awarded the contract for practically all of the standard and special machine tools, and for the jigs, fixtures, and gauges required to mass-produce the Enfield rifle, to the firm of Robbins & Lawrence in Windsor, Vermont.

What was lacking among the European mechanics whom Colt had been unable to employ was the intense and daring mechanical imagination which foreign commentators repeatedly remarked as a characteristic of the American workman, and which remained such a distinctive feature of our industrial system that, no matter how decisively England maintained her world leadership in the scientific development of machines, America—as the London *Times* itself observed in 1878—nevertheless developed "more that is new and practical in mechanism than all Europe combined."

The whole subject of American mechanical history— or, to be more inclusive, technological history—has been too much neglected, especially those aspects of it which reflect its relationship to cultural history as a whole. The very materials from which such a history could be written are scattered, and in many cases have been lost. The scientist or the technical expert has little interest in regional or national variants in mechanism, as such; he is concerned chiefly with the discovery of mechanical principles (which have no nationality) and their efficient application.

Yet it is evident that machinery developed very differently in different countries. In the abstract, technology may be technology wherever it exists, but in actual practice its internationalism is a myth, or at best an ideal which has never been attained. During the nineteenth century wide divergence in national and regional practice existed, and much may be learned from a consideration of those differences of which evidence still remains. As early as 1840 the English author of a *True Guide* to the United States, published in London for the benefit of British mechanics and laborers who were planning to emigrate, summed up his experience of four years' work and five thousand miles of travel in the new nation by warning that mechanics from the "Old Country" should be prepared to meet with "new and peculiar, if not improved, modes and ideas, and make up his mind also to their immediate adoption." But unfortunately the author does not discuss the "new and peculiar" modes and ideas in any detail.

There is, however, valuable evidence regarding such differences in one branch of mechanics in John Richards' *Treatise on the Construction and Operation of Woodworking Machinery*, published in London in 1872. Richards was a native of Pennsylvania who lived much of his life abroad and was known throughout the world as a designer and builder of all kinds of machinery. As head of the American firm of Richards, London, & Kelley and of the English firm of Richards and Atkinson of Manchester, and as the designer and builder of machinery for the Russian Royal Arsenal, he originated over a thousand different machines and was familiar with contemporary practice in many lands.

Much of his book is of interest only to the specialists for whom it was intended, but there are a number of passages which bear on the development of the vernacular tradition. Richards says, for example, that the distinction between English and American woodworking machinery at that time was perhaps the greatest that had "ever existed in a system of machines both directed to the same, or nearly the same, purposes." Most of the basic machines for wood conversion had been invented at the end of the eighteenth century in England by Samuel Bentham. But from then on the development took place chiefly in the United States, largely because wood was so much more widely used here, not only in building houses, bridges, and ships but even in framing steam engines and in other capacities where iron was used in Europe. In 1844 a number of American machines were imported into England, but—according to Richards—since "the ruling idea in these machines was economy in cost and rapid performance in the hands of skilled men, neither of which elements fitted them for the English market," practically no use was made by English builders of the modifications they might have suggested. It was not until after the Crystal Palace Exhibition in 1851, where the performance of the American machines was amply demonstrated, that English engineers adopted the American improvements.

Necessity, coupled with what Richards called "a strong ingenuity and boldness of plan," had led to the development in America of an entire system of machines for sawing, planing, boring, mortising, and tenoning, plus hundreds of special machines for manufacturing carriages, plows, furniture, joiner's work, bent work, and so on.

What Richards meant by ingenuity and boldness can best be understood by reference to specific machines which he describes. One of these was the reciprocating mortising machine; that is, a machine designed to drive a chisel back and forth into the wood to cut out a square hole. Reciprocating motion in a machine always involves more vibration—and consequent wear—than rotary motion, and at the high speeds required in wood machines the jarring is severe. A skilled engineer, Richards observed, who was conversant with all the principles of the operation and the difficulties to be encountered, would not be inclined to attempt construction of reciprocating mortising machines, and European builders avoided them. But in the United States, "either through an ignorance of the difficulties to be encountered, a greater boldness in such things, or the high price of labour," they were extensively made and generally used.

Another example was the "muley-saw mill," which

originated in, and was largely confined to, the Western states. This was an unprecedented device which seemed to defy all the accepted notions about reciprocating—as distinguished from circular—saws. The blades of reciprocating saws had always been operated under tension—that is, tightly stretched between upper and lower frames, which must be strong enough to stand heavy transverse and compressive strain as they moved up and down. The weight of these frames tended to limit the rate of teeth movement of the saw, thereby reducing the saw's efficiency. The muley-saw was simply an expedient to increase the cutting speed of the blade by dispensing with the heavy-tension frame and all possible weight in the reciprocating parts. The blade was left slack, merely guided—above and below the log—by light lateral supports of wood which prevented it from bending. The result was, surprisingly, that the lumber was "cut more true, as to dimensions, than that cut on mills of any other kind; just the opposite of what would be expected from the plan of operating a saw without tension."

Repeatedly through Richards' book one encounters evidence that Americans produced bold and original machines "which upon theoretical deductions would scarcely have been made." This does not, however, mean that all American machinery approached the high level of mechanical perfection which was standard in England. It did not, for a number of reasons. For one thing, European machines were less likely to be improvised than those made in the United States; they were rarely made for the personal use of the designer, or even of the buyer, but rather for a workman employed by the buyer, and this required that they be made to operate as nearly as possible without the intelligence of the workman, even if the original cost was high. In the United States, however, machines were frequently made for the designer's own use, and were usually sold, as Richards noted, *"only to those who use them and understand their use."* Most of the early American wood-working machines, for example, were designed and built by carpenters, cabinetmakers, and shipbuilders for their own use. To these men iron was a new material. They had in mind "no constants, or rules for proportions, like an engineer or machinist, but blindly supplied a shaft here, a pulley there, with bolts and framing to support them," very much as they would have made a house or a piece of furniture.

As Richards puts it, the carpenter carried out his architectural ideas in framing his woodworking machines; "the metal was disposed in scrolls and network, and all conceivable forms except those that the strains would indicate, figures of vines and shrubbery, 'pomegranates and lily-work' were raised in relief, the whole was painted in gorgeous hues, and as if to cap the climax, the rough iron surfaces were generally finished off with a coat of transparent varnish." (See Fig. 1.) In ways like this the cultivated tradition in America, acting through the agency of craft techniques, interacted with the vernacular. But the influence of the cultivated tradition was largely confined thus to surfaces; the carpenter-builders may have trimmed their woodworking machines with extravagant and uncouth decorations, but the operation of their machines was not open to such criticism. We have it on Richards' authority that nowhere in the world had machines for making doors, sash, and joiner work generally, equaled those made by these carpenter-builders. If they lacked the finish and elaborateness of European machines, that was characteristic of a tradition in which, as Richards said, "the movement and

Figure 1: Decorative Motifs in Machine Design
(*Above left*) Scroll saw; Warren Aldrich, Chicago, Illinois (from an advertisement published in 1858); (*above right*) iron planer; Putnam Machine Co., Fitchburg, Massachusetts (from an advertisement published in 1858); (*right*) scroll saw; Trump Brothers, Wilmington, Delaware, 1876 (from *Manufacturer and Builder*, May 1876); (*below*) circular saw mill; Lane and Bodley, Cincinnati, Ohio, 1872 (from Richards, *Treatise on . . . Woodworking Machines*, London, 1872)

application of the cutting edge was the prime object, everything else unimportant."

Actually, whatever was built or made in the vernacular
was likely to be marked by constraint and simplicity. There
was no room in such a tradition for diffuseness, there were no
resources to spare for the ornate, and it was merely sound
sense to design a thing as economically as one could. But in
the United States these qualities seem to have become especially characteristic. We had to have machines and tools that
would work well in a rough land, would economize labor, and
would save the owner from running to far-off shops for re-
pairs. This meant light, simple, tough tools. But as time went
on even elaborate machinery took on distinctive qualities.
W. F. Durfee, one of the judges at the Centennial, commended
the metalworking machines made by Pratt and Whitney of
Hartford, Connecticut, for "the admirable character of their
general design, which shows the result of careful study and
large experience applied to the determination of the proportion and union of parts in the several tools, with the view of
eliminating unnecessary details, thus at once cheapening their
construction and improving their qualities as working machines."

The great Corliss steam engine in the Centennial's Machinery Hall was a contemporary masterpiece of this tradition
in design. The largest and most powerful engine that had ever
been built up to that time, it was installed at the exhibition to
provide power for all the lathes, grinders, drills, weaving machines, printing presses, and other machinery displayed by
the various exhibitors. It weighed altogether 1,700,000
pounds, yet so perfectly was it made that it worked almost as
quietly and with as little vibration as a watch.

In large engines of this kind it had long been customary for the designers to strive for architectural or other ornamental effects. Important engines were usually framed with elaborate Gothic arches or Corinthian columns (see Plate I); struts and braces which by every engineering requirement should have been straight lines were often disposed in graceful curves. By contrast with such engines the Corliss design was unequivocally severe, and before the exhibition was opened to the public many commentators, including the editor of the *Scientific American,* thought that it would therefore be disappointing to the general public.

But to anyone who reads the mass of contemporary comment on the exhibition it is obvious that the commentators need not have worried. Even those who, like the correspondent of the *Manufacturer and Builder,* had at first criticized "the undoubted clumsiness of the design," grudgingly admitted after the exhibition opened that the engine looked "much better in motion than it did when standing still."

People said all the fine things that duty required about the pictures and statues in Memorial Hall, but in the presence of the Corliss engine they were exalted. It stood there at the center of the twelve-acre building, towering forty feet above its platform, not an idealization but an unmitigated fact. Yet to the thousands who saw it, it was more than merely the motive power for the miles of shafting which belted their energy to machines throughout the building. (See Frontispiece.)

Consciously or unconsciously, each visitor in his own way testified to its aesthetic impact. Sixty years later the Midwestern poet, Harriet Monroe, remembered being taken from Chicago to Philadelphia to visit the Centennial and recorded that she, at sixteen, was far more impressed by the Corliss engine "turning its great wheels massively" than by any of the art exhibitions. "Josiah Allen's wife," the perennially popular humorist-philosopher of *Samantha at the Centennial* and a dozen later "Samantha" books, had spoken for thousands of ordinary citizens when she wrote that "that great 'Careless Enjun' alone was enough to run anybody's idees up into majestic heights and run 'em round and round into lofty circles and spears of thought they hadn't never thought of runnin' into before." And the French sculptor Bartholdi said in an official report to his government that the engine had "the beauty and almost the grace of the human form." It was such engines which led a London *Times* correspondent to report that "the American mechanizes as an old Greek sculptured, as the Venetian painted." Even the Brahminic *Atlantic Monthly* concluded rhetorically that "surely here, and not in literature, science, or art, is the true evidence of man's creative power; here is Prometheus unbound."

Not often were the technological elements of our environment welded into such a vernacular masterpiece. One could scarcely expect the millennium in the turbulent life of nineteenth-century America. But it is essential to realize that in the very decades which our cultural historians have called the ugliest and bleakest in our history—the years of "chromo-civilization" and the "Gilded Age"—American people had developed skills and knowledge which enabled them to create patterns of clean, organic, and indigenous beauty out of the crude materials of the technological environment.

Most people, of course, failed to recognize in such patterns the substance of art. Inherited notions of beauty and the influences of education interfered with any such recognition. A typical account of the Centennial recorded that "although the first thought would be that no arrangement of axes, hatchets, picks, shovels, etc., could be made that would be pleasing to the eye," an exhibit of such articles was nevertheless "attractive."

Such an attitude inevitably encouraged those attempts to decorate machinery which we have already noted. So prevalent were architectural details in nineteenth-century machinery that it has frequently been assumed that the early designers themselves were originally architects, but there is considerable evidence that this was not the case. Drawings of new machines—other than rough sketches on boards, or chalk marks on the floor—were seldom used in the early years of the nineteenth century. Toward the middle of the century, to be sure, advertisements occasionally appear like that of G. P. Randall, "Architect and Builder," who announced in the pages of a Vermont newspaper in 1846 that he would design not only churches, residences, and bridges, but also "simple and complicated machinery, stoves, etc." But early machines were designed out of the inventor's head, as it were, and changes were made as the work progressed. Since most of these machines were built largely of wood (metal and metal-working facilities being scarce), machine building came into the realm of the cabinetmaker, who had the necessary knowledge and tools. The United States Patent Office for many years required a small-sized working model of an invention instead of the formal drawings required today, and a cabinetmaker usually made the model if the inventor himself did not do so. Since the patterns for the finished machine would closely resemble the model, patternmaking gradually developed as a branch of the cabinetmaker's trade. Accustomed to making furniture, and acquainted with architectural detail through the making of woodwork "trim" for house builders, the skilled craftsman quite naturally embellished the prosaic machine patterns with scrollwork, claw feet, delicately carved legs, and fluted columns.

Opposed to this transferred ornamental habit there was no tradition, no codified grammar, of technological design, but only an intuitive sense of appropriate form. William Sellers, of Philadelphia, for instance (whom the English designer Whitworth is said to have called the greatest mechanical engineer in the world), simply went on the theory that "if a machine was right, it would *look* right." (See Fig. 2.) John Fritz, one of the important figures in the development of the Bessemer process in the United States, was typical of the empirical engineers. One of his favorite remarks after he had finished work on a new machine which he had designed was: "Now, boys, we have got her done, let's start her up and see why she doesn't work." By and large American mechanical engineers adopted original methods of design, taking the problem presented to them and working out the design (as Joseph M. Wilson expressed it) "without any blind adherence to old established forms or precedents."

This empirical attitude was characteristic of almost all early efforts to pattern the technological environment. The men who designed and built the clipper ships of the 1840s and 1850s worked in much the same way as Sellers did in the designing of his machine tools, and the essential characteristics of their designs were the same. Economy of line, lightness, strength, and freedom from meaningless ornament made Donald McKay's *Flying Cloud* and *Sovereign of the Seas* not

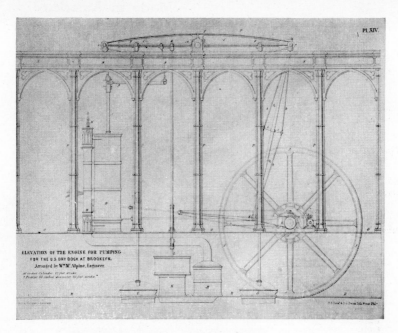

Plate I: Architectural Elements in Machine Design
(*Above*) Gothic frame of steam engine designed by William Mc-Alpine for U. S. Drydock at Brooklyn; (*below*) Corinthian frame of steam engine designed by J. T. Sutton and Co. (From Oliver Byrne, *The American Engineer, Draftsman, and Machinist's Assistant*, Philadelphia, 1853)

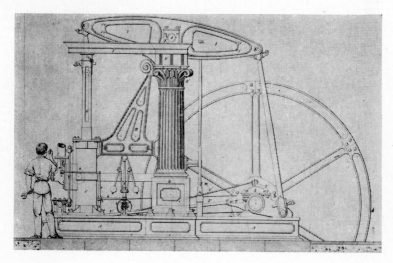

Plate II: Model Room of George Steers, Ship Designer

In this room, surrounded by models of ships which he and other designers had built, Steers worked until his death in 1856. On the back wall, above his drafting table, are the models of five of his most famous ships, including the prize-winning yacht *America* (second from top), the steamship *Adriatic* (third from top), and the schooner *Pride of the Seas* (bottom). At the upper left of the picture is a model of Donald McKay's *Flying Cloud*. (From *Frank Leslie's New York Journal,* February 1857) only two of the swiftest sailing ships of their time but also two of the most beautiful vessels that ever sailed the ocean seas.

The day of the clippers was brief. During the very years when they were the monarchs of the seas, steamships were being developed and perfected to a point where they would inevitably drive the clippers out of existence. But in

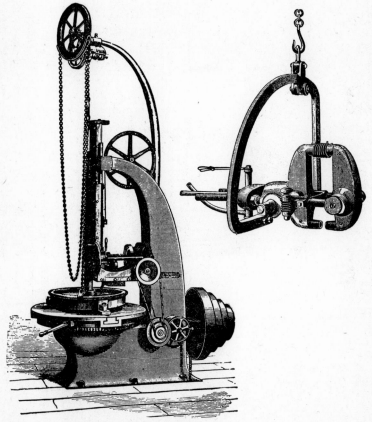

Figure 2: Vernacular Machine Design
(*Left*) Car-wheel boring mill, and (*right*) portable riveting machine, both designed by William Sellers (from *The Masterpieces of the Centennial International Exhibition*, Philadelphia, 1877)

Figure 3: Western River Steamboat—1830s
Drawn by James Andrews from a sketch made on the Ohio River by David Stevenson, published in Stevenson's Sketch of the Civil Engineering of North America, London, 1838

steamship design, likewise, the vernacular tradition developed its characteristic qualities.

On the Ohio and Mississippi a distinctive type of vessel was developed on principles which had been worked out by a man whose name scarcely ever appears in the history books: Henry Miller Shreve. Attempts by Robert Fulton and other Easterners to design steamboats for the Western rivers had ended in several costly failures. Shreve had grown up on the rivers, working as bargeman and later as captain of the *Enterprise*, the first steamer that ever ascended the Mississippi to Louisville. He knew what the rivers required, and when he built the *Washington* in 1816 it was in every essential respect unlike any other steam vessel then known. Previously, the boilers had always been placed in the hold of the vessel and the cylinders set upright. Shreve set his machinery on the deck, thus permitting the use of flat-bottomed, shallow hulls similar to the keelboats which had long been familiar on Western rivers, and placed the cylinders in a horizontal position. Further, he designed and built a high-pressure engine, rather than the low-pressure variety customary in the East and in Europe. And the success of the *Washington* established Shreve's system as the basis of all Western steamboats for many years. (See Fig. 3.)

Nevertheless, there were countless variants in the design of American river steamers. In 1838 an English engineer, David Stevenson, reported in his *Sketch of the Civil Engineering of North America* that after minutely examining all the most approved American steamboats he could trace no *general* principles which had served as guides for their construction.

Every American steamboat builder holds opinions of his own [he wrote], which are generally founded, not on theoretical principles, but on deductions drawn from a close examination of the practical effects of the different arrangements and proportions adopted in the construction of different steamboats . . . ; and the natural consequence is, that, even at this day, no two steamboats are alike, and few of them have attained the age of six months without undergoing some material alteration.

In transatlantic navigation, of course, these shallow-draft boats would be useless, and in that field English builders took a quick lead. But even here the vernacular tradition modified the design of American ships. In 1853 Captain Mackinnon of the Royal Navy crossed on the American Collins liner *Baltic*, built by Jacob Bell, of New York, and shortly thereafter published an article comparing the *Baltic's* design and performance with those of English ships. Basically, he found, the American ship was superior. An English vessel would have a heavy bow with a vast bowsprit, "an absolute excrescence," the captain angrily called it, "a bow-plunging, speed-stopping, money-spending, and absurd acquiescence in old-fashioned prejudices about appearance. . . ." But American ships were hampered by no such devotion to traditional design. They had, instead, a long and gently graduated bow without a bowsprit, with the result that they rode the waves gently even in a heavy sea, without shipping water and without the shock and stagger of the blunt-bowed Britishers.

The *Baltic* and the other American steamships of the early fifties were designed and built by the same shipyards that were turning out the famous clippers. Steam clippers and sailing clippers were constructed side by side. Of course the steamships, not being intended to carry an immense spread of canvas, could be much narrower than any sailing vessel that had ever been designed. But the contemporary newspapers in maritime cities throughout the world were full of descriptions of sailing clippers which sound very much like Captain Mackinnon's account of the steamship *Baltic*. The Mauritius *Commercial Gazeteer* (December 7, 1855) said the bow of the *Herald of the Morning*, designed by Samuel Pook, of New York, was "so sharp as to take the form of a razor, the keel forming the edge; there are no rails at the bow, which is quite unencumbered."

The clipper ships were not any one man's invention. Rather, they were a composite creation, the product of literally scores of keen minds. McKay himself declared in an interview that before making the model of his *Stag Hound* (1850) he had familiarized himself with "all the celebrated clipper models." The designer did not know how his ship would perform until it was actually put to the test. He borrowed ideas from vessels which were under sail and combined them with his own intuitive sense of the lines which were appropriate to the requirements of the ships he intended to build. George Steers, designer of the schooner-yacht *America* which won the international yacht race in 1851 and brought to this country the prize cup which is still called by its name, was particularly proud of a model he was working on shortly before his death. It tapered so beautifully from the center that the eye could not find the exact center spot—"just like the well-formed leg of a woman," from which, he said, he had borrowed his idea. (See Plate II.)

Magnificent as these ships were, the railroad locomotive was the dominant symbol of technological progress during the nineteenth century. As would be expected, the design and performance of American locomotives revealed the characteristics of the vernacular tradition and consequently differed considerably from contemporary European engines. We can perhaps get the clearest sense of this difference by referring to accounts of contemporary American civil engineers. These experts profoundly admired English locomotives, as they did all English machinery. United States Commissioner William Anderson, in his official report on railway apparatus exhibited at the Universal Exposition in Paris, 1878, stated that "the locomotives exhibited in the British section were, as may be said of the machinery exhibits of the United Kingdom generally, remarkable for the skill, the directness, the strong common sense, and the faithfulness illustrated in their construction." And Charles Barnard, writing in 1879, flatly asserted that "the finest piece of steam mechanism in the world is undoubtedly the English locomotive engine."

Barnard goes on to describe these engines: a cylindrical boiler and a capacious firebox, resting upon a massive and rigid frame of iron plates, which in turn was supported by wheels of extraordinary size and strength. In front there might be a pair of smaller wheels, but these like the larger ones were fastened by their axles to the rigid frame which supported the boiler. "One cannot," he wrote, "fail to admire the thoroughly English solidity and stability of the machine. . . . Every part of the mechanism is admirable—strong, accurate, and fitted to its work with marvellous precision."

But the moment the English locomotive was taken from its island lines—relatively straight, and as level as money and labor could make them—and was used in, say, Canada or Australia, it exhibited a number of defects, especially a certain want of pliability. For in those countries, as in the United States, distances were so vast, territory was so thinly populated, capital resources were so limited, and speed of construction was so essential, that the railroads had to negotiate considerable grades and abrupt curves without too much insistence on a straight line or a level roadbed. On such winding and uneven roads the English locomotive was either derailed by the curves, or wrenched and twisted by having only three of its four wheels on the track at one time.

To cope with American roadbeds a very different locomotive was developed which, to anyone accustomed to English engines, would seem a "crazy affair, as loose-jointed as a basket." It had no massive frame. In Barnard's words:

> The framework is light and open, and yet strong. The supporting springs that take the weight of the machine from the axles are not secured directly to the frame, but to the levers extending both across and along the engine. . . . The engine is thus hung upon the fulcrums of a system of levers, balanced equally in every direction. Let the road follow its own wayward will, be low here and high there . . . the basket-like flexibility of the frame and its supports . . . adjusts the engine to its road at every instant of its journey.

Further, it had a group of small wheels at the front—the pilot truck, or track feeler—which was designed to carry the engine around sharp curves. This truck was not only supported on equalizing bars and levers, as were the driving wheels, but also incorporated an arrangement which shifted the weight of the engine so that, like a circus rider, the engine leaned inward on curves to counteract centrifugal force. (See Plate III.)

The characteristics of the American locomotive had appeared early. The first really successful railroad locomotive in the world—George Stephenson's *Rocket*—was built in England in 1829, yet in the very next year H. L. B. Lewis, of New

York, was advertising his invention of a simple contrivance, consisting of wheels attached to the front and rear of the engine, "so arranged that they have a horizontal and lateral motion, so as to admit of their adapting their position to any curve in the track, or any inequality on the top sides of the rails." Two years later, in 1832, Jervis designed the *Brother Jonathan*—the first locomotive to use the lead-truck principle. Five years later Garrett and Eastwick built the *Hercules*, the first engine on which a driving-wheel equalizer invented by Joseph Harrison, Jr., was used; the weight of the engine rested upon the center of a separate frame, the driving-wheel axles being placed in pedestals or supports which allowed the wheels to adjust to uneven track. In 1842 Eastwick and Harrison's *Mercury* combined a highly flexible system of truck suspension with a further development of the equalized driving-wheel arrangement, and an extremely light frame. From that point onward, the essential characteristics of the American locomotive rapidly developed.[1]

For about twenty years after 1850, it is true, extraneous attempts were made to apply "art" to the iron horse. In large measure this art consisted in architectural detail, used in constructing the engine cabs which after 1850 became common on American locomotives. Baldwin's eight-wheeled engine of that year had a cab with large decorative panels on the sides, Corinthian columns supporting an ornamental cornice, and Gothic arched windows. As late as 1868 the *Nathaniel McKay*,

[1] The difference between American and British locomotives early in the twentieth century was thus described by the English railroad expert, Vaughan Pendred, in *The Railway Locomotive*, New York, 1908, p. X: "The British locomotive is, above all others, simple, strong, and carefully finished. . . . The American locomotive is the incarnate spirit of opportunism. . . . In Europe complication is favored rather than disliked. . . . In all cases the national character appears to stamp itself on machinery of every kind."

designed by and named after the son of the clipper-ship designer, Donald McKay, retained the Gothic point in its cab windows. But by 1875 the return of the clean, functional form is reflected in the restrained and attractive design of John C. Davis' engine for the Baltimore and Ohio. (See Plate III.)

The characteristics of economy, simplicity, and flexibility which the products of the vernacular displayed so clearly in the United States are closely related to the design of the American system of industrial production itself. There is a clue to this relationship in the comment already quoted from the catalogue of London's Crystal Palace Exhibition in 1851: that productive labor in the United States was "applied with direct reference to increasing the number or quantity of articles suited to the wants of a whole people."

Let us return for a moment to those long-barreled rifles which Washington's frontiersmen demonstrated on Cambridge Common. Each of those rifles was made by hand, and because they were handmade, no two were exactly alike. If more guns were needed, skilled craftsmen had to be found to make them, and each gun that was made had to be shaped and fitted with individual care.

As a matter of fact, in 1798, when war with France seemed imminent, the government found itself in need of large quantities of rifles. To meet that need, Eli Whitney, of Connecticut, agreed to manufacture ten thousand guns in two years—an undreamed-of quantity in a land where skilled gunsmiths were rare. To achieve this task Whitney proposed "to substitute correct and effective operations of machinery for that skill of the artist which is acquired only by long experience."

The story of how Whitney successfully worked out his system of machine-made, standardized, interchangeable parts is less well known than his invention of the cotton gin, but is of primary importance in the history of modern civilization. Le Blanc, the Frenchman, had previously experimented with the idea of assembling muskets from machine-made parts, but had not carried the idea through. But quite apart from the question of who deserves the credit for inventing such a system, the fact remains that in America it was rapidly developed and was soon applied to a number of manufactures. By the early 1870s it had been applied so extensively to the manufacture of sewing machines, for example, that 600,000 were made and sold in a single year. Firearms, agricultural machinery, watches, and even locomotives were produced by this so-called American system of manufacture.

There is no need to describe here in detail the development of this system, or how it works in specific cases. The essential point in the present context is that it had collaborated with all the other factors we have considered to strengthen and accentuate the characteristic qualities of the American vernacular tradition. On the one hand, if rifles, reapers, sewing machines, and watches had not already been characterized by simplicity and plainness, it would have been considerably more difficult to apply the new system in the first place; on the other hand, once the system was applied, it inevitably encouraged further simplification and further stripping away of non-essentials. (An American cast-steel plow, as manufactured by the famous Collins Company of Hartford in the early seventies, weighed only forty pounds; whereas a contemporary English wrought-iron plow, which could cut a furrow of equal width and depth, weighed two hundred and fifty pounds.) Furthermore, an industrial structure based upon such a system is pointless unless it turns out large quantities of goods. To some people mass production still seems necessarily to imply inferior products, but there is no technological reason why it should not always produce superior goods. When mass-produced American watches were subjected to comparative tests at the Centennial, only twenty-five years after the new system had been introduced in their manufacture, two different makes surpassed the best performances of fine Swiss watches. There is, to be sure, nothing in the mass-production process which insures that its machines will necessarily be used to turn out the highest-quality products; but the quality can be high if the creators and owners of the machine so desire. Furthermore, the products are uniform and can be made available to more people and at lower prices than is otherwise possible.

The rapidity with which America adopted the new manufacturing procedure, and the relative slowness with which it was accepted in Europe, may well have had some connection with another peculiarity of the American industrial system. Writing in 1841, the English mechanical authority Robert Willis noted that in Great Britain power was transmitted from the prime mover (a steam engine, water wheel, or turbine) to the various machines in different parts of a factory by means of long shafts and toothed gear wheels, but in America by large belts, moving rapidly and quietly. Toothed-wheel transmission is by nature a rigid setup; if the location of the machinery is changed, new shafts and new gears must be arranged. But a system of belts and pulleys is comparatively flexible; the arrangement of machinery can be changed with considerable freedom. It was therefore relatively

easy for American manufacturers to rearrange existing factories in a manner appropriate to the new system of interchangeable parts.[2]

Mass production as we know it today, however, depends
as much upon mechanical handling of materials as upon interchangeable parts, and the development of mechanical conveyors and their use in an integrated manufacturing procedure
can be traced to an even earlier date than Whitney's system.
Thirteen years before Whitney set up his armory in New
Haven, Oliver Evans built a flour mill in Newcastle County,
Delaware, in which he installed belt conveyors, screw conveyors, endless-chain bucket elevators, and, as Joseph W. Roe
has noted, nearly all of the modern transporting devices in
substantially their present form. A few years later these devices were installed in Thomas Ellicott's mill near Baltimore
(see Fig. 4), in which, as Evans wrote, they performed "every
necessary movement of the grain and meal, from one part of
the mill to another, or from one machine to another, through
all the various operations, from the time the grain is emptied
from the Wagoner's bag, or from the measure on board the
ship, until it is completely manufactured into flour . . .
ready for packing into barrels, for sale or exportation. All of
which is performed by the force of water, without the aid of
manual labor, except to set the different machines in motion."

It is this system of mechanical handling plus the system
of interchangeable parts which united to make modern mass
production, and it is strange that so little attention has been
paid to their development by the historians of our civilization.

[2]By 1878 the American system of belt and pulley transmission was being adopted in Europe. See William T. Porter, "Machines and Machine
Tools," *Reports of the United States Commissioners to the Paris Universal Exposition, 1878*, Washington, 1880, Vol. IV.

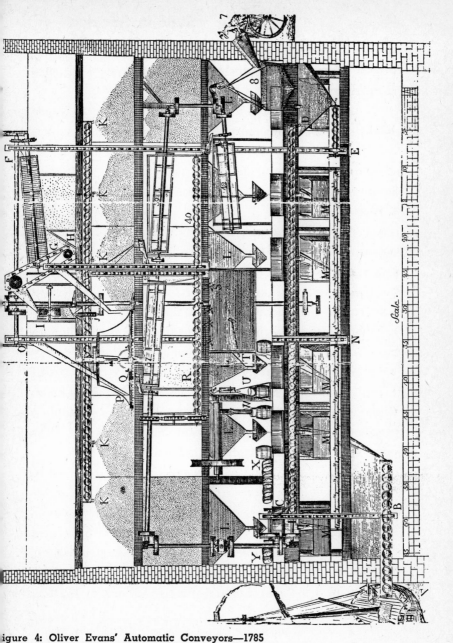

Figure 4: Oliver Evans' Automatic Conveyors—1785

A diagrammatic drawing of Thomas Ellicott's grain mill, near Baltimore, in which automatic machine production was achieved by the use of the conveyors, elevators, hopper-boys, and descenders invented by Oliver Evans (from Evans' *The Young Mill-Wright and Miller's Guide,* Philadelphia, 1795)

Whitney is usually spoken of only as the inventor of the cotton gin, and Evans—if he is mentioned at all—is referred to as the inventor of an ungainly, amphibious steam carriage called *Eructor Amphibolis.* But it is their contributions to the design of the industrial structure itself, to the fundamental principles of mass production, that command our attention here. For it is to them that we owe the manufacturing system which made the products of technological design available to great numbers of people.

It was Henry Ford who finally combined Whitney's system of interchangeable parts and Evans' system of mechanical conveyors to create the modern system of power-driven assembly-line manufacture. When the French engineers, Arnold and Faurote, published their study of *Ford Methods and Ford Shops* in 1915 they described in some detail the Ford system of motor and chassis assembly. Ford practice, they noted, was to place the most suitable component of an assembly on elevated ways or rails, and carry or push it past successive stationary sources of component supply and past successive groups of workmen who fixed the various components to the basic part of the assembly. Since the components were perfectly gauged and absolutely interchangeable, each piece could be affixed in a predetermined time and the whole assembly could be chain-driven along the rails at a uniform rate.

Arnold and Faurote stated that Ford had introduced this system in 1914, and they credited it as "the very first example of chain-driving an assembly in progress of assembling." Ford himself, writing in 1923, said he had installed the first moving assembly line (for flywheel magnetos) "along about April 1, 1913." But revolutionary as the Ford assembly line was, it rested upon a conception which had long been developing in American industry. For the idea of conveying a job mechanically past workmen at fixed stations, each of whom performs a special operation, came directly from the Chicago meat packers, and the basic procedure in their plants had originated in the hog-slaughtering houses of Cincinnati almost eighty years before Ford adapted it.

The earliest detailed account of the Cincinnati slaughterhouse procedure seems to be that published in 1861 by Charles L. Flint. According to Flint, the carcasses of the hogs were slid from the bleeding platform (where their throats had been cut) into a long scalding vat, floated along through it to a lever-operated contrivance which lifted them out onto the higher end of a long, inclined table down which they were slid past eight or nine pairs of men, each of whom had some special job to do in the process of shaving and cleaning the hog. At the end of the table the carcass was hung from a hook on the rim of a huge horizontal wheel, about six feet above the floor, which revolved around a perpendicular shaft. As soon as the hog was swung on its hook the wheel turned one eighth of its circuit, bringing the next hook to the table to receive its carcass and carrying the first carcass a distance of four feet to the workers who performed the first operation in the process of gutting it. Successive turns carried the carcass to other workers who in turn performed their jobs until finally, just before the hook returned to the table for another hog, the gutted and washed carcass was lifted off and carried to another part of the building and hung up to cool.

Sometime in the early sixties the horizontal wheel was replaced by an overhead railway loop, around which hooks traveled on pulleys, carrying the carcass past the workers'

Figure 5: Origin of the Assembly Line—Hog Slaughtering in 1860s
Interior of Cincinnati slaughterhouse showing line production and mechanical handling of materials (from *One Hundred Years Progress of the United States*, Hartford, 1872; an earlier but less detailed picture of the overhead-rail conveyor was published in *Harper's Weekly*, January 11, 1868)

EXPRESS PASSENGER-TRAIN ENGINE, MIDLAND RAILWAY.

ate III: English and American Locomotives—1875

(*Above*) The express passenger engine, built for the Midland Railway, typi-
fies the massive and rigid construction of English locomotives of the period
(from *The Scientific American Supplement, No. 27*, July 1, 1876); (*below*) the
Baltimore and Ohio express engine, designed by John C. Davis, master
machinist, is typical of the light and flexible locomotives developed in America
(from *The Railway Journal*, November 17, 1876)

Plate IV: Carpenter-Gothic
The "Lace House" on Main Street, opposite the railroad station, Blackhawk, Colorado. Built by Frederick Fiske (photograph reproduced by courtesy of the Denver Public Library, Western History Collection)

stations until, at the end of the loop, they swung off on a straightaway along which they conveyed it to the cooling chamber. (See Fig. 5.) Thus it was no longer necessary to carry the carcass by hand from the end of the dis-assembly line to the storage room, as it had been with the wheel conveyor. But in all essential respects the principle of the mechanized assembly line remained unchanged.

Just when the system Flint describes was introduced we do not know, but his account indicates that it was already well established in Cincinnati by 1860, and there is clear evidence that in principle, at least, it originated much earlier. When Harriet Martineau visited Cincinnati in 1835 she was driven about the town by Dr. Daniel Drake (of whom more in a later chapter), who showed her the slaughterhouses on Deer Creek. She did not want to see inside, but the doctor described their method of operation and she recorded what he told her.

> One man [she noted] drives into one pen or chamber the reluctant hogs, to be knocked on the head by another whose mallet is for ever going. A third sticks the throats, after which they are *conveyed by some clever device* to the cutting-up room, and thence to the pickling, and thence to the packing and branding. [Italics mine.]

One wishes Miss Martineau had been able to stomach the "reeking carcasses" and had seen and described the clever device which conveyed them from station to station. But whatever it was, a horizontal wheel or other conveyor, it is clear that the basic system must have been essentially the same as that described by Flint.

Our lack of precise knowledge about the origin of the system is an indication of the extent to which we have hitherto neglected the underlying technological factors of our civilization. Up until recently it has frequently been asserted that the

system Ford took over from the meat packers and made the
core of modern mass-production industry had originated in
the seventies or eighties and had thus been a product of the
surge of industrialization which is held to have transformed
America in the last quarter of the nineteenth century. Siegfried Giedion, in his newly published history of mechanization, dates the system from the late sixties or early seventies,
on the basis of patent-office records and such information as
he was able to get from Cincinnati's local historians. Yet Miss
Martineau's account is pretty conclusive evidence that the
industrial system which Giedion justly calls "the dominant
principle of the twentieth century" had in all its essentials
been put into actual practice more than sixty-five years before
that fateful century began. Whatever the precise date may
have been, the evidence at hand is sufficient to emphasize that
the increasing tempo of industrialization in late nineteenth-
century America was a development of technological factors
which were already deeply rooted in our national experience
during the "agrarian" decades of the thirties and forties. It
should effectively remind us that the technology of mass production is as indigenous to the United States as the husking
bee.

All this emphasis on mechanical and technological
factors in nineteenth-century America may seem to ignore the
fact that until 1860 the United States was primarily an agricultural country. But the proportion of people engaged in
agriculture, or the relative value of agricultural and manufactured products, is not the most significant index of the role
of technology in a nation's life.

Before the American land could be a union in fact as

well as in name, the land itself had to be made smaller and more compact than it had been when it took Washington nine days to proceed from Philadelphia to Cambridge to take command of the Revolutionary Army. A number of forces contributed to this contraction and unification of the continent. There were threats from the outside which drove the people to unite in self-protection; there was a vast increase in population to fill the empty spaces; there were the people's common interests in development of new land, in conquest of the wilderness; there was the homesick need of the pioneer to keep in touch with those left behind in the settled regions; there was the invasion of Washington by the frontier in the person of Andrew Jackson; and there was the belief in Union of dynamic idealists like Lincoln. But, as the technological historian Roger Burlingame has said, "without the continuous, inevitable progress of technology—of which, indeed, very few were conscious—all these causes would have failed to operate."

Before the Declaration of Independence there were apparently only two steam engines in the thirteen colonies: one at Passaic, New Jersey, in a copper mine and the other in a Philadelphia brewery. England had forbidden the colonies to engage in most industries, in an effort to keep them dependent on British manufactures. But once the Revolution was achieved, industrial expansion and technological invention proceeded at a rapid rate. As a matter of fact, in the seventeen years between the end of the Revolutionary War (1783) and the end of the century, three major technological achievements had already laid the foundations for future national unification. Whitney's cotton gin unified the South by giving it a new source of wealth—cotton—and a common interest in slavery as a means of exploiting it. Slater's reproduction of English textile machinery in New England began the Industrial Revolution in that section and linked it economically to the South, whose cotton fields supplied the raw materials for the mills. And finally Fitch's steamboats—later promoted by Livingston and Fulton and ingeniously adapted to shallow rivers by Henry Shreve—enabled the pioneer to settle the West and at the same time bound him inextricably to the East. McCormick's reaper later made the East and the South dependent on the West for food, and the railroads and other subsequent inventions implemented and strengthened the interdependence of all these diverse regions.

The importance of these factors becomes clear when we remember that the unity of no other nation in history rested to a similar degree upon technological foundations. In the light of that fact the characteristics of the vernacular assume a new significance. For it is clear that they had inadvertently become *national* in a way that had nothing to do with the naïve nationalism which patriots had self-consciously demanded from our literature and our art.

It was this tradition in which were developed, and kept universally available, certain elements of design and certain principles of structure which were a direct, uninhibited response to the new environment and which finally had decisive influence in the hands of men of skill and vision. This stream of art often failed to create beauty of its own. But its patterns at least reflected actuality, however ugly that actuality often was; and the forms evolved in it were firmly rooted in contemporary experience.

3

Two Traditions in Conflict

It was in the various branches of technology that the vernacular tradition first and most uninhibitedly displayed its characteristics, and we have therefore attempted to define it in terms of tools and machines. But even in machine design, as we have seen, it interacted with the tradition of cultivated taste which flowed into our national life from the reservoirs of western European culture. Actually the two traditions mingle from the beginning in all branches of the arts; it is in their interpenetration and in their alternate ascendancy in the work of different men and different periods that the history of American art consists.

To make clear the nature of this interaction, let us turn for a moment to a consideration of the art of building. Throughout the Western world during the nineteenth century there was a disastrous separation between engineering and architecture.[1] Academic architecture, swept along on the flood of classic, Gothic, and Renaissance revivals which culminated in eclecticism, became more and more archaeologically-minded as the century progressed. It was ornament, not con-

---

[1]The phrase is Talbot Hamlin's in his magnificent history of *Architecture Through the Ages.*

struction, that it adopted as its province, and architects seemed increasingly to share the belief of James Ferguson—one of the century's most influential writers on the subject—that "where the engineer leaves off the art of the architect begins." Given the engineer's structural materials, the architect had merely to arrange them "artistically," as the phrase was, and then add ornament.

In the United States it was in such academic architecture that the tradition of cultivated taste found expression. Moreover, it was this tradition that produced some of the most attractive buildings of the century. Richard Upjohn's Trinity Church at the head of Wall Street in New York, Minard Lafever's Holy Trinity in Brooklyn, and James Renwick's St. Patrick's Cathedral on Fifth Avenue are all charmingly successful imitations of medieval Gothic forms, and the national Capitol in Washington, with its vast dome, is an impressive echo of classic styles. The very success of such buildings, however, did much to establish in America the dichotomy between architecture and engineering. If Renwick could get away with Gothic nave vaults of papier-mâché painted to look like stone, and if Thomas U. Walter's dome for the Capitol could be so impressive in spite of the structural dishonesty of its iron members, disguised as masonry, why should architecture concern itself with the logic of structural expression?

The development of academic styles necessarily figures largely in the history of the practice of architecture in the United States, and we can learn much about our cultural limitations and aspirations from the way in which we tried to adapt a variety of imported forms and styles to our needs. But, taken by themselves, without reference to the enormous quantity of non-academic and non-professional building which our people produced, these borrowed modes mislead rather than inform us about American civilization, however charming they may be. More significant, from our point of view, are the constructive techniques of the vernacular tradition, which can be seen in their purest form in the technological features of construction—in engineering itself.

National unity, in a land so vast and geographically diverse as ours, could not have been achieved without roads, bridges, canals, railroads, and other means of intercommunication, and farsighted Americans early in our history were well aware that the consolidation and expansion of the nation as a political, social, and economic unit would depend upon technological developments. As early as 1785 Washington was preoccupied with the necessity for developing inland navigation in order to bring the Western settlements in close connection with the Atlantic states. "Without this," he argued, "I can easily conceive they will have different views, separate interests, and other connections." And Thomas Pope, shipbuilder and bridge designer, explicitly stated in his *Treatise on Bridge Architecture* (1811) that no real physical union of the country could take place without "the building of bridges, the digging of canals, and the making of sound turnpike roads."

The speed with which canals and bridges were constructed in America was astonishing to Europeans. With the coming of the canals and railroads it was necessary to span rivers, streams, and chasms cheaply and rapidly, and new techniques were used ingeniously to meet the new needs.[2]

[2]It was the "ingenious novelty of invention" displayed in American engineering works to which the Englishman, John Weale, hoped to call attention in the illustrated folio he published in London in 1841. See

David Stevenson, the English civil engineer, traveled widely in this country in the thirties and was struck by the temporary and apparently unfinished state of our canals. "Undressed slopes of cuttings and embankments," he wrote, "roughly built rubble arches, stone parapet-walls coped with timber, and canal locks wholly constructed of that material, everywhere offend the eye accustomed to view European workmanship." But, he added, although the works were wanting in finish, they served their purpose efficiently, and they had the advantage that, as traffic increased, they could be enlarged and improved "without the mortification of destroying expensive and substantial works of masonry." Had some of the Erie barge canal's locks not been originally built of stone, the canal would, he pointed out, have been converted into a ship canal long before. But most construction was of wood, in bridges as well as in canal locks and aqueducts, and all kinds of experiments were tried with it. Most important, the techniques developed in wood construction were carried over into later work in more durable materials.

By the seventies, for instance, it had become apparent that the practice of American engineers in iron bridges differed widely from that of their European contemporaries. European bridge builders had always aimed to build structures as strong and safe and durable as possible, cost and speed of construction having been secondary considerations. For hundreds of years before the introduction of iron as a building material, massive stone-arch bridges had been painstakingly erected across European rivers. It had been only natural, therefore,

---

The Public Works of the United States of America, edited by William Strickland, Edward Gill, and Henry R. Campbell, London, 1841, with prefatory "Advertisement" by John Weale.

that when in 1793–96 Rowland Burdon built the famous cast-iron bridge at Sunderland, England (based on plans worked out some years before by Thomas Paine, the great propagandist of the American Revolution), he had adapted the methods of stone vaulting to iron construction. The six ribs which formed the 236-foot arch were made up of cast-iron panels which served roughly the same structural function as the wedge-shaped stones in a masonry arch. Even in later bridges European engineers tended to perpetuate in iron the proportions which had been familiar in stonework.

The contrast between European and American practice was made clear in a paper read by Thomas C. Clarke before a meeting of the American Institute of Mining Engineers in 1876. In America the aim of the builders had necessarily been to erect a bridge as rapidly and as cheaply as possible. Lack of capital and the necessity for haste led the early railroad-bridge builder, like the canal builder, to use the most abundant material—wood—and the same influences prompted him to design the bridge so that it could be put together with the utmost rapidity. Hence, as Clarke said, when we began to build our iron bridges, we copied the proportions already established as the most economical in wooden trusses instead of copying the more massive proportions of stone; and rather than rivet the separate parts of the bridge together on the scaffolds (as a mason would cement together the separate stones), we copied the techniques of timber construction—using tenons and sliding joints for the compressive members, and pins and eyebars for those in tension. (See Fig. 6.)

The marked feature of the American method, according to Clarke, was the special use of special machine tools, by which the sizes and lengths of all the parts were fitted with the utmost exactness at the place of manufacture. In other words, the parts of the bridge were prefabricated by machinery and could be rapidly assembled on the spot; whereas in the European system of riveted lattice construction assembly was often tediously slow.

The proportions adopted by American designers and their methods of construction both resulted in great economy of material. The result was that when, for instance, English, continental, and American bridge builders submitted competing designs in 1876 for a bridge over the Minamidic River on

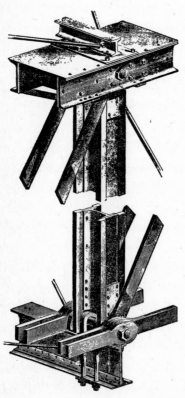

Figure 6: Detail of Iron Bridge Construction
The Point Bridge, Pittsburgh, built by the American Bridge Company, 1875 (from *The Masterpieces of the Centennial International Exhibition*, Philadelphia, 1877)

the Intercolonial Railway of Canada, the American plans called on the average for roughly half the weight of materials required by their competitors. Similarly, when Roebling had completed the Niagara Suspension Bridge (1851–55)—the first large railroad suspension span in the world—he was able to write in his report to the directors of the company: "The work which you did me the honor to entrust to my charge has cost less than $400,000. The same object accomplished in Europe would have cost four millions without securing a better purpose, or insuring greater safety."

The early builders of wooden-truss bridges, like the early designers of machinery, had worked by rule of thumb. The carpenter-builder had a feel for the strength of timber but no precise knowledge of its capacity to bear loads. Not until 1847—when Squire Whipple, of Utica, New York, published his analysis of bridge building—was there any source of accurate quantitative information on stresses in bridge trusses. The consequence was that some early bridges were uneconomically strong; but the rivalry between the patentees of various wooden trusses in the early days, and the subsequent competition between the various iron-bridge manufacturing companies (like Keystone, Phoenix, and Baltimore) constantly encouraged economy of materials and standardization of design.

In the realm of house building, as in bridge building, the prevalence of wood construction in America as opposed to the stone or brick construction of Europe led to significant differences in architectural fundamentals.

In the twenty-five years immediately preceding the Revolutionary War the tide of Adam's and Chambers' classic revival architecture, which had already swept Gothic, Tudor, and Jacobean ideas out of favor in Britain, reached its height in the American colonies. Almost all the early classic revival buildings in England had been of stone or of brick faced with stucco. But in America the plentifulness of wood had resulted in the development of more skilled carpenters than masons; so the New England builder usually approximated in wood the stonework details he found illustrated in the English books he imported. But modifications of the original designs began to appear almost immediately. Cornices became smaller and more delicate, mantels became daintier, and all the decorative details took on more and more the essential characteristics of wood.

But far more important than these modifications of borrowed forms was the way in which wood construction co-operated with the social system to undermine the cultivated tradition and develop new and more flexible forms. As would be expected, the cultivated classes regarded wood as an inferior material. For one thing it was perishable, and subject to the dangers of storm and fire. But from the earliest days of the Republic there were other and weightier arguments in favor of brick and stone. The article on architecture in *The New and Complete American Encyclopaedia* (New York, 1805) baldly put it thus:

> Considered politically, there is this good attending brick buildings: from durable habitations, in which more money has been spent, and more of the refined tastes gratified, an affection for the soil is increased. . . . But the last and highest consideration which strikes us is that emigration would be less easy, and not so common amongst us, were a finer spirit of building to prevail. The facility with which we *may* move, is a strong incentive to that love of change which it particularly interests us to repress in our citizens.

But change was irresistible under democratic political institutions. Ruskin might appropriately argue in Britain that the right to have a house express one's character and history belonged to its first builder and should be respected by his children. But among the majority of Americans there were few who would have agreed with him that it was "an evil sign" when a people built their houses to last for one generation only, and it was inevitable that in the United States the facility of wood construction would be exploited.

Technologically, the most important contribution in building was the anonymous development of the so-called balloon frame, a revolutionary method of wood construction which appeared early in the nineteenth century in the vernacular realm of utilitarian architecture. No historian of our architecture considered this invention worthy of notice until Siegfried Giedion, in the Norton Lectures at Harvard in 1939, emphasized its importance as marking the point at which industrialization began to penetrate housing. But despite the refusal of academic architecture to concern itself with such a utilitarian development, there are a number of sources for information about the role it played in American life.

For hundreds of years men had made wood frames for houses out of heavy timbers (often a foot or more thick) which were joined together by cutting down the end of one timber to form a tenon which could be fitted into a hole, or mortise, which had been cut out of the other timber. If the joint had to support a pull, rather than a thrust, the two pieces were fastened together with a wooden peg driven through auger holes.

With the invention of nail-making machinery early in the nineteenth century, and the resulting availability of cheap nails, the way was open to the development in the United

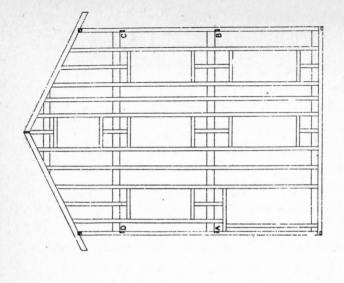

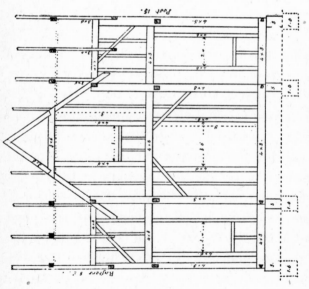

Figure 7: Balloon Frame and Traditional Frame

(*Left*) Framing plan for "English style" cottage, with 4" x 8" beams and 4" x 6" and 3" x 6" studs, mortise and tenon joints (from William H. Ranlett, *The Architect, A Series of Original Designs*, New York, 1847); (*right*) framing plan of two-story balloon-frame house, with 2" x 4" studs and corner posts of two 2" x 4"'s nailed together (from James H. Monckton, *The National Carpenter and Builder*, New York, 1873)

States of a new construction which soon replaced the old type
and which has been used throughout the country ever since.
This was the balloon frame (so nicknamed, in contempt for
its lightness, by traditional carpenters and builders), which
the mid-century builders G. E. and F .W. Woodward described
as characterized by light sticks, which did not require labori-
ous mortising and tenoning, and (in language very reminiscent of that used in contemporary descriptions of American
locomotives) by "a close basket-like manner of construction."
The balloon-frame house is nailed together with light studs
only two inches by four inches, but is so tied and strengthened
that every nail holds to its utmost strength. (See Fig. 7.)

Credit for the invention apparently belongs to a carpenter-builder named Augustine Deodat Taylor, who in 1833
built St. Mary's Catholic Church in Chicago—the first balloon-
frame building ever built. Giedion and others have credited it
to another Chicagoan, but the recent researches of Walker
Field, first published in 1942, seem to establish Taylor as the
real originator. Throughout the nineteenth century, however,
the new construction developed anonymously.

The first professional architect who recognized its importance, so far as I have discovered, was Gervase Wheeler,
an Englishman who came to the States to practice in the 1840s.
His book, *Homes for the People* (published in 1855), was
the first architectural publication to quote the description of
balloon framing which Solon Robinson had given at a meeting
of the American Institute and which had been reported in the
New York *Tribune*, January 18, 1855. Robinson himself,
who was apparently the first person to describe the new system
of construction, was a farmer who had migrated from Connecticut to Indiana in 1834, and he had seen how these lightly

framed buildings, erected on the open wind-swept prairies, stood as firm as any of the old frames of New England with posts and beams sixteen inches square. How long they might endure he did not know, but for all practical purposes they were substantial enough to meet the needs of those who were building towns in the wilderness. When another member of the Institute expressed doubts about the long-term durability of the balloon-frame structures, in spite of their admitted strength, Robinson replied: "Sir, we are Christians, you know, and therefore we take no thought for the morrow."

Yet, in spite of Gervase Wheeler's interest in the new method of construction, it was generally ignored by professional architects. As one of the most successful of them put it in 1879:

> It sometimes happens, in localities remote from large cities or large towns, that persons are obliged to do with make-shifts, to get a home at all. It was such a condition of things that led the well-disposed pioneer of the West to adopt the method called "Balloon framing", which is really no framing at all. . . .

It was the carpenter-builders and the farmers who developed it, and its role in American life was best understood by men like Robinson and one of the anonymous authors of *The Great Industries of the United States* (published in Hartford in 1873), who hailed it as "the most important contribution to our domestic architecture which the spirit of economy, and a scientific adaptation of means to ends, have given the modern world." There was, he thought, hardly a better evidence of the American spirit than the prompt adaptation to new conditions reflected in the introduction of this new method of building. And he demonstrated his understanding of its relationship with other aspects of technological advance when he added that "our methods of construction, like our means of transportation, have passed into the railroad phase of development."

Here, then, were the roots of the vernacular tradition in building. Here were the same characteristics which we have already traced in technological design: simplicity, lightness, strength of construction, and wide availability.

These balloon-frame buildings were often designed and constructed without reference to any requirements other than those of utility, and they were often appallingly unattractive. Professional architects usually regarded them with horror. To Calvert Vaux, for instance, who, like Gervase Wheeler, had come to the United States with the best available English training and had devoted his life to the realization in this country of his ideals of his art, such houses seemed to have been constructed without any sense of proportion or the slightest apparent desire to make them agreeable objects in the landscape. These "bare, bald white cubes," as he called them in 1857, struck him as monotonous evidence of a life spent "with little or no cultivation of the higher natural perceptions." And like many of his cultivated contemporaries, he set about doing his best to educate the American people in sifting, testing, and improving all suitable architectural forms and modes of the past. He recommends, for instance, Moorish arcades and verandas and Chinese balconies and trellises added to what he calls the "irregular Italian" or to the "later modifications of the Gothic."

But Vaux, again like a number of his contemporaries, was at least vaguely aware of the basic problem represented by the conflict between the cultivated academic tradition and the square boxes which were springing up in every direction.

Republicanism, he argued, "tacitly, but none the less practically, demanded of art to thrive in the open air, in all weathers,
for the benefit of all, if it was worth anything, and if not, to
perish as a troublesome encumbrance." The balloon-frame
houses might trouble him because of their builders' apparent
lack of capacity for enjoying what is really desirable in life,
but he nevertheless recognized that they were rooted in the
lives of the people, "simply and unceremoniously" reflecting
both the migratory, independent spirit which pervaded Americans and the economic opportunity which made it possible
for almost every storekeeper and mechanic to build his own
home.

Vaux was typical, in a sense, of a whole group of professionals to whom it was obvious that the forms and modes
of the past could not be slavishly copied in this country. The
past, they proclaimed, should be regarded as a servant, not
as a master. Yet no matter how devoutly they professed, as
William M. Woollett did, that "architectural effect should be
obtained by the natural combinations and workings of the
constructive portions of the structure, and not by adding or
planting on of these features," they nevertheless were capable
of the kind of alteration of old houses illustrated in the accompanying plates from Woollett's book. (See Fig. 8.) Calvert
Vaux was willing enough to quote Emerson's exhortation to
the American architect to "study with hope and love the precise thing to be done by him, considering the climate, the soil,
the length of the day, the wants of the people, the habit and
form of government." Indeed, many professionals felt in a
vague sort of way that American architecture would develop
some distinctive characteristics, but they generally agreed
with Vaux that whatever these characteristics might ultimately

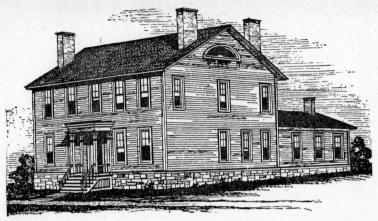

VIEW BEFORE ALTERATION

Figure 8: The Vernacular Succumbs to Cultivated Taste
According to William M. Woollett, the architect who did the remodeling, "the not very attractive-looking structure" shown in the upper picture was in first-class condition and was "withal a good, comfortable house in which to live." The alterations shown in the lower picture were designed merely "to slightly improve its appearance without destroying the date and character of the building" (from Woollett's *Old Homes Made New*, New York, 1878)

VIEW AFTER ALTERATION

turn out to be, they could "hardly be expected to depend much on the employment of really new forms."

Clearly it could not be from men so disposed and so bound to tradition that fundamental innovations would come. Those would continue to develop anonymously in haphazard response to social necessity, as did balloon-framing. But as the anonymous and revolutionary contributions of the vernacular tradition became established in building construction, they inevitably influenced and modified, and were modified by, the ideas and practice of the professional architects. There is no more charming evidence of the interaction of the two traditions than the carpenter-Gothic houses (like the delightful "Lace House" in Blackhawk, Colorado, Plate IV), built in all parts of the country during the middle decades of the century. The fanciful and sometimes highly elaborate scrollwork overlies a balloon-frame structure in much the same way that the carpenter's scrollwork overlay the bold, simple mechanism of many American woodworking machines.

The essential point, however, is that through all the various revivals which were borrowed from Europe by the professional architects in the United States—whether it were Asher Benjamin's Greek style, Alexander Jackson Davis' and Upjohn's Gothic, or Vaux's Italian—certain characteristics recur which distinguish the American examples from their European contemporaries; and these characteristics clearly reflect the recurring influence of the vernacular tradition.

One of these characteristics is the plane surface—the flat wall of wood, or brick, or stone. The simple clapboard wall, for instance, which was evolved in response to the lack of lime in the colonies, has dominated American wood construction for three centuries. There have been, of course, numerous instances in the United States of cluttered and elaborate wall surfaces, in wood as well as in other materials. But in general, even in the worst moments of nineteenth-century eclecticism, American buildings differed from those of England, Germany, or France in being less given to surface richness. Similarly, early in the century, when classic styles had been revived, in Europe it was chiefly the magnificence of Roman forms which had been imitated, while in the United States (except momentarily in a few urban centers in the East) it was the serenity and severity of Greek forms which had appeared in churches, houses, and courthouses throughout the country.

Newspapers, farm journals, family magazines, and many books of the period offer ample evidence of the attitude which is expressed in the buildings themselves. There is a whole literature, for example, on the general subject of rural architecture, some of it by trained architects but much of it simply by farmers or "friends of agriculture" who had enough ingenuity and good sense to plan houses which met practical needs. Almost all of this literature expresses pragmatic contempt for "Gothic castles with piecrust battlements," "fantastical and puerile 'bird cages' with gewgaw carvings," and other follies which, as D. J. Browne told his fellow farmers at an American Institute meeting in the forties, were at variance with the simplicity of our manners, with our climate, and with reason and sound taste.

Nowhere did the interaction of the vernacular and the cultivated tradition find clearer expression than in the popular books on architecture which appeared in the middle of the century. One of the most amusing and enlightening of these was Lewis F. Allen's *Rural Architecture,* published in New

York in 1852, a forgotten volume which did more to shape
the course of ordinary house building than many a more pretentious and less salty book. Allen was a farmer in western
New York State (and an uncle, incidentally, of Grover
Cleveland) who had no formal training as an architect, and
whose contempt for the professionals sprang from a conviction
that they showed no understanding of the purposes to which a
rural home should be adapted. He therefore took it upon himself to instruct his neighbors in the fundamentals of house
building, so that they would have their own notions about it,
"and not be subject to the caprice and government of such as
profess to exclusive knowledge." He was concerned, he said,
only with the shape, arrangement, and accommodation of the
building, not with modes and styles of exterior finish. The
latter, so long as they suited those who adopted them, were of
little consequence, he felt, and could therefore safely be left
to the architects.

The fundamental principles which Allen keeps reiterat-
ing throughout his book—whether in connection with farmhouses themselves, or barns, or poultry houses, or rabbit
hutches—are all summed up in his definition of good taste. It
is a definition which in our day may sound commonplace
enough, but which most academic architects of his day overlooked. Good taste, Allen believed, demanded both a fitness to
the purpose for which a thing was intended and a harmony
between the various parts. Any product of good taste would
be both "pleasing to the eye, as addressed to the sense, and
satisfactory to the mind, as appropriate to the object for which
it is required." No style of architecture or finish could be
really *bad*, he insisted, if utility were duly consulted and
complied with. Provided there was a harmony amongst them

even the meanest buildings on a farm derived a dignity from "the character of utility or necessity which they maintain."

Planting himself on these convictions, he mercilessly attacked the meaningless current styles which the architects of the cultivated tradition were exploiting. At the slightest excuse he laid into "the ambitious cottage, with its covert expression of humility" such as those which men like Vaux and Downing were building. "What," he asks, "are the benefits of a parcel of needless gables and peaked windows, running up like owls ears above the eaves of a house, except to create expense, and invite leakage and decay?" He detested all the "gewgawgery" of the haberdasher-built houses of his time and maintained stoutly that all buildings should show for themselves what they were built of, rather than masquerade as something else.

Being altogether untutored in draftsmanship, Allen had to employ a Buffalo architect to draw up the elevations and plans of his houses for illustrations in his book, and—as might be imagined—the results were not satisfactory. Throughout the text Allen snipes at the architect's renderings. For instance, he objects to the diamond-paned windows with which the draftsman dressed up his design for a poultry house; "but," he sourly remarks, "as he had, no doubt, an eye to the 'picturesque,' we let it pass, only remarking that if we were building the house on our own account, there should be no such nonsense about it." (See Fig. 9.)

But the significance of his book is not confined to its attacks upon frippery and pretense. Its positive contribution is that all the plans for buildings which it offers have their origin in the life to be lived, or the jobs to be done, within them. The layout of buildings, arrangement of rooms, pro-

Figure 9: Vernacular Buildings in Cultivated Dress
Farm house planned by Lewis F. Allen, as rendered by Otis and Brown, architects, of Buffalo. As usual, the architects insisted upon fashionable decoration. The design, Allen remarked in his book, "is rather florid . . but the cut and moulded trimmings may be left off by those who prefer a plain finish. Such, indeed, is our own taste" (from Allen's *Rural Architecture,* New

vision for light and ventilation—all are managed with an eye to the comfort, convenience, and pleasure of actual farm living rather than to stylistic design.

Another book which should be better known to students of American architecture is Orson S. Fowler's *A Home for All, or, The Gravel Wall and Octagon Mode of Building*, originally published in New York in 1849. Fowler was, in a way, typical of the reformer-enthusiasts who flourished in the forties and fifties. For a generation he and his brother Lorenzo were the most active boosters of phrenology—the "science" based on the belief that mental faculties and character traits are revealed by the conformation of the skull—and he traveled throughout the country lecturing and selling copies of the books and magazines which he and his brother wrote and published.

It was on one of his Western trips that Fowler came across a method of building which, combined with certain phrenological conceptions of his own, produced a system of building examples of which can still be seen in many Hudson Valley towns and elsewhere. Fowler was convinced that, from all points of view, an octagonal form was the ideal one for a home. For one thing it provided considerably more enclosed space than a square or rectangle of the same circumference, and hence was economically superior. Furthermore, it permitted floor plans which, he argued persuasively, were phrenologically sound and which made housekeeping less of a burden than it had to be in houses of other shapes. The trouble was, simply, that its obtuse angles were harder to frame than the right angles of conventional houses.

The solution to this problem he found, however, when

he saw houses near Janesville, Wisconsin, built of lime, gravel, and sand. But let him tell it in his own words:

> I visited Milton [Wisconsin], to examine the house put up by Mr. Goodrich, the original discoverer of this mode of building, and found his walls as hard as stone itself, and harder than brick walls. I pounded them with the hammer, and examined them thoroughly, till fully satisfied as to their solidity and strength. Mr. Goodrich offered to allow me to strike with a sledge, as hard as I pleased, upon the inside of his parlor walls for six cents per blow, which he said would repair all damages. He said in making his discovery he reasoned thus: Has nature not provided some other building material on these prairies but wood, which is scarce? . . . Let me see what we have. Lime abounds on them everywhere. So does coarse gravel. Will they not do? I will try. He first built an academy not larger than a school house. . . . It stood; it hardened with age. He erected a blacksmith's shop, and finally a block of stores and dwellings; and his plan was copied extensively. And he deserves to be immortalized, for the superiority of his plan must revolutionize building, and especially enable poor men to build their own houses.

Here was a method of construction (in reality an empirical rediscovery of Roman concrete, and one of the earliest uses of this material for domestic architecture in modern times) which was easily adapted to octagonal houses, and Fowler at once set out to sell the idea to his countrymen. His own house at Fishkill, New York, was a sight-seers' objective for many years, until seepage from a cesspool made it a typhoid breeder and broke the old man's heart. In the meantime, however, hundreds of houses had been built according to his proposals, and his book did a great deal to promote a method of construction which, quite apart from his octagonal plan, had a share in the development of what later became ferro-concrete architecture.

Like Lewis F. Allen, Fowler had no use for fancy

trimmings, and one of the things he liked about his "gravel walls" was the plain surfaces they presented. Nature, he reminded his readers, "never puts on anything *exclusively* for ornament *as such*. She appends only what is useful, and even absolutely *necessary*," and that should be the law of design.

This brings us to another recurring characteristic which —like the plane surface—distinguishes American domestic architecture from its European counterpart: flexibility of ground plan. This flexibility may be traced from its origins in the early eighteenth-century practice of adding ells and lean-tos to the central-chimney houses on up through the nineteenth-century development of sliding doors which came into American house design with the Greek revival in the late 1820s and were extensively used thereafter. Yet to Wilhelm Bode, the German critic, these sliding doors seemed a novelty at the time of his visit to the Chicago World's Fair in 1893.

Openness and flexibility have been characteristic of American house plans for three hundred years, and have to a great extent resulted from the influence of the vernacular tradition. It is possible to trace a part of their development in the records of academic architecture, especially in summer cottages and country homes where architect and client felt relatively free to develop independent solutions. But for many of the most daring innovations one must turn to such unlikely and neglected sources as, for example, a volume produced in the sixties by Catherine Beecher and her more eminent sister, Harriet Beecher Stowe. Here, in *The American Woman's Home* (New York, 1869), these worthy and earnest ladies laid down the specifications for what they called "a Christian house; that is, a house contrived [notice the verb] for the express purpose of enabling every member of a family to labor with the hands for the common good, and by modes at once healthful, economical, and tasteful." The house they contrived is a remarkable job. They planned it for mass use, and deliberately acknowledged the industrial environment by arguing that, owing to the railroads, men working in cities could build such a house and rear families in the country. The over-all plan, and every detail, aims—in Miss Beecher's words —at "economizing time, labor, and expense by the close packing of conveniences." (See Fig. 10.)

As in Frank Lloyd Wright's Suntop Homes at Ardmore seventy years later, all the heating, plumbing, and storage facilities are concentrated in a central unit—at the darkest part of the house—leaving the well-lighted outer parts free for family life. The kitchen and stove room, the arrangement of which the authors liken to a cook's galley on a steamship (from which, indeed, they probably got the idea) are an extraordinarily advanced piece of compact, functional planning. The glazed sliding doors between stove room and kitchen serve to shut out heat and smells and to let in light. The whole house is artificially ventilated by a system of flues connected with the stove; the stove warms the air in the flues, thus setting up a current in them, which both draws off the heat and smells of the kitchen (and of the water-closet room on the second floor) and draws fresh air from outdoors to supply all the rooms of the house.

Particularly interesting, since it seems to be the earliest recorded use of a movable partition in an American house, is the screen on rollers by means of which the large room to the left of the entrance could serve as a big, airy sleeping room at night; then in the morning, when the screen is rolled to the middle of the room, as a sitting room on one side of the screen

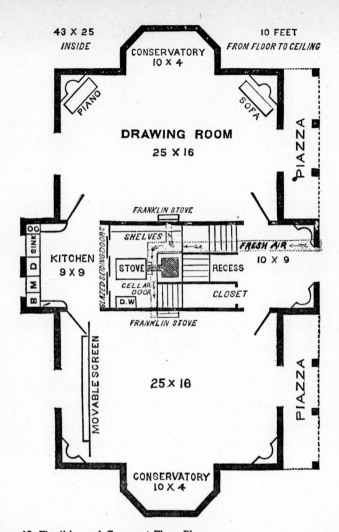

Figure 10: Flexible and Compact Floor Plan
Floor plan of house designed by Catherine Beecher and Harriet Beecher Stowe. Note movable screen partition in room to left of entrance and the compact kitchen and stove-room unit. The counter-height working surface in the kitchen included a breadboard (B), molding board and meatboard (M), and drainboard (D). Beneath this continuous work surface were bins, drawers, and cupboards for flour, meal, towels, and utensils; above it were open shelves extending to the ceiling (from Beecher and Stowe, *The American Woman's Home*, New York, 1869)

and a breakfast room on the other; and finally, through the day, a large parlor on the front side and a sewing room behind. By means of this movable partition and the compact kitchen and stove room, the useless spaces usually devoted to kitchen, entries, hall, back stairs, pantry, etc., would all be economized. It is, on the whole, a radical interior plan, broadly prophetic of features of the best twentieth-century design. But the ladies got nowhere with the exterior; that remained strictly conventional. Working from the inside out, they—like Allen and other nameless exponents of the vernacular tradition—did not have the requisite experience and training to evolve a suitable exterior shell for their creation. The chances are, indeed, that they were not much concerned about relating the exterior to the interior. Even among professional designers it was assumed that although the ground plans of a house should be made to conform to the necessities and requirements of those who were to occupy it, those plans did not, as the architect S. B. Reed said, "decide, or even indicate, the style, character, or expense of the outside dress that may be put upon them."

But it was the gradual pressure of flexible and open plans, co-operating with the freedom and facility of the vernacular balloon-frame construction, which encouraged a few architects to abandon the stagnation of academic traditions and to evolve new solutions to the problems of house building.

A writer in *Putnam's Magazine* in 1854 declared that splendors of architecture were not to be looked for in America (except in the shape of bridges and aqueducts) until such time as we learned that twenty or thirty families might live in a palace by pooling their wealth and building one capacious dwelling, while if each built separately they would be compelled to live in inconvenient and unattractive houses. The problem which the writer was facing was one which is still much agitated: how can we provide adequate housing for the masses of our people? As a matter of fact his suggested solution (an idea which he caught from the vast hotels of his pre-apartment-house period) is basically the same as the one which Lewis Mumford and others have advocated in our time: dividing up the expense of major installations, such as heating units and water mains, among a number of families to reduce the per capita investment. But the other approach to the problem —mass-produced portable and prefabricated housing—about which we hear even more today, goes back at least as far.

Balloon-frame construction, as we have seen, early in the last century made substantial houses much more widely available than they had been before. But maximum availability could be achieved only when the building industry adopted mass-production techniques similar to those developed in the manufacture of firearms, machinery, and watches. In recent years, particularly as a result of the war-stimulated demand for emergency housing of workers, we have learned a great deal about prefabrication of houses and about portable and demountable buildings. One gathers from present-day writers on architecture and construction that these are almost exclusively twentieth-century developments. (The John B. Pierce Foundation, for example, published in 1943 a *History of Prefabrication*, by Alfred Bruce and Harold Sandbank, which mentions no case of precut or sectional buildings before 1892.) Certainly many important features of modern technique are of recent origin, but the theory of prefabrication itself, and its pioneer practice, go back well into the nineteenth century. Hewn-timber houses and buildings were shipped ready-cut to all parts of the world, as we know from early records. The old Seamen's Chapel, or Mission House, in Honolulu, was sent from Boston around Cape Horn in a whaling ship in 1820.

Even some of the most revolutionary current methods were proposed more than a hundred years ago by a weird Pittsburgh genius named John Adolphus Etzler. He described them at considerable length in a long memorial to Congress and in a book called *The Paradise within the Reach of All Men, without Labor, by Powers of Nature and Machinery*, first published in this country in 1833, reissued a number of times in England, and rather scornfully reviewed by Henry Thoreau in the leading article of the *Democratic Review* for November 1843. Etzler described, for instance, how wood, if "cut and ground to dust and then cemented with a liquor," could be molded into any shape and dried so as to become a solid, consistent substance which could be dyed and polished. Thus, he announced, "we may mould and bake any form of any size, entire walls, floors, ceilings, roofs, . . . furnitures, . . . kitchen utensils, pieces of machineries." He proposed the construction of huge, air-conditioned apartment buildings, to be made of "large solid masses, baked or cast in one piece . . . so as to join and hook into each other firmly."

Apparently Etzler's schemes never came to anything much, and the man himself was so completely lost sight of that a popular American writer of the seventies—confused by the numerous English editions of the book—referred to him as "Mr. Etzler, of England." But prefabrication on a less ambitious scale managed to make considerable headway during the next few years. Thomas P. Kettell observed in 1861 that "the settler on the new lands of the West is now not always required to plunge into the wilderness and rear his first shelter from logs, but may have his house sent from Chicago or other cities by railroad, and put up to await his coming." By 1873 an anonymous writer was able to say that with the opening of the West, with the new methods of transportation, and with the application of machinery to lessening the expenditure of labor, domestic architecture had "partaken fully" of the spirit of the age; the Western prairies, he said, were dotted over with houses which had been "shipped there all made, and the various pieces numbered, so that they could be put up complete, by anyone." One of the most interesting of the United States exhibits at the Paris Universal Exposition of 1867 was a balloon-frame farmhouse which had been shipped in sections by its manufacturer, Colonel Lyman Bridges, of Chicago, and assembled at the exposition. Bridges had, for a number of years, been in the business of supplying settlers in the West with portable, prefabricated buildings of this type. According to his own testimony at the time, the majority of his customers ordered houses of from two to four rooms, which cost from two hundred to six hundred dollars, but about one out of seven bought more pretentious houses which sold at prices up to a thousand dollars. Schoolhouses, also, were supplied to pioneer villages (usually of a standardized 24′ × 36′ floor plan— costing a thousand dollars), and stores of various styles and sizes could be had at prices ranging from five hundred to two thousand dollars. Similarly, D. N. Skillings and D. B. Flint manufactured and sold in Boston and New York in the early sixties farmhouses, barns, hospitals and barracks for the Union armies, depots for the Adams Express Company, all made in sections, any one of which could be applied to any building of their make (on the general principle of interchangeable parts).

Ready-Made Houses.

Col. DERROM'S PATENT.

The great want of our day is CHEAP HOMES for the people.

These can be made of fire-resisting materials if desired, with little extra cost.

Cottages, Villas, and other Constructions.

Contracts taken to erect Buildings of any style or size.

DOLLARS CAN BE SAVED BY THIS SYSTEM.

Particularly adapted for Camp Grounds, Seaside and Summer Resorts, Pioneer Settlements, the West Indies, Etc., Etc.

The most simple mode yet produced of Sectional Portable Buildings,

Neat, Effective, and Cheap.

THE BEST SECTIONAL BUILDINGS EXTANT.

Neat, Convenient, and Cheap; used for Residences, Temporary or Permanent.

For particulars, address

A. DERROM, CONSULTING ARCHITECT,

Room 44, Tribune Building,

NEW YORK.

☞ PAY YOUR POSTAGE.

Figure 11: Prefabricated Houses as Advertised in 1876

(From *The Manufacturer and Builder*, February, 1876)

It is difficult to trace the development of prefabrication. Source material for such history (such as catalogues and advertisements) is ephemeral, and no one thus far seems to have bothered to collect the available scraps. But by the seventies the system was well established. Derrom's Ready-Made Houses were widely advertised in 1876. (See Fig. 11.) The Ducker Portable House Company, of New York, published an extensive catalogue of buildings made up of strong, light, wood-framed sections—covered with an indurated, waterproof fiber—which locked together without the use of nails, screws, or any other appliance. William H. Wahl, writing in the eighties, said that the manufacture of portable houses had become an important industry in the United States. According to his account, they were extensively used by builders of such public works as railroads and canals; by the Army (as barracks, hospitals, etc.); and by miners, sportsmen, photographers, and others. Railway stations, storehouses, bathing houses, pavilions, fruit stands, summer kitchens, and outbuildings of every description were available, and one could buy substantial summer cottages "of many styles and as elaborately finished outside and inside as may be wished." By 1897, when the Klondike gold rush began, a New York company immediately shipped a large number of houses overland, and began loading a vessel to carry more of them to Seattle via Cape Horn, all of them ready-made in sections so that they could be carried easily in boats up the Yukon or packed on sleds.

Unfortunately these early experiments with prefabricated houses did not lead to a thoroughgoing modernization of the building industry. For one thing carpenters and builders early organized to resist the adoption of a house-manufacturing method which threatened to deprive many of them of jobs. Perhaps equally important, the architects must have quietly done all they could to discourage people from buying the mass-produced products which threatened not only to deprive their profession of work, but also to standardize architectural forms and characteristics which seemed to them incompatible with good taste. We have seen how the vernacular tradition in purely technological design ran afoul of the cultivated tradition during the early days of machine design when inventors had to turn to cabinetmakers and architects for patternmaking. But that was simply the result of the inevitable fumbling for methods and techniques which characterizes early procedure in any new field. House design was quite a different matter; it was not a new field, and it had long been the province of the architects—who had the weight and prestige of the cultivated tradition behind them.

Here, then, and in the development of balloon-framing, were the makings for a showdown between the two traditions. The inevitable clash was marked by all the features which we have come to recognize as misfortunes in the social and artistic history of the United States. On the one hand, the emergent vernacular tradition—neglected as it was by the architects— was free to evolve solutions for problems inherent in the new civilization's environment; but its freedom was bought at the cost of losing all contact with the humane tradition of western European art. On the other hand, the cultivated tradition, refusing to adapt itself to the new environment, turned in upon itself—marrying itself to its own past; and the more it did so, the more anemic and impotent it became. The results of this conflict, at the worst, were on the one hand the bare, unimaginative, depressing houses which stalked both sides of Main Street in Western manufacturing and mining towns, and on the other hand the pointlessly mendacious pseudo-classical and pseudo-Renaissance public buildings which were pompously erected in the proudest cities of the land.

Yet, however much weight the cultivated tradition had, it was a dead weight. In the long run the vernacular, with its creative vitality, was certain to exert increasing influence. At first, of course, this influence was felt almost exclusively in those areas where the new civilization was least subject to the restraining influence of the older culture. In geographical terms this meant the new industrial centers, particularly in the Midwest and West; in social terms it meant the fields of inexpensive housing and of commercial and industrial structures. It was precisely in these subartistic areas that balloon-frame construction and prefabrication of buildings were developed (both of them, apparently, first in Chicago, and both of them for the satisfaction of plain people's needs); and it was largely in such utilitarian structures as factories, grain elevators, and warehouses that a tradition was developed of direct, unembarrassed simplicity and common-sense adaptation of form to function.

In these areas also there emerged yet another major achievement of the vernacular: the expressive use of the iron or steel skeleton. In order to understand the relationship of this architectural advance to the vernacular tradition as a whole, we must turn for a moment to an even earlier development: the use of iron as a building material.

The first building in which iron columns replaced the masonry of the outer walls as the support of the various floors was a five-story factory erected by James Bogardus in New York in 1848. Boulton and Watt in England had used cast-iron beams and columns in interior construction forty-seven years earlier, but Bogardus was the first to employ exterior iron columns as supports in place of brick or stone columns or walls. From 1850 on he designed and built a great number of buildings of this type, using prefabrication techniques much like those which we have already mentioned in the discussion of the construction of American iron bridges. (See Fig. 12.)

The discovery of gold in California gave the necessary impetus for the development of Bogardus' invention. Previously he had been unable to persuade American or English capitalists to invest in his project, but when the rush to California set in there was suddenly a huge market. Wrought-iron parts for buildings which were shipped to San Francisco by his English competitors required a month to assemble, but the buildings Bogardus sent out by the shipload could be put up in a day.

Throughout the next thirty years iron was widely used in the United States; but in spite of the fact that Bogardus had hoped from the start to introduce it in domestic architecture, its use (other than in hidden or disguised structural members —as, for instance, in the dome of the Capitol at Washington) was largely confined to warehouses, office buildings, and other structures which were often regarded as beneath the notice of official architecture. Iron, as iron, was suspect.[3]

[3]The professional architect's attitude toward iron as a structural material is plainly revealed in Minard Lafever's *The Architectural Instructor*, New York, 1856, pp. 405–07. Iron, Lafever wrote, was suitable for "warehouses, crystal palaces, banks, and printing establishments" and also "for the interior structure and decoration" of other buildings where fireproof construction was desirable and where floors and galleries required strong support with a minimum of material. For such decorative details as window pediments and cornices, he pointed out, iron when painted and sanded "has the ornate and massive appearance almost of carved stone."

To the custodians of the cultivated tradition the new material offered nothing. Ruskin, after all, had made it clear that "true architecture does not admit iron as a constructive material" because the sense of proportion and the laws of

Figure 12: The Sun Iron Building, Baltimore
Designed by James Bogardus (from G. W. Howard, *The Monumental City, Its Past History and Present Resources*, Baltimore, 1873)

structure had always been based on the use of clay, wood, and stone; a metallic framework would inevitably create a flimsy appearance. Indeed, such works as the cast-iron central spire of Rouen Cathedral and the roofs and pillars of iron railroad stations were, he flatly asserted, "not architecture at all." In 1869 the editors of *Appleton's Journal,* one of the most influential of all the magazines which were trying to improve America's taste in the arts, announced that the use of iron in architecture was "utterly destructive to its dignity." Seven years later Richard Morris Hunt, architect of a number of Fifth Avenue châteaux and Newport villas, and a staunch advocate of "art education for the masses," echoed Ruskin in his official report on the architecture of the Centennial Exhibition when he said that because the main building was built of glass and iron there was "a total absence of anything like monumental grandeur or even apparent substantiality" about it. The author of *Gems of the Centennial Exhibition* (1877) went even further, asserting that there was an "utter lack of beauty and picturesqueness in all iron-frame buildings," and that iron columns and girders, filled in with plate glass, could only produce an inartistic effect.

But to those who, like the authors of *The Great Industries of the United States,* had living contact with the everyday world of machines and trade about them, the use of iron seemed "one of the chief improvements of modern times." It was clear enough to them, to be sure, that the architects of the sixties and seventies had not yet evolved a satisfactory treatment of the new material; but they knew that it had potentialities which should not be neglected. They saw that London's Crystal Palace of 1851 had pointed the way toward exciting new architectural forms and methods of treatment. Here, they

J. B. & J. M. CORNELL,

PLAIN & ORNAMENTAL IRON WORKS,

Office and Wareroom, Nos. 139, 141 & 143 Centre St., New York.

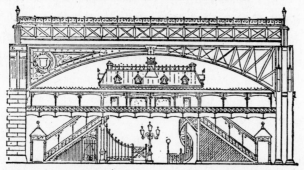

—(Estimates Furnished for Iron Work of all kinds on application.)—

FIRE-PROOF BUILDINGS,
IRON FRONTS,
Railroad Buildings, Stations, Depots
and Warehouses,
BRIDGES, ROOFS & FLOORS,
ELEVATED RAILROADS,
Solid Wrought Iron Rolled Beams,
Angles and Tees,

PATENT LIGHT SIDEWALKS, FLOORS,
ROOFS AND AREAS,
REVOLVING SHUTTERS,
FIRE-PROOF CEILINGS AND FLOORS,
Cornell's Fire-Proof Lath,
DOORS, SKYLIGHTS, STAIRS, COLUMNS, COR-
NICES, LINTELS, SHUTTERS, RAILINGS,
GATES, ETC., ETC

BURGLAR-PROOF SAFES AND VAULTS.

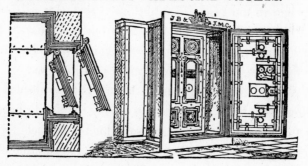

Figure 13: Iron Fronts to Order
(From advertisement in *The Vermont Business Directory,*
Boston, 1881)

wrote, was a material whose tensile strength permitted its use in slender pillars and thin sheets, allowing "an unprecedented proportion of space for windows"; a material which was cheap, handy, strong, safe, and easily movable. No sentimental, Ruskinish objections could, in their view, prevent the increased use of a material with such advantages, and the time would surely come when increased knowledge would lead to its scientific use.

Meanwhile, however, the chief recommendation of iron as an architectural material was the ease with which it could "embody any architectural design." From the architectural rather than the engineering point of view, it was the "iron front" rather than the iron frame that was most interesting, and huge factories were built in Baltimore, New York, Chicago, and other cities to make iron fronts for buildings throughout the country. (See Fig. 13.) Little attention has been paid to this aspect of our architectural history, and the available information has never been collected. Casual research reveals, however, that twenty iron-front buildings, all designed by the architects Van Osdel and Bauman, were built in Chicago in the year 1856, the iron fronts for all but two of which were made (if not designed) by D. D. Badger & Co. of New York. The other two, one of which was a bank, were made by Stone, Boomer, and Bouton of Chicago.

A few fine, intelligently handled examples of iron buildings were built anonymously during the third quarter of the century, such as the warehouses which have recently been restored as part of the Jefferson Memorial Park on the old St. Louis waterfront. But most architects who used iron at all continued to treat it as nearly as possible as if it were stone, casting it in Corinthian columns and Romanesque or Gothic arches. (See Plate V.) In cities like Chicago and Baltimore there were by 1870 many commercial buildings with iron fronts which were modeled as nearly as possible in the forms and proportions of stone, with only such modifications as the nature of iron made necessary. Such imitation of old forms in new materials is apparently an inevitable stage of development. When sheets of galvanized steel were used to cover the fronts of wooden-frame buildings in the eighties, they were stamped in patterns resembling stone and brick and iron. (See Fig. 14.) Worse still, when Chicago was rebuilt after the fire of 1871, and stone was reintroduced in place of the iron which had melted and buckled so quickly in the fire, the forms which had themselves been modified metal imitations of stone construction were now in turn imitated in masonry which was painted to look exactly like cast iron.

Nevertheless, the essential scheme of a metal frame was becoming firmly established, and the way was being prepared for the development of the steel-skeleton architecture which —in skyscrapers and great factories—later appeared as one of the most distinctive achievements of American art. With the increasing use of steel during the seventies and eighties, new techniques of construction had been evolved. In 1874 James B. Eads completed the famous steel-arch bridge across the Mississippi at St. Louis—the first bridge in the world in which steel was extensively used, and a structure which served as an important stimulus to the development of the Chicago School of Architecture in the eighties and nineties. The engineering problems presented by Eads' design and solved by him in carrying it out, and the honesty and majesty of the finished structure, marked it at once as a monument in the history of bridge building. But it was more than that. From this bridge

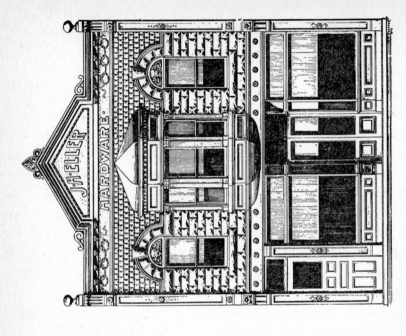

Figure 14: Stamped Metal Fronts—Circa 1890
(From *General Catalogue No. 24*, The Eller Manufacturing Company, Canton, Ohio. Reproduced with permission of the Milcor Steel Company, Cleveland, Ohio.)

Louis Sullivan, the greatest of the Chicago architects of the end of the century, caught his vision of the power of the creative dreamer—"he who possessed the power of vision needed to harness the intellect, to make science do his will, to make the emotions serve him."

One of the first buildings in which the steel skeleton was used without any self-supporting walls was William LeBaron Jenney's Leiter Building (1889) at the corner of Van Buren and State streets, Chicago. Unlike Jenney's earlier Home Insurance Company Building (1883–85), which was the first "skyscraper" actually erected, the Leiter Building displays practically no reminiscences of academic architectural styles; as in Jenney's proposed building for the Hercules Manufacturing Company, the huge squares of the steel skeleton give shape and form to the exterior. Wide areas of glass screen the interior from the weather, and there is so little ornament that the eye is not distracted from the clean, strong shape of the building. (See Plate VI.) To many contemporary critics it was of no account as architecture, but the anonymous author of *Industrial Chicago* (1891) admired its light, airy, yet substantial appearance and astutely observed that it was constructed "with the same science and all the careful inspection" that would be used in the construction of a steel bridge of the first order.

It would be wrong to give the impression that engineering construction in the United States surpassed the achievements of contemporary Europe. As in the case of machine building, the truth seems to be quite the contrary. According to Giedion, French engineers achieved the most audacious and brilliant constructions during the period from 1855 to 1900, Cottancin's and Dutert's Galerie des Machines and the

Eiffel Tower at the Paris Exhibition of 1889 marking the climax and conclusion of a long development. But it was in the United States, and specifically in Chicago during the eighties and nineties, that the science of the engineer and the creative genius of the artist combined to produce a new urban architecture: the clear-cut, open skyscrapers of Jenney, of Burnham and Root, and of Adler and Sullivan.

While emphasizing the engineers' role in developing new techniques and forms we should not, however, lose sight of the fact that architecture, rightly conceived, has always concerned itself with more than mere construction, and that the engineers had by no means taken over the large-scale humanizing and planning functions of the architect. The result inevitably was that whenever vernacular forms were in competition with the work of the best-cultivated architects people were likely to prefer the latter. So, for example, the success of the vernacular in Chicago's business district during the eighties and early nineties was for a time almost completely obscured by the academic brilliance of the cultivated tradition as displayed at the Chicago World's Fair of 1893. Returning to the classic forms which had dominated our official architecture in the first decades of the century, the architects erected an impressive group of buildings which, according to the glowing tribute of Hubert H. Bancroft, the Western historian, were "a triumph of the aesthetical." It has often been said that the Chicago Fair set back American architecture thirty years; and in a sense it did. Certainly there was more originality of design in Sullivan's Transportation Building than in the scholarly classic revival buildings which dominated the exhibition. But in another sense the fair was a significant achievement. Never before had Americans seen a group of buildings so skillfully harmonized; nowhere else had they been able to wander down one apparently endless vista of beautifully correlated façades, then turn a corner and face another, and never encounter a discordant detail. It was this over-all planning, this total effect, which made the borrowed, academic style so impressive to the thousands who visited the fair. So long as the fine achievements of the vernacular remained isolated and unrelated phenomena, they inevitably failed to capture the public imagination on so vast a scale.

The century ended with academic architecture in the ascendancy, and with McKim, Mead, and White as the leading practitioners of the art. But despite the elegance and echoed charm of such buildings as the Boston Public Library (1887–95) and New York's Pennsylvania Railroad Station (1906–10), the work of men like McKim, who operated in the cultivated tradition, had less relation to the vital contemporary forces of American life, and to its future, than even the crudest, least ingratiating examples of small-town dwellings or the most materialistically functional office buildings. And meanwhile, however thoroughly Louis Sullivan's work was eclipsed by his Eastern contemporaries, he for one had fused the vital impulses of the vernacular into what he liked to describe as *organic* architecture (a word which he loved for its sense of "a ten-fingered grasp of reality"). The vision he had caught from the great St. Louis bridge was given concrete expression in his buildings. "With me," he wrote to Claude Bragdon, "architecture is not an art, but a religion, and that religion but a part of the greater religion of Democracy." Here, close to the vernacular roots, was the first flowering of an architecture indigenous to modern civilization.

4

The Practical and the Æsthetic

It is neither necessary nor possible in this book to analyze in detail the interaction of the cultivated and vernacular traditions in nineteenth-century architecture. Enough has been said to suggest the limitations of a historical or critical approach which confines its attention to the development in the United States of the western European tradition, and to indicate that wherever modern civilization has been freely accepted the characteristics of the vernacular tradition have appeared in whatever patterns people have created.

It is not a question of which examples of architecture (or painting, or literature) are "best" or "finest"; such absolute qualitative judgments are meaningless unless they are made in relation to specific criteria of judgment. By the standards of the academic tradition Memorial Hall at the Centennial Exhibition (now the Pennsylvania Museum in Fairmount Park) was a "finer" building than others which, by the standards of good facilities for exhibiting things, were far finer than it was. A striking instance of the latter was the Pomological Annex, a temporary structure which has been neglected in all discussions of the Centennial's architecture and of which only one picture seems to have been made, but which deserves attention for the striking way in which its form and spirit prefigure those of many modern buildings. (See Plate VII.) The only contemporary description of it which has come to light speaks apologetically of the fact that it was designed without any effort at ornamentation, for purely utilitarian purposes. The walls rose solid to a height convenient for purposes of display, but above that point they were simply glass screens of continuous sash. The interior was light, airy, and cheerful, painted white, with a roof supported by plain joists and girders. In short, the annex was an intelligently designed structure, without any of the pretense that infected the other exhibition buildings. Even the Main Building and Machinery Hall, for all that they were competent engineering designs in iron, were dressed up in meretricious ornament copied from stone and wood forms.

Indeed, in the United States, as throughout the Western world, one of the most characteristic features of the interaction of the two traditions in the industrial and plastic arts was the way in which the materials and methods of technology were employed to perpetuate the forms and modes of craftsmanship. Nothing could be more marked, for instance, than the contrast which frequently existed between the clean, functional design of nineteenth-century machines and the unreasonable fussiness of the objects they were used to manufacture. Industrialization has often been accused of cheapening everything it touched, but the case was often precisely the opposite. Manufacturers in Europe and in America often went to a great deal of extra trouble and expense in order to satisfy cultivated taste by turning out machine-made lighting fixtures, hardware, mantel decorations, furniture, and other ornamental objects which were designed to be beautiful in the same way that handicraft objects were beautiful. (See Fig. 15.) It was not until the twentieth century that the custodians of culture acquired any confidence in the aesthetic merit of forms which were appropriate to machine manufacture. And by that time they faced the tremendous task of undoing the work of their predecessors who had so diligently labored to undermine popular esteem for the vernacular. Schools and museums and books and magazines had so long and so arduously taught people to despise the indigenous products of their environment that it was difficult to persuade them to cherish suddenly what they had so long ignored. Many Americans were—and for that matter are—timid or indifferent in their relationships with the so-called fine arts; it is only in those areas which are outside the scope of the cultivated tradition that they universally felt—and feel—themselves to be on sure ground. As one of our art historians has said, the dealer who put on the market an automobile as inept and clumsy in design as nine out of ten public monuments would be unable to sell it. But this fact is noted as an indication only of the average American's lack of artistic sense, the historian clearly assuming that a beautiful monument is inherently more artistic than a beautiful automobile. Elsewhere in the same volume, for example, it is admitted that automobiles, airplanes, and locomotives are perhaps "the most satisfying aesthetically" of all modern products, but they are excluded from consideration on the grounds that they are in the realm of industrial design, not art.

This exclusive doctrine of art's domain is closely allied to another doctrine which has had considerable vogue in one form or another for many years. This is the doctrine, alluded to earlier in this book, which maintains that art cannot exist

Figure 15: Decorative Art in Cast Iron—Circa 1880
Iron washstands and garden seat by J. L. Mott Iron Works (from the *Illustrated Catalogue of the Plumbing and Sanitary Department of the J. L. Mott Iron Works*, New York, 1881; and Philip T. Sandhurst, *Industrial and Fine Arts*, Philadelphia, 1879)

except in the neighborhood of a wealthy and aristocratic class. As applied to the post-Civil War period, for instance, the theory is that the newly rich, "fired with the innate human passion for conspicuous waste," surrounded themselves with luxury and patronized art. Being alien to the aristocratic tradition, the theory continues, they did these things crudely; and yet the collections of Mr. Morgan, Mr. Altman, and Mrs. Gardner, for example, are nevertheless held to have "greatly enriched American cultural resources." This, it seems to me, is a weird mismarriage of Veblen and snobbery! It is hard to believe that those who hold such a theory have any basic objection either to conspicuous waste or to the idea that the artist is by nature a sponge to absorb such waste. One suspects that the thing they are interested in is whether the particular sponges they happen to like are doing the absorbing.

The doctrine of artistic exclusiveness has a sturdy history. In J. L. Blake's *Family Encyclopedia* (1834) the orthodox view is bluntly revealed in the statement that "a general love of coarse pleasures" distinguishes the multitude from the more polite classes, and "the inferior orders of society are therefore disqualified from deciding upon the merits of the fine arts." That was the cant phrase of a camp follower of the cultivated tradition. But less than ten years later the vernacular found its first important defender.

Horatio Greenough (1805–52) has been known almost exclusively as the sculptor of a vast, almost naked Washington which horrified his contemporaries. All of his completed work was sentimentally imitative of classical sculpture; one could scarcely find an American artist whose work more clearly reflected the impotence of creative talent working in alien but admired forms. But in recent years it has become clear that Greenough's place in the history of art in the United States has little relation to his statues. It is his life, and his ideas, which now seem important.

Discouraged by the popular reaction to the statue of Washington which he had brought over from his studio in Florence in November 1842 ("A grand martial Magog," Philip Hone called it, "undressed, with a napkin lying in his lap"), and disappointed by the inadequate setting provided for it, Greenough nevertheless was a staunch and loyal democrat. He wrote to his brother Henry from Wilmington, Delaware, in the spring of '43: "If I succeed in placing my Washington in a good light, I may dissolve my connection with the Government. I have enjoyed as much as any artist ever enjoyed in my profession. . . . My heart will always yearn after America." Having gone to Rome to study sculpture directly after finishing his studies at Harvard in 1825, he spent most of his time abroad (chiefly at Florence) until 1851, making only occasional trips to the United States. Italy appealed to him, as to all our early sculptors, because skilled marble workers were available there. But Europe was never his home, and he missed what he called the "world of living and acting men." In Liverpool, for instance, he spoke of the contrast between Englishmen and Americans and how the former had "a kind of groomed neatness which seems to be the result of police interference,—an expression of respectable servitude." Again, in Vienna he noted "the sort of military view taken of life" which "sweetens subordination to all classes. . . . I believe that we found our institutions upon hope, they upon experience. We hoist the sail and are seasick; they anchor and dance." Although, as he wrote shortly before he died in 1852, he had been inoculated to some extent during his travels with the various ways of thinking of men of different races, creeds, and forms of civilization, he had nevertheless retained "nearly the same proportion of original Yankee conviction to afterthought that you will find of matrix to pebbles in the puddingstones of Roxbury, Mass."

In 1851 political troubles in Florence had led him to give up his studio there and return with his family to the United States. Here he was caught up immediately by the spirit of active power which seemed to him the characteristic feature of American life. And he began work on a book which appeared in incomplete form in 1852 (the year of his death).

This extraordinary little volume—*The Travels, Observations, and Experience of a Yankee Stonecutter*—included several essays and lectures which Greenough had written some years earlier during visits to America, and which had been published in periodicals.

Writing in the *Democratic Review* for July 1843, Greenough had early declared his impatience with the doctrine of exclusiveness in art. Just as the British aristocracy had come to regard the masses as "a flock to be fed, and defended, and cherished, for the sake of their mutton," he wrote, so also the Academies of Fine Arts in Europe had made "a band of educandi the basis of a hierarchy." But Greenough could not accept such dogma. "It is the great multitude for whom all really great things are done and said and suffered," he maintained. And he added, with a humility rare in men whose own work has been damned: "The great multitude desires the best of everything, and in the long run is the best judge of it." And again: "The monuments, the pictures, the statues of the republic will represent what the people love and wish for,—not what they can be made to accept. . . ."

Despite the recent revival of interest in Greenough's ideas, his writings have never been reprinted in their entirety and copies of his book are available in only a very few libraries.[1] It will be necessary, therefore, to quote here those passages which will convey some notion of the alertness of his observation and the flavor of his genius; for this neglected writer was possessed of one of the wisest and most farseeing critical talents in American literature.

The subjects of his various chapters seem strangely assorted at first glance: "Chastity," "American Art," "Social Theories," "Aesthetics at Washington," "American Architecture." Yet all the essays are essentially related to one another; they are all, as he said of his book, meant to be signs that he, for one, "born by the grace of God in this land, found life a cheerful thing, and not that sad and dreadful task with whose prospect they scared my youth."

Living in an age of transcendentalists and social visionaries, he clung stoutly to the actual. "For these reasons," he wrote in his essay on Fourier and the other social reformers of Europe and America, "do I mistrust the theorist. Nine times in ten hath he no wholesome, working, organic relation with God's ground or with his fellow-men. . . . Nine times in ten doth he sit perched upon an income which is a dead branch of the living tree of industry, and with his belly distended by the east wind, and his heart sour with the ambition that hath struck inward, doth he spout generalities." The real test of Fourier's theoretical writings, Greenough felt, would be to read them in a German beerhouse in New York, or amid

---

[1] Some of his best essays were reprinted early in 1948 in a small collection entitled *Form and Function*, edited by Harold A. Small and published by the University of California Press.

throngs of low-browed and big-jawed Hibernians, stepping here on shore with vast appetite and a faith that removes mountains. "I love the concrete, my brother! and I can look Sir Isaac Newton in the eye without flinching; I kneel to Willy Shakespeare, who guessed to a drop how much oil goes to a Lombard's salad. Give me the man who, seated in that fog bank between the North Sea and the Irish Channel, held horses at the playhouse and found it in his head to teach kings how to wear a crown! . . . That's the mind that I will follow, not only because he is substantial, hath an *avoirdupois,* a perfume and a taste, but because he is multiform, elastic, not procrustean, not monomaniacal."

With an elaborate (and not altogether successful) figure of speech in this same essay Greenough probes once more for the heart of his belief. The fruit of the tree of civilization, he says, is knowledge, or science, and the seeds within it are wisdom; but the fruit must be plucked from the tree and consigned to "that earth which we all despise so truly—the hearts and heads of common men; there must it find the soil and moisture, blood and tears, which burst its rind and evolve the godhead within."

Greenough was bound by no reverence for the conventional view of any subject. He denounces the notion of chastity, for instance, as any but a negative and relative virtue. "I know that it comes from very far east and is very old—I am, however, from very far west, and . . . disposed to look narrowly into the matter."

As for architecture, Greenough felt that Americans had mauled and misused Gothic and Greek and Roman and, even where we had succeeded in actually copying, had produced something which was only a make-believe. The number and variety of our experiments with architectural styles was a witness of our dissatisfaction with them; their expense, a witness of the strength of our desire for excellence. And the talents and abilities of the men employed were an indication that the failure to create a satisfactory architecture lay in the system, not in the men.

The Mint in Philadelphia, for instance, was in reality built to house vast engines and printing and coining machines, and the furnaces to operate them. Its Chestnut Street front, however, was a "maimed quotation of a passage of Greek eloquence, relating to something else," while in the rear rose a huge brick chimney, talking everyday English and warning you that the façade was to be taken with some grains of allowance.

However, let us turn, says Greenough, to a structure of our own, one which by its nature and uses commands us to reject authority:

> Observe a ship at sea! What Academy of Design, what research of connoisseurship, what imitation of the Greeks produced this marvel of construction? Here is the result of the study of man upon the great deep, where Nature spake of the laws of building . . . in wind and waves, and he bent all his mind to hear and to obey. . . . If this anatomic connection and proportion has been attained in ships, in machines, and, in spite of false principles, in such buildings as make a departure from it fatal, as in bridges and in scaffolding, why should we fear its use in all construction!

Greenough looked about him with eyes unclouded by the cant and conventions of aesthetic tradition.

> The men who have reduced locomotion to its simplest elements, in the trotting wagon and the yacht America, are nearer to Athens at this moment than they who would bend the Greek temple to every use. I contend for Greek principles, not Greek

things. If a flat sail goes nearest the wind, a bellying sail, though picturesque, must be given up. The slender harness, and tall gaunt wheels, are not only effective, they are beautiful for they respect the beauty of a horse, and do not uselessly tax him.

Looking at the skeletons and skins of animals, birds, and fish, he found a variety and a beauty which led him to observe that there is "no arbitrary law of proportion, no unbending model of form in them. It is neither the presence nor the absence of this or that part or shape or color that wins our eye in natural objects; it is the consistency and harmony of the parts juxtaposed, the subordination of details to masses, and of masses to the whole." And from these direct, unborrowed observations of the world around him he deduced a theory which anticipates—even in its phrasing—the famous theory of which Louis Sullivan became the apostle a half century later: "If there be any principle of structure more plainly inculcated in the works of the Creator than all others, it is the principle of unflinching adaptation of forms to function."

In all structures which are by their nature purely scientific—such as fortifications, bridges, and ships—we had, as Greenough saw it, been emancipated from the authority of tradition "by the stern organic requirements of the works." If an artist would compare American vehicles and ships with those of England, he maintained, he would see that "the mechanics of the United States had outstripped the artists." In the American trotting wagon he would see the old-fashioned and pompous coach dealt with "as the old-fashioned palatial display must yet be dealt with in this land. . . . The redundant must be pared down, the superfluous dropped, the necessary itself reduced to its simplest expression. . . ."

The quality which Greenough admired in the work of

American mechanics was quite the opposite of that which appeared in "art-manufacture"; he made it perfectly clear that it was not to be confused with the crude plagiarisms of "steam artisans." Nor was it the cheap product of mere naïve materialism; for the style the mechanics had achieved was really the dearest of all styles. "It costs the thought of men," he wrote, "much, very much thought, untiring investigation, ceaseless experiment. Its simplicity is not the simplicity of emptiness or of poverty: its simplicity is that of justness, I had almost said, of justice."

The simplicity Greenough admired was the simplicity which resulted from knowledge and understanding, from science. Embellishment of any kind was to him the product of ignorance or superstition, and was hence to be avoided even at the risk of nakedness; for in nakedness he recognized "the majesty of the essential, without the trappings of pretension."

Greenough never elaborated a theory of aesthetics to bolster his judgments, but he did state his position briefly, and far more cogently than he has been given credit for. In essence his idea was this: man is not gifted, as brutes are, with an instinctive sense of completeness. Being aware, through his *senses*, that there is a rhythm and harmony in the universe beyond any adaptation of means to ends which his *reason* can measure, man seeks to perfect his own approximation to the essential by crowning it with a wreath of measured and musical, yet non-rational (or as he put it, "non-demonstrable") additions of ornament. In other words man applies embellishment to the products of his rational and scientific designing, hoping thereby to make them more *beautiful*, more in keeping with the many-sided and full and rich harmony which he senses but does not understand in nature. But, says Greenough, this many-sided harmony in nature is in reality a many-sided response to the call for many functions, not an aesthetical utterance of the Godhead. If we find an apparent embellishment in nature, we can assume that it appears to be such only because we do not yet know enough to understand the function to which it is adapted.

"I base my opinion of embellishment," he wrote, "upon the hypothesis that there is not one truth in religion, another in the mathematics, and a third in physics and in art; but that there is one truth even as one God, and that organization is his utterance." Here, then, was the basis for his admiration of the functional forms achieved by mechanics and engineers, and for his distrust of all those theories which asserted that this or that form or color was beautiful *per se*—theories which, he maintained, could be held only by those who arrogate to themselves godship; and to one with Greenough's faith in democracy it seemed clear that "once that false step is taken, human-godship or tyranny is inevitable." Here, too, was the first reasoned defense of the vernacular in the arts.

Few of Greenough's articulate contemporaries shared his interest in and enthusiasm for the aesthetic qualities of the forms of the emerging vernacular. There were, of course, striking analogies between his ideas about American art and those of some of the great writers of his time. Emerson, especially, was hospitable to his ideas; "when one has once got his thought," he wrote to William Emerson, "it will stick by you." And Greenough's admiration for Emerson is indicated by the fact that he sought his opinion of the material to be included in *The Travels, Observations, and Experience of a*

Yankee Stonecutter, saying that he would publish nothing till he had Emerson's advice. But the only mid-century art critic who came anywhere near Greenough's discovery of the new art forms was James Jackson Jarves, who in 1864 published *The Art Idea: Sculpture, Painting, and Architecture in America.* Jarves had traveled a great deal (he established the first newspaper in the Hawaiian Islands in 1840), and had studied and collected Italian art. He recognized that "our ocean clippers, river steamers, and industrial machines . . . bespeak an enterprise, invention, and development of the practical arts" which was indigenous to our civilization. But he regretfully concluded that, "were we annihilated tomorrow, nothing could be learned of us, as a distinctive race" from our architecture or our other arts.

For the most part, however, Jarves and his contemporaries who wrote about the arts inevitably thought in terms of the cultivated tradition. Art, in that tradition, was centuries old; its products were housed in the public and private museums and libraries of Europe and America; its history had been explored and recorded by great scholars; great writers from Vasari to Ruskin had interpreted it to the world; and schools and academies had codified and institutionalized its patterns and forms. The vernacular, on the other hand, was only beginning to take shape. Its characteristics were not established; its products were scattered and impromptu; it had no textbooks or histories.

In the United States, as in Europe, those whose innate responsiveness to patterns of shape, sound, texture, color, or ideas developed into a literate, self-conscious interest quite naturally turned for education to the libraries, the museums, the galleries, and the schools of the cultivated tradition.

The consequence was that the more interested in art Americans became, the more firmly they subjugated themselves to a tradition which not only was alien to the seminal forces in modern civilization but which also tended to discourage any appreciation of the emergent indigenous forms and patterns. They came to feel that American civilization and art were mutually incompatible. George Parsons Lathrop, writing in the late seventies, declared that America's "practical" civilization had "imperilled the higher development of the aesthetic," and that in the United States the museums of fine arts were defending art against what he scornfully called "an enlightened age" just as the monasteries had once protected it from the Dark Ages. And Henry T. Tuckerman, whose *American Artist Life* (1870) was an early and sympathetic study of our artistic progress, came to the conclusion that even if the adverse influences of our civilization did not altogether extinguish the love of art, or quell the talent for it, they did at least limit the development of both among us.

Yet even the most ardent apostles of the cultivated tradition recognized what Lathrop called the American's "inborn responsiveness to the artistic." Tuckerman, surveying the American scene at the beginning of the Gilded Age, noted that there were pianos in wilderness log cabins; daguerreotypes, photographs, engravings, and lithographs everywhere; stereoscopes in every parlor. Singers and instrumentalists drew a large box office in towns and cities throughout the land; vast quantities of sheet music were sold; art exhibits drew crowds; and art unions, picture raffles, art clubs, and art journals were ubiquitous. To play the piano with "superficial dexterity," to sketch from nature, to own "a tolerable landscape or engraving," and to read Ruskin, were all common social phenomena. The level of all this artistic activity was very mediocre, Tuckerman thought, but even so it represented "a somewhat remarkable interest in the subject."

This interest the custodians of the cultivated tradition tried in many ways to foster. To them, for instance, the Centennial Exhibition of 1876 offered no hint of that emerging vernacular whose characteristics appear in retrospect to have been so clearly illustrated in the Corliss engine; they saw it only as a chance for Americans to absorb at last—from the foreign exhibit of fine arts and art manufacture—the splendors and charms of the European tradition. Here at last was the opportunity demanded by Eugene Benson in *Appleton's Journal* six years earlier, to replace the "common, pretentious, and ugly objects of our everyday life" by those from abroad which would "soften manners and counteract the now unmitigated exercise and influence of mere industrialism." There was, of course, industrialism to counteract in Europe too. But there, at least, it was not unmitigated.

Robert Underwood Johnson, writing in 1923, remembered that not only he and his wife but the whole country got their "first bent toward the aesthetic" from the Centennial, and William H. Ellsworth in his recollections of *A Golden Age of Authors* (1919) recalled that the Centennial had not only "implanted an appreciation of art which was new to the American people," but had also stimulated a whole generation of new artists.

There is evidence enough to support these claims. E. A. Abbey acknowledged the debt he owed to the foreign contemporary paintings which he saw there—particularly those in the English section. Many of his young contemporaries were correspondingly impressed by the work of the Paris and

Munich schools; in the fall of 1876 Dwight William Tryon auctioned off all his unsold pictures and sketches, made two thousand dollars, and set out for Paris to study with a pupil of Ingres. A number of American painters had, of course, been deeply influenced by contemporary European styles long before the Centennial. William Merritt Chase and other American students had met regularly with Frank Duveneck in the smoke-filled rooms of the Max Emanuel Café in Munich in the early seventies to discuss art over huge flagons of beer; both Inness and W. M. Hunt had long shown the influence of French painting, and Saint-Gaudens and Olin Warner had studied at the Ecole des Beaux Arts. But never before the Centennial had so many American artists been so overwhelmed by the work of their European contemporaries.

Three years later S. G. W. Benjamin was reporting that there was everywhere apparent "a deeper appreciation of the supreme importance of the ideal in art, and a gathering of forces for a new advance against the strongholds of the materialism that wars against the culture of the ideal." For one thing, a widespread interest in decorative art had been excited at Philadelphia by the exhibits of tiles, furniture, textiles, and decorative objects by William Morris, De Morgan, and Alma-Tadema, and by the work of the Kensington School of Design. A number of our ablest artists—including Abbey, Saint-Gaudens, Elihu Vedder, and Stanford White—founded the famous Tile Club the year after the exhibition (at which Minton tiles had been the rage), and in the following decade a number of schools of industrial art and normal schools for training art teachers were established throughout the country.

There was a great deal of talk about "applied art"; and "art" *was* applied, with a vengeance—to everything the culture collectors could get their hands on. *Harper's Bazaar* (in its leading article for the issue of July 1, 1876) urged its fair readers to clip poems out of periodicals, paste them in "a pretty scrap album for the library table," and then "stick on all sorts of little ornaments . . . monograms, little gilt devices cut from envelope bands, flowers—anything at all that is pretty." Bric-a-brac and fretwork, in George W. Curtis' phrase, became "a consolation and joy beyond music or poetry" to many people, and two years after the Centennial the sale of jig-saw blades had leaped from a few thousand a year to about five hundred thousand a month.

Even before the Centennial the progress of art manufacture in the United States had been encouraging to those whose hatred of the ugliness of early machine civilization led them, like Morris and Ruskin in England, to attempt to revive and perpetuate the forms and the spirit of handicraft. When foreign exhibitors at Philadelphia sent only their less ornate products, because they thought Americans would prefer the plainer things, some of our commentators were bitterly offended. "Even gorgeous articles of luxury," as Walter Smith smugly recorded, "such as only princes in Europe could purchase, were sold to wealthy persons here." And he was borne out by the French critic Simonin, who warned his countrymen, in an article about the Centennial which appeared in the *Revue des Deux Mondes*, that the Americans were continually borrowing the methods and skilled processes of continental workmen and were already producing *bijouterie*, artistic bronzes, luxurious furniture, gold and silver ware, and artificial flowers which had "the veritable stamp of solidity and good taste." Nor was Simonin the last Frenchman to worry about these matters. In 1884 Monsieur Lourdelet, vice-presi-

dent of the Society of Commercial Geography in Paris, excit-
edly urged his compatriots to abandon their inefficient craft
techniques in making bronzes, furniture, and artificial flowers
and adopt the system he had seen in America, where they used
"elevators" to move materials from one floor to another in
factories, and where "nearly everything is done by steam,
even the carving." To be sure, he added, "the taste, perhaps,
is not perfect . . . ; it is not, perhaps, the best expression of
art"; but American manufacturers, he warned, were sending
designers to Europe all the time in search of "purer" ideas,
and their products were cutting heavily into the French
market in South America as well as the United States.

As an example of this American work we may take a
brass corona chandelier made by Mitchell, Vance and Company of New York. (See Fig. 16.) Here, according to Walter
Smith's survey of the masterpieces of the Centennial, was an
example of American industrial art workmanship which
Europeans might look at with pleasure and profit. Smith never
tired of repeating the Kensington doctrine that good design
calls for "honesty in construction, fitness of ornament to material, and decorative subordination"; and it was these very
qualities, he said, which made this chandelier thoroughly
satisfactory. Similarly he declared that the beauty of musical
instruments should always lie rather in their shape and adaptation to their purpose than in the richness of their ornamentation, and as an example of an instrument "free from all the
abortions in the shape of ornament with which many pretentious instruments are disfigured" he selected the Mason
& Hamlin organ which is illustrated in Fig. 17.

Nothing could show more vividly than these comments
the difference between the Kensingtonian doctrine of "subor-

Figure 16: Industrial Art Workmanship—1876
Brass Chandelier by Mitchell, Vance and Co., New York (from *Masterpieces of the Centennial International Exhibition*, Philadelphia, 1876)

Figure 17: "Decoration Subordinated to Use"
Mason & Hamlin organ exhibited at the Centennial (from *The
Masterpieces of the Centennial International Exhibition*, Philadelphia, 1877, in which Walter Smith singled it out as an example of
an instrument "free from all the abortions in the shape of ornament
with which many pretentious instruments are disfigured")

dinating decoration to use" and Greenough's doctrine of functionalism. Nowhere better than in such examples of art manufacture can we see the fruits of that tradition which had dedicated itself to persuading the Americans that they were a "raw and noisy and obtrusive people" who could be saved only by placing themselves under the influence of the past and reverently studying specimens of the arts of luxury from Europe. This is what happens when, as Howells said, "the mass of common men have been afraid to apply their own simplicity, naturalness, and honesty to the appreciation of the beautiful. They have cast about for the instruction of someone who professed to know better, and who browbeat wholesome commonsense into the self-distrust that ends in sophistication."

5

The Figure in the Carpet

It was only in areas from which the propaganda of culture was completely excluded that the vernacular aesthetic of the machine was wholeheartedly accepted. The present-day interest in Shaker crafts and architecture, no matter how carelessly the antique collectors and folk-art enthusiasts may lump them with the quaint survivals of an agrarian era, is essentially a recognition of the vitality and strength of vernacular forms evolved without any reference to the cultivated tradition. The Shakers had no fear of the machine. Their communities actually seem to have produced more mechanics and inventors per capita than most other towns and villages of comparable size. In the Shaker laundry and dairy at Canterbury, New Hampshire, at least as early as 1868 there was a stationary steam engine that did "all the work of lifting, lowering, turning, washing, ironing, drying, churning, etc."—which indicates a degree of mechanization not achieved in commercial laundries for some years thereafter. Indeed it is a noteworthy fact that the mechanical and inventive faculties which have so long been claimed as the peculiar virtue of rugged individualism turn out on inspection to have been a distinctive characteristic not only of the

Shakers but of a number of other nineteenth-century socialist communities as well. Charles Nordhoff traveled across the country in the early 1870s, visiting and collecting data on the Shakers, Perfectionists, Rappists, and others, and reported his findings in *The Communistic Societies of the United States* (1875). No one, he says, who visited a society which had been for some time in existence could fail to be struck with "the amount of ingenuity, inventive skill, and business talent developed among men from whom, in the outer world, one would not expect such qualities."

At the Shaker colony in New Gloucester, Maine, Elder Hewitt Chandler was the inventor of a mowing machine which was manufactured by the society, and of other machines which were used in making oak staves for molasses hogsheads. At the Oneida community the Perfectionists had contrived all the machines for making traps, including a very ingenious one for making the links for the chains, machines for measuring silk thread as it was wound on spools, and machines for testing the strength of thread. The severity and stripped utility of all Shaker objects (their furniture is never decorated with stencils or painted designs as are chairs and chests made in a true folk tradition like that of the Pennsylvania Dutch) was in perfect harmony with machine work. But its plain forms,— though admired by "outsiders" for their utility—could scarcely have seemed beautiful to people who were accustomed to the ornamental design of the cultivated tradition. When Nordhoff, for instance, visited the Shaker settlement at New Lebanon, he was depressed by what seemed to him to be the homeliness of the buildings, which struck him as "mere factories or human hives." He asked Elder Frederick Evans whether, if they were to build anew, they could not "aim at

some architectural effect, some beauty of design." Evans' reply was a direct, though negative, statement of the deliberate
rejection of embellishment which Greenough had achieved in
theory and the Shakers in practice. "No," he replied with
great positiveness. "The beautiful, as you call it, is absurd and
abnormal. It has no business with us. The divine has no right
to waste money upon what you would call beauty, in his house
or his daily life." If they built anew, he added, they would
design their buildings with an eye to "more light, a more
equal distribution of heat, and a more general care for protection and comfort, because these things tend to health and long
life. But no beauty."

Shaker art was thus much more closely identified with
the vernacular than with what the antiquaries call the folk
arts. In its simplicity, lightness, linear clarity, and mechanical
ingenuity it was sensitive to the technological environment,
and its social aims were in harmony with equalitarian democracy. It had a share in molding the new tradition.

But the tradition was certainly not appreciated or understood by those in Elder Evans' time who were interested
in encouraging an American style of decorative art. To be
sure, Emerson's essays and lectures were quite widely known
among the cultivated classes, and Emerson had expressed
some ideas about art which had a touch of Greenough in them.
In *The Conduct of Life* (1860), for instance, he had said, in
the essay on "Beauty," that "outside embellishment is de-
formity. . . . Hence our taste in building rejects paint, and
all shifts, and shows the original grain of the wood . . . ,"
and had pronounced it as "a rule of widest application, true
in plant, true in a loaf of bread, that in the construction of any
fabric or organism, any real increase of fitness to its end, is an

increase of beauty." But few, if any, of Emerson's readers then were free enough from cultivated preconceptions about design to grasp the literal truth of his idea. One may doubt, indeed, whether Emerson himself, in spite of his fondness for a man who liked a good barn as well as a great tragedy, would have been able to see in the New Lebanon buildings the application of his own rule. That perception had to wait for another sixty years, and for the intuitive grasp of a painter like Charles Sheeler, working in a medium for which Emerson had little use.

In the meantime culture-conscious Americans, in their search for suitable decorative arts, as in their search for a suitable architecture, overlooked the products of the vernacular. Just as Washington Irving had filled his pseudo-Gothic Sunnyside with furnishings many of which were pure Georgian, people everywhere tried to adapt assorted available styles to their everyday requirements. Far from being plain, the various fads and fashions which were encouraged by our cultural teachers—from A. J. Downing's Elizabethan and Gothic hybrids to the Eastlake-Morris styles which were so well advertised at the Centennial—were elaborate and ornate. It was left to industrial commercial folk to appreciate the plywood (or, as it was then called, "pressed-work") furniture, made out of thin sheets of wood glued together and then heated and pressed in molds, which in the seventies was replacing the old-fashioned solid, high-backed chairs and ponderous tables. It was one of the anonymous authors of *The Great Industries of the United States* who pointed out the relationship between these "lighter articles and more graceful forms" and the lightness and strength of balloon-frame construction.

No one in the mid-century had a greater influence on American taste in architecture and decoration than Downing. He published a number of books which sold widely, and his influence was further spread through the work of disciples like Calvert Vaux and Frederick Law Olmstead, the designer of New York's Central Park. On the whole his influence was healthy, and he did much to encourage the formation of what he liked to call a free and manly school of republican tastes and manners as opposed to transplanting "the meaningless conventionalities of the realms of foreign caste." But he was aware that to many people memory is dearer than hope, and he instinctively shared the tastes of these "natural conservatives," as he called them, "whom Providence has wisely distributed, even in the most democratic governments, to steady the otherwise too impetuous and unsteady onward movements of those who, in their love for progress, would obliterate the past, even in its hold on the feelings and imaginations of our race." He was happy to assure such people that they were under no obligation to be interested in an architecture related to their own time. They were quite free, he said, to surround themselves with the "forms and symbols" of some former age.

Downing was not unaware of the importance of the purely functional elements in design, but he was not prepared to follow Greenough (or the Shakers) into a rejection of all embellishment.

> A head of grain [he insisted], one of the most useful of vegetable forms, is not so beautiful as a rose; an ass, one of the most useful of animals, is not so beautiful as a gazelle; a cotton-mill, one of the most useful of modern structures, is not so beautiful as the temple of Vesta. . . .

Therefore it was an undeniable truth, he argued, that the beautiful was intrinsically something distinct from the useful, and it was consequently inevitable that many people would be unsatisfied with mere utilitarian design and would "yearn, with an instinct as strong as for life itself, for the manifestation of a higher attribute of matter." With the result in Downing's own case, for example, that though he lays it down as a general law of design that "the material should *appear* to be what it is," when he gets down to cases he nevertheless specifies that woodwork should be "oak or other dark wood, varnished, *or it should be painted and grained to resemble it.*" (Italics mine.)

Downing and his followers all opposed the brightness which was characteristic of American interiors. "Soft and delicate tints," "cool and sober tones," "fawn or neutral shades"—these are the recurrent phrases in their prescriptions for wallpapers, drapery, and carpets. (See Fig. 18.) They agreed with Edgar Allan Poe, who had told the readers of *Burton's Gentleman's Magazine* in 1840 that "glare is a leading error in the philosophy of American household decoration," and had lamented that no one here, least of all the money aristocracy, understood "the spirituality of a British *boudoir.*"

Poe's article about house furnishings suggests some interesting points about the relationship between the vernacular tradition and popular taste in interior decoration. It reminds us that the very concept of decoration, whatever its nature, is incompatible with the vernacular's unembellished utility. There could not be any such thing as vernacular decoration, in the sense which we have here attributed to that term. But the democratic-technological environment which determined the characteristics of vernacular design also imposed certain qualities upon decorative patterns wherever they occurred.

Take the matter of carpets, for example. According to Poe, whose taste in these matters was molded altogether by his affinity for a romantic if decadent aristocracy, the soul of every room is the carpet. From it should be deduced not only the hues but the forms of all other objects.

> Everyone knows [he went on] that a large floor *may* have a covering of large figures, and that a small one *must* have a covering of small—yet this is not all the knowledge in the world.

Figure 18: Interior Decoration
A. J. Downing's sketch of "a neat and simple style of finishing the parlor of a substantial house" (from Downing's *The Architecture of Country Houses*, New York, 1850)

As regards texture, the Saxony is alone admissible. . . . In brief, distinct grounds and vivid circular or cycloid figures, *of no meaning*, are here Median laws. The abomination of flowers, or representations of well-known objects of any kind, should not be endured within the limits of Christendom. . . . As for those antique floor-cloths still occasionally seen in the dwellings of the rabble—cloths of huge, sprawling and radiating devices, stripe-interspersed, and glorious with all hues, among which no ground is intelligible—these are but the wicked invention of a race of time-servers and money-lovers —children of Baal and worshippers of Mammon—Benthams, who, to spare thought and economize fancy, first cruelly invented the Kaleidoscope, and then established joint-stock companies to twirl it by steam.

Everyone, it seems, who wanted to "improve" American taste in decoration—in Poe's time and for many years thereafter—tried to discourage the popular taste for bright light, cheerful color, and for realistic forms in ornamental design. In *High Life in New York* (1854), Mrs. Ann S. Stephens ridiculed the fashionable dining room where "everything glittered and shone so it fairly took away my appetite," and the parlor whose carpet was "the brightest and softest thing I ever did see . . . enough to make a feller stun blind to look at it, the figgers on it were so allfired gaudy." And in the seventies cultivated writers were still objecting to flower patterns in carpets and to rugs which were "the best imitation of landscape painting that can be woven in dyed wool."

In this opposition to realism in fabric design, cultivated Americans were reflecting the opinion of the most respectable English authorities. They were fond of quoting, for example, from Sir Matthew Digby Wyatt, Slade professor of fine arts at Cambridge and author of a learned volume on *Industrial Arts of the Nineteenth Century* (1853). Sir Digby thus put the

case against floral designs in upholstery and carpets in his
painfully academic prose:

> The moment one is impressed with the idea of walking or sit-
> ting upon what no person in his senses would think of walking
> or sitting on, a painful sense of impropriety is experienced,
> proportioned in intensity to the vivacity with which this mis-
> appropriation of judicious design is expressed in the fabric.

But in spite of all cultivated objections, realistic representations of natural forms continued to suit the popular
taste. If carpets were to be colorful, people in general shared
Walt Whitman's preference for figures closely imitated from
nature: the deep and pale reds of autumn leaves, the green
of pines, the bright yellow of hickory. "How much better,"
Whitman had written in 1862, "than the tasteless, meaningless, and every way inartistical diagrams that we walk over,
now, in the most fashionably carpeted parlors."

Similarly, people continued to be "violently enamored
of gas and of glass" in spite of Poe's or anyone else's objections. At the Centennial the furnished rooms exhibited by
American firms were full of glass (one New York manufacturer exhibited furniture all made of mirrors), and looked,
as one disapproving observer remarked, like the bridal chambers of hotels or the saloons of steamboats. Indeed, it may well
be that the popular ideal of interior decoration found its most
accessible symbol in the cabins of the Mississippi steamboats
which Mark Twain delighted to describe. The subdued tones
and the air of repose encouraged by Downing, Vaux, and their
successors had no place in the "snow-white cabin; porcelain
knob and oil-picture on every stateroom door; curving patterns of filigree-work touched up with gilding . . . ; big
chandeliers every little way, each an April shower of glittering

glass-drops"; nor, for that matter, in the ladies' cabin, with its "pink and white Wilton carpet, as soft as mush, and glorified with a ravishing pattern of gigantic flowers."

Marietta Holley's "Samantha Allen" had a carpet in her parlor in Jonesville which would have perfectly suited Whitman's taste and have horrified Poe. In affectionate detail she describes its "green ground work that looks just like moss, with clusters of leaves all scattered over it, crimson and gold colored and russet brown, that look for all the world as if they might have fell offen the maple trees out in the yard in the fall of the year." Here is the same insistence upon meaningful design and the realistic representation of natural forms which we will later encounter as an important characteristic of the vernacular attitude toward painting.

The Centennial brought to America an impressive display of English decorative arts. The *Illustrated London News* had told its readers that Great Britain certainly would carry off the prizes in the departments of art furniture and ceramics. And so, indeed, she did. For a decade and more thereafter, America had her share of conscience-smitten women (to use the phrase of a later female authority on decoration) who went in for "art" wallpaper, "art" furniture, and "art" textiles. But it wasn't many years before Eastlake and Morris were forgotten, and the floral wallpaper, floral carpets, and floral upholstery against which they had inveighed were back in fashion.

Some light on this is shed in an essay by Mary Gay Humphreys on "The Progress of American Decorative Art," which appeared in the London *Art Journal* in 1893. Faced, at the close of the century, with the same popular preferences which had been opposed from the beginning by various exponents of cultivated taste, she concluded that since we were short on museums, private collections, noble houses, and other "depositories of accumulated treasures of Art," and since our "foraging-ground" for such materials was across many thousand miles of water, we had been thrown more or less on our own resources. Our designers had been driven to seek their inspirations in natural forms and had thus contracted an "allegiance to nature," as Miss Humphreys called it, "which the most determined theorist on the subject of conventional decoration" could not overcome. The consequence, she admitted, was that "in purely American work the boundaries between realism and conventionality are far less rigidly defined than elsewhere."

In this area of the arts, as in the others we have looked at, the vernacular and the cultivated traditions interacted. Even in a curtain designed by the painter John La Farge, appliqué and embroidery were used to define a realistic perspective landscape. But by the end of the century we had gone a long way toward accumulating on this side of the Atlantic enough "treasures of art" to threaten to suffocate not only the patterns which had evolved in the vernacular tradition but even the popular taste for realistic decorative designs. Too many of us, convinced that the useful and the aesthetic were antithetical and that our genius lay with the former, had comfortably decided—like the editor of *Harper's Magazine* in 1859—that "what is fine in the buildings of the old countries we can borrow; their statues and their pictures we will be able in good time to buy." Borrow and buy we did, filling our homes as well as our museums with the plunder, and sending generations of our children to school to study the uprooted masterpieces of another civilization. In that cultural climate

Emerson's essay on "Art" must have seemed like pure vapor. Perhaps only in our own time, when the achievements of the vernacular have begun to be recognized, has that strange essay found its audience. At all events, it is worth extracting these paragraphs as a postscript to this chapter:

> The old tragic Necessity, which lowers on the brows even of the Venuses and Cupids of the antique . . . —namely that they were inevitable; that the artist was drunk with a passion for form which he could not resist, and which vented itself in these fine extravagances—no longer dignifies the chisel or the pencil. But the artist and connoisseur now seek in art the exhibition of their talent, or an asylum from the evils of life. Men are not well pleased with the figure they make in their own imaginations, and they flee to art, and convey their better sense in an oratorio, a statue, or a picture. Art makes the same effort which a sensual prosperity makes; namely to detach the beautiful from the useful, to do up the work as unavoidable, and, hating it, to pass on to enjoyment.

> Now men do not see nature to be beautiful, and they go to make a statue which shall be. They abhor men as tasteless, dull, and unconvertible, and console themselves with color bags and blocks of marble. They reject life as prosaic, and create a death which they call poetic. . . . Beauty must come back to the useful arts, and the distinction between the fine and the useful arts be forgotten. . . . In nature all is useful, all is beautiful. It is therefore beautiful because it is alive, moving, reproductive; it is therefore useful because it is symmetrical and fair.

> Beauty will not come at the call of a legislature, nor will it repeat in England or America its history in Greece. . . . It is in vain that we look for genius to reiterate its miracles in the old arts; it is its instinct to find beauty and holiness in new and necessary facts, in the field and roadside, in the shop and mill.

Emerson wrote these words a generation before the Corliss engine or the Eads bridge were built. Indeed, it was to be several years before Emerson's friend Greenough identified specific manifestations of the vernacular, in the clipper ships, for example, and in machines and scaffolding. But by a characteristically perceptive insight Emerson grasped the inevitability of a new tradition in art. He faced the stubborn fact that art could never be at home in the new civilization if it clung to forms which were no longer alive and reproductive.

6

To Make All Things New

Throughout the nineteenth century, as we have already observed, both writers and readers had been actively interested in the creation of an American literature. Longfellow had made a plea for a native American poetry as early as 1825, but like many others he had thought chiefly in terms of substituting native New England birds for the skylarks and nightingales of English poetry, and he soon perceived the futility of that kind of superficial nationalism. Other writers followed William Gilmore Simms in the belief that "to be *national* in literature, one must needs be *sectional*." But as Melville said in the mid-century, the usual mistake of those Americans who looked forward to the coming of a literary genius among us was that "they somehow fancy he will come in the costume of Queen Elizabeth's day."

However popular these fallacies may once have been, they need not concern us here. They had, after all, no influence except among second- and third-rate authors. We can learn more from another and more enduring attitude toward the problem, namely faith in "the West" as the source of the distinctively American element in character and therefore in literature. It was truly a national faith, shared by many who otherwise had little in common. In *Israel Potter*, written four

years after *Moby Dick,* Melville ascribed the peculiarly American quality of Ethan Allen to his "essentially Western" spirit,
that spirit which "is, or will be (for no other is, or can be),
the true American one." When Thoreau went out for a walk
he found that, though he turned round and round irresolute,
his instinct inevitably led him to walk southwest or west.
"Eastward I go only by force; but westward I go free. . . . I
must walk toward Oregon, and not toward Europe. And that
way the nation is moving. . . ." And Whitman saw in "the
grandeur and superb monotony" of the Western prairies the
home of America's "distinctive ideas and distinctive realities."

    One of the most interesting expressions of the typical
popular confidence in the West appeared in an anonymous
article called "Forty Days in a Western Hotel" which was
published in *Putnam's Magazine* in December 1854. It pulls
together so many of the threads of the vernacular tradition
as we have defined it, and weaves them so skillfully into the
fabric of the Western faith, that it is worth quoting here at
some length.

> I saw in the West [the author wrote], no signs of quiet enjoy-
> ment of life as it passes. . . . At present the inhabitants are
> hewing wood and drawing water—laying the foundations of a
> civilization which is yet to be, and such as has never been be-
> fore. . . . Though men do not write books there, or paint
> pictures, there is no lack, in our western world, of mind. The
> genius of this new country is necessarily mechanical. Our
> greatest thinkers are not in the library, nor the capitol, but in
> the machine shop. . . . The youth of this country are learn-
> ing the sciences, not as theories, but with reference to their
> applications to the arts. . . . Even literature is cultivated for
> its jobs; and the fine arts are followed as a trade. . . .
> The American mind will be brought to maturity along the
> chain of the great lakes, the banks of the Mississippi, the Mis-

souri, and their tributaries in the far northwest. There, on the rolling plains, will be formed a republic of letters which, not governed like that on our seaboard by the great literary powers of Europe, shall be free indeed.

This is a quite different attitude from that of Thoreau, for example, to whom the West was really only another name for the wild, for the forests and savage wilderness from which civilization could draw nourishment and renewed vigor. It suggests, rather, an aspect of the West which should be sharply distinguished from the frontier as it was defined so effectively by Frederick Jackson Turner. Turner's theory, first presented in 1893, dealt with the effects upon our history of the area of free land, moving westward as the wilderness was settled, where savagery and civilization were continually in tension. His book, *The Frontier in American History,* was a tremendously fruitful one and much of the best recent historical work has owed a great deal to its insights and suggestions. But the frontier has since come to be thought of chiefly as Thoreau thought of it—as geographical wilderness; it is this conception of the West which has underlain most of the recent analyses of the significance of the frontier in our history and literature.

The writer in *Putnam's,* however, fastens on the Westerner's utilitarian attitude toward the arts and sciences, his mechanical bent, and his freedom from European influence. In Boston or Charleston it was easy enough for a writer to agree with Longfellow's brother-in-law, Tom Appleton, that Europe was "the home of his protoplasm." But beyond the centers of cultivation and good breeding—and not just on the advancing frontier either—men were to a considerable extent free from European precedents and forces. The man of the industrial town, the man in the machine shop, had placed himself as completely as Turner's frontiersman "under influences destructive to many of the gains of civilization" and looked at things just as independently and with as little regard or appreciation for the best Old World experience. The new environment was the product of both frontier democracy and machine civilization, and from it inevitably emerged new attitudes toward writing, and new themes which would interweave to make a fabric whose texture would seem harsh and garish to those who were familiar with the great tradition of English literature.

Anyone who reads widely in American nineteenth-century literature must be struck with the reiteration, in a variety of terms and in many different contexts, of an attitude which was foreshadowed by William Ellery Channing in 1830. The aristocratic institutions of the Old World, Channing declared, had all tended to throw obscurity over "what we most need to know, and that is the worth and claims of a human being." But in America, he thought, man was not hidden from us by so many disguises as in Europe, and he therefore hoped that our literature would explore and develop that consciousness of our own nature which teaches us at once self-respect and respect for others.

Channing knew well enough that his prosperous Boston contemporaries were fearful of the political power of "the labouring classes," and he also knew that their fear was justified in so far as the masses could be used as tools. He insisted nevertheless that it was the vices of the prosperous which bring about a community's downfall, and he denounced those who used the French Revolution as a horrible example of what happens when the mob has power. The saddest aspect of the age, he said in 1840, "is that which undoubtedly contributes to social order. . . . It is the selfish prudence which is never tired of the labour of accumulation, and which keeps men steady, regular, respectable drudges from morning to night."

It may well be true (as has recently been argued by Arthur M. Schlesinger, Jr.) that Channing in the long run sabotaged the liberal principles of his day by urging reform only in ways in which it could not practically be achieved. Certainly his talk about "the Elevation of the Soul" in the *Lectures on the Elevation of the Labouring Portion of the Community* (1840) is either complacent or naïve. But he was not frightened or dismayed by the outcropping of violent revolutionary activity in Europe in the forties, and it would be unfair to assume that it was only because the ocean separated his world from the world of violence that he could hail it as "the dawning of that great principle, that the individual is not made to be the instrument of others . . . ; and that he belongs to himself and to God, and to no human superior."

It has been fashionable in recent years to emphasize the economic rather than the moral and religious elements in democratic thought, and criticism has therefore tended to ignore one of the basic motives in American life and literature. Channing's Unitarian liberalism was only one manifestation of an impulse which recurs in many different forms. The socialist communities and religious sects of the nineteenth century frequently gave expression to related attitudes. Among the Campbellites and their followers in western Pennsylvania and Ohio, for instance, it led to a belief in democratic America as the new Jerusalem, "a new political heaven and a new political earth," where each man would interpret the Bible for himself and sectarianism would be dissolved into divine unity. One of the leading Campbellites was a man named Walter Scott, described by a fellow preacher as one of the first on this continent "who took the old field-notes of the apostles and run [sic] the original survey, beginning at Jerusalem." Scott's most important book, *The Messiahship,* was published in Cincinnati in 1860, and salted down amid its arguments touching baptism, the symbolism of the scriptures, and other theological matters, there are repeated evidences of the democratic faith. "Everything in old society nearly, that is truly desirable," Scott wrote, "is royal or aristocratic; the people cannot reach it; it belongs, if it is good, to the rich; if bad, to the poor." But Luther and Washington had given us "a *new* religion and a *new* society in a *new* world."

Among our writers this attitude produced a widespread interest in reaching a large audience rather than a select few. On one level it prompted Catharine Maria Sedgwick's pious query, "If the poet and painter cannot bring down their arts to the level of the poor, are there none to be God's interpreters to them?" On quite a different level it led Melville, in his enthusiasm for Hawthorne's *Mosses,* to call upon America to recognize those of her writers "who breathe that unshackled, democratic spirit of Christianity in all things, which now takes the practical lead in this world." And in still another form— and one which reflected little enthusiasm for democracy—it found expression in Poe's defense of the short prose tale as the form which, next to lyric poetry, "should best fulfill the demands of high genius." The tale, he pointed out, permitted the writer a vast variety of modes or inflections of thought and expression in a form "more appreciable by the mass of mankind" than any other. Similarly, in a letter to Charles

Anthon, written in June 1844, Poe outlined his interest in establishing a magazine of his own which would satisfy the contemporary demand for "the curt, the terse, the well-timed, the readily-diffused, in preference to the old forms of the verbose and ponderous and the inaccessible."

Forty years later elements of the same basic attitude found expression in Mark Twain's famous letter to Andrew Lang. "I have never tried in even one single instance," he wrote in 1889, "to help cultivate the cultivated classes. I was not equipped for it, either by native gifts or training. And I never had any ambition in that direction, but always hunted for bigger game—the masses." He had his fling, too, at the critics who assumed that if a book didn't meet the standards of the cultivated class it was valueless. If a critic should start a religion, he went on, it would not have any object but to convert angels, and where was the use of that? The thin top crust of humanity—the cultivated—were worth pacifying and coddling and nourishing with delicacies, to be sure, but for himself Mark Twain could see no satisfaction in feeding the overfed. He was only half in jest when he argued that "It is not that little minority who are already saved that are best worth trying to uplift, I should think, but the mighty mass of the uncultivated who are underneath." His friend, William Dean Howells, meant something very similar when he said two years later that art must make friends with need, or perish. It would be a suicidal mistake, he insisted, for art to take itself from the many and give itself to the few, for "the art which . . . disdains the office of teacher is one of the last refuges of the aristocratic spirit which is disappearing from politics and society, and is now seeking to shelter itself in aesthetics." The same basic attitude is still current in our own time, as when Upton Sinclair, defending his novels against a recent academic review in the *Atlantic Monthly*, retorted that "somebody has to write for the masses and not just for the Harvard professors."

This concern with the ethical uses of the arts in a democratic society had, of course, received its most explicit statement in the works of Emerson and Whitman. "Art," said Emerson, "has not yet come to its maturity if it do not put itself abreast with the most potent influences of the world, if it is not practical and moral, if it do not stand in connection with the conscience, if it do not make the poor and uncultivated feel that it addresses them with a voice of lofty cheer." And Whitman, rebelling against everything represented by the popular conception of culture, had demanded "a programme . . . drawn out, not for a single class alone, or for the parlors or lecture-rooms, but with an eye to practical life, the West, the working-man, the facts of farms and jack-planes and engineers. . . . I should demand of this programme or theory a scope generous enough to include the widest human area."

The aesthetic problems involved in this attitude need not be elaborated here. For the moment it is necessary only to indicate that over a period of many years concern with the availability of the arts and with the ethical and (in the non-sectarian, even anti-church sense) religious purposes of literature was shared by so many American writers. The opposite tendency also existed, to be sure. There were always people who wanted to preserve the arts inviolate from contact with the vulgar masses. (*Appleton's* in 1869 dismissed scornfully any and all arguments in favor of what it called "the multiplication of poor copies of inferior pictures by means of chrome-lithography," just as the aesthetic snobs of our own day refuse to countenance even the best contemporary color reproductions of paintings.) There were always some who acknowledged no connection between art and use. But through all the changes in literary fashion, among the so-called romanticists equally with the realists, and in all sections of the country, American writers—with a few notable exceptions—would have agreed with the doctrine which Orestes Brownson had expounded in 1843: that the literature of America should breathe a free, noble, and generous spirit, give expression to the love of man as man, and impart to all who came under its influence "the needed wisdom to labor for the moral, the religious, the intellectual, and the physical well-being of all men."

As one would expect, this attitude toward the functions of the arts was reflected in the subject matter with which our writers concerned themselves. At its worst it led to the attempt to sugar-coat useful knowledge and to insinuate all sorts of dry erudition and historical lore into fictional form. It was this sort of thing which led *Appleton's Journal* to protest that Harriet Beecher Stowe's *Oldtown Folks* was a sample of what it unhappily admitted was a distinctively American kind of fiction which gave expression to the utilitarianism of the people. At its best, however, it led to a realization of the importance of everyday life, to a stalwart reckoning with the actualities of our civilization.

"Give me insight into today," Emerson had said in his Phi Beta Kappa address at Harvard in 1837, "and you may have the antique and future worlds. What would we really know the meaning of? The meal in the firkin; the milk in the

pan; the ballad in the street; the news of the boat; the glance
of the eye; the form and gait of the body. . . ." And ten
years later, in the essay on "The Poet" he cast his belief into
the form of a challenge which has become a landmark in our
cultural history:

> Time and nature yield us many gifts, but not yet the timely
> man, the new religion, the reconciler, whom all things await.
> . . . We have yet had no genius in America, with tyrannous
> eye, which knew the incomparable value of our materials, and
> saw in the barbarism and materialism of our times, another
> carnival of the same gods whose picture he so much admires
> in Homer; then in the Middle Age; then in Calvinism. Banks
> and tariffs, the newspaper and caucus, Methodism and Uni-
> tarianism, are flat and dull to dull people, but rest on the same
> foundations of wonder as the town of Troy and the temple of
> Delphi, and are as swiftly passing away. Our log-rolling, our
> stumps and their politics, our fisheries, our Negroes and
> Indians, our boats and our repudiations, the wrath of rogues
> and the pusillanimity of honest men, the northern trade, the
> southern planting, the western clearing, Oregon and Texas,
> are yet unsung.

It was left to Walt Whitman to take up Emerson's challenge and explore the full range of his conception of a poet.
But American writers both before and after Emerson were
preoccupied with the actualities of everyday life and tried,
with whatever limitations of understanding, to know their
meaning. Our first professional novelist, Charles Brockden
Brown, announced himself as "one of those who would rather
travel into the mind of a ploughman than into the interior of
Africa." Margaret Fuller, during her term as book reviewer
for Horace Greeley's *Tribune* in the mid-forties, chanced on
an anonymous novel called *Ellen* which, though coarsely
written, she fastened upon as a genuine example of an increasingly common type of fiction. It was, she observed, a tran-

script of the "crimes, calumnies, excitements, half-blind love of right, and honest indignation" which were characteristic of the uncultivated classes. Further, it gave a picture of the kind of life which Cooper or Miss Sedgwick "might see, as the writer did, but could hardly believe in enough to speak of it with such fidelity." Yet even Miss Sedgwick, for all her sentimental fondness for uplift, understood something of the intrinsic dignity of the human being. In one of her contributions to the *Token* she stated a belief (to which many of her novels and tales bore witness) that every family, however insignificant in the stranger's eye, has a world of its own which offers a richer field for exploring the infinite story of human relations than the deeds of gods and heroes. And thirty years later, out of a very different background, we have Edward Eggleston's declaration, in the preface to *The Circuit Rider* (1874)—a landmark in the realistic representation of the lawless frontier—that no man is worthy to be called a novelist "who does not endeavor with his whole soul to produce the higher form of history, by writing truly of men as they are, and dispassionately of those forms of life that come within his scope. . . . The story of any true life is wholesome, if only the writer will tell it simply. . . ."

Much has been made by both social and literary historians of the sentimental rot—the "pure Cinderella with a touch of Bluebeard," as Della T. Lutes defined it—which has formed such a large part of the reading matter of the American people. But this emphasis on the trashy melodramatic novels and stories which have been written and read in such numbers from the days of *Charlotte Temple* and Mrs. E. D. E. N. Southworth to the present had tended to obscure the fact that an opposite tendency has also existed, much of it outside the limits of what is commonly regarded as literature even in its broad sense.

Constance Rourke was the first to point out that the long delay in the development of the novel as a literary form in America may have resulted in part at least from the fact that its function was fulfilled by other forms of reading matter. She called attention in her essay on the Shakers to the controversial literature which sprang up between members of the communities and their critics in the "outside world." As an example she used the pamphlets written by Mary Dyer and her husband during their controversy over the children and property which he took with him when he joined the Shaker community at New Lebanon. Both husband and wife, as Miss Rourke noted, had the gift for portraying concrete instances that good novelists possess, and both frequently quoted sworn testimony of neighbors and friends who likewise had an eye for specific details and a sense of narrative pace. The Dyers and the Shakers were the center of all these events and episodes, but their story emerged against a three-dimensional background built up out of domestic habits, the rise of errant personalities, and vivid discussion of sexual relationships revealing considerable psychological insight. Indeed, Miss Rourke was quite accurate in saying that in these pamphlets the very substance of the novel was exhibited "with far more candor than in any English novel of the period or indeed of the entire nineteenth century. Only Fielding or Smollett could have matched it."

From the earliest times there have been personal narratives of life in the new country, vivid records of individual adaptations to new environments. There were the narratives of Indian captivity, of which Mrs. Mary Jemison's was per-

haps the most widely read, full of high and terrible adventure
and loaded with specific details about how to get along in the
wilderness and about the charms and miseries of savage life.
There were the minute psychological revelations of the innumerable religious autobiographies and biographies, well
represented by those collected in Jonathan Edwards' *Faithful
Narrative of the Surprising Work of God* (1737) and later in
the camp-meeting testimonies of the saved and damned. There
were the wild and bloody narratives of border violence like
Virgil Stewart's *History of the Detection, Conviction, Life,
and Designs of John A. Murel* (1835).

At every stage in our history there have been conflicts
and conquests—religious, political, and economic—out of
which have come such personal narratives, set against a lively
background of social struggle and development. The "anti-
rent" agitation in New York in the 1840s, the abolitionist
movement of the pre-Civil War years, the Mormon controversy, the populist movement, and the exploration and
settlement of the West all furnished materials for pamphlets,
newspaper articles, and books by the men and women who
participated in them. *Pat Crowe, His Story, Confession and
Reformation*, a paper-bound booklet published in 1906, is set
against the background of popular resentment against the
beef trust at the end of the century, and is typical of the best
of these personal narratives. Crowe had kidnaped Eddie
Cudahy, son of the Omaha packer, in 1900—the very year in
which the trust succeeded in eliminating competition in buying, so as to fix prices—and had demanded and collected
twenty-five thousand dollars' ransom. The first part of the
paper-bound booklet contains Crowe's own direct, undrama-
tized narrative of the affair ("I want to start right by con-

fessing in plain English that I was guilty of the kidnapping"); a reprint of a magazine article by W. H. Hodge, claiming that the Omaha jury which acquitted Crowe didn't consider the question of guilt but only the question "Isn't it all right to rob a member of the beef trust if you can?"; and Crowe's reply, defending the verdict as "the most popular ever returned in Nebraska." But the most interesting part of the book is the full text of the "Address to the Jury" by which Crowe's attorney, Albert S. Ritchie, had swayed the jurors to acquit a guilty man. There is a dramatic immediacy about it, a sense of social forces shaping the lives of the individuals present in the courtroom at that very moment, which surpasses any scenes in the plays or novels of the period. "Much as I admire my friend, the county attorney here, who shows so much enthusiasm and warmth for Mr. Cudahy and for the State, so mingled that you cannot distinguish them . . ." Ritchie begins, thrusting his words deep down into the popular resentment against the rising power of industrial monopoly; and as he speaks the courtroom scene comes alive, and the popular attitudes are clear. "If you will give me a million dollars," he continued, "and make me a vice-president of the Cudahy Packing Company, I can pretty near move the social world in the City of Omaha." It becomes plain as the drama unfolds that the jury's vote was not to acquit Crowe but to indict monopoly.

Such narratives were, however, only one of the many kinds of writing which our literary histories have neglected but which have performed the double function of satisfying the demands of the reading public and at the same time exploring the techniques for coping with new ways of life in a new environment. The almanacs which hung on a nail in almost every kitchen evolved a pattern of anecdote, comment, and humor with a distinctly native flavor. Melville had grown up on Webster's *Albany Almanacs* in the thirties and rediscovered them years later with relish. And Hamlin Garland was only one of thousands of Americans who in the sixties, seventies, and eighties pored over the testimonials in the almanacs distributed by the makers of Hostetter's Bitters and Allen's Cherry Pectoral, dwelling on their realistic accounts of the aches and pains of humankind and their heartening statements of cures.

Something of this same clinical interest attached to the "doctor books" and collections of recipes which were as universally owned as the Bible and far more widely read. But these books have another and greater importance to us. The most famous was probably *Dr. Chase's Recipes: or, Information for Everybody*, which was first published in 1863 and in the next thirteen years sold over seven hundred thousand copies. The author, A. W. Chase, of Ann Arbor, Michigan, had been in the drug and grocery business for a number of years when he decided to study medicine. Thereupon he put together a pamphlet containing recipes he had learned in his business, and for seven years traveled "between New York and Iowa" selling the pamphlets and pumping everyone he met for useful information in every practical field. The material thus collected made up the book, divided into departments for merchants and grocers, tanners and harness makers, painters, blacksmiths, gunsmiths, home bakers and cooks, and others.

Apparently the recipes gave satisfaction; the book contains innumerable testimonials from professors at the University of Michigan and other worthy citizens. But the clue to its universal popularity is contained in a review of it which appeared in the Syracuse (New York) *Journal*. For, as the paper said, the eight hundred recipes were "interspersed with sufficient wit and wisdom to make it interesting as a general reading book, besides the fact that it embraces only such subjects as have a practical adaptability to 'Everybody's' everyday use." It is not an inconsiderable social phenomenon that three quarters of a million Americans of the Gilded Age paid out a dollar and a quarter for a "reading book" dealing solely with such matters of everyday usefulness as how Byron Rose, of Madison, Ohio, tanned and finished horsehides for harness leather, how elm bark made a horrendous tapeworm "come away" from the daughter of Mr. E. Fish, of Beardstown, Illinois, and how C. Keller, gunsmith, of Evansville, Indiana, browned his gun barrels.

The public welcomed any useful and informative book, and Dr. Chase had many rivals in the race to supply the demand. One of the most successful was Thomas E. Hill, of Aurora, Illinois, an industrious and enthusiastic penmanship teacher who became publisher and editor of the local newspaper, mayor of the town, and author of *Hill's Manual of Social and Business Forms,* which went through thirty-nine editions in the ten years following its publication in 1873. Hill subtitled his book "A Guide to Correct Writing" and dedicated it to "the millions who would, and may, easily and gracefully express the right thought." It is also a bible of decorous social deportment and correct business and legal procedures, combined with a guide to the refinements of culture. But it is more than merely another of that vast number of books which appeared in England and America during the nineteenth century, designed to feed the middle-class appetite for self-improvement and self-culture. Hill devised a distinctive formula which fitted into the native American interest in specific detail. The models he offers as guides—to the mother writing to a teacher to excuse her child from school, the inventor applying for a patent, and the man who wants to mortgage the family farm—are in all cases apparently genuine letters or documents, most of them bearing the names of actual people and places. The man who wanted to write his will could model it on that of Warren P. Holden, of Bennington, Vermont. The young man on his travels could get ideas for his letter home from one written by Alfred T. Weeks, during a visit to the "old home" in Cambridge, New York, to his family in the West. The boy who wanted to become an apprentice could study the agreement made between fourteen-year-old Allan Ellis, of Pittsburgh, and the blacksmith Marcus Moran. And the pioneer settler who wanted to encourage a friend in the East to emigrate could be guided by the letter Martin Fuller, of Big Stranger, Kansas, wrote to Chas. W. Canfield of Toledo, Ohio.

These letters and documents still retain something of the fascination they must have had for the men and women who dog-eared and almost wore out their copies of the *Manual*. The book offered, in effect, a vast panorama of the nation at work and at play, settling new country, building towns and factories, burying the dead, giving parties, courting, organizing village lyceums and "protective associations" against horse thieves, with real people—your own neighbors—as the actors. In Hill's section on "How the United States Are Governed" the operations of legislatures are illustrated by a detailed and stubbornly realistic narrative of a freshman congressman's schooling in the techniques of introducing a bill, pushing it

through committee by lobbying and by deals with other con-
gressmen, and finally bringing it to a vote. There is no more
vivid and unvarnished picture of American politics in our
literature than Hill's straightforward, saltily satirical account
of how Representative Smith of the Tenth District of Wisconsin got a federal appropriation for a dam across a non-
navigable stream on which he wanted to operate a steamship
line.

One of the most significant features of such books as
those by Chase and Hill is that they achieved national scope
by radiating outward from a Midwestern center and localizing
themselves in so many specific places, and that they compre-
hended such a diversity of activities and occupations in terms
of concrete events in the lives of individual citizens. It was a
vernacular technique to which the cultivated literary tradition
made no contribution but from which—as Whitman demonstrated—it could draw vitality.

It is high time these vernacular sources were fully explored in other fields. Years before Chase and Hill, for example, and five years before *Leaves of Grass* itself, a frontier
physician named Daniel Drake had published a book which
should be recognized as a landmark in our literary history.
It bore the ungainly title, *A Systematic Treatise, Historical,
Etiological, and Practical, on the Principal Diseases of the
Interior Valley of North America,* and it was first published in
Cincinnati in 1850. Drake was a crusty, indefatigable doctor,
born and raised in a Kentucky frontier settlement. During
the academic year he quarreled with his fellow professors on
the staff of the medical college he had helped to establish, and
in the summers, for thirty years, pursued evidence out of
which to build his theory of the relationship of disease to

climate, geography, and social environment. On horseback and on foot if there were no other means of transportation he traveled more than thirty thousand miles from the Great Lakes to the Gulf, and from the Alleghenies to the Rockies, talking with every physician he met, mingling with all kinds of people, making notes on climate, soil, and wind, employing topographical engineers and draftsmen to make plans of the localities noted for specific diseases, recording the occupations, habits, racial and social backgrounds of the people, and relating all this to the incidence of yellow fever, pneumonia, intermittent fever, and other diseases.

His work is one of the monuments in the development of American medical science, but that is not what concerns us here. The point is that Drake's book played a part in the development of techniques for recording the sprawling divergences of American life in concrete, local, and factual terms.

In contrast with the tradition of actuality which was developed in these non-literary forms, there were, of course, quite different tendencies in much of the fiction and poetry which was most popular with American readers. The "Choice Selections from the Poets" which Hill included in his *Manual* offer a fair sample of the kind of thing his readers wanted as a relief from the frequently harsh realities of life in booming towns and cities and on lonely farms. "How dear to this heart are the scenes of my childhood" was in this sense the theme song of the century. It appeared over and over again, in Whittier's

> *God pity them both! and pity us all*
> *Who vainly the dreams of youth recall;*

and in Florence Percy's

> *Backward, turn backward, O Time, in your flight,*
> *Make me a child again, just for tonight.*

Looking back to youth, for many Americans, meant
looking eastward—either to some longer-settled region in
this country, or to Europe itself. Time-past did not extend
downward into a wealth of accumulated experience on the
ground where you stood but stretched backward across plains
and mountains and perhaps the sea. In youth, and in his
buoyant moods, the American faced west. The boys Hamlin
Garland grew up with during the sixties and seventies in the
lumber town at the mouth of the Black River in Wisconsin
and on the prairies of Iowa all talked of Colorado, never of
New England, and his father's favorite song was "Freedom's
Star":

> *Then o'er the hills in legions, boys,*
> *Fair freedom's star*
> *Points to the sunset regions, boys,*
> *Ha, ha, ha-ha!*

But to Garland's mother, as to many pioneer women, moving
West meant "not so much the acquisition of a new home as
the loss of all her friends and relatives." And even his father
in some moods talked nostalgically of the East while refusing
to revisit it—proudly saying "I never take the back trail."
There were moods in every American which required him to
hold onto the elastic threads connecting him with the cultivated
tradition, however thin they had been stretched.

It was these moods that were exploited by the publishers
who brought out editions of the English novelists and poets

and to which many minor American writers gave expression. Ralph L. Rusk, in his definitive study of *The Literature of the Middle Western Frontier,* has pointed out that although there were few people on the frontier in the thirties who read about any subject but politics, there was nevertheless a good market in the more settled communities for the work of the English romantic sentimentalists like Felicia Hemans and Thomas Moore, and that both Scott and Byron enjoyed an unparalleled popularity. By 1840, indeed, there were steamboats on the Ohio and Mississippi which bore such names as *Lady of the Lake, Marmion, Corsair,* and *Mazeppa*—a rather touching evidence of the compelling need somehow to relate the vernacular environment to the cultivated tradition, even if only by such a superficial device as a label.

The sentimental novels which formed such a large part of nineteenth-century reading matter both in England and America offer some instructive evidence of the divergence between English and American attitudes. The most notable trend in their development during the seventy years after the founding of the federal government was the increasing tendency to make fiction out of what exists, rather than out of things wished for and dreamed of. The stock figures of the early American novels in this class were the seduced maiden, the captivating libertine, the mercenary parents, and the reformed rake—all borrowed straight from Richardson's *Pamela, Clarissa,* and *Sir Charles Grandison.* The heroines were delicate, full of sensibility, devoted to the thankless task of refining and spiritualizing man, winning, if successful, an adoring and reclaimed husband, but ready otherwise to reclaim the sinner by an uncomplaining, lingering decline which would "teach how innocence should die." By mid-century, however, the heroines were typified by Mrs. C. L. Hentz's Rena, who was "very fond of the poetry of the kitchen, such as the beating the whites of eggs," and the novels themselves frequently revolved—like Elizabeth Wetherell's *Queechy*— around plain domestic duties and hard work.[1]

In some measure this change was the result of the conscious effort of a number of women writers "to do good," as Sarah Josepha Hale put it, "especially to and for our sex." Mrs. Hale was for forty years the editor of *Godey's Lady's Book,* and month after month she hammered home to her feminine readers the message which Ola E. Winslow summarized thus: "You have a mind; cultivate it. Home is woman's proper sphere; stay in it. Woman's influence is profound; exercise it." As Miss Winslow says, women like Mrs. Hale and Catharine Maria Sedgwick did what the women's rights leaders, or idealists like Emerson and Whitman couldn't possibly have done for the same audience, stripping off layer after layer of romance and moonlight from the literature of the average woman reader, and helping her to plant her feet solidly on the American earth.

But the trend toward reality in the novels, and the emergence of the heroine who had two hands and knew how to use them, probably owed even more to the tradition which was developed in the non-literary personal narratives which were referred to earlier in this chapter—to Mrs. Jemison's story, for instance, or to such narratives as that of Deborah Sampson, published in 1797 under the title *The Female Review: or, The Memoirs of an American Young Lady*. Deborah had disguised herself as a man and served as a soldier in the

[1]For a fascinating survey of these books see the volume by Herbert R. Brown cited in the bibliography.

Continental Army for more than two years, during which time, as the book assures us, "she performed the duties of every department and preserved her chastity inviolate."

What was true of the sentimental novels was also true of the sensational fiction of dark and gruesome texture which was so widely read, especially by young men. In the novels of George Lippard, for example, this sensational matter took on characteristics directly related to the kind of social drama illustrated in Pat Crowe's confessions. Lippard, who was a friend of Poe's and whose work may possibly have influenced him, wrote a number of melodramatic tales of vice in large cities and in 1850 founded a semisocialist "Brotherhood of the Union" which aimed to wipe out the sources of poverty and crime. *New York: Its Upper Ten and Lower Millions* (Cincinnati, 1854) is a loosely organized narrative dealing with the fulfillment of the terms of an eccentric will left by a wealthy New Yorker who committed suicide in 1823. The plot evolves through a series of episodes involving sex crimes, murders, robberies, kidnaping, and political intrigue, and the settings include brothels, slums, gambling dens, and the palaces of the rich. But through all this there is woven a thread of flamboyant yet effective preaching of Lippard's romantic socialism, with savage attacks on ministers and priests who preach a clockwork gospel "invented some years ago for the purpose of supplying the masses with *something to believe* and themselves with a good salary" while ignoring "the true Word . . . which enjoins the establishment of the kingdom of God, *on earth*, in the physical and intellectual welfare of the greatest portion of mankind."

The hero of the book (if it has a single hero) is Arthur Dermoyne, intelligent shoemaker who refuses to enter a pro-

fession because, as he says, "I cannot separate myself from
that nine-tenths of the human family who seem to have been
born to work and die." His dream is to lead a group of workmen out of the city shops to the West where they can build a
community in which "every man will have a place to work
and every one will receive the fruits of his labor," and where,
without priest or monopolist or slaveholder, they can worship
"that Christ who was himself a workman, even as he is now the
workman's God." But the most interesting point is that when
one of the other characters charges Dermoyne with having
absorbed the doctrines of the French school (presumably those
of Fourier, whose socialist theories were widely known in
America at the time), he replies that they were the ideas of his
Pennsylvania-Dutch forebears who had emigrated from Germany to William Penn's colony a hundred and fifty years before. It was an assertion of Lippard's consciousness of the
native roots of his faith.

Of all the strands which are woven into the fabric of
vernacular American writing, humor might seem to have least
connection with the religious faith in democracy which moti-
vated so many of our writers. Yet the two are closely related.
In her book on *American Humor* (1921), Miss Rourke
showed, for instance, how the comic spirit co-operated "to
fulfill the biblical cry running through much of the revivalism
of the time: 'to make all things new.'" Humor, especially the
frontier variety, served as a leveling agent, deflating lofty
notions and tossing aside all alien traditions, partly out of
sheer delight in destruction but also as a part of the necessary
process of clearing the ground for new growth. As one of the
burlesque writers of the sixties said, the thing he and his fellow

humorists were doing for literature was "simplifying matters —stripping them of their excrescences," the very thing that American mechanics and builders were doing in machine design and house construction.

Miss Rourke has pointed out that the central figures in the humorous writing of the period of national expansion were the representatives of racial or regional elements of the new society—the Yankee, the backwoodsman, the Negro— broadly drawn types which emerged from and belonged to the mass of the people and to the insurgent and revolutionary class. They formed a "comic trio," each member of which took on coloring from the other two as the types developed, though they never blended into a single symbol. Each represented a class which had been torn from all roots in an established culture and which willingly or unwillingly had become wanderers. And as their world is created—in the monologues of Yankee Hill, the sayings of Seba Smith's Major Jack Downing, the tall tales of the Crockett almanacs, Johnson J. Hooper's "campaign biography" of Captain Simon Suggs, and the Negro minstrelsy of Jim Crow, Zip Coon, and Dan Tucker—it takes form as a richly detailed panorama of the raw realities of American life which provides a setting for repeated comic triumphs of sharp wit or outlandish rascality, frequently operating in terms of the wildest fantasy.

Much of this humorous writing had its sources in oral tales—the stories about legendary figures like Davy Crockett and Mike Fink and the tall stories which were swapped around campfires in the wilderness, in country stores and taverns, on steamboats and trains. And these tales were often grotesque and humorous handlings of the same everyday materials which we have encountered in other vernacular forms. An Englishman riding in a stagecoach between Wheeling and Zanesville in the forties, for example, listened to his fellow passengers swapping yarns which blended outrageous and exuberant fantasy with the same class of factual material which Daniel Drake was amassing for his monumental treatise. "The unhealthy condition of some of the Western rivers, the Illinois in particular, was the subject of their discourse," he recorded.

> One asserted that he had known a man to be so dreadfully affected with the ague, from sleeping in the fall on its banks, that he shook . . . all the teeth out of his head. This was matched by another, who said there was a man from his State, who had gone to Illinois to settle, and the ague seized him so terribly hard that he shook off all his clothes . . . and could not keep a garment whole, for it unravelled the very web, thread by thread, till it was all destroyed.

And the climax was capped by still a third who told of a friend of his who got the ague so bad that he shook his whole house down about his ears and buried himself in the ruins.

Similarly the humorous writings, like other forms of the vernacular, all have panoramic sweep. The inclusive realism of the backgrounds against which the sagas of Simon Suggs, Sut Lovingood, and the others are set is another manifestation of the same impulse to encompass and localize the diversities of the American environment which we have traced in the "doctor books" and in Hill's famous *Manual*. Like Dr. Drake, and Dr. Chase too, for that matter, the authors of the humorous classics of the frontier were peripatetic. A. B. Longstreet, the author of *Georgia Scenes*, and Johnson Hooper were both lawyers who had traveled the circuit in their regions. George W. Harris, creator of Sut Lovingood, had learned to know Tennessee as a jeweler's apprentice, river-boat captain,

silversmith, postmaster, hunter, journalist, and inventor. It is
no wonder that their books reveal every aspect of the life of
the frontier.

Much has been made of the quality of wild exaggeration
in these humorous narratives. Exaggeration has, indeed, been
repeatedly specified as the significant element in all characteristically American humor. And it does form a large part of
our humorous tradition. On that famous January morning
when it was so all screwen cold that the very daybreak froze
fast as it was trying to dawn, Davy Crockett (as the 1854
Crockett Almanac tells us) decided something must be done
or creation itself would be done for. So he took up a fresh
bear and beat the animal against the ice "till the hot ile began
to walk out on him at all sides."

> I then took an' held him over the airth's axes [Davy re-
> counted] an' squeezed him till I'd thawed 'em loose, poured
> out about a ton on't over the sun's face, give the airth's cog-
> wheel one kick backward till I got the sun loose—whistled
> "Push along, keep movin'!" an' in about fifteen seconds the
> airth gave a grunt, an' began movin'. The sun walked up
> beautiful, salutin' me with sich a wind o' gratitude that it
> made me sneeze. I lit my pipe by the blaze o' his top-knot,
> shouldered my bear, an' walked home, introducin' people to
> the fresh daylight with a piece of sunrise in my pocket.

Something of this same quality has appeared in less
genuinely poetic form in much of our oratory, and has always
provided our humorists with grist. As far back as the middle
of the eighteenth century Mather Byles, the grandson of old
Increase Mather, had created a satirical portrait of Richard
Stentor, who was "moderately speaking, Nine Foot high, and
Four in Diameter," and who delivered an oration in praise of
Beacon Hill, hailing it as "so pompous, magnificent, illustri-
ous, and lofty-towering, that, as I twirl around my Arm with

the artful Flourish of an Orator, I seem to feel my Knuckles rebound from the blew vault of Heaven. . . ." And the tradition of oratorical bombast was still fair game for the humorists a century and a quarter later when Orpheus C. Kerr travestied their technique in his delightfully anticlimactic: "The sun rushed up the eastern sky in a state of patriotic combustion, and as the dew fell upon the grassy hillsides, the mountains lifted their heads and were rather green." But in all the grandiose oratory which democratic politics produced, and in all the non-literary humorous writings, there was an expansive gusto, an inventive and nervy handling of language, and a bold contempt for ordered forms which offered a healthy contrast to the sterile decorousness of most of the cultivated literature of the period. It was from such sources that Mark Twain drew, and it is to them that we can trace many of those elements in his style and manner which made him the first writer of international stature who is thoroughly and completely American.

These Western and frontier elements of vernacular literature were of great importance, as many of our historians and critics have realized. But they were not the sole elements of the tradition. We should not let the brilliance of Turner's theory blind us to other aspects of the emerging cultural patterns. Yet even H. L. Mencken, whose historical and critical study of the American language has been one of the most stimulating achievements of contemporary scholarship, seems to have pursued his investigations chiefly along the trails lighted by the Western star. It is to the influence of "the great open spaces" that he assigns the credit for the distinctive characteristics of American speech in the nineteenth century. To be sure, he acknowledges that "the slums of the great

Eastern cities" continued to provide what could be called frontier conditions even after the frontier had vanished at the end of the century, and in another place he urges intensive studies of American slang and of "American trade argots" as well as further investigation "of the novelties introduced into the language by the great movement into the West." But throughout his books the emphasis is placed upon the frontier as the source of the American elements in our language.

And so it is, if you focus your interest on the flashier neologisms like *sockdolager*, *hornswoggle*, or *absquatulate*. But many of the frontier words were more startling than useful, and their total contribution to the American language as it is now used has probably been overemphasized. At all events, when Mencken draws up a list of words to illustrate the current, twentieth-century differences between American and English usage on the level of everyday speech, remarkably few of the American words appear to have had their origins on the frontier. Most of them, on the contrary, come from technological and industrial sources—as in the case of such railroad terms as *caboose*, *freight car*, and *roundhouse* (in English usage, *brake-van*, *goods wagon*, and *running shed*)—or from the world of trades and commerce, as with *ashman*, *clapboard*, and *truck farmer* (in England, *dustman*, *weatherboard*, and *market gardener*). Even a casual search through lists of American words and phrases will turn up a number which are plainly of vernacular origin in the special sense that we have applied to that term. For example: *to know the ropes* (from sailing ships), *to pan out* (from mining), *single-track mind*, *jerk-water*, and *to clear the track* (from railroads), *claw hammer* (slang for full-dress tailcoat, from carpenter's tool). It is amusing to note, furthermore, that many political terms of American origin are borrowings from technology: we speak of political organizations as *machines,* and politics is full of such terms as *steering committee, logrolling, pump priming, to steamroller,* and *to engineer.*

The romantic glamor of the frontier has apparently bewitched even the iconoclastic sage of Baltimore into neglecting a lead which was suggested by a British observer of our language more than a hundred years ago. For in 1837, as Mencken himself has noted, Captain Marryat remarked on the tendency in America for technical words and phrases to enter into general speech by metaphor, as an example of which he offered the transformation of "straining at a gnat and swallowing a camel" into "straining at a gate and swallowing a sawmill." Elsewhere Mencken quotes a specimen of frontier brag which illustrates the same phenomenon: "I'm the ginewine article, a real double-acting engine, and I can out-run, out-jump, etc., etc." Perhaps after all Howells was right when he said that American writers would find the sources of a vital native language not only in the great open spaces but in both "the shops and fields."

Granted the purposes which were so much a part of the vernacular tradition and granted the universal appeal of its subject matter, it was inevitable that—side by side with the development of new oral and written forms for handling its materials—there would be a corresponding development of techniques for distribution of its products. The plays and variety shows in which the figures of the comic trio were developed were taken by traveling theatrical troupes into the remotest settlements. P. T. Barnum's "Grand Scientific and Musical Theater," his first traveling show, toured the South-

Plate V: Gothic Tracery in Iron and Glass
The Grover and Baker Sewing Machine Company's building at
495 Broadway, New York (from the *New York Illustrated News*,
August 25, 1860)

L. Z LEITER'S BUILDING,
STATE, VAN BUREN AND CONGRESS STREETS, CHICAGO.
W. L. B. JENNEY, ARCHITECT.

Plate VI: The Architecture of the Steel Skeleton

(*Above*) William LeBaron Jenney's Leiter Building, Chicago, 1889; (*below*) Jenney's proposed building for the Hercules Manufacturing Co.—1888 (both drawings from *The Inland Architect and News Record*)

THE PROPOSED HERCULES MANUFACTURING BUILDING, CHICAGO.
W. L. B. JENNEY, ARCHITECT AND ENGINEER.

ern states in two wagons, and from the earliest days similar troupes gave performances on canalboats and flatboats, and later on the elaborate showboats which plied the Western rivers. The characteristics of oral literature, its personal and anecdotal flavor, its racy and colloquial style, were developed in the Lyceum lecture circuits established by such men as Josiah Holbrook and James Redpath and later in the Chautauqua camps and tent shows. Almost all the prominent writers of the period from 1830 to 1924 had traveled across the country at least once, lecturing at village Lyceums or at Chautauquas. Never before in history had so many authors had firsthand contact with such vast audiences in so many diverse communities.

In book publishing also there were significant developments. Both Dr. Chase and Thomas E. Hill, for example, set up their own special printing and publishing establishments to handle their books, and neither was satisfied with the conventional process of distribution through bookstores. As Chase announced in his preface, his book was sold "only by Travelling Agents, that all may have a chance to purchase; for if left at the bookstores, or by advertisement only, not one in fifty would ever see it."

Subscription publishing, as this method was called, was an important development in the latter half of the century. It is described in *The Great Industries of the United States* (1873) as a fairly new branch of the book business, which was becoming more popular every year because it was the best, if not the only, means of introducing books to a large circle of readers, "especially in interior towns which are remote from book-publishing and book-selling centers." Essentially it was simply an industrialized extension of the earlier system (described in 1841 by S. G. Goodrich, the bookseller and publisher) whereby peddlers—mostly from Connecticut, apparently—bought books and almanacs wholesale from some supplier like the Pearl Street Bookstore in New York, and then traveled by horse and wagon through the Southern and Western states, selling them at any house where they could find "a sucker." But in subscription publishing the traveling agents carried with them samples only, taking orders for later delivery.

That the new method was successful, and that it was admirably suited to the vernacular forms, is indicated by the fact that it was a subscription publisher who brought out all Mark Twain's early books. Not long after *The Innocents Abroad* was published by the American Publishing Company in Hartford, Twain wrote to its proprietor, Elisha Bliss, that everywhere he went on his lecture tours he found that an agent had been there before him and many people had read the book. "It is easy to see, when one travels around," he added, "that one must be endowed with a deal of genuine generalship in order to maneuver a publication whose line of battle stretches from end to end of a great continent, and whose foragers and skirmishers invest every hamlet and besiege every village hidden away in all the vast space between."

Important as all these factors were in the development of the vernacular, the most serviceable vehicle of all was journalism. No literary vehicle is more flexible than the newspaper, and none responds more directly to the tastes and preferences of its readers. Many of the writers who have figured in the development of a distinctively American litera-ture—Whitman and Mark Twain among them—have at some time been newspapermen or newspaper contributors.

It is a notable fact that the essential feature of the success of cheap journalism in England and America, first exploited in the United States by Benjamin H. Day's New York *Sun* (1833) and the other penny dailies of the thirties, turned out to be human-interest stories: non-political local news about people who were—or might be—known to the reader. It was the same principle which Chase and Hill were later to rely on in their books. It was precisely what Mark Twain, out in Virginia City in the mad mining days, had in mind when he wrote to his sister in St. Louis that she would never make a good reporter because she didn't appreciate the interest that attaches to names. "An item is of no use," he told her, "unless it speaks of some *person*, and not then, unless that person's *name* is distinctly mentioned. The most interesting letter . . . is one that treats of *persons* . . . rather than the public events of the day." American journalism from the beginning has demonstrated that we are more interested in what local individuals do, and what they say about politics, than we are in what goes on in the rest of the world, or what really happens in politics. From Ben Franklin's *Dogood Papers* to Finley Dunne's *Mr. Dooley* and on down to Will Rogers and thence to Winchell, Pegler, and Eleanor Roosevelt, Americans have been specialists in personal journalism.

So we have come full circle and are back again to the individual human being whose worth, Channing had said, it should be the function of our literature to show. We have seen how, in a variety of subliterary ways, the vernacular tradition improvised techniques to tear away the disguises from men living under democratic institutions in a machine age. But the search for new forms and techniques was by no means confined to these subliterary areas.

Think, for a moment, of the eminent American writers of the nineteenth century and notice how many of them are difficult to classify in terms of the literary forms in which they worked. Was Melville a novelist? Certainly not in the sense that Thackeray, Flaubert, or even Tolstoy were novelists. *Typee, Omoo,* and *Mardi* are not novels by any definition, and *Moby Dick* itself is—in form—altogether unlike any other book ever written, a compound of tragic drama, treatise on whaling technology, allegory, philosophical speculations, adventure narrative, and seamanship manual. Were Emerson and Thoreau essayists and poets? But Emerson's essays are really oral lectures, and his stature as a writer depends fully as much on the *Journals* as upon the essays; it is the *Journals* after all which come closest to being the kind of "Montaigne's book" he wanted, "full of fun, poetry, business, divinity, philosophy, anecdote, smut." Thoreau's masterpiece, *Walden,* is part poetic record of a personal adventure, part a philosophy of rebellion against social conformity, and part the record of a reporter-naturalist. For years Whitman's *Leaves of Grass* was only reluctantly admitted to be poetry. ("Confused, inarticulate, and surging in a mad kind of rhythm which sounds as if hexameters were trying to bubble through sewage," Professor Barrett Wendell of Harvard's English department called it in his *Literary History of America* in 1900.) The author of *Huckleberry Finn, Life on the Mississippi, Personal Recollections of Joan of Arc,* and *Roughing It* is hard to label in terms of the forms he worked in. Even Hawthorne and Poe, who on first thought are easily classified as writers of fiction, were the creators of a new form: the modern short story.

The influence of vernacular elements is notable in the work of all these writers. Charles Olson recently called attention to the fact that the whaling ship, which Melville wrote about in *Moby Dick*, was one of the most highly developed industrial machines of its time, and it is significant that it was in writing this book that Melville for the first and only time succeeded in fusing the techniques of reporting and of allegory, which, as Professor Matthiessen has said, were his two contrasting methods of dealing with material.

The vernacular elements in Emerson's writing are no less important for being less obvious. Constance Rourke was the first to call attention to the relationship between his lectures and the oral and communal dialogues of the humorists, the lyrical strain which had sounded in the midst of Jack Downing's Yankee lingo, "the air of wonder, the rhapsodic speech" of Western tall talk. But the relationship had been sensed in Emerson's own time. Two newspaper accounts of his lectures were included, side by side with samples of Down East and frontier humor, in *Yankee Smith's American Broad Grins*, one of innumerable such collections brought out in the fifties and sixties. One of the accounts, in spite of its self-consciously arty journalism, moves very close to the rhapsodic boasting of the frontier demigods, in its picture of the gentle Yankee speaker as "a spiritual shuttle, vibrating between the unheard of and the unutterable."

> Like a child he shakes his rattle over the edge of chaos, and swings on the gates of the past, and sits like a nightingale in a golden ring, suspended by a silver cord from a nail driven into the zenith.

One is reminded of Lowell's less ebullient description of the lectures as "a chaos full of shooting stars, a jumble of creative forces."

Emerson learned his techniques the hard way, in small

towns and villages all over the land where he gave Lyceum lectures. In spite of his shy and withdrawn nature and his predilection for contemplation rather than action he never lost his conviction that his audience must include the great mass of people who "understand what's what as well as the little mass." He had scathing contempt for the "pert gentlemen" who assumed that the whole object was "to manage 'the great mass' and they, forsooth, are behind the curtain with the Deity and mean to help manage."

Emerson's lectures—like the published essays which were based upon them—were loosely organized as compared with the formal prose of a contemporary like Lowell. But they had a vitality and flexibility which his oral medium required. His friend Carlyle objected that his paragraphs were square bags of duck shot rather than beaten ingots, and he himself seems to have felt occasionally that his essays should have had more continuity. But fundamentally Emerson cared little for the purely literary values. He put his writing to different tests, measuring it against values inherent in the vernacular environment.

Out in Beloit, Wisconsin, for instance, on a January day in 1856 when the temperature was down somewhere between twenty and thirty degrees below zero, he made this entry in his journal:

> This climate and people are a new test for the wares of a man
> of letters. All his thin, watery matter freezes; 'tis only the
> smallest portion of alcohol that remains good. At the lyceum,
> the stout Illinoian, after a short trial, walks out of the hall.
> The Committee tell you that the people want a hearty laugh.
> . . . Well, I think with Governor Reynolds, the people are
> always right (in a sense), and that the man of letters is to say,
> These are the new conditions to which I must conform. The
> architect who is asked to build a house to go upon the sea,

must not build a Parthenon, or a square house, but a ship. And Shakespeare, or Franklin, or Aesop, coming to Illinois, would say, I must give my wisdom a comic form, instead of tragics or elegiacs, and well I know to do it, and he is no master who cannot vary his forms, and carry his own end triumphantly through the most difficult.

That is a typically Emersonian passage not only in the freshness of its imagery but also in its modesty and honesty. The Illinoian walked out on him, and the Illinoian was the very man he was after. The Illinoian wanted a laugh. Very well, then, that was a fact which genius should accept and turn to its own account.

To be sure, Emerson was never able to give comic form to his own genius—as Mark Twain was later to do in the same vernacular medium of the platform lecture. But, as he said of the sailor preacher, Father Taylor, he did succeed in making abstractions "accessible and effectual" to hearers who were not much given to reading philosophical essays, and in the process of doing so he created a personal idiom more instant and supple than any in our literature before him. What matter if he could not meet the cultivated tradition's standard of polished and finished prose? "Only that good profits which we can taste with all doors open, and which serves all men."

Whitman, too, drew on vernacular oral techniques in evolving a form suited to his purposes. Faced with the vast panorama of American life, the poet, he insisted, must abandon conventional poetic form and rhyme and seek a more flexible, more eligible medium of expression, "enlarging, adapting itself to comprehend the size of the whole people." The form of expression which had most powerfully moved him and which contributed most to his own style was the "passionate unstudied oratory" of men like the Quaker

preacher Elias Hicks, to whom he had listened as a boy on
Long Island, and Emerson's friend Father Taylor. Dilating
confidently in the oratorical rhythms of a language which, as
Emerson described it, was compounded from the *Bhagvat-
Geeta* and the New York *Herald,* Whitman sometimes lapsed
into such unconscious burlesque as the exclamatory line from
"Night on the Prairie":

> *How plenteous! how spiritual! how resumé!*

But at its rare best the instrument he had created was the most
flexible and powerful medium yet created for expressing the
American scene. Even in the much-deprecated "catalogue
passages" there are such visually and emotionally concise,
reportorial lines as these from Section 15 of "Song of Myself":

> *The carpenter dresses his plank, the tongue of his fore-
>   plane whistles its wild ascending lisp. . . .*
> *The jour printer with gray head and gaunt jaws works
>   at his case,*
> *He turns his quid of tobacco while his eyes blur with
>   the manuscript;*
> *The malformed limbs are tied to the surgeon's table,*
> *What is removed drops horribly in a pail. . . .*

The extent of the influence of vernacular forces on the
major writers of nineteenth-century America is only briefly
suggested by the instances given here. Nothing has been said
of the journalistic origins of the short story form which Hawthorne and Poe created; nor have we attempted to explore
such obvious areas as the influence upon Whitman and Mark
Twain of their years as newspaper editors. But enough has
been said, perhaps, to indicate that a considerable part of the
characteristically American quality in the work of our major

writers stems from the influence of the vernacular tradition. Wherever we look in the writing of the nineteenth century we are likely to encounter one or more of the vernacular characteristics of utilitarian ethics, concern with the value of the individual, and the panoramic effort to comprehend a diversity of people and places in specific local and factual terms; and we are sure to find these characteristics developed in writing aimed at wide audiences—in personal narratives (from outright autobiographies like Franklin's to books like Melville's *Typee* and *Redburn* and Mark Twain's *Huckleberry Finn* and *Life on the Mississippi*), in books of information, in humorous writing, and in journalism.

Now let us see how some of these same vernacular qualities have manifested themselves in American painting, where the medium of expression is less subject to utilitarian demands than the written word.

7

Seeing Is Believing

After visiting the art gallery at the Philadelphia Centennial, William James wrote to his brother Henry to tell him how pleased he was with the high average of the American paintings. The great majority of them were landscapes, he noted, and in almost every case the animating spirit was "a perfectly sincere effort to reproduce a natural aspect" which in some special way had affected the painter's sensibility.

James's description of the animating spirit in these paintings is significant. It emphasizes the literalness in American paintings which almost all critics agreed was characteristic, whether or not they approved of it. William Dean Howells felt that the American paintings were "too often unstoried, like our scenery," and that their subjects "were seen, not deeply felt and thought." Similarly, the *Art Journal's* critic preferred the English landscape paintings to the American because so many of the best of ours appeared like pictures seen in the camera. (An odd converse to this statement appears in a comment by Hermann Wilhelm Vogel, one of the German judges, on the exhibit at Photographic Hall: the Americans, he noted, expect from the photographer "work which in

Europe would belong to the artist.") As early as 1856 John Ruskin, complaining of the ugliness of some American paintings he had just seen, acidly noted that he could see "that they were *true* studies and that the ugliness of the country must be Unfathomable." The art critic James Jackson Jarves, too, objected to the literalness of our painters, and gave as an example Bierstadt's "Rocky Mountains," in which the realism was so factual "that the botanist and geologist can find work in his rocks and vegetation." And in 1879 S. G. W. Benjamin was complaining that the influence which had given birth to our landscape art had been prosaic, exacting, and uninspiring.

The "topographical and mechanical" notions of art to which Benjamin and the others objected, had—as a matter of fact—been come by honestly enough in the case of many of the painters. An extraordinary large percentage of American artists were originally apt in, or dependent upon, mechanical skill; Peale, Durand, Palmer, Chapman, and Kensett were all disciplined for pictorial work by workmanship in machinery, watchmaking, carving, or engraving. Several of our early sculptors, too, were mechanics by training. Joel Tanner Hart was a stonemason before he did his bust of Henry Clay (1847), based on exact measurements and a number of daguerreotype studies, and he later invented and patented a measuring machine to make his work more precise. Hiram Powers, late in his career, liked to reminisce in Florence about his early training in America as a mechanic simplifying and improving a machine for cutting clock wheels, and finishing brass plates for organ stops so smoothly and accurately that when one was laid on another and then raised, it would lift the other—as he proudly put it—"by mere cohesive attraction." So mechanically did Powers work in marble that he could sum up his philosophy of art by saying baldly that "He that can copy a potato precisely can copy a face precisely." The limitations of Powers' once-famous "Greek Slave" and other statues are evident enough to anyone who has seen them. But—like the familiar and universally popular "Rogers Groups" of the sixties[1]—they serve to illustrate the same sort of perfectly sincere effort to reproduce nature which James noted in American landscape painting.

In one of the most interesting recent (1936) studies of American painting Alan Burroughs makes it clear that a distinctively American—as distinguished from the parent English—approach to art had become apparent as early as 1750; and this distinction appeared not in the South but in New England, where the "best society" (that is, the patrons of art) was in close contact with the yeomanry. In painting, as in furniture design and architecture, there was a new emphasis on simplicity, reality, and serviceability. In the work of Copley, Smibert, and the other mid-eighteenth-century New England portrait painters, Burroughs writes, "what took the place of beauty and consciously artistic structure was simply good eyesight." And if one traces the course of American painting thereafter, it becomes clear that the only attitude which is traditional in American art is, as Burroughs concludes, "dependence on fact." There are, of course, different kinds of realism: realism of the eye, of the emotions, and of the mind; but there is only one fundamental attitude which permits any kind of realism, and that is respect for the thing seen, the feeling aroused, or the attendant thought.

[1]Typical examples were "The Returned Volunteer," "The Council of War," and "Weighing the Baby." John Rogers, their creator, had studied civil engineering, worked in a New Hampshire machine shop, and been boss of a railroad repair shop in the West.

This respect, this dependence upon fact, appears variously in the work of both the ablest and the least accomplished technicians. To analyze it carefully and fully would require more space than we have here at our disposal; but it will be familiar to anyone who has seen the work, for example, of William Sidney Mount, Winslow Homer, Thomas Eakins, or of the numerous so-called primitive painters.

American primitive paintings have been eagerly collected and frequently exhibited during the past few years, and more than a hundred of the best of them (from widely scattered private and public collections) have been reproduced by Jean Lipman in a handsome volume published by the Oxford University Press in 1942. Miss Lipman admires these paintings primarily because of what she calls their "purely aesthetic qualities of abstract design," which, she asserts, "entirely accounts for" the widespread contemporary interest in them. One may suppose, therefore, that she has selected for inclusion those pictures which best illustrate those qualities.

Yet anyone who examines the pictures soon discovers that there are two quite divergent types among them. On the one hand there are some which are indeed highly abstract and free from any apparent concern with visual reality, such as the formal little landscapes and still-life groups, frequently executed by means of stencils, or the conventionalized memorials like the one by Eunice Pinney (see Plate VIII), reproduced from Miss Lipman's own collection. These are in every sense abstract patterns of forms and colors. There is no optical reality about them.

On the other hand, a sizable majority of the paintings seem to represent a quite different attitude upon the part of the artist. In them one senses a diligent and often rather touching effort to make a literal and detailed record of the thing seen. Joseph H. Headley's oil on wood painting of Poestenkill (see Plate VIII) is obviously an attempt to record specific houses, barns, fences, roads, and landscape. Whatever deviations from actuality such a painting contains are imposed by the painter's lack of technical mastery. They are not the result of indifference to exact appearance, or of an instinctive preference for abstract design. If one of the barns in the painting is red, one feels sure that Headley did not paint it so because his sense of design required it but because that particular barn in Poestenkill in 1850 was red.

The point I am insisting on here is that in the two different types of primitives the absence of an accurate "representation of normal visible reality," which Miss Lipman and many other contemporary critics admire, results from two quite different causes. In pictures like Eunice Pinney's "Memorial" the painter had no intention of representing optical reality; she was out to create a lugubrious design, not a picture of a specific tomb. But in paintings like Headley's, actuality was the painter's primary concern—so much so that, within the limits of his craftsmanship, he often represented it even if he couldn't see it from where he stood, just because he *knew* it was there.

As one would expect, these two opposed attitudes are reflected in the kind of subject matter chosen. When the painter was concerned primarily with abstract design he drew his subjects from literature, or copied conventional designs in popular prints and pictures, or simply arranged stencils in agreeable patterns. But when the painter was concerned primarily with actuality, he turned for his subjects to real landscapes and to houses, ships, trains, and people that he knew.

In the former case composition is primarily the product of the artist's design sense, and the details are selected in terms of the design. In the latter, the composition exists almost independently of the artist; in a sense he merely selects or discovers it. One painter imposes a satisfying design upon pleasing conventionalized elements; the other imposes upon himself a satisfying relationship with an already existing design.

Those primitives in which fact is subordinate to design are always on the fringes of the cultivated tradition, and many of them are echoes if not mere unskilled imitations of professional work. The anonymous painting of "The Runaway Horse" (Plate 43 in Miss Lipman's volume) is an obvious echo of the academic English landscape school; Edward Hicks's notable "Penn's Treaty with the Indians" (Plate 69) is a memory image of Benjamin West's much-reproduced painting of the same scene; and the anonymous painting of "Cleveland's Public Square" (Plate 62) was certainly done by someone familiar with the expert aquatint engravings of the early nineteenth century. Amy, in Louisa May Alcott's *Little Women,* was in a sense the type of all the cultivated primitives. When she took up "poker-sketching," you may remember, "Raphael's face was found boldly executed on the under side of the moulding board, and Bacchus on the head of a beer barrel," and her later paintings were of swarthy boys and dark-eyed madonnas suggesting Murillo or "buxom ladies and dropsical infants" which were meant to look like Rubens. Even when she got the mania for "sketching from nature" she haunted river, field, and wood, "sighing for ruins to copy."

It seems clear, then, that there are two distinct categories of paintings which are generally lumped together as American primitives: unprofessional paintings reflecting the impact on the artist of some aspect of the cultivated tradition, and paintings which, seeking to reproduce optical reality, create a tone and feeling which relate directly to the thing seen.

These same qualities appear also in the work of our professional painters. Two pictures which provide a striking example of these divergent approaches were included in the loan exhibition, "Life In America," which was shown at the Metropolitan Museum of Art during the New York World's Fair in 1939, and are illustrated on facing pages of the catalogue of that exhibition. James M. Hart's "The Old Schoolhouse" and Henry Inman's "Dismissal of School on an October Afternoon" are very similar in subject matter and were both painted in the 1840s. (See Plate IX.) Both contain a country schoolhouse among trees at the right of the scene, a group of children in the center foreground, and at the left a stream flowing into a distant landscape of hills and fields. In Inman's painting the whole effect is misty; the October atmosphere is an essential part of the artist's intention. The schoolhouse is partly obscured by trees; the children, though nearer to the artist than in Hart's painting, are less clearly observed and seem to be on loan from an inferior canvas by Sir Thomas Lawrence or George Romney; and the distant hills and fields are reminiscent of many of the romantic English landscapes of the period. Hart's schoolhouse, on the other hand, is sharply defined, revealing the warped and split clapboards and each shingle of the roof; the children look as country children may well have looked, not too tidy; and the landscape is familiar farmland.

Both Inman and Hart learned to paint in upstate New York, but Inman was taught by John Wesley Jarvis, the fashionable portrait painter, and became so successful that,

Plate VII: The Pomological Annex at the Centennial

This picture, from Thompson Westcott's *Centennial Portfolio*, Philadelphia, 1876, is the only surviving record of the building. Of Agricultural Hall, in the background at the left, Westcott remarked that the exterior displayed "ornamentation sufficient to make the edifice attractive"

Plate VIII: Two Types of Primitive Painting

(*Above*) *Memorial*, a water color by Eunice Pinney, done about
1815 (reproduced with permission from the collection of Jean and
Howard Lipman); (*below*) *Poestenkill—Winter*, an oil-on-wood
painting by Joseph H. Headley, done about 1850 (©Halladay-
Thomas Collection; reproduced with permission)

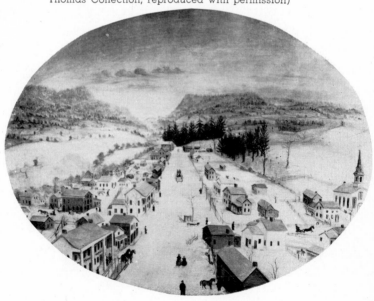

under the patronage of wealthy admirers, he went to England in 1844 (the year before "Dismissal of School" was painted) and was warmly received by Mulready, Leslie, and other fashionable English artists. Hart, however, learned painting as a trade, both from his brother William, who was a carriage painter, and as an apprentice to a sign and banner painter. It was not until after "The Old Schoolhouse" was painted that he went to Düsseldorf for formal training.

No question of relative merit is involved in this discussion of these two canvases. The point is simply to demonstrate that the same diverse streams of art which we find in our architecture can be traced also in American painting. The fact happens to be that all during the nineteenth century and well into the twentieth art critics here and abroad have admired few of those painters, European or American, who have been dominated by a devotion to literal representation. Those who loved and understood the western European tradition of painting, and those who worked in it, were naturally drawn to Americans like Whistler and Mary Cassatt, whose work—done chiefly abroad—related directly to the development of that tradition. When Edgar P. Richardson made his scholarly study of *The Way of Western Art* (1939), he was concerned to "relate American art to the tradition to which it belongs." Inevitably, therefore, he omitted William Sidney Mount altogether, and gave only about a page each to Winslow Homer and Thomas Eakins.

Yet Homer and Eakins are towering figures in American painting, as Richardson would undoubtedly agree, and Mount's clear, explicit genre pictures and open-air landscapes are more and more coming to be recognized as an important link in a characteristic American tradition of precise representation. In 1846 Mount wrote in his journal: "There has been enough written on ideality and the grand style of Art, etc., to divert the artist from the true study of natural objects." But Mount was not to be diverted. Note after note in his journal records that his pictures were painted "out of doors," "on the spot," or "in the open air," and he designed an "artist's waggon," or portable studio with large glass windows, "to sketch and paint in during windy and rainy weather." It is this outdoor clarity which makes "Long Island Farmhouse" (Metropolitan) one of Mount's most effective paintings: an honest, literal record of plain structures in November sunlight.

Eakins saw his subjects with the eye of a trained scientist, rather than a mere observer, but his knowledge and understanding of them never led him to compromise with the absolute integrity of visual reality. As Lloyd Goodrich has said, he "worked from the core of reality out into art." Or, to say it another way, he knew—as Whitman knew—that "out from the well-tended concrete and physical—and in them and from them only—radiate the spiritual and heroic."

His interests were strongly scientific and mechanical. When, during his brief sojourn as an art student in Paris, he visited the International Exposition of 1867, it was the exhibits of locomotives and machinery which attracted him, rather than the art galleries. Throughout his life the most creative influence on his painting was the study of anatomy, in which he became almost a professional, contributing papers on his research to the published *Proceedings of the Academy of Natural Sciences of Philadelphia*. One of these papers, on "The Differential Action of Certain Muscles Passing More Than One Joint" (1894), clearly shows Eakins' mechanical-scientific bent. Having observed the muscles in a horse's leg when the beast was straining to start a horsecar, he noticed that they did not act as they would if they conformed to the description of them in standard works on muscular action. He therefore constructed "a model of the entire limb with flat pieces of half-inch pine board, catgut for tendons and ligaments, and rubber bands for muscles, all attached to their places and properly restrained." With this mechanism and with dissection on the leg of a dead horse, he demonstrated the true action of the muscles and showed how they must be considered not only in relation to the bones to which they are attached, "but with relation to the whole movement of the animal. . . . One is never sure," he concluded, "that he understands the least movement of an animal, unless he can connect it with the whole muscular system, making, in fact, a complete circuit of all the strains. . . . On the lines of the mighty and simple strains dominating the movement, and felt intuitively and studied out by him, the master artist groups, with full intention, his muscular forms. No detail contradicts. His men and animals live."

This interest in anatomical movement also led Eakins to carry out important experiments with photography. Muybridge's photographs of galloping horses, taken in California with a battery of twenty-four cameras, attracted a great deal of interest, and in 1884 (partly through Eakins' influence) he was invited to continue his experiments at the University of Pennsylvania. Eakins himself designed and helped to build a special camera which recorded successive phases of motion on a single film, thus approximating the effect of a series of movie stills.

Eakins' ideal of a painting was one in which "you can

see what o'clock it is, afternoon or morning, if it's hot or cold, winter or summer, and what kind of people are there, and what they are doing, and why they are doing it." The great painter, he believed, learns what nature does with light, color, and form and appropriates these tools to his own use. They serve him, as he wrote to his father, as "a canoe of his own, smaller than Nature's, but big enough for every purpose," in which he can sail parallel to nature. But if the painter ever thinks he can "sail another fashion from Nature or make a better shaped boat, he'll capsize or stick in the mud." To many of Eakins' contemporaries, here and abroad, the study of light and atmosphere became an end in itself; but to him it was, like his knowledge of anatomy, merely an instrument. Speaking of the role of anatomical dissection in his teaching at the Pennsylvania Academy of Fine Arts he made it clear that for anatomy as such he cared nothing whatever. Dissection was hard and dirty work, of value to the artist simply because it increased his knowledge of how animals and human beings are put together and thus enabled him to "imitate" them. "Even to refine upon natural beauty—to idealize," he added, "one must understand what it is that he is idealizing; otherwise his idealization—I don't like the word, by the way —becomes distortion, and distortion is ugliness."

Eakins himself did not idealize; the unparalleled series of portraits he painted in the eighties and nineties are a record of his relentless understanding of human character and his objective respect for it. And "Max Schmitt in a Single Scull" (Metropolitan Museum of Art), with its precise representation of the light-modeled forms of the Girard Avenue Bridge in the background, and "The Agnew Clinic" (University of Pennsylvania), with the figure of Dr. Agnew standing out sharply against the background of student observers, are masterpieces of scientific realism in our nineteenth-century painting. Nor are they isolated phenomena, as they have sometimes been presumed to be. Something of the same point of view toward reality, with less depth of emotional understanding but none the less unmistakably, had appeared earlier in Audubon's paintings of animals and birds, and reappeared in isolated works of Eakins' own time, like Henry Alexander's "The Laboratory of Thomas Price" (Metropolitan Museum).

Related to Eakins' scientific realism was another pictorial approach which might be called reportorial or journalistic realism. The painter who best represented this approach was Winslow Homer, who found his way into painting through work as an illustrator-correspondent for *Ballou's Pictorial* and *Harper's Weekly* during the Civil War. It is in his early paintings, especially, that one senses the reporter's concern with visual accuracy. Precise and tight in brushwork, these pictures of rural schools, factories, and home scenes were less concerned with interpretation than were Eakins' paintings, but they searched out and recorded significant surfaces and forms with an integrity which not even Eakins could surpass. In "The Morning Bell," for instance, there is something suggestive of Eakins in the way angular planes of light and shadow are employed to record the factory and the plank footbridge leading to it across the millpond. It is apparent that here, as in many of the unschooled primitive paintings of the same mid-century period, the arrangement of forms and colors was discovered and reported by the painter, rather than created by him. "When I have selected the thing carefully," Homer insisted, "I paint it exactly as it appears."

The tradition, if I may call it that, of respect for actu-

ality can be traced in the work of many other painters than
those mentioned here. It is clear that factualism has been a
powerful force in the visual arts in this country, and that even
when the influence of French painting asserted itself here at
the turn of the century, men like Luks, Glackens, and Sloan
(all of whom had, incidentally, been influenced by Eakins'
teaching and all of whom also had been newspaper artists,
trained in pictorial journalism) applied the techniques which
they learned from abroad in reporting precisely and honestly
what they saw about them.

Nor does the matter rest there. Horatio Greenough said
a century ago that America had been born in the Age of
Reason, and had been fed from the beginning with "the stout
bread and meat of fact"; America was Europe's giant off-
spring, to be sure, but "every wry face the bantling ever made
had been daguerreotyped." And this domination by fact is
still effective. It appears most blatantly, perhaps, in the work
of some of our popular illustrators like John Falter and Norman Rockwell. In describing his methods of painting Rockwell recently said, in words reminiscent of those quoted from
Winslow Homer, "It has never been natural for me to deviate
from the facts of anything before me. . . . If a model has
worn a red sweater, I have painted it red—I couldn't possibly
have made it green. I have tried again and again to take such
liberties, but with little success." And even an artist like
George Grosz, who came here from Germany in 1932, found
that his work became, as he described it, "more realistic."
"I became easily influenced," he wrote ten years later, "by
the great sense of fact in America."

But dependence on fact does not in itself make a tradition of art. At most it is only the traditional basis of an atti-

tude toward painting, or sculpture, or architecture, or literature. Nor does "the American scene" or American subject matter provide the basis for an American tradition. Neither patriotic pictures like Leutze's "Washington Crossing the Delaware" nor the work of local-colorists like Grant Wood or Thomas Benton has sufficed.

The determinant in such a tradition in any art is, as Constance Rourke said of painting, not subject but form. It is by the use of form "that the individual artist makes his art distinctive. It is the consistent print of form in successive periods which gives a national tradition its character." Going one step beyond this, it is the consistent print of form which gives character to a civilization, and it is therefore to forms that we must look for the emergence of the vernacular tradition in our painting.

Seen from this perspective, it is no mere coincidence that good eyesight and respect for optical reality have been so large an element of American painting. Instinctively artists have known that they must discover forms which are significant to their contemporaries, and the search for such forms —indigenous to the new civilization—demanded respect for the thing seen and put a premium on good eyesight, on honest reporting, and on scientific analysis. America has, to be sure, produced important painters—and painters whose work was in other ways as distinctively American as Homer's or Eakins' —whose achievements depended not at all upon these qualities. But these have been isolated figures who, like Albert Pinkham Ryder, sought to express their own inner worlds of imagination rather than the concrete reality of the world about them.

Inevitably, perhaps, those Americans who achieved the

greatest technical mastery in painting were those like Whistler, Mary Cassatt, and La Farge who turned from the crude actualities of American life to the heritage of Europe and the Orient. And it was probably also inevitable that their work, divorced from dominant concerns of contemporary life and lacking the inner integrity of Ryder's dream canvases, should seem somehow thin and lacking in substance. On the other hand it was likewise inevitable that those who worked outside the older traditions would, like Mount, Homer, and Eakins, and even Ryder himself, have had to cope with technical limitations which sometimes encumber the structural interest of their work.

It is these limitations, one suspects, which in our own time lead a painter like Charles Sheeler to deny any stimulus from Homer or Eakins. Certainly the painters from whom Sheeler learned most have all been Europeans. But anyone who looks at his work will recognize that although the modes in which he paints have their chief source in France, in postimpressionism and cubism, the forms which give character to his work are the product of the vernacular tradition—the unself-conscious architecture of barns and factories, the unornamented furniture and buildings of the Shakers, the structure of ships and machines. His large drawing of "The Open Door" and the much earlier tempera painting of the "Bucks County Barn" (Plate X) are technically fine compositions, almost abstract in quality, not unrelated to the spatial and linear studies of the postimpressionists and cubists. But in a very real sense they have roots in the tradition of respect for actuality. They have something in common with even such utilitarian pictures as the lithographs which illustrated so many of the county histories published in the nineteenth century. Notice, for instance, in the detail from the anonymous 1878 lithograph of the "Residence and Stock Farm of J. F. Blair & Son" (Plate X) how the group of barns is rendered in terms of planes of light and shadow.

Many twentieth-century painters, in both Europe and America, have been primarily concerned with the problems of achieving formal strength. In Europe this interest in the elements of structure in painting led chiefly to the study of primitive art of all kinds—African sculpture, medieval stained glass, and prehistoric pictographs. In America it led chiefly to increased interest in vernacular forms, particularly those of technology and industry. Even Lyonel Feininger, who spent most of his creative life in Germany before the war, as a member of the Bauhaus group, used cubist line and plane to express that love of mechanical and architectural form which he had developed as a young man in New York. (See especially "Side Wheeler" in the Detroit Institute of Arts, and "Old American Locomotive," both illustrated in the catalogue of the Museum of Modern Art's Feininger-Hartley exhibit in 1944.) It is not without significance that the good eyesight which goes into the discovery of such forms was in Sheeler's case supplemented by his meticulous and careful work as a photographer. Not that he confuses the art of photography with the art of painting; no one has more concretely defined the scope of each. But his eye, like Eakins' before him, had been disciplined in part by the exactness of the camera lens. Whatever rank may be assigned to Sheeler's paintings, it seems clear that in them, as effectively as in those of any of his contemporaries, the cultivated and vernacular traditions have merged into a distinctive creation.

8

The Artist's Dilemma

In the preceding chapters we have distinguished two different traditions of art in nineteenth-century America, one inherited from the older culture of Europe and the other emerging in direct response to the actualities of a machine civilization in a political democracy. We have observed how these traditions interacted, each modifying the other, and how a number of influences—geographical, political, psychological, and social—have variously favored and resisted the development of each. And finally we have seen that it was in the unself-conscious tradition of vernacular expression that American people dealt most successfully with the new and necessary facts of the emerging civilization.

Up to this point, then, we have been exploring a method of approach to the problem of the arts in America. Now let us see how that method might be applied to a consideration of the arts themselves. In what ways might it help us to understand why our literature, for instance, has always seemed less American than our history? What light can it shed on the resistances which the American environment offered to the creative imagination of the individual artist?

The arts are rooted in the civilization which produces

them, shaped in its image. Ranged behind the great master-pieces of the past—the temples of Greece, the paintings of the Italian Renaissance, the plays of Shakespeare—there had in each case been an immense and complete reality of which they were the imaginative projection. For a moment in the history of man's psychological adaptation to his environment he had achieved an apparently stable synthesis of his knowledge and belief, and the structure of society itself—as embodied in its political, social, economic, and religious institutions—seemed to reflect a coherent and enduring view of human destiny.

But in American civilization, as Emerson intuitively perceived and as Walt Whitman explicitly asserted, there was no such equilibrium between what men knew and what they believed, between fact and faith. As Whitman pointed out in *Democratic Vistas* (1871) our political institutions were based upon government of, by, and for those very people whom many of our social institutions encouraged us to dis-trust. The best-educated and most highly cultivated portion of the community looked upon the masses of people as a vulgar, untidy lump of humanity, with "gaunt and ill-bred" vices and virtues. At the same time our economic institutions and many of the social relationships of everyday life were being shaped by a technology and science which were at odds with the creeds and dogmas of our religious institutions and with the traditional amenities of cultivated society. The revolutionary impact of the twin forces of democracy and science had only begun to be felt. The spirit of the new civilization, irresistibly reshaping the foundations of man's consciousness of himself and his world, still moved almost unnoticed beneath the sur-face of American life.

It was his awareness of this amorphous, self-contra-

dictory quality in our civilization which brought Whitman to
the recognition that there could be "no complete or epical
presentation" of America until its distinctive spirit had per-
meated all aspects of its life. "How much is still to be dis-
entangled, freed!" he said in *Democratic Vistas*. "How long
it takes to make this American world see that it is, in itself,
the final authority and reliance!"

> We see the sons and daughters of the New World, ignorant of
> its genius, not yet inaugurating the native, the universal, and
> the near, still importing the distant, the partial, and the dead.
> We see London, Paris, Italy—not original, superb, as where
> they belong—but second-hand here, where they do not belong.
> We see the shreds of Hebrews, Romans, Greeks; but where,
> on her own soil, do we see, in any faithful, highest, proud
> expression, America herself? I sometimes question whether
> she has a corner in her own house.

In such a situation, he argued, America required "a
new theory of literary composition for imaginative works."
The poet must no longer be expected to round out and complete his vision in an artistic unity. The reader, not the poet,
must himself or herself construct the finished poem—"the text
furnishing the hints, the clue, the start or frame-work. Not the
book needs so much to be the complete thing, but the reader
of the book does." As he had said in the preface to the original
edition of *Leaves of Grass* (1855), "the expression of the
American poet is to be transcendant and new. It is to be in-
direct, and not direct or descriptive or epic. Let the age and
wars of other nations be chanted, and their eras and characters
be illustrated, and that finish the verse. Not so the great psalm
of the republic. Here the theme is creative and has vista." So
also, near the end of his life, he said: "I round and finish little,
if anything, and could not, consistently with my scheme. . . .

I seek less to state or display any theme or thought, and more to bring you, reader, into the atmosphere of the theme or thought—there to pursue your own flight."

In other words, Whitman saw that the function of the creative imagination in the new civilization differed essentially from that which was fulfilled in the older culture by artistic sensibility.

> . . . *each man and each woman of you I lead upon a knoll,*
> *My left hand hooking you around the waist,*
> *My right hand pointing to landscapes of continents and the public road.*
> *Not I, not any one else can travel that road for you,*
> *You must travel it for yourself.*
> *It is not far, it is within reach,*
> *Perhaps you have been on it since you were born and did not know.*

It is not the artist who "rounds and finishes" that speaks in this passage from the "Song of Myself." It is rather the man who believed in the necessity of giving "positive place, identity" to his vision of America's destiny, revealing to each man the inner meaning and direction of an inchoate, revolutionary "future-founding" age.

To insist upon this aspect of Whitman's genius is not to deny that there are passages in his verse—and indeed whole poems—which rise into the concentrated intensity of lyric poetry. But there are many other passages—which an "artist" would have trimmed away, but which form an integral part of his design—where he is essentially the announcer with a megaphone on a cosmic sight-seeing bus, pointing out the landmarks to his fellow passengers as they roll along the open road. Few critics have been willing enough to take Whitman at his word when he asserted that no one can get at the real meaning of his *Leaves* "who insists upon viewing them as a literary performance, or attempt at such performance, or as aiming mainly toward art or aestheticism."

Probably no one who was driven solely, or even primarily, by the passion to integrate experience and give it order in artistic form could have flooded himself so completely, and even delightedly, as Whitman did "with the immediate age as with vast oceanic tides." Certainly there has been a marked tendency throughout our history for Americans with artistic talent to withdraw from direct contact with the everyday life about them. From Copley and Benjamin West to Whistler, Sargent, and Mary Cassatt it was almost habitual for American-born painters to become expatriates, and from the time of Greenough and Hiram Powers our sculptors have spent much of their creative lives abroad. In the field of literature, Henry James was the first eminent writer to become an actual expatriate, but many of his predecessors from Irving on down lived for considerable periods in England or on the Continent, and Lafcadio Hearn went to live in Japan. Even when our artists have not actually left the country, however, they have frequently sought some other means of isolating themselves from American society—whether in a lonely cabin at Walden Pond, like Thoreau, in an enclosed garden in Amherst, Massachusetts, like Emily Dickinson, or in a private solitude of vision like Albert Pinkham Ryder.

The work of any one of the writers or artists whom we have mentioned would provide us with ample material to illustrate the nature of the resistances which American civilization opposed to the artistic imagination. Yet we will do better, perhaps, to concentrate our attention here on someone who, for all that he was an essentially solitary and lonely genius, did not permit himself to become either a recluse or an expatriate.

Like most of his contemporaries, Nathaniel Hawthorne as a young man shared in the enthusiasm for creating a national literature, "hewing it, as it were, out of the unwrought granite of our intellectual quarries," discovering, if need be, new forms which would not be merely an "interminably repeated . . . reproduction of the images that were molded by our great fathers of song and fiction." As time passed, however, and as he concentrated more and more on the specific problems involved in shaping his own stories and novels, he made fewer and fewer overt references to the general problem of indigenous literary forms. Yet it would be a mistake to infer from this that he—or any other American artist— escaped the fundamental artistic problem involved in the conflict between the two traditions. Actually he ran head on into it. Over and over again in the prefaces to his books he reminded his readers of the difficulties involved in writing fiction about a land where actualities were "so terribly insisted upon" as they were—and needs must be—in America.

> In the old countries [he wrote in the preface to *The Blithedale Romance*], with which fiction has long been conversant, a certain conventional privilege seems to be awarded to the romancer; his work is not put exactly side by side with nature. . . . Among ourselves, on the contrary, there is as yet no such Faery Land, so like the real world that, in a suitable remoteness, one cannot well tell the difference, but with an atmosphere of strange enchantment, beheld through which the

inhabitants have a propriety of their own. This atmosphere is
what the American romancer needs.

It was in an effort to provide something of this atmosphere that Hawthorne always contrived settings for his novels
which were somewhat removed from the everyday world about
him—remote either in time or place from the main current of
contemporary life. Even in *The House of the Seven Gables,*
which—as Henry James observed—contained more of the
"literal actuality" of American life than any of his other
books, he deliberately intertwined the past and present
through the agency of what he described as "a legend prolong-
ing itself, from an epoch now gray in the distance, down into
our own broad daylight, and bringing along with it some of
its legendary mist"—a mist which would float almost im-
perceptibly about the characters and events of the novel to
create the necessary atmosphere of strange enchantment.

Yet Hawthorne knew that his books were weakened by
his inability to cope with the crude but vital elements of the
emerging civilization. There was profound conviction behind
his statement that, though he was unable to bring his creative
imagination to bear on the world of commerce and trade in
which for three years he played a part as surveyor of customs
for the port of Salem, the fault was his own. "The page of life
which was laid out before me," he wrote, "seemed dull and
commonplace only because I had not fathomed its deeper
import. A better book than I shall ever write was there. . . ."

One is struck by the fact that when he turned in his
fiction to portraying the artist's role in American society he
characteristically chose for his protagonists men who worked
in art forms which were firmly rooted in the technological

environment. Holgrave, for instance, in *The House of the Seven Gables*, was a daguerreotypist—a practitioner of the most "up-to-date" and scientific art; the hero of "Drowne's Wooden Image" was a carver of figureheads for ships; and in "The Artist of the Beautiful," Hawthorne's most elaborate allegory of the artist's role, Owen Warland was a young mechanical genius whose dream—and ultimate triumph—was "to spiritualize machinery, and to combine with the new species of life and motion thus produced a beauty that should attain to the ideal."

The sense of the past which permeates Hawthorne's novels and tales tends to obscure the relationships between his art and the main currents of life in his own time. Yet, if we follow the development in his fiction of the theme of conflict between past and present we will discover that it is closely related to his awareness of the artist's problem in the new civilization. In its barest form the theme was first stated in an idea for a story which he recorded in his notebook sometime during 1844. What he there proposed was "to represent the influence Dead Men have among living affairs." Dead men, he observed, by the terms of their wills control the disposition of wealth; the opinions of dead judges dominate the law courts. In short, "Dead Men's opinions in all things control the living truth; we believe in Dead Men's religion; we laugh at Dead Men's jokes; we cry at Dead Men's pathos; everywhere and in all matters, Dead Men tyranize inexorably over us."

It was in *The House of the Seven Gables* (1851) that this theme found its most complete embodiment. The very language of the notebook entry appears there, considerably elaborated, in a speech which Hawthorne put into the mouth of Holgrave, the daguerreotypist, but which sums up the theme of the entire novel.

> "Shall we never, never get rid of this Past?" cried he. . . .
> "It lies upon the Present like a giant's dead body! In fact, the case is just as if a young giant were compelled to waste all his strength in carrying about the corpse of the old giant, his grandfather. . . . Just think a moment, and it will startle you to see what slaves we are to bygone times,—to Death, if we give the matter the right word!"

Then follows an expanded version of the passage quoted above from the notebook, with this significant addition: "I ought to have said, too, that we live in dead men's houses; as, for instance, in this of the Seven Gables."

> "But we shall live to see the day, I trust," went on the artist, "when no man shall build his house for posterity. . . . If each generation were allowed and expected to build its own houses, that single change . . . would imply almost every reform which society is now suffering for. . . . This old Pyncheon house . . . in my view, is expressive of that odious and abominable past, with all its bad influences, against which I have just been declaiming. I dwell in it for a while, that I may know the better how to hate it."

It is true that the idea as stated here is intended as an expression of Holgrave's character and is not presented as the author's own view. Indeed, speaking in his own person, Hawthorne in part disclaims it. Yet Holgrave, as we have seen, was one of the characters through whom Hawthorne projected his concept of the artist's role in America. Further, in a passage of the novel where Hawthorne comments in his own right on Holgrave's character, he explicitly states that "in his culture and want of culture . . . the artist might fitly enough stand forth as the representative of many compeers in his native land." And finally, the same ideas, in very nearly the same words, are expressed by another character in the novel who is also in some degree a projection of the author's own personality. For Clifford, the broken and defeated lover of the beautiful in whom Hawthorne represented many of those aspects of the artistic temperament which he recognized in himself, echoes Holgrave in his impassioned exclamation that the chief obstructions to human happiness are "these heaps of bricks and stones, consolidated with mortar, or hewn timber" which men build for themselves to die in and for their posterity to be miserable in.

Here, then, is the theme of conflict between past and present, fused in an architectural symbol which always had a peculiar fascination for Hawthorne. Long before he began to work on *The House of the Seven Gables* he had made something of a hobby of visiting old houses which had fallen into decay as the fortunes of the original owner declined. They seemed to him to suggest with special force the folly of attempting to establish hereditary patterns of family life amid the fluctuations of a democratic society. And when he first went abroad—two years after *The House of the Seven Gables* appeared—his impressions of England and Italy almost invariably crystallized around some architectural symbol of the older cultures.

Of course any American going abroad for the first time would inevitably receive his first and most overwhelming impressions of European culture from the buildings which embodied its aspirations and triumphs. Architecture, after all, is the most public and tangible expression of a civilization. As Catharine Maria Sedgwick had said, during her first visit to England in 1839, a miracle was wrought in the presence of a building like Winchester Cathedral, and the poems and paintings which had before seemed mere shadows—"a kind of magic mirrors, showing false images"—were suddenly revealed as divine forms "for the perpetual preservation of the beautiful creations of nature and art." But to Hawthorne the buildings of Europe had a special significance, deeply colored by the artistic problem with which he was so profoundly concerned.

His English and Italian notebooks are full of comments which embroider the theme he had explored in *The House of the Seven Gables*. Having observed in Coventry and other English towns that many buildings had "modern fronts" superimposed on Elizabethan frames and interiors, he remarked that they offered "a good emblem" of what England itself really was. Modern civilization, as he saw it there, was essentially only a modification of the old. The new elements in it were not only based and supported on the sturdy old things but were "often limited and impeded" by them. And yet, he concluded, "this antiquity is so massive that there seems to be no means of getting rid of it, without tearing the whole structure of society to pieces."

The great cathedrals and public buildings which still remained in their original glory filled him with the sense that "a flood of uncomprehended beauty" was pouring down on him. But he could not help feeling that the architecture of Westminster Hall, for instance, had more to do with the past than with the future. "Its beauty and magnificence," he noted, "are made out of ideas that are gone by." Still less was he impressed with Sir Charles Barry's adjacent attempt to resuscitate Gothic forms in the new Houses of Parliament. Granted that Barry had achieved magnificence, he said, he had nevertheless "contrived all his effects with malice afore-thought," and thus missed the crowning glory "which God, out of his pure grace, mixes up with only the simple-hearted, best efforts of men."

From one point of view Hawthorne's comments on art are evidence of a philistinism which is only slightly less in-sensitive than that which still shocks the cultivated readers of Mark Twain's *A Tramp Abroad.* But the significant thing about them, in our present context, is that whenever he specu-lated about the arts of the Old World he tended to link them in his imagination with his own problems as an artist. On two separate occasions he went to see the Elgin marbles and the Assyrian and Egyptian statuary at the British Museum. Both times his thought recurred to the theme of the domination of the past as fused in the architectural symbol. "I wished," he wrote after the first visit, "that the whole Past might be swept away, and each generation compelled to bury and destroy whatever it had produced. . . . When we quit a house, we are expected to make it clean for the next occupant. . . ." Seeing them again six months later he found himself wishing that the marbles and the frieze of the Parthenon itself "were all burnt into lime, and that the granite Egyptian statues were hewn and squared into building stones. . . . The present is burthened too much with the past. We have not time, in our earthly existence, to appreciate what is warm with life, and immediately around us."

If we bear in mind his sense that modern civilization in England was overwhelmed by the past, there is a special interest in his remarks about the iron and glass architecture of the famous Crystal Palace. His opinion of it differed on the several occasions that he saw it; at first it seemed to him that no edifice built of glass could be anything but an overgrown conservatory, while two years later he decided that it was "positively a very beautiful object." But the thing that particularly impressed him was that this earliest masterpiece of iron architecture was uncongenial with the English character, "destitute of mass, weight, and shadow, unsusceptible of ivy, lichens, or any mellowness from age." One cannot miss the echo of that comment in the preface to *The Marble Faun* where he gave his most definite statement of the artists' problem in America. No author, without a trial, he wrote, could conceive of the difficulty of dealing with an environment which offered no shadow or mystery. "Romance and poetry, ivy, lichens, and wall-flowers, need ruin to make them grow."

In *The Marble Faun,* written in England after a two-year visit to Italy, the theme of conflict between past and present is transformed into somewhat different terms. As it emerges there it is a study of conflict between European and American civilization as revealed in the fortunes of two young American artists who have gone to live in Rome. The theme as it develops in this instance is a subsidiary element of the novel, but the parallels it suggests are worth exploring. It was in Rome that Hawthorne himself had first come to the realization that "it needs the native air to give life a reality"—a truth, he recorded in his notebook, which he took home to himself regretfully, since he had little inclination to go back to the realities of his own. Hiram Powers and the other self-exiled American artists whom he had met there had seemed to him to be caught in the situation where they were always deferring the reality of life to a future moment, till by and by there would either be no future or they would go back to

America and find that life had "shifted whatever of reality it had" to the country where they had lived as expatriates.

This realization permeates Hawthorne's handling of the theme of conflict in his novel. The theme as he develops it there is elaborated most explicitly in his portrayal of Hilda, the young New England painter who—like so many of her artistic countrymen—had gone to live in Italy in the belief that it was the only country where art could really flourish. Hilda is represented as passing through three distinct phases as an artist. Back in New England she had shown real talent and had done some very creditable work. Once arrived in Italy, however, she "seemed to have entirely lost the impulse of original design, which brought her thither."

> No doubt [Hawthorne continued] the girl's early dreams had been of sending forms and hues of beauty into the visible world out of her own mind . . . through conceptions and by methods individual to herself. But more and more, as she grew familiar with the miracles of art that enrich so many galleries in Rome, Hilda had ceased to consider herself as an original artist. . . . It had probably happened in many other instances, as it did in Hilda's case, that she ceased to aim at original achievement in consequence of the very gifts which so exquisitely fitted her to profit by familiarity with the works of the mighty old masters.

That Hawthorne's own wife was a talented copyist of paintings may account for the elaborate justification which he subsequently offers for Hilda's abandoning her youthful ambitions. Granting all the noble and unselfish merits which he ascribes to her "for thus sacrificing herself to the devout recognition of the highest excellence" in the art of the past, there remains the inescapable fact that her youthful dreams were not unlike Hawthorne's own, and that he represents them as being drained from her by her subjection to the masterpieces of European culture. Nor is there any reason to suppose that Hawthorne was not fully aware of the implications of Hilda's change. For in the denouement of the novel Hilda arrives at a third stage in her development. Caught in a web of evil and wrongdoing which had not been of her own making, she grew "sadly critical" of many of the paintings she had formerly so much admired; she developed a new perceptive faculty which "penetrated the canvas like a steel probe, and found but a crust of paint over an emptiness." In the end she marries Kenyon, a young American sculptor to whom it had long seemed that in Italy, where generation after generation lived in the same house, "all the weary and dreary Past were piled upon the back of the Present," and when they decide to return to America, Hawthorne explains their decision in the very words he had used in his notebooks to describe the situation in which expatriates like Powers—and perhaps to some degree he also, now—found themselves.

When he returned to the United States in 1860 Hawthorne had already begun work on a novel which was to develop the international theme not as a minor element in the story but as its principle feature. The novel was never finished, but a number of unfinished versions of it remained in manuscript when he died in 1864, and some of these have since been published.

We cannot know what form Hawthorne might ultimately have given to his theme if failing health and the heartbreaking distractions of the Civil War had not prevented him from concentrating his full powers upon it, but we do know, from the number of attempts he made and the determination with which he persisted, that the theme was important to him. What he originally had in mind was to tell the story of a young American who has it in his power to join together the mysteriously broken thread of a tradition, part of which is known in England and part in the United States. In one version, for example, the hero was a descendant of a man who, wishing to disconnect himself from the past, emigrated from England to the new world and began life there under a new name. His descendant is fascinated by the strange legends woven around a small key which had been handed down from generation to generation in the American branch of the family. According to the legend, the key will open a cabinet containing a document that will clear up the mystery of his family's hereditary origin. The climax of the story is to be reached when, during a visit to England, he is led by a series of strange events to an old mansion which contains the very cabinet in which the secret is hidden.

The simple outline of the story had been suggested to Hawthorne by the number of Americans who had come to him while he was United States consul at Liverpool and asked him to help them establish their claims to some English estate. In his published account of his consular experiences he mentioned several instances of what he called "this diseased American appetite for English soil," and dwelt on them at some length because it seemed to him that they revealed a weakness which lay deep in the hearts of many of his countrymen. "The American," he observed, "is often conscious of the deep-rooted sympathies that belong more fitly to times gone by, and feels a blind, pathetic tendency to wander back again." But of all the "stray Americans" whom he had encountered at the consulate, the one that interested him most was an old man whose story oddly paralleled that of Herman Melville's *Israel Potter*. For years the old fellow had been

wandering around England trying to earn or beg enough
money "to get home to Ninety-Second Street, Philadelphia."

> His manner and accent [Hawthorne remarked] did not quite
> convince me that he was an American, and I told him so; but
> he steadfastly affirmed,—"Sir, I was born and have lived in
> Ninety-Second Street, Philadelphia," and then went on to de-
> scribe some public edifices, and other local objects with which
> he used to be familiar, adding, with a simplicity that touched
> me very closely, "Sir, I had rather be there than here!" . . .
> If, as I believe, the tale was fact, how very strange and sad
> was this old man's fate! Homeless on a foreign shore, looking
> always toward his country, . . . and at last dying and sur-
> rendering his clay to be a portion of the soil whence he could
> not escape in his lifetime.

Against the background of his experiences in the consulate and in Italy it was inevitable, then, that in planning his
novel Hawthorne always conceived of the American's attempt
to establish a firm link with the past as ending in some form
of failure or disillusionment. He might find the cabinet which
held the secret, but when he fitted his key to the lock he would
discover something which he had better never have known.
And curiously enough, the cabinet itself was fused in Hawthorne's imagination with the symbol which he so persistently
associated with the domination of the past. For as he described
it to himself it was one of those tall, stately, and elaborate
pieces "that are rather articles of architecture" than of furniture—a miniature mansion "with pillars, an entrance, a lofty
flight of steps, windows, and everything perfect."

But however the details of plot were to be worked out,
it is clear that in the end the American would return to his
own land. For the moral of the tale, as Hawthorne explicitly
stated it at one stage of his experiment with the theme, was:
"Let the past alone; do not seek to renew it; . . . and be

assured that the right way can never be that which leads you back to the identical shapes that you long ago left behind you."

By thus isolating from its context in his work as a whole the single theme of the past's tyranny over the present we are able to throw into sharp focus the nature of Hawthorne's response to the civilization of his own time. It becomes clear that he fully sensed the necessity for new artistic forms suited to the unlineaged realities of a democratic and industrial social system. Yet every quality of his temperament which fitted him to be an artist in the traditional sense unfitted him to deal with the crude materials out of which the new forms could be created. The artistic sensibility and poetic insight which in *The Scarlet Letter* he could put to such effective use among the shadowy scenes of an imagined past were apparently useless in dealing with the glaring and turbulent realities of the present. Yet Hawthorne never lost his sense of the inherent value in the materials which proved so intractable to his genius. Late in his life he plied the young William Dean Howells with many questions about the West and said he would like to see some part of the country on which the "damned shadow" of Europe had not fallen. If his own experience finally convinced him that the arts as we had known them provided no tools powerful enough to shape the unwrought granite of American life, it never deluded him into thinking that the forms created by an older civilization could be imposed upon the actualities of the new one. "There is reason to suspect," he wrote in his last completed novel, "that a people are waning to decay and ruin the moment that their life becomes fascinating either in the poet's imagination or the painter's eye." There is a kind of magnificent courage in that observation. It is the statement of an artist who, like many others in his time, had gone down to defeat at the hands of immitigable facts, but who—unlike many of the others—had not turned and run.

The dilemma in which Hawthorne found himself was deeply colored by many factors peculiar to his own personality and to his own particular New England heritage. But the tension created by the conflict between inherited forms and present experience has been a dominant element, consciously or unconsciously, in the work of every creative artist who has attempted to deal with the American environment, whatever the artistic medium.

Thus we come face to face with the central fact in the development of the arts in America, whether we think in terms of the individual artist or of the people whose vision of life the artist finally expresses. For what men believed to be beautiful they knew—in their inmost hearts, at least—to be false. To paraphrase one of Hawthorne's most revealing remarks about old houses like the Pyncheon mansion, there was something so massive, stable, and almost irresistibly imposing in the forms which embodied the spirit of western European culture that their very existence seemed to give them a right to survive—at least, so excellent a counterfeit of right that few men had moral force enough to question it.

In Europe throughout the nineteenth century this right seemed to be substantiated by the fact that the foundations upon which the traditional forms had been erected had not been wholly wrecked by the upheaval of the Industrial Revolution. But in America the traditional forms stood on quicksand, no matter how earnestly the custodians of culture worked to put foundations under them, and something of the illusion of permanence departed from them. Furthermore it was in America, as we have seen, that the unembellished simplicity of vernacular forms, unself-consciously evolved by people who had no choice but to deal directly with the elements of the new environment, first emerged as a vivid challenge to creative artists. It was, of course, still possible for the minor poet, painter, or architect to create charming and delightful echoes of the past in conventional patterns. It is only when the creative imagination goes beyond talent and approaches genius that it becomes a moral force capable of rejecting all counterfeit majesty and confronting the naked majesty of the essential.

9

Space and Chance

When Hawthorne saw the great Gothic cathedrals of England in mid-century, he felt that they must be the most wonderful works that man had yet achieved. But there was something about those masterpieces of an earlier civilization which was alien to him, with which he could not feel at home. No matter how familiar he might become with their vast, intricate, yet harmonious shapes, he knew that he would never be able adequately to comprehend them, and would always be "remotely excluded from the interior mystery" of their beauty and grandeur.

A half century later one of the greatest American novelists found himself similarly excluded from the "mystery" of the great buildings which symbolized some of the strongest forces in contemporary American civilization—New York's skyscrapers. Henry James, revisiting America in 1904–06 after having lived abroad for more than twenty years, felt that the huge buildings—the most piercing notes, as he called them, in that "concert of the expensively provisional" which was the metropolis—left him staring at them "as at a world of immovably-closed doors." Behind those doors, to be sure, there was immense material for the artist, but he reluctantly concluded that it was beyond the reach of a writer who, like himself, had "so early and so fatally" withdrawn from contacts which might have initiated him into the life which the skyscrapers symbolized.

In these parallel reactions it is the shift of viewpoint which measures the change from the mid-nineteenth to the early twentieth century. It was common enough in Hawthorne's time for the American artist to be conscious that he was outside the European tradition and to try by whatever means he could devise to get inside. As for the vernacular tradition growing up around him, in so far as it had taken on any definite character, he either consciously rejected and resisted it, or simply took it for granted. Whatever influence it had upon his work was unconsciously assimilated. It would never have occurred to him to regret that he could not "get inside" such a formative tradition because it would not have occurred to him that it had anything whatever to do with art. By the time James revisited America in the early twentieth century, however, the vitality and energy of the vernacular had effectively displayed themselves in so many forms that the situation was almost exactly reversed. Artists like James, thoroughly immersed in the cultivated tradition, began to feel the need to make fruitful contact with the emerging tradition. But as James's career makes clear, the gap between the two was so wide that it could not easily be bridged.

Educated chiefly in Europe, lacking any close connection with the vital commercial, industrial, and technical elements of American life, James early discovered that the American scene was too restricted to supply materials for his art. As he wrote to Charles Eliot Norton in 1871, after returning to America from a year abroad, he concluded after looking

about him that "the face of nature and civilization in this our
country is to a certain point a very sufficient literary field. But
it will yield its secrets only to a really *grasping* imagination."
James *did* look about him, but as Hartley Grattan pointed out
some years ago, in what is still one of the most perceptive
studies of the novelist, he did not look in the places where we
now know—and a few even then knew—that the secret and
tremendous drives in American life were to be found. It was
in the new factories, the new cities, the hustle and bustle of
commerce and manufacturing and transportation that the
American secret was hidden; business was a closed field for
James, whose interest was in the leisure class—which in the
America of the seventies was very small and almost exclusively feminine. In other words, by training and by taste
he was concerned with the cultivated tradition. For it was
"matured and established" manners, customs, usages, habits,
and forms which, as he wrote to Howells, were the very stuff
upon which a novelist, in James's sense, must work. It was
inevitable that James, who of all American writers contributed
most to the development of the novel as a form of western
European literature, taking rank with George Sand, Balzac,
Flaubert, and the other nineteenth-century masters, should
have preferred "the denser, richer, warmer European spec-
tacle" to life in America. In a famous passage from his critical
study of Hawthorne (1879) he enumerated the essential
"items of high civilization" which were lacking in the United
States:

> No sovereign, no court, no personal loyalty, no aristocracy,
> no church, no clergy, no army, no diplomatic service, no
> country gentlemen, no palaces, no castles, no manners, nor
> old country-houses, nor parsonages, nor thatched cottages, nor

Plate IX: The Vernacular and Cultivated Traditions in Painting
(*Above*) *The Old Schoolhouse* by James M. Hart, 1849 (reproduced with permission from the collection of Ira W. Martin); (*below*) *Dismissal of School on an October Afternoon*, by Henry Inman, 1845 (reproduced with permission of the Museum of Fine Arts, Boston, M. and M. Karolik Collection)

Plate X: The Painter's Discovery of Vernacular Forms
(*Above*) *Bucks County Barn—1923*, water color with pencil by Charles Sheeler (reproduced with permission from the collection of Whitney Museum of American Art); (*below*) Ohio Barns—1878, detail of lithograph of *Residence and Stock Farm of J. F. Blair & Son* in Williams' *History of Ashtabula County, Ohio*, Philadelphia, 1878.

ivied ruins; no cathedrals, nor abbeys, nor little Norman churches; no great Universities, nor public schools—no Oxford, nor Eton, nor Harrow; no literature, no novels, no museums, no pictures, no political society, no sporting class—no Epsom nor Ascot!

Not that he believed these things were necessarily the proper subjects of fiction. As Grattan said, he simply found that without these things present to him in the surrounding air, his characters existed in a void. It was inevitable that he chose England as his residence, and ultimately became a British subject.

The recent revival of interest in James has done much to combat the jingoistic prejudice which for a number of years condemned him for "deserting" America and which underrated his artistic achievements on the basis that they were un-American. There was, to be sure, much in America that he disliked, much which he could not understand, and much of which he was afraid. Back in England, at his home in Rye, after his last trip to the United States, he remembered his homeland as giving "an immense impression of material and political power; but almost cruelly charmless, in effect, and calculated to make one crouch, ever afterwards, as cravenly as possible, at Lamb House, Rye." But James was too acute, and too brilliantly analytical, to confuse the issue as his detractors have done. What was taking place in America, as he observed, was "a perpetual repudiation of the past, so far as there had been a past to repudiate." But this repudiation—or as he elsewhere calls it, "the will to grow at no matter what or whose expense"—was not an exclusively American phenomenon. He had seen it, and hated it, on the other side of the world in a thousand places and forms; he was, indeed, aware that it was "the pipe to which humanity is actually dancing." In the United States, however, there was a difference; here, as he phrased it, it was a question of "scale and space and chance, margin and elbow-room." To some extent he meant this in the purely geographical sense. As he said in another connection, the nation seemed to him "too large for any human convenience," so large in fact that it could "scarce, in the scheme of Providence, have been meant to be dealt with" as he was trying to deal with it. But geography wasn't the whole of it. The bourgeois "will to grow" had more chance in America than in England, for instance, because here the influence of the aristocracy had been suppressed, and "a bourgeoisie without an aristocracy to worry it is of course a very different thing from a bourgeoisie struggling *in* that shade."

Actually, as we have repeatedly seen, and as James knew, Americans were by no means out from under the shadow of the cultivated tradition. Strether, the symbolic American of *The Ambassadors,* had fallen so deeply under the spell of Europe on his first visit that he had returned with the resolve to raise up "a temple of taste" by preserving, cherishing, and extending the germs of "the higher culture" he had seen abroad. And many of James's contemporaries had the same idea, as witness the founding of art schools and art museums and the wholesale acquisition of European *objets d'art* for American collections like that of Mrs. Jack Gardner in Boston. It was the success of these efforts, steadily increasing in audacity and ingenuity in the quarter century after the Centennial, which was usually meant when people in the early 1900s referred admiringly to the increasing culture of America.

Curiously enough it was three of James's English contemporaries in literature who, on their visits to this country, were able to see beneath surfaces and discover, as he had failed to do, the real sources of creative energy in modern civilization. Oscar Wilde, who might be presumed to have been even less well equipped than James to cope with the vernacular environment, made some amazingly acute observations in a lecture entitled "Impressions of America" which he first delivered in September 1883, shortly after returning to England.

There was little beauty to be found in American cities, he said—nothing like "the lovely relics of a beautiful age" which were to be found in Oxford, Cambridge, Salisbury, or Winchester. And whatever beauty there was could be found "only where the American has not attempted to create it." Wherever the Americans had consciously sought to produce beauty, he went on, they had signally failed. Where they had succeeded—unconsciously—was in the field of applied science:

> There is no country in the world [he told his British audiences] where machinery is so lovely as in America. I have always wished to believe that the line of strength and the line of beauty are one. That wish was realized when I contemplated American machinery. It was not until I had seen the waterworks at Chicago that I realized the wonders of machinery; the rise and fall of the steel rods, the symmetrical motion of great wheels is the most beautifully rhythmic thing I have ever seen.

But if cultivated Americans ever read what Wilde had said about them, they apparently assumed that he was merely being witty or paradoxical, for they continued to ignore the vernacular. Thirty years later the novelist Arnold Bennett reported that the most exacerbating experience that had be-

fallen him during his visit to the United States had been to
hear

> in discreetly lighted and luxurious drawing rooms, amid
> various mural proofs of trained taste, and usually from the lips
> of an elegantly Europeanized American woman with a sad,
> agreeable smile: "There is no art in the United States. . . . I
> feel like an exile." A number of these exiles, each believing
> himself or herself to be a solitary lamp in the awful darkness,
> are dotted up and down the great cities. . . . They associate
> art with Florentine frames, matinee hats, distant museums,
> and clever talk full of allusions to the dead.

It did not occur to them, he added (any more than it had to
Henry James) to search for American art in the architecture
of railroad stations or in the draftsmanship and sketch-writing
of newspapers and magazines, because—as he scornfully put
it—they had not the wit to learn that genuine art flourishes
best in the atmosphere of genuine popular demand.

H. G. Wells, in a book about America published in the
very year that Henry James left it for the last time, had been
oppressed by the same sort of talk. At a meeting of a Boston
book collectors' club which he attended it came to him with
a horrible quality of conviction "that the mind of the world
was dead, and that this was a distribution of the souvenirs";
and it seemed to him that all so-called American refinement,
mysteriously enchanting and ineffectual as it was, was pervaded with "that Boston of the mind and heart" which, having eyes, did not see and, having powers, achieved nothing. It
was an oppressive fact, but a fact none the less, that the full
sensing of what was ripe and good in the past carried with it
the quality of discriminating against the present and the
future.

Outside of the realms dominated by this Boston of the
mind and heart, however, there were signs which made Wells

hopeful. There were the dynamos and turbines at the Niagara hydroelectric plant. Best of all there were men like Pierrepont Noyes, president of the Oneida Company—manufacturers of traps and plated silver. Noyes showed Wells around the factories; showed him the processes of manufacturing panther traps, bear traps, fox traps, and others; told him how the trap trade of all North America was in Oneida's hands, how they fought and won against British traps in South America and Burma. Time after time Wells tried to get Noyes going on politics. (His father, John Humphrey Noyes, the founder of the Oneida Community, had after all been a communist, even if a "non-political" one.) But the attempts came to nothing. As Wells described it, making a new world was to Noyes a mere rhetorical flourish about futile and troublesome activities, and politicians were merely a disreputable sort of parasite upon honorable people who made traps and chains and plated spoons. To see a man "so firmly gripped by the romantic constructive and adventurous element of business, so little concerned about personal riches or wealth," taught Wells something which he had never before understood about the American character—and which many people still do not comprehend. To such a man, Wells gathered, America was just "the impartial space, the large liberty," (space and chance, James had called it) in which Oneida grew. With America as a state or nation, in the European sense, such men had no concern. Yet back in 1906 Wells suspected—and he may still have been right—that it was with the services of such men that the World State, and peace, would one day be built.[1]

[1]Hugo Munsterberg, professor of psychology at Harvard, in a book about America published in Germany in 1904, commented in similar

Underlying the devotion of men like Noyes to their manufacturing enterprises there was, of course, a whole-hearted acceptance of the industrial and technological environment which was instinctive with almost all Americans when they were not consciously struggling in the shadow of an imported (or transplanted) culture. As Joseph Wood Krutch once remarked, Europeans learned to use the machine as a middle-aged man learns to drive a car—dubiously and without ceasing to feel that it is alien to his nature; but Americans took to it with the enthusiasm of youth and manipulated its levers as if they were the muscles of their own bodies.

The American's affection for machinery has always been an outstanding characteristic. There is an amusing story, preserved by Julia Neal, of a Negro who received his freedom from the Shakers at South Union, Kentucky, in the early 1830s and went along with some of the Shaker merchants on a trip down the Mississippi to New Orleans. On the return trip he left his companions at Nashville and took a job on a river steamer at fifteen dollars per month. When the Shakers admonished him about leaving his religion he replied: "Talk to me about Eternal Life! Why Jesus Christ never saw a steamboat." Howard Paul, in some American sketches published in England in 1853, commented on the enthusiasm and devotion which the members of American fire companies lavished on their machines. The nearest thing to it in England,

---

terms on the American attitude toward business. "The economic life means to the American a realizing of efforts which are in themselves precious. It is not the means to an end, but is its own end. . . . The merchant in Europe does not feel himself to be a free creator like the artist or scholar. . . . The American merchant works for money in exactly the sense that a great painter works for money; the high price which is paid for his picture is a very welcome indication of the general appreciation of his art." *The Americans*, translated by Edwin B. Holt, New York, 1904, pp. 237–38.

he said, was the devotion to favorite horses on Derby Day.
The same sort of intense affection has been lavished on railroad locomotives, river steamers, automobiles, airplanes, and
countless other machines and engines.

It is no accident that one of the most eloquent and moving elegies in American literature, Lee Strout White's "Farewell, My Lovely," is a lament for the passing of the Model-T
Ford car. No other people in the world have adopted the automobile with such fervor as the Americans. In great part, of
course, it was economic and geographic factors which accounted for the tremendous growth of the automobile industry
here as compared with Europe.

To paraphrase the conclusions of David L. Cohn in his
informal history of the automobile age, from 1900 to 1942
the industry produced 69,000,000 automobiles whose *wholesale* value was $44,000,000,000; to accommodate those cars
we built hundreds of thousands of miles of road connecting
500,000 square miles of our national territory; fabulous industries were created or vastly expanded to serve the car,
including petroleum, rubber, tourism, and installment finance;
millions of people earned their living by making cars or serv-
icing them and millions more used cars as an essential part of
their daily lives. These are, as Mr. Cohn says, stupendous
economic and social facts, "not comparable to anything else
in our national life or in the experience of any other people."
But, as Bergen Evans recently argued with some plausibility,
there is really no economic excuse for the amount of money
and time which the average American citizen spends on and
in his car. The whole business of car owning long ago ex-
ceeded the bounds of reason and took on the color and characteristics of something much closer to a love affair than a

business proposition. And who counts the cost of a love affair?

Three reasons are commonly given for the American's passionate attachment to his car: that it serves him as a sort of mechanized magic carpet (in 1940, the last non-war year for which figures are available, the American people drove their cars an estimated four hundred and ninety-eight *billion* passenger miles—an average of almost four thousand miles for every man, woman, and child in the country); that it vicariously gratifies his lust for power; and that it serves as a symbol of social prestige. All these are undoubtedly elements in the phenomenon, but there are at least two others which are even more important. For one thing, automobiles provide the majority of people with their most impressive firsthand experience of the machine civilization which shapes their lives. C. F. Hirschfeld estimated that in 1930 more than three quarters of the nation's prime-mover capacity (steam, hydro-electric, internal combustion, and all) was located under the hoods of pleasure cars! The defense plants, war machines, and airplanes built since then may well have reduced this percentage, but it is nevertheless true that an astounding proportion of the total mechanical power which our civilization has produced is owned and controlled by individual citizens.

The psychological results of this fact have never been adequately considered. Obviously the person who knows how to clean his own fuel-pump filter and to adjust his ignition timing will be hard to convince that "the machine" is his master. Merely understanding a few of your car's idiosyncrasies—the particular way to tease its worn-out windshield wiper into renewed activity, or the exact amount of pressure on the foot pedal which the brakes' adjustment requires— gives you a kind of secret intimacy with mechanical power which deprives it of the irrational terrors with which some people still like to scare themselves.

But in addition to providing a sense of familiarity with and personal control over "the machine," automobiles also happen to be among the most beautiful objects which modern civilization has produced, in spite of the chromium academicism of bulbous streamlining which the professional designers have imposed upon so many of them. Along with the skyscrapers, the grain elevators, the suspension bridges, and the huge transport planes, they are among the most aesthetically satisfying products of technology—and of all these objects they are the only ones which the average citizen can own.

In the early years, of course, the design of automobiles reflected the conflicting influences of the vernacular and cultivated traditions even more clearly than it now does. Only reluctantly was the essentially technological character of the car acknowledged. Back in 1896, when cars were still a rarity, Charles Duryea advertised his Duryea Motor Carriage as "having a 'complete appearance'—not a 'carriage-without-a-horse look'—and yet not a machine in appearance." But of course it *was* a machine, and no satisfactory solution of its design could disguise that fact.

When the history of automobile design is someday written, the Model-T Ford will surely turn out to have been one of the most effective contributions to the evolution of a distinctively automotive design. Here was a naked, undisguised machine for transportation, as free from extraneous ornament, as perfectly adapted to mass-production techniques of manufacture as its modern successor in popular affection, the honest-to-God army jeep. If there ever was an unabashed

product of the vernacular tradition as this book has defined
it, the Model-T Ford was it.

Once established (in 1909), the design of the Model-T
was almost immutable, granted the business principle to which
Ford adhered for so many years. What he set out to do was to
manufacture a dependable, inexpensive, simple, and "completely utilitarian" car to meet the needs of "the ninety-five
percent" of the population who could not afford fancy trimmings. Writing in 1923, he put it this way:

> It is considered good manufacturing practice, and not bad
> ethics, occasionally to change designs so that old models will
> become obsolete and new ones will have to be bought. . . .
> Our principle of business is precisely to the contrary. We can-
> not conceive how to serve the customer unless we make for
> him something that, as far as we can provide, will last forever.
> . . . We never make an improvement that renders any pre-
> vious model obsolete. The parts of a specific model are not
> only interchangeable with all other cars of that model, but they
> are interchangeable with similar parts on all cars that we
> have turned out. You can take a car of ten years ago, and buy-
> ing today's parts, make it with very little expense into a car
> of today.

From the beginning, of course, some people were dis-
satisfied with the stripped utilitarianism of the Model-T's
appearance. Industries grew up to supply the aesthetic de-
ficiencies of the dowdy Ford, offering fancy radiator caps,
wire wheels, special mudguards, and other ornamental gadg-
ets. In 1916 a company in Detroit manufactured a complete
transformation for Model-T. Heretofore, their advertisement
said, "You have had to choose either Ford dependability and
economy and put up with its appearance or pay a higher price
for a better appearing car and stand its extravagant upkeep."
Now, for $260, you could get a beautiful, luxuriously up-

holstered Beau Brummel Body to fit any Ford chassis. But of
the millions of Model-T's sold, far and away the majority
were appreciated for what they were, and were left in their
natal, unornamented state.

For those who couldn't stomach the Ford's unasham-
edly vernacular design, there were a number of cars which
carried on for several years the Duryea tradition of disguis-
ing or minimizing the mechanical nature of the automobile,
at least in their advertising. There was the Apperson, with its
"Old English Coach of 1820 lines," for instance, whose
bright red with black trimmings was advertised as "an exact
duplicate of color study as used in the latter days of George
III before railroads had spanned countries." Yet by 1916 at
the latest the basic "streamline" design of the modern car had
been pretty generally adopted. (See Plate XI.) As the magazine *Motor World* summarized it in December 1916, "The
year gone by has not been a remarkable one for engineering
achievement. There has been no great change, no upheaval, in
design or construction." What changes had been made were
chiefly the addition of such "selling features" as dashboard
clocks, Boyce Moto-Meters (on radiator caps to indicate water
temperature), cigar lighters (not yet called cigarette lighters),
and other items designed to make the cars more "attractive
and comfortable." Closed cars were rapidly increasing in
popularity; seventeen makes were regularly equipped with
detachable closed and open tops for summer and winter, and
sedans were being made in increasing numbers. But the important fact was that, as any group of illustrations of 1916
models will show, automobiles by then looked like automobiles and nothing else.

The relative success of automobile design in thus early

rejecting the influence of the cultivated tradition can be traced to a number of influences. For one thing, once the "horseless carriage" idea was overcome it was recognized that a car was an altogether new kind of vehicle, undeniably a machine, and as such it was enthusiastically welcomed by all but a few of the conservatively wealthy. (It was the big, expensive cars which held on longest to the carriage and coach styles.) For another thing, the mass-production techniques which Ford introduced into the business tended, as they always do in the long run, to simplify and standardize design.

Indeed it was chiefly the automobile industry as created by Ford which, by the 1920s, seemed to many people to symbolize America. The Frenchman, André Siegfried, for instance, announced with "heart burnings and regrets" in 1927 that Americans were creating, on a vast scale, "an entirely original social structure which bears only a superficial resemblance to the European"—and the basis of that structure, as he saw it, was "Fordism." By Fordism, of course, he meant industrial mass production, which, as he rightly feared, meant doom for the kind of society to which he, as a European, was accustomed.

For in Europe as well as in America the influence of Fordism was strong. What appealed to American artists and travelers abroad was, of course, "the Europe of 'dreaming spires,' divine Gothic, moss-grown castles, quaint villages, special crafts, folk songs, gay peasant costumes, and working-men who love Wagner with their beer," but, as Charles Beard wrote in 1929, only a blind man could contend that that was any longer the creative and dynamic Europe. The truth was, as he pointed out, that Europe was at war with herself, and that the American invasion—spearheaded during the twenties by tourists, expatriates, and commercial and financial expansionists—was merely adding weight to the winning side.

Actually, Europe had been at war with herself in this sense ever since the Industrial Revolution got under way in England toward the end of the eighteenth century. That America had by the late 1920s become synonymous with modern civilization, while Europe was still regarded (and on the whole regarded herself) as the custodian of the older culture, was—as James had observed—merely the result of the fact that here the new forces had found more space and chance. But the inevitable result was that when Europeans became aware of the new civilization's growing domination in their own countries they tended to identify it with American influence.

To some extent, of course, it *was* American influence. Industrial mass production, though it was the logical and inevitable outgrowth of forces which had their origins in eighteenth-century Europe, evolved so much more rapidly in the United States that its techniques were largely of American origin by the time Europe began to adopt it on a large scale.

The first great American influence on European industry was not "Fordism" however, but "Taylorism," and it is revealing to look briefly at what that influence involved. It began in 1903, when the Philadelphia engineer and inventor Frederick Winslow Taylor published an article called "Shop Management" in the *Transactions of the American Society of Mechanical Engineers*. The article was translated and published in almost every European country, as was the book *The Principles of Scientific Management* (1911) in which Taylor subsequently expanded his ideas.

If Taylor is remembered now, it is usually only as the

man who introduced time and motion studies into factory management, but his contribution was a much more significant one than that. What it involved was a recognition that the worker was an integral part of the industrial process—that increased productivity involved not only the improvement of machines and of factory layout but also the increased efficiency of the men and women who tended them. Essentially, as Taylor said in his testimony before a special congressional investigating committee in 1912, scientific management was not a mere bunch of efficiency devices. It was, rather, an attitude toward production which involved a complete mental revolution on the part of both workers and management. Both must take their eyes off the division of the surplus resulting from their joint labors and concentrate instead on increasing the surplus. Both must substitute "exact scientific investigation and knowledge" for individual judgments or opinions, either of the workman or boss, in all matters relating to production.

In other words, Taylor was working toward a unifying conception of the total industrial process, based on scientific rather than empirical knowledge. By many of his contemporaries, however, his system was accepted as simply a new kind of wage system or a collection of "efficiency devices" in the crude sense, and Taylor himself was partly to blame for the misunderstanding. To get his system adopted, he had to sell the idea to management and he therefore tended to emphasize the ways in which it would increase management's immediate profits. Labor, consequently, got the notion that the system exploited the workers, and labor leaders viciously attacked the man who proposed it. Labor's attacks in turn led Taylor, who was hotheaded and frequently tactless, to say and do things which confirmed the impression that he was anti-labor.

Taylor never formally stated his basic philosophy, but there are enough scattered clues to indicate the democratic bases of his thought. In his book, for instance, he thus summarized the characteristics of the kind of industrial system he advocated as distinguished from current practice:

> Science, not rule of thumb.
> Harmony, not discord.
> Cooperation, not individualism.
> Maximum output, in place of restricted output.
> The development of each man to his greatest efficiency and prosperity.

These are social objectives, far removed from the "public be damned" attitude of the finance-capitalists who, at that time, were largely in control of American industry. But Taylor made his outlook even clearer in a letter written in the same year that his book was published. In it he pointed out that workmen and employers are only two of the parties in the industrial process; that it is the whole people who eventually pay both wages and profits; and that "the rights of the people are therefore greater than those of either employer or employee." The aim of scientific management was, therefore, the broadly social one of maximum production in the interests of the whole people. That maximum was to be achieved by over-all planning in terms of exact knowledge of all production factors—including the workers.

What Taylor's work amounted to was the systematic formalization of industrial procedures which up to that time had evolved in hit-or-miss fashion out of the everyday experience of many scattered shops and factories. That it failed to achieve the harmony and co-operation which he aimed at was perhaps inevitable in a time when the entire industrial and economic system was thought of as something distinct from the rest of human life, having nothing to do with the values expressed in political and social institutions, to say nothing of the arts. Full recognition of the interrelationships between the industrial system and the rest of society had to await the now famous experiments undertaken in the late twenties by F. J. Roethlisberger of Harvard and W. J. Dickson of the Western Electric Company at Western Electric's Hawthorne plant in Chicago. Those experiments, together with the subsequent studies directed by Elton Mayo, make it clear that Taylor's emphasis on techniques to promote human efficiency must give way to an emphasis on techniques of human cooperation.

But in his own time it was, as we have said, Taylor's efficiency techniques which were seized upon by industry, and it was these which were borrowed most eagerly in Europe. The pressures toward increased industrial efficiency growing out of the First World War created widespread interest in American methods of production, and as Taylor's biographer, F. B. Copley, has shown, Taylorism became the focal point of that interest. In France the Michelin Foundation sought to promote Taylorism by courses given in the advanced technical colleges and by public lectures, and in a circular dated February 26, 1918, signed by Clemenceau, the French Ministry of War declared "an imperative necessity" that all heads of military establishments should study Taylorism, and ordered that in every plant there should be created a planning department whose directors should consult Taylor's books. In Vienna there appeared a periodical called *Taylor-Zeitschrift*. In Russia *Pravda* for April 28, 1918, carried a long article by Lenin on "The Urgent Problems of Soviet Rule" in which he de-

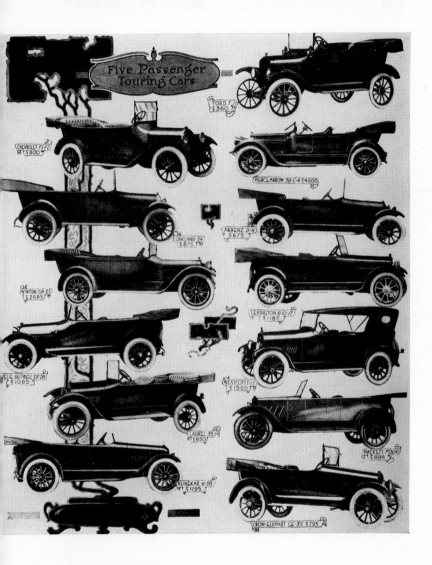

late XI: Automobile Design—1916

A page of five-passenger touring cars from the "Before the Show" issue of the magazine *Motor World* (courtesy of the Chilton Company)

Plate XII: Flexible Factory Layout

Portable conveyor, electrically operated, receives stampings from chute of one punch press, carries them upward on cleated belt, and deposits them on tray by operator of next press, and so on through progressive operations (photograph of Press-Veyor installation at Dodge Tool and Manufacturing clared that the new Russia "should try out every scientific and progressive suggestion of the Taylor system."

The spread of Taylorism and later of Fordism to Europe and the rest of the world has, of course, been more often lamented than welcomed by those who cherish the values inherent in the older cultures. To many it has seemed, as it did to André Siegfried, that mankind was giving up a system in which the individual was considered as an independent ego, and substituting for it one which sacrificed the individual to material conquests. Certainly there is little enough in the history of the rise of Fascism in Italy and Germany, or of Soviet Communism in Russia, to contradict this gloomy view. It is no wonder, after the horrors of the last fifteen years, that the "Americanization" of Europe or Asia is regarded with dread—if to Americanize means merely to adopt or imitate our technology rather than to adopt those attitudes and motives which made that technology possible.

That it has meant this, in many instances, is one of the greatest tragedies of our time, a tragedy which results from a fundamental misconception of the American experience. For underlying that experience and running through every phase of our history, as we have seen in our tracing of the vernacular tradition, the technological influences have been inextricably interwoven with those of democracy. It was our democratic political and social institutions that gave our industrial system its special characteristics, while at the same time it was our technological achievements that strengthened and extended our political and social democracy. Neither could have existed without the other in anything like its present form.

It would be pointless to defend such an assertion as anything more than a useful generalization. The present writer has no interest in trying to foster the notion that American industrialists have been uniformly democratic and humane. It is absurd, however, to assume as many people do that industrial technology is everywhere the same in its character and influence. Anyone who reads the British government's recent postwar surveys of the need for increased productivity in British industry, or who studies the so-called Monet plan for industrial modernization in France, will find ample evidence of the astonishing divergences between British and French technology and that of the United States. Only in the most superficial sense is it true that an automobile plant or electric motor factory is the same sort of thing in Britain or France as in America. Even the most cursory reading of prewar and postwar technical and industrial publications will confirm the impression that both in its administrative aspects and in its technology American industry has been shaped by vernacular influences to a much greater degree than that of Europe.

It will be apparent, for instance, that the differences between European and American technical practice grow out of the differing social contexts in which industry has developed there and here. Consider in this connection the conclusions of Wallace Clark, consulting management engineer, after three and a half years of experience in France, Germany, England, Poland, and several other countries during the boom years of 1927–30. He was impressed by the fact that European industrialists had long persisted in the belief "that the purchase of the most efficient machinery and equipment" was all that was required to bring them American prosperity, and were only beginning to learn that the attitudes and methods of American management were "quite as important as machines and processes." Throughout Europe he found that there was a barrier between the administrator and the practical mechanic which was almost never crossed. Plant executives, from the superintendent up, invariably had engineering degrees which represented good theoretical training, but they had seldom had any actual shop experience. Workers, on the other hand, had so little reason to expect promotion to positions of responsibility that they did nothing to fit themselves for it. There were of course, variations in this pattern from place to place, but as Mr. Clark piles up illustrations of his point in plant after plant and country after country it becomes apparent that the degree to which the gap between management and worker is unbridgeable in any nation reflects the relative rigidity of class lines in other social spheres. Not, as he said, that executives in European industry actively opposed promotions from the ranks when he suggested them. It was simply that under normal circumstances such things were very rare. To put it in Mr. Clark's own words, "it does not occur to anyone that they can be done."

What this means is that in countries where distinctions between social classes were established by long tradition before modern industrialism was introduced, the technology of production tends to be administered by an elite which deliberately cuts itself off from practical experience. In America, on the other hand, despite the increasing concentration of economic power which industrial development has produced in this as in other countries, control of production is still largely in the hands of men who have had actual shop experience.

Similarly, vernacular influences have molded the technology of American industry, with the result that the organization of production still retains its characteristic flexibility and adaptability. In an earlier chapter we noted how belts and pulleys were early substituted for toothed gears and shafts in transmitting power in American factories, thus permitting greater flexibility in layout. At the Centennial Exhibition in 1876 one of the most striking inventions exhibited was the Stow flexible shaft (Fig. 19)—ancestor of the cordlike shaft on a modern dentist's drill—which, with its various attachments, enabled power to be transmitted readily to all positions and applied in any desired direction. Two years later, at the Paris exhibition, the London *Times* correspondent singled it out as the very type of Yankee contrivances. Watching its operator holding what seemed at first sight to be a small garden hose with an auger at its end, with which he could bore

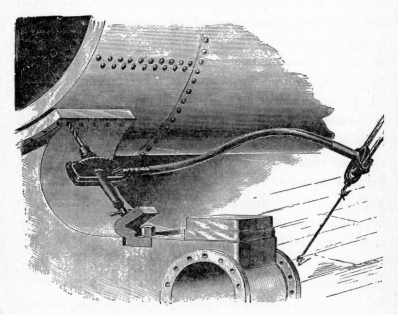

Figure 19: Flexible Power
   The Stow flexible shaft (from *The Masterpieces of the Centennial*, Philadelphia, 1877)

in every direction, the *Times* writer declared that it "upsets all one's ideas of rigidity."

With the coming of the electric motor, flexibility of factory layout was further increased. When each machine and power tool had its own direct source of power, and it was no longer necessary to arrange them in relation to fixed lines of shafting, the old standard factory aisles could be broken up and the machines could be grouped in functional units.

The degree to which this flexibility has been carried in recent years can be illustrated by the setup in a plant like that of the Spicer Manufacturing Company of Toledo, Ohio, makers of truck and bus parts, which was described by Mike Kallaher in the June 1943 issue of *Factory*. The nature of the company's business requires major changes in its production lines every four or five months, and lesser changes—involving on the average twenty machines—every week. The plant is housed in a one-story building with monitor roof so constructed as to provide adequate natural light in all parts of the interior, thus imposing no limitations on the location of machines because of light requirements. The factory floor is made of asphalt-impregnated wood blocks over which heavy machines can be slid without injury to them or to the floor. Suspended from the roof at regular intervals are electric power ducts, which can be plugged into at any point. The machines themselves, each driven by an individual motor, get their electric current from the overhead ducts through lead-in wires carried in flexible cable rather than in rigid pipe, as in other plants. This system does not make for tidiness of appearance, but it saves a lot of pipe-fitting time when changes in layout are made. As a result of these various features it is possible for a tractor and its operator and one millwright to

haul and shove a machine from one location to another in a
very brief time, the electrician merely pulling the plug out of
one junction box on the overhead ducts and plugging it into
another. A department of fifty machines, many of them heavy
gear cutters, was thus moved in a single day by two tractors
plus their operators, two millwrights, and two electricians.[2]

This factory is, of course, a somewhat special case.
Many plants do not require such frequent changes of layout.
But throughout American industry one can find evidence of
essentially the same sort of adaptability. The magazine which
contained the description of the Spicer plant carried in the
same issue an article on the decentralization of the mainte-
nance department at a Douglas Aircraft Company plant, an
outgrowth of the need for more flexible operations; and an
entire section of the magazine was devoted to a review of
portable factory equipment which had been introduced during
the preceding year. Another technical magazine, *Mill and
Factory*, brought out a special 684-page issue in May 1947,
in which were presented thousands of recently introduced
devices and techniques, many of which—like portable conveyor systems, shop trucks and tractors, and free-moving
cranes—greatly increase the flexibility of plant layout. (See
Plate XII.)

The most notable recent development in this area may
well be the new theory of machine design recently proposed
by two young Canadian physicists, Eric W. Leaver and John
J. Brown, both of whom worked for a number of years in the
United States. Their experience in Canada's wartime radar

---

[2]For an earlier example of the same sort of flexible layout, with belt-
driven machines, see "Migration of Presses into Grouped Production
Units," *The Iron Age*, November 13, 1930, which describes practices at
the Acklin Stamping Company of Toledo, Ohio.

program stimulated their interest in the application of electronics to industrial processes. Up till now, they argued in an article in *Fortune* (November 1946), machines have been designed to turn out a certain *product* rather than to perform a certain function, and this point of view has resulted in increasingly uneconomic specialization. As an example of this they mention a machine made during the war to mass-produce aircraft cylinder heads.

> It was ninety feet long, a marvel of precision and ingenuity, and cost in the neighborhood of $100,000. Rough castings went in one end, and finished cylinder heads dropped out the other at the rate of one a minute. The machine is now just scrap metal; that type of cylinder head is no longer made.

What Leaver and Brown propose is a theory of design which concentrates on basic operations rather than on products. Briefly summarized, their idea is that machines should be made up of groups of small units plugged together, each unit designed to perform one function. Various combinations of these basic units will comprise machines to make the various parts of a given product. A number of such machines, electronically controlled and linked by conveyors, will produce and assemble a complete product.

In discussing the significance of their proposal, they and the editors of *Fortune* place the chief emphasis on the automatism which would be achieved in a factory that used such machines—the H. G. Wellsian concept of a factory whose production floor, "as clean, spacious, and continuously operating as a hydroelectric plant," is barren of men, the only human presences being a few engineers and technicians who walk about on a balcony before a great wall of master control panels. But automatic production is by no means new. In the processing of raw materials it was achieved more than a century and a half ago, as we know from the accounts of Oliver Evans' flour mill (quoted in Chapter 2), and it has been common practice in bulk manufacturing—of bread, gasoline, and many other products—for a number of years. Even in large-scale assembly operations it is well beyond the experimental stage.

Almost thirty years ago the A. O. Smith Corporation of Milwaukee, Wisconsin, completed an automatic factory for manufacturing automobile frames, and by 1930 the company's assistant works manager, A. W. Redlin, was able to report to the members of the American Society of Mechanical Engineers that every operation from raw steel stock to the assembled and painted frame, including nearly all handling, was done with automatic machinery. The scope of the engineering imagination involved in designing such a factory is suggested by the fact that each frame was composed of more than a hundred parts, and that fabricating and assembling those parts required more than five hundred separate operations, all of which had to be perfectly synchronized. The raw materials had to be automatically tested by special machines and then distributed mechanically to more than a hundred different places in the plant, where as many different machines fabricated the various parts. These parts in turn had to be conveyed mechanically to meet on precise schedule at one place where other machines automatically assembled them at the rate of a completed frame every eight seconds. In a twenty-four-hour day the plant could turn out ten thousand frames, the machines performing approximately four million synchronized, automatic operations.

Yet for all the engineering genius displayed in the A. O. Smith factory, its automatism may well prove to have been a dead-end solution to an essentially anachronistic problem. Nothing, surely, could be more inflexible, more mechanically rigid, than a factory so arranged. Nowhere in modern industry has mechanical specialization been carried so far.

From our point of view, therefore, it is not the automatic feature of the Leaver and Brown proposal that is significant, but their idea that machines should be "highly adaptable, with easily detachable components designed to be shuffled and rearranged at any time to build an entirely different product." This interchangeability of basic units would permit a factory to accommodate itself to changes in the market with an ease unknown in contemporary production, and would remove one of the most binding restrictions on the introduction of new products. The great problem with mass production has always been that the cost of the plant can be justified only by large demand. But for a new product the demand is rarely great. Leaver and Brown take as an instance the dilemma of the manufacturers of helicopters. The present small demand for these aircraft would undoubtedly increase if the price could be cut to that of an automobile. But the only way to get the price down is to mass-produce, and that would involve an investment of millions of dollars in specialized machines. If such an investment were made now, when helicopter design is changing rapidly, the whole factory might be obsolete before a single helicopter was sold. Under a system of flexible machine units, however, changes in design could easily be made.

Putting the Leaver and Brown proposal into practice would create some painful social and economic consequences, including technological unemployment and the scrapping of costly current equipment—consequences which cannot be lightly dismissed. But the suggestion commands our attention here because it so dramatically extends the traditional adaptability and flexibility of American industry.

Signs of the same sort of adaptability appear also in recent developments in the administrative and financial branches of industry. One of the most interesting experiments along this line got its start in 1940 when a young physicist named Richard S. Morse set out to organize a company which would depend for its economic success on turning out one new process or product after another. At first glance there may not appear to be anything very revolutionary about that. Introducing new products and processes has long been a source of profit to manufacturers and businessmen, and has kept our economic system supple and expanding. But if the history of American business demonstrates anything, it demonstrates that once a company turns out an idea which is a financial success it tends to lose interest in other ideas and concentrate on exploiting the successful one already launched. As Mr. Kettering of the General Motors research laboratories once put it, "the human family in industry is always looking for a park bench along the road of progress where it can sit down and rest."

Despite the loud wailing of some of our crusading liberals, there is no unholy conspiracy of corporate evil involved in the reluctance of an established producer to introduce a new process or product. He faces the prospect of putting out of business some of his equipment, of having to spend money to train men in new processes, of having to shut down his plant, of incurring expenses for new machinery, and hence of losing money. Even with an automatic factory like that proposed by Leaver and Brown, change would involve the risk of some losses, and in present practice the losses are often great.

Obviously these are disquieting prospects, and it is not surprising that few businessmen feel they can afford to act in terms of the perfectly obvious but remote fact that such losses would be temporary, and that in the long run an improved product or process would be more profitable than the old one.

As long as business remained in the hands of a great many relatively small companies, many of which went bankrupt or simply went out of business every generation and were replaced by new enterprises, the economic system as a whole did not suffer much from the natural tendency of established business to shy away from new talent and new techniques. In a highly competitive field there was nearly always someone who would take a chance on the long-run profits, someone who would be able to take Mr. Kettering's advice that the surest way to sell a new device to one company is to sell it first to a competitor.

But what if there is no competitor? The history of American business has been the story of a larger and larger proportion of our economic activity coming under the control of fewer and fewer large corporations. This long-term trend was markedly accelerated by the recent war, and the restrictive pressures—the clogs on progress—inevitably have become greater and greater. On all sides we see symptoms of hardening of the economic arteries, from devices aimed at getting around the anti-trust laws to an increasing reliance on salesmanship.

Everyone agrees, of course, that we must continue to have a healthy and expanding economy, with the rising standard of living it implies. But only constant, progressive change in the techniques of manufacture and distribution can keep the economic system healthy. And that is why it is worth look-

ing at a company which, like Morse's National Research Corporation, is trying to find an organizational basis which will
make change profitable.

Basically, Morse's company is designed as a producing
unit built around scientific and technical research. The core
of the company is to be ideas rather than products. His intention is that production should stimulate research rather than
that research should merely assist production. If things go
according to plan the company will set up subsidiary companies to manufacture the products or to exploit the processes
which the research outfit develops. (Only one such subsidiary
had been set up when this chapter was written, but others were
in the offing.) Obviously, if the subsidiaries are very successful there will be a tendency for the tail to wag the dog unless
the parent company automatically divests itself of its interests
in the subsidiary after a fixed interval, and some such arrangement is inevitable if the parent company is to be put in a position where continued profits require the constant development
of new methods and new products.

Since creative scientific research is "a young man's
game," as Vannevar Bush has said, a company sparked by research must remain in the control of young men. Morse long
ago decided that high salaries and early retirement for research men were essential to the future of his company, and it
is probable that the older members of the original outfit will
move over into administrative positions in the subsidiaries as
those are set up, thus making room for younger research men
to replace them.

Whatever the outcome of this particular experiment in
enterprise, it calls attention to the continuing need for fresh
solutions to the conflict between the profit-making necessities

of established units in our business system and the experimentation and innovation which renews the system's lifeblood. Whether or not this particular solution works, interest in the problem is widespread. Edwin H. Land of the Polaroid Corporation took this sort of organizational scheme as the subject of his talk at the Standard Oil Development Company's 1944 forum on the "Future of Industrial Research." More recently, in 1946, a group of businessmen and scientists, originally led by Ralph E. Flanders—machine-tool manufacturer, former president of the Federal Reserve Bank of Boston, and senator from Vermont—formed the American Research and Development Corporation to provide financial support and research facilities for small companies trying to introduce "new ideas and developments which give promise of expanded production and employment, and an increased standard of living for the American people." These and other recent financial and organizational experiments, coupled with technological proposals like those of Mr. Leaver and Mr. Brown, suggest that the adaptability and flexibility of American industry are by no means played out, and that the one-time bugaboo of a "mature economy" was more a depression-born slogan than an industrial reality. As long as our civilization rests upon an industrial system which remains quick on its feet and readily adaptable there will be space and chance for those who are "firmly gripped by the romantic constructive and adventurous element of business." The danger comes, as the so-called Americanization of Europe and a number of grim episodes in our own history have demonstrated, when the instruments of technological civilization come under the control of those who use them to perpetuate the forms and values of a moribund social structure.

10

Stone, Steel, and Jazz

A civilization shaped by technical and industrial forces like those we have considered in the last chapter, working in collaboration with social and political institutions which —in spite of two world wars and a cataclysmic depression— have retained a degree of democratic equality and personal liberty unparalleled elsewhere, implies cultural values and artistic forms which are not only different from those appropriate to the agricultural and handicraft-commercial civilizations of the past, but have also originated in an altogether different way. For the process by which technological civilization has taken form has reversed that which operated in earlier cultures.

Hitherto, as Santayana pointed out in *Reason in Society* (1905), civilization has consisted in the diffusion and dilution of habits arising in privileged centers: "It has not sprung from the people; it has arisen in their midst by a variation from them, and it has afterward imposed itself on them from above." But civilization in America, in so far as it can be identified with the vernacular influences this book has sought to define, *has* sprung from the people. What was "imposed on them from above" was the transplanted traditions of an older culture.

From the point of view of those who have been trained in the cultivated tradition, the emergence of a civilization from popular roots has been a phenomenon of dubious merit. The fear of what is often called "popular culture," in all its manifestations, is a notable feature of much historical and critical writing. To Santayana himself it seemed certain that "a state composed exclusively of such workers and peasants as make up the bulk of modern nations would be an utterly barbarous state." Indeed, those who think of culture as "the diffusion of habits arising in privileged centers" are led almost unavoidably to the conclusion reached by an anonymous writer in *Harper's* in 1928, that the future of culture in America is "clearly quite hopeless" because there is no church or aristocracy or other authority to modify or restrain what is assumed to be the human race's "natural taste for bathos."

Back in the 1880s this attitude was already firmly established. Cultivated people everywhere tended to agree with writers like Sir Edmund Gosse that it was from America that the real threat to established values came.

> Up to the present time, in all parts of the world [Sir Edmund wrote in 1889], the masses of uneducated or semi-educated persons . . . though they cannot and do not appreciate the classics of their race, have been content to acknowledge their traditional supremacy. Of late there have been certain signs, especially in America, of a revolt of the mob against our literary masters. . . . The revolution against taste, once begun, will land us in irreparable chaos.

Here was one aspect of that "perpetual repudiation of the past" that Henry James had observed. But what Gosse did not see, and could not have accounted for if he had seen, was that this revolt was by no means confined to the mob. Eight years before Gosse wrote, the conservative and staid *North American Review* had published Walt Whitman's famous essay on "The Poetry of the Future" in which he argued that until America produced its own great poetry the "feudalistic, anti-republican poetry" of Shakespeare and the other great writers of the past "will have to be accepted, such as they are, and thankful they are no worse." Even the decorous William Dean Howells was publicly asserting a few years later that at least three fifths of the literature called classic, in all langauges, was as dead as the people who wrote it and was preserved only by "a superstitious piety." What was happening, of course, was much more than a mere revolution *against* taste. It was a revolution *in* taste—and it had its roots in the changing bases of civilization itself.

The man who, perhaps more clearly than anyone else in his time, understood what was going on was the engineer, George S. Morison, designer of the first of the great bridges across the Mississippi at Memphis and of many other bridges throughout the country. A powerful man, physically and intellectually, Morison had early abandoned what promised to be a successful career in law to go into engineering. He went to work under Octave Chanute, chief engineer of the Kansas City bridge, in 1867, and by the time the bridge was completed in June 1869, Morison had risen to be associate engineer. By 1875 he was internationally famous as the man who—eighty-six days after fire destroyed the great wooden trestle which carried the Erie Railroad across the Genesee River at Portage—had designed and constructed the steel bridge which replaced it, and at the time of his death in 1903 he was widely recognized as one of the world's great engineers.

Plate XIII: Engineering Without Architecture
The George Washington Bridge over the Hudson River (photograph courtesy the Port of New York Authority)

Plate XIV: Engineering and Architecture
(*Above left*) The George Washington Bridge towers as originally
planned (Cass Gilbert's design, courtesy of the Port of New York
Authority); (*above right*) Robinson and Steinman's Proposed Lib-
erty Bridge over the Narrows, New York Harbor (from Steinman
and Watson, *Bridges and Their Builders*, G. P. Putnam's Sons, New
York, 1941, courtesy of David B. Steinman); (*below*) the Bronx-
Whitestone Bridge; Aymar Embury, II, architect (courtesy of the
Triborough Bridge and Tunnel Authority)

Oddly enough, however, few people remember Morison's book, *The New Epoch as Developed by the Manufacture of Power,* published just after he died but completed—and the preface dated—in Chicago in 1898. It is a strange, forcefully clear book, and an important one, though no historian of our civilization, so far as the present writer has discovered, has taken any note of it. Briefly, it argued that with the discovery of ways to manufacture power mankind entered a new ethnical epoch which would transform civilization. What ultimate form the new epoch would take he did not specify, but he saw clearly that the new mechanical and technical era would in the long run bring about fundamental changes in men's relationship with one another and with their environment. In many ways, he realized, the new epoch would inevitably open as an era of destruction. By its very nature it would destroy "many of the conditions which give most interest to the history of the past, and many of the traditions which people hold most dear." There would be destruction in both the physical and intellectual world—of customs and ideas, systems of thought, and methods of education as well as of old buildings, old boundaries, and old monuments. How this destruction would occur, and how much time it would take, he did not care to guess. The important thing, he argued, was that it would come—"not because the things which are destroyed are themselves bad, but because however good and useful they may have been in the past, they are not adaptable to fulfill the requirements of the new epoch."

Meanwhile there was danger. Some time might elapse after the old had been destroyed before the new was established in its place, and the trouble would lie in the gap between the two. "The next two or three centuries," he warned, "may have periods of war, insurrection, and other trials, which it would be well if the world could avoid." One of the greatest dangers, in this connection, would be the fact that the new epoch would destroy ignorance, spreading education not only to all classes in civilized countries but to savage and barbarous races as well. The most terrible period of all would be that time "when the number of half-educated people is greatest, when the world is full of people who do not know enough to recognize their limitations, but know too much to follow loyally the direction of better qualified leaders."

Whatever the limitations of Morison's 134-page historical essay, it nevertheless succeeded as few if any of its more ponderous successors have done in diagnosing the causes of unrest and chaos in our time. If we bear his thesis in mind we will no longer have any difficulty in understanding the link between Gosse and other cultivated writers of the genteel tradition in the eighties and nineties and their vigorous critics in the 1920s. On the surface, of course, men like J. E. Spingarn, H. L. Mencken, and Ludwig Lewisohn were in open rebellion against almost everything that the exponents of the genteel tradition had stood for. But essentially the writers of the twenties were, in Lewisohn's phrase, trying as their predecessors had done to awaken Americans to "the peril of cutting ourselves off from the historic culture of mankind." Even Irving Babbitt and the new humanists were doing their best to reinforce traditional standards which would correct that "unrestraint and violation of the law of measure" which was at the root of our cultural deficiency. The finest literary talent of a generation was dedicated to the task of setting up some authority which would restrain what inevitably seemed, to anyone who cherished the values inherent in European culture, to be the American's "natural taste for bathos."

Almost nobody among our writers seemed to realize, as Morison did, that destruction of those values was inevitable, however regrettable it might be, and that the great job to be done was to help discover and establish those new values, based upon the actualities of political democracy and industrial technology, which must one day—after who knows what misery and devastation—take their place. Those who sensed that this was so were left to struggle with the problem alone, till many were overcome by the fear of futility. There is no more pitiful record of this fearful loneliness than Sherwood Anderson's *Perhaps Women* (1931). Listen to the note of desperation in these words, for instance:

> . . . when mechanical invention followed mechanical invention . . . I at least had not tried to get out of it all by fleeing to Europe.
>
> I had at least not gone to Paris, to sit eternally in cafes, talking of art.
>
> I had stuck and yet . . . all my efforts had been efforts to escape.
>
> Time and again I had told the story of the American man crushed and puzzled by the age of the machine. I had told the story until I was tired of telling it. I had retreated from the city to the town, from the town to the farm.

Watching an intricate machine at work, Anderson thought that the men who designed and built it might "some day be known to be as important in the life swing of mankind as the man who built the Cathedral of Chartres." And yet, he asked, can man, being man, actually stand, naked in his inefficiency before the efficient machine? And his answer was no, it cannot be done—not yet in any event. "They are too complex and beautiful for me. My manhood cannot stand up against them yet."

In his loneliness Anderson questioned whether men any longer had the power to make new values to replace those which the machine was destroying, and the point of his book was the despairing hope that perhaps women could do it for them. But he at least faced up to the challenge, which one woman had thrown at him, to "go and look" at the factories and machines which were shaping the new age, and to "stay looking."

Those who might have been expected to help in the exploration of new values too often spent their time ridiculing or denouncing or lamenting what they called America's bourgeois taste. People like James Truslow Adams, whose study of the downfall of the Puritan theocracy in colonial New England should have taught him better, wrote articles urging "the upper class" to refine and elevate the middle class and not be swamped by its "obscurantist prejudices, its narrow and ignoble prepossessions, its dogmatism, self-righteousness, self-sufficiency." In an article published in a popular monthly in 1932—after Radio City and the George Washington Bridge had both been built—one of the future editors of the *Reader's Digest* declared that anyone who looked at American architecture and manners could see that for a decade or more we had been in the throes of an "uprising of serfs." The middle class, he announced, had delusions of upper-class grandeur to which it was giving expression in structures like the Automat restaurant up near the Bronx with its huge cathedral window and elaborate vestibule, in huge, "insincerely magnificent" movie palaces such as New York's Roxy and Paramount, and in overelaborate business offices designed to cater to what he contemptuously called "the demand for the dignity of industrial pursuits."

That demand was real enough, and the amount of money spent in an effort to satisfy it is a measure of its intensity. It is certainly true that there were plenty of inappropriate guesses as to how that dignity should be expressed. But the failure to find appropriate expressions, in architecture and elsewhere, should not have been taken as evidence that the demand itself was contemptible. The onus for buildings like the Roxy, the Gothic Automat, and the ornate business offices belonged not to those who demanded beautiful surroundings for recreation and work without knowing how to achieve them, but to those who could not, or would not, share Louis Sullivan's faith that it was the architect's job to affirm that which the people really wish to affirm—namely, the best that is in them. For as Sullivan knew, "the people want true buildings, but do not know how to get them so long as architects betray them with architectural phrases."

As one looks back at the twenties and thirties in the light of the argument which this book has developed, there is something rather touching about the desperate efforts Americans made to put utilitarian architecture behind them and to build beautiful things. We had been effectively taught, by those who we readily agreed were our betters in aesthetic matters, that what was useful was not beautiful. The architecture of the Chicago school—the highest manifestation of the vernacular tradition yet achieved—was discussed by Thomas E. Tallmadge in a chapter of his 1927 history of American architecture entitled "Louis Sullivan and the Lost Cause." Such architecture was doomed, he said, because of its demand for originality and for freedom from traditional styles. "What is the culture and genius of America?" he asked; and promptly answered, "It is European."[1]

It was no wonder, then, that the ordinary citizen who wanted beauty in his dwelling frequently turned, not to the vernacular for inspiration, but to the cultivated tradition, convinced that to be beautiful a design must be both European and useless. It was in this mood that Americans built during the twenties those genial horrors that Charles Merz described in *The American Bandwagon:* the Italian wells that pumped no water, the Spanish balconies for houses with no rooms upstairs, and all the rest of the amiable but pointless lies of the Coral Gables era.

There were, of course, fine things being done all through this period. We were still building grain elevators and industrial plants which, as the German architect Walter Gropius had written in the *Jahrbuch des Deutschen Werkbundes* in 1913, had a natural integrity deriving from their designers' independent and clear vision of these grand, impressive forms, and which were "not obscured by sentimental reverence for tradition nor by other intellectual scruples which prostrate our contemporary European design." But in the twenties this mechanical architecture, as Lewis Mumford pointed out at the time, had a vocabulary without a literature. When it stepped beyond the elements of its grammar—that is, when it moved from pure engineering construction into the field of architecture proper, it usually could only "translate badly into its own tongue the noble poems and epics which the Romans and Greeks and medieval builders left behind them."

[1]Nine years later, in a revised edition of his book, Mr. Tallmadge changed the title of his chapter on Sullivan to "Louis Sullivan, Parent and Prophet"—a change which concisely expresses the shift in "official" attitudes toward the vernacular from the twenties to the thirties.

A dispassionate study of the relationships between engineering and architecture in the twentieth century would be of great value to an understanding of our civilization. What apparently happened was that the engineers, feeling the need for something more than the purely utilitarian satisfactions which their designs provided, turned to the architects for help, while at the same time the architects, sensing the vitality of engineering construction in contrast with the sterility of traditional architecture, turned increasingly to the problems of giving architectonic expression to the forms evolved by the engineers.

Any study of these interrelationships would, to be sure, have to reckon with certain questions which are posed by such a structure as the George Washington suspension bridge across the Hudson at New York. As it stands, the bridge is concededly one of the most beautiful structures in America. Other great suspension bridges, like the Golden Gate Bridge, have more spectacular settings; but there is something about the George Washington's lofty yet sturdy towers, curving cables, and slender floor which, as the eminent bridge designer David B. Steinman has said, has made this bridge, to the younger generation of Americans, a symbol of our civilization. (See Plate XIII.) Yet, as it stands, the bridge is unfinished; the original design worked out by the engineers and the consulting architect has never been completed.

The bridge as originally designed was the work of O. H. Amman, chief engineer; Allston Dana, engineer of design; and Cass Gilbert, architect. According to the *First Progress Report* on the bridge, issued by the Port of New York Authority January 1, 1928, the guiding motives of the design, from the engineering point of view, were "purity of type, simplicity of structural arrangement, and ease and expediency of construction"—motives which, as we have frequently observed, are characteristic of the vernacular tradition. But, the *Report* continues, in designing this bridge "it was realized that more than the usual attention must be paid to the aesthetic side," because of its monumental size and conspicuous location and because the bridge "should be handed down to posterity as a truly monumental structure, which will cast credit upon the aesthetic sense of the present generation." Here were the reverence for tradition and the intellectual scruples which Gropius had lamented in European design, and which appeared in America wherever the cultivated tradition retained influence. The general outlines and proportions were purely vernacular in origin, dictated, as the *Report* said, "by engineering requirements." But the towers, anchorages, and approaches "called for careful architectural treatment and dignified appearance." It was here, especially in the towers, that the cultivated tradition would be called upon to create the beauty which it was assumed the vernacular alone could not achieve. The steel skeletons of the towers, designed to carry the entire dead and live load of the completed structure, were nevertheless to be imbedded in a concrete casing faced with granite, in the design of which the architect had decorated the main arch with imposts, springers, and voussoirs and had provided other ornamental details which had no reference to the structural forces at work. (See Plate XIV.)

However, as the 635-foot steel skeletons of the towers rose from the shores of the river, something unprecedented happened. The "unexpected" functional beauty of the naked steelwork fascinated people, and there was a widespread popular protest against applying the masonry covering which, according to the original plan, was to be the chief element in the aesthetic appeal of the bridge.[2] So far as the present writer knows, the Port of New York Authority has never taken formal action to abandon the original design, and it is still theoretically possible that the towers will be cased in concrete and stone.[3] The protest which prevented the "aesthetic" treatment of the towers was, after all, almost entirely a popular one, and the time may come when our betters in these matters will decide to go ahead with the design which they believed would best cast credit on our generation's taste. For to many people, apparently, it still seems difficult to believe that pure mathematics and engineering expediency can by themselves produce something beautiful. Even Chief Engineer Amman himself, in his final report on the bridge in 1933, still insisted that the appearance of the towers would be "materially enhanced by an encasement with an architectural treatment" like Cass Gilbert's, though he admitted that the steel towers as they stand lent the structure "a much more satisfactory appearance"

[2]After this chapter was written the author came upon a discussion of this incident in Le Corbusier's recent book, *When the Cathedrals Were White* (1947). M. Le Corbusier agrees that the George Washington is "the most beautiful bridge in the world," and that it would have been utterly spoiled if the towers had been faced with stone "molded and sculptured in 'Beaux Arts' style" as the architect had planned. But he seems to have picked up an impression that it was the farseeing wisdom of a single "sensitive" individual which caused the original design to be abandoned. Further, he fails to consider the implications of the fact that the bridge as it stands is a *pure* engineering achievement in the sense that the designer had no aesthetic intentions, but was merely solving functional problems and providing a structure upon which the aesthetic "treatment" could be hung.

[3]The fact that Cass Gilbert's designs for the anchorages and approaches of the bridge were ultimately discarded in favor of much simpler designs by Aymar Embury II suggests, however, that Gilbert's designs for the towers may also have been permanently shelved. The Port Authority will not, however, make public any information on this point.

than he or anyone else connected with the project had anticipated.

Nor is Mr. Amman the only civil engineer who is unable to accept the statement made fifty years ago by George S. Morison, past president of their society, that "architecture, which as a fine art would consign itself to the museum, . . . will find its highest development in correct construction." For even in suspension bridges designed since the George Washington, the engineers have usually felt the need of some sort of architectural treatment for the towers, such as the step-back of Joseph Strauss's Golden Gate Bridge or the steel cupola and spire indicated in Robinson's and Steinman's studies for the proposed Liberty Bridge over the Narrows of New York Harbor. (See Plate XIV.) On the other hand, when architects have had a large part in bridge design they have shown increased confidence in the aesthetic force of unadorned engineering forms, as witness the design by Aymar Embury II of the sheet-steel towers of the Bronx-Whitestone Bridge (see Plate XIV). Mr. Embury, it is perhaps worth noting, was trained as an engineer before he began his work as an architect.

One of the most illuminating architectural careers of this period was that of Raymond M. Hood, who died in 1934. The buildings Hood designed from 1914 to the time of his death offer a startling record of the change from architecture conceived in terms of the cultivated tradition to architecture as the exaltation of vernacular forms.

Born in Pawtucket, Rhode Island, educated at Brown University and the Massachusetts Institute of Technology, Hood worked for a year as a draftsman in the office of Cram, Goodhue and Ferguson, then went to the Beaux Arts in Paris.

After his return to this country in 1911, he worked for a while in an architect's office in Pittsburgh, then in 1914 set up as an architect on his own in New York. For years he found little work to do, managing to keep himself going only with sustaining jobs like designing radiator covers. In 1922, however, he suddenly leapt into fame as the co-author of the prize-winning design in the Chicago *Tribune's* $50,000 competition. (See Plate XV.) The contrast between Hood's and Howell's tower, with its drapery of Gothic flying buttresses, and the design submitted in the same competition by the Finnish architect Eliel Saarinen, has often been pointed out. Saarinen's design—"a soaring pile of receding pyramidal masses"— made no compromise with the essential nature of a skyscraper; Hood's tried its best to hide the fact that it was made of concrete and steel and glass.

How much Hood's later work was influenced by the bold design which was defeated by his own in the *Tribune* competition it is impossible now to say. His next big skyscraper was the black and gold American Radiator Tower in New York (1924), which was simpler than the Tribune Tower but essentially in the same vein. Even as late as 1929, in the Scranton Masonic Temple, he was still echoing the Gothic which he had learned in the office of Cram, Goodhue and Ferguson. Then suddenly in 1930 he produced the Daily News Building, with its red stripes accentuating the vertical quality of its step-backed mass, and a year later the McGraw-Hill Building (his favorite) in which the wide strips of windows are separated by horizontal bands of green-blue. (See Plate XV) Those two great buildings were the last, except for his undetermined share of the Rockefeller Center project, before he died.

What happened to Hood between the Tribune Tower and the McGraw-Hill Building would make a profoundly interesting study. No doubt it was in part the influence of his friend Joseph Urban which encouraged him to use color as an integral part of design. It is probable too that his partnership with the engineer André Fouilhoux taught him a great deal about steel, concrete, and glass construction. But such influences do not by any means answer the questions which his astonishing career raises. What we need to know, and someday may know when Hood's life is properly written, is what he meant when he said, late in life, to Kenneth Murchison, "This beauty stuff is all bunk." On the evidence of his two greatest buildings it seems safe to assume that he meant something very like what the Shaker elder, Frederick Evans, had meant back in the 1870s when he told Charles Nordhoff that Shaker buildings ignored "architectural effect and beauty of design" because what people called "beautiful" was "absurd and abnormal." Like the Shakers, the designer of the McGraw-Hill Building had an eye to "more light, a more equal distribution of heat, and a more general care for protection and comfort. . . . But no beauty"—if beauty was something apart from such things as these.

In all branches of architecture the influence of the vernacular has been increasingly effective during the past twenty years. First the depression and then the war created pressures which tended to overcome the retarding influence of the cultivated tradition and to encourage a bold acceptance of vernacular forms and techniques. There is increasing awareness that the best work in American architecture grows directly out of the democratic and technological necessities which force us to think in terms of economy, simplification, and fitness for human purposes.

Writing in 1941, Talbot Hamlin listed some of the architectural high spots of the preceding five years: the Farm Security Administration's camps for migratory workers; the Hunter College building; Rockefeller Center; the Bronx-Whitestone Bridge; the new buildings of the Massachusetts General Hospital; the Kaufman house—Falling Water; the planned community of Greenbelt, Maryland; the Norris Dam and its powerhouse; the high school at Idaho Springs, Colorado; the Santa Rita housing project at Austin, Texas; and Frank Lloyd Wright's buildings for the Taliesin Fellowship. Of all these structures, as Mr. Hamlin observed, only Wright's Kaufman house was a private dwelling; all the rest were designed for some socially constructive purpose.

In a technical discussion of the FSA camps in a professional architectural journal Mr. Hamlin observed that the details of actual construction of these buildings were of extraordinary interest "because they show how the need for economy, creatively conceived, can itself become a means to new and beautiful architectural forms," as, for example, in the use of ventilating louvers as an important element of design in the Utilities Building at the Woodville, California, camp. (See Plate XVI.)

> Apparently [he continued] the San Francisco architectural office of the FSA approached every problem of architectural design, in big as in little ways, with complete freshness and innocence of mind. It had no fixed ideas as to windows or doors or interiors or exteriors. Nothing seems to have inhibited its logical approach to each problem; no foreordained picture of what had been done or what was usual held it back.

Very much the same sort of freedom characterizes the best of our industrial plants, especially those built during the recent war, and here too it is economy which provided the impetus to imaginative construction. The late Albert Kahn, engineer and architect of such magnificent structures as the Chrysler Tank Arsenal in Detroit (see Plate XVI), the Olds Foundry at Lansing, Michigan, and many others, stated the matter very clearly in an article written for the *Atlantic Monthly* in 1942. Strict economy must, by the nature of the case, prevail in designing factories, especially those which were then called "defense projects." All non-essentials, everything which is not "purely utilitarian," must be eliminated.

> The very observance of this requirement, however, often makes for successful design [Mr. Kahn continued]. As a rule, the most direct and straightforward solution produces the best-looking structure. . . . Just as the mere clothing of the skeleton of a modern airplane by designers with an eye for line and a sense of fitness produces an object of beauty, so the frank expression of the functional, the structural, element of the industrial building makes for success.[4]

The triumph during the second quarter of this century of vernacular forms which emerged from a hundred years of firsthand experiments in patterning the elements of a new environment could be traced in many fields besides construction. In writing, for example, it would be easy to show how the tradition of reportorial journalism which first attained literary quality more than a hundred years ago in Dana's *Two Years Before the Mast* had become, since Mark Twain's time, one of the principal shaping forces in our literature and could be traced as clearly in John Dos Passos' *U.S.A.* trilogy

[4]It is interesting to observe how the structural forms of Kahn's steel and glass factories were prefigured seventy years earlier in the temporary wood and glass exhibition building shown in Plate VII.

as in John Gunther's *Inside U.S.A.* Indeed, journalism in this sense has become a distinctively American phenomenon. As Georges Bataille recently said in the critical journal which he publishes in France, writing like John Hersey's account of the atom bomb's aftermath in Hiroshima illustrates a characteristic American effort "to give reportage a foundation of rigorously factual detail" which is almost unknown elsewhere.

In the movies, again, one could observe the origin and development of an almost purely vernacular art form, the direct product of technology and the commercial organization of popular culture. Those who were sensitive to the changing character of our civilization had anticipated something like the movies long before the technical means had been discovered. As early as 1888 David Goodman Croly, newspaper editor and sociologist, wrote a curious book called *Glimpses of the Future* in which—fifty years before publication of *Finnegan's Wake*—he prophesied the disintegration of the novel as an art form and suggested the use of colored pictures (in his day, chromo-lithographs of course) to take the place of descriptions of people and places, and of phonographs to reproduce the conversations between characters. That was as near as he could come, at that stage of technical development, to foreseeing the Technicolor talking picture. But the point worth noting is that long before movie cameras or color film had been invented those who were aware of the vital forces in the new civilization recognized that the traditional art forms would be superseded by forms appropriate to a technological environment.

A study of the development of the movies, furthermore, would provide a striking example of the interaction between the cultivated and vernacular traditions. Earlier in this book that interaction was discussed in terms of architecture, and we saw how the forms which had been inherited from an older civilization were modified by such vernacular influences as balloon-frame construction. In the case of the movies, however, the process was reversed, and a vernacular form was modified by cultivated influences. In the early stages movies were produced without any conscious aesthetic aim; the men and women who made them were in the business of providing mass entertainment in a medium which had been created by machines and science. Then, sometime in the twenties, cultivated critics began discussing the films of D. W. Griffith and Charlie Chaplin as artistic achievements of the first rank. The movie makers themselves began to wonder if they weren't artists and shouldn't behave as such, and artists who had been trained in the techniques of older art forms like the theater began to move over into movie making. With the coming of the talking picture in the late twenties the movies became more and more like photographed plays, and the confusion between what can properly be called cinema values and those of the theater still marks much of Hollywood's output in spite of the success of such movies as *The Informer* and a few of the great documentary films like Pare Lorentz' *The River*.

The role of the vernacular in creating new art forms and altering the basis of old ones could be traced, too, in other fields: in modern dance, in the evolution of the animated cartoon, of the comic strip, and of the radio serial, and in the effect of photographic techniques and movie scenarios upon fiction and poetry. But it is in music, especially in the music loosely known as jazz, that we can most clearly perceive both the extent to which vernacular forms and techniques have

Plate XV: "This Beauty Stuff Is All Bunk."

(*Left*) The Chicago Tribune Tower, by Raymond Hood—1922 (photograph courtesy of the Chicago Tribune); (*right*) the McGraw-Hill Building, by Raymond Hood—1931 (photograph courtesy of McGraw-Hill Studio)

Plate XVI: The Triumph of Vernacular Form
(*Above*) Utilities Building, FSA Camp, Woodville, California (photograph courtesy of Library of Congress, Prints and Photographs Division); (*below*) Chrysler Tank Arsenal, designed by Albert Kahn (photograph by Hedrich-Blessing, courtesy of *Architectural Forum* and Hedrich-Blessing Studio)

succeeded in modifying older traditions and the degree to which the newer forms and techniques are still limited.

Jazz is a subject about which many people have very intemperate opinions, and it will be well, for the purposes of this present discussion, if we can avoid the heated controversies which constantly rage not only between those who dislike it and those who like it, but even between the various cults of its admirers. We may as well avoid, in so far as possible, such bitterly disputed points as the precise relationship between jazz and the music of primitive African tribes and the extent to which jazz has been improved or degraded by its divergence from the instrumental music produced by colored bands in New Orleans sporting houses fifty years ago.

To begin with, then, let us agree that by jazz we mean American popular dance music, exclusive of waltzes, *as it has been performed* for the past quarter century or so. By this definition we mean to include not only the spontaneous instrumental or vocal improvising called hot jazz, epitomized by such a performer as Louis Armstrong, but also the carefully rehearsed performances, featuring improvised solos and "breaks," which professional dance bands like Benny Goodman's or Tommy Dorsey's give to everything they play— whether it be Tin Pan Alley tunes composed in the old operetta or ballad traditions, or melodies lifted from western European concert music, or pieces composed by Tin Pan Alley in imitation of hot-jazz improvisations. In this broad sense jazz is a product of the interaction of the vernacular and cultivated traditions, but its distinctive characteristics as a form of musical expression are purely vernacular.

Jazz is fundamentally a performer's art, and in this it marks itself off decisively from the music of the western

European tradition. The composer, who is the dominant figure in Western concert music, is of almost no importance to jazz, for in jazz—in its most distinctive form—invention and performance occur simultaneously as the players have their way with the melodic or rhythmic pattern. It is true, of course, that musical improvisation has flourished in other cultures, and that even Western music of the cultivated tradition had its roots in improvisatory processes. But never before have conditions favored the universal availability of a performer art. The emergence of jazz as what might be called the folk music of the American people is inextricably bound up with such technological advances as phonographic recording and radio broadcasting.

Nor is it only in making jazz available that these technological devices have been important. In the early development of jazz, for example, the player piano not only contributed to the dissemination of ragtime (a rhythmic type which popularized many of the elements of jazz) but also imposed certain characteristics of rhythmic precision and even of tonal quality which became distinctive elements of its techniques. Anyone familiar with the playing of accomplished jazz pianists knows how they can use "pianola" style, though usually only for humorous effect in these latter, more sophisticated days. Similarly, the microphone of the recording and broadcasting studios has had its effect upon the instrumental and vocal performance of jazz. The vocal techniques of singers as diverse as Louis Armstrong and Bing Crosby, Bessie Smith and Dinah Shore, have been devised—often with remarkable inventiveness and sensitivity—to exploit the full range of possibilities in the microphone, and it is largely to the microphone's limitations and possibilities that the typical jazz band owes both its characteristic make-up and its distinctive instrumental techniques. Indeed, these techniques have become such an integral part of jazz that it is seldom performed without the use of a microphone even in small quarters like night clubs and even when the band is not on the air.

It was precisely with the beginning of recorded jazz, in 1918 and the years immediately following, that the instrumentation of jazz bands began to undergo the changes which in the early twenties produced the orchestral combination that is still standard. As long as jazz remained a localized phenomenon in the Storyville district of New Orleans, it retained the instrumentation which had first crystallized with Buddy Bolden's band in the 1890s: a combination of trumpet, valve trombone, clarinet, string bass, drums, and banjo. But as it spread to other parts of the country, and as recordings became increasingly popular after the phenomenal success which Victor made with its records by the Original Dixieland Band in 1918, new instruments were added (notably the piano and saxophone) and the balance of instruments within the ensemble underwent important changes. From about 1921 on the standard jazz orchestra has consisted of three units: the brass (trumpets and trombones), the reeds (saxophones and a clarinet), and the rhythm section (piano, guitar or banjo, string bass or tuba, and drums). All kinds of variants have been tried on this basic arrangement; big "symphonic" bands have been organized, and there have been recurrent experiments with various "small band" combinations built around a piano, and even some highly successful trios, quartets, sextets, and so on. But the three-unit instrumentation remains the standard for both hot and sweet (or commercial) bands.

One of the most interesting aspects of jazz instrumenta-

tion is that the rhythm section tends to remain intact, whatever
variations may be made in the other units. A fifteen-piece band
has four men in the rhythm section, and so has an eight-piece
band. What this amounts to, of course, is a recognition of the
fundamentally rhythmic nature of jazz. For it is its rhythmic
structure that distinguishes it from other types of music.

It is precisely this distinctive rhythmic structure which
makes jazz such an extraordinarily effective musical form in
our civilization, and we will be better able to understand its
significance if we acquaint ourselves with the two rhythmic
characteristics which give it its special quality.[5] These characteristics are syncopation and polyrhythm.

Syncopation, in the simplest terms, is the upsetting of
rhythmic expectation by accenting a normally unstressed beat
and depriving a normally stressed beat of its emphasis. As
such it is a device which is fairly common in western European
music, and consequently people who do not understand jazz
frequently assume that jazz performance has merely borrowed
a stock effect from traditional music and done it to death. But
in a Brahms quartet, for example, syncopation is a special
effect, consciously used for its striking qualities, whereas in
jazz it is—as Winthrop Sargeant says—"a basic structural
ingredient which permeates the entire musical idiom."

Even so, syncopation by no means accounts for the
special nature of jazz. If it did, musicians trained exclusively
in the cultivated tradition would produce jazz merely by continuously employing a device with which they are already
familiar—whereas all they would actually produce would be

---

[5]Far and away the most useful analysis of jazz as a musical form is
that by Winthrop Sargeant in the revised and enlarged edition of his
book, *Jazz: Hot and Hybrid*, published in 1946. I draw heavily on Mr.
Sargeant's work in this chapter.

corn. For in addition to syncopation jazz is characterized by superimposing of conflicting rhythms which creates a peculiar form of polyrhythm. This polyrhythm, as Don Knowlton was apparently the first to recognize, consists of imposing a *one* —two—three rhythmical element upon the fundamental one —two—three—four rhythm which underlies all jazz.

This formula of three-over-four, with its interplay of two different rhythms, seldom is baldly stated in jazz melody, but it almost invariably affects jazz phraseology and gives it its unique stamp. Here, as in the case of syncopation, we are using a term which is familiar in the cultivated tradition of Western music; but, as with syncopation, the term has a distinctive meaning in relation to jazz. As Sargeant points out, the commonest form of polyrhythm in European concert music —two-over-three—*never* appears in jazz, and the almost universal three-over-four of jazz is very rare indeed in Western music. Furthermore, in European polyrhythm there is no upset of normal rhythmic expectation; strong beats remain stressed and no accent is placed upon unstressed beats. But jazz polyrhythm has the effect of displacing accents in somewhat the same way that syncopation does so.

The domination of jazz by these two characteristics means, as Sargeant makes clear, that the relation between jazz rhythms and those of music composed in the western European tradition is "so slight as to be negligible." In other respects, of course, jazz has been strongly influenced by the cultivated tradition. Both its scalar and harmonic structure are largely borrowed or adapted from western European sources, though even in these aspects jazz has developed certain peculiarities —notably the "barbershop" or "close" harmony which it shares with other types of American music including that of the cowboys and the hillbillies.[6] But rhythmically jazz is a distinctive phenomenon.

The source of jazz polyrhythm is almost certainly to be found in the Afro-American folk music of the Southern Negroes. But from the point of view of our discussion, the important fact is that almost all American popular music, the commercial "sweet" as well as the hot variety, has whole-heartedly adopted both polyrhythm and syncopation, *and that both of these are devices for upsetting expected patterns.* In other words this music which originated in America and spread from there to the rest of the world depends for its distinctive quality upon two rhythmic devices which contribute to a single effect: the interruption of an established pattern of alternation between stressed and unstressed beats.

This interruption of rhythmic regularity in jazz is perhaps most clearly exemplified by the so-called "break" or "hot lick"—the improvised solo bridge passage of two or four measures which frequently fills the interval between two melodic phrases. During the break the fundamental four-four beat is silenced and the solo goes off on its independent rhythmic and melodic tangents, until suddenly the band picks up the basic four-four beat again right where it would have been if it had never been interrupted. The effect is brilliantly described in the following paragraph from Winthrop Sargeant's book:

> In this process the fundamental rhythm is not really destroyed. The perceptive listener holds in his mind a continuation of its

[6]Sargeant makes a convincing case for the idea that this barbershop harmony is not an echo of the post-Wagnerian chromatic effects of European music, but was developed from the structural characteristics of accompanying instruments like the guitar and banjo. It merely uses the chords you get by sliding the hand up and down the neck of the instrument while holding the fingers in the same relative position. Cf. *Jazz: Hot and Hybrid*, pp. 198–200.

regular pulse even though the orchestra has stopped marking it. . . . The situation during the silent pulses is one that challenges the listener to hold his bearings. . . . If he does not feel the challenge, or is perfectly content to lose himself, then he is one of those who will never understand the appeal of jazz. The challenge is backed up by the chaotic behavior of the solo instrument playing the break. It does everything possible to throw the listener off his guard. It syncopates; it accents everything *but* the normal pulse of the fundamental rhythm. . . . The listener feels all the exhilaration of a battle.

It is essentially this same sort of battle between unexpected, challenging melodic rhythms and the regularity of the fundamental beat which characterizes all jazz. In hot jazz, when almost all the players are improvising all the time and nobody really knows what anybody is going to do next, the exhilaration is more intense than in rehearsed performances spiced with improvised solos and breaks. But the difference is one of degree, not of kind.

Now a musical form which exploits and encourages this kind of free-for-all might logically be expected to be chaotic and disorderly in the extreme. As Louis Armstrong once wrote, you would think "that if every man in a big sixteen-piece band had his own way and could play as he wanted, all you would get would be a lot of jumbled up, crazy noise." And with ordinary performers that is exactly what you would get— which is why most orchestras play from scores in which, with varying degrees of success, an arranger has incorporated hot phrasing. But, as Armstrong concludes, when you have "a real bunch of swing players" they can pick up and follow one another's improvisations "all by ear and sheer musical instinct." It is the essence of good jazz performance to be able to cut loose from the score, and to know—or feel—"just when to leave it and when to get back on it."

Benny Goodman, explaining the basis of organization for the famous band he got together in 1934, put the matter thus: what he wanted was, first of all, "a good rhythm section that would kick out, or jump, or rock or swing," and secondly, musical arrangements that would be adequate vehicles for such a rhythmic section and at the same time would "give the men a chance to play solos and express the music in their own individual way." In other words, Goodman intuitively recognized that it is the rhythmic structure of jazz which reconciles the demands of group performance (the arrangement) and individual expression (the solos).

What we have here, then, is an art form which within its own well-recognized limits comes closer than any other we have devised to reconciling the conflict which Emerson long ago recognized as the fundamental problem in modern civilization—the conflict between the claims of the individual and of the group. Everybody in a first-class jazz band seems to be —and has all the satisfaction of feeling that he is—going his own way, uninhibited by a prescribed musical pattern, and at the same time all are performing in a dazzlingly precise creative unison. The thing that holds them together is the very thing they are all so busy flouting: the fundamental four-four beat. In this one artistic form, if nowhere else, Americans have found a way to give expression to the Emersonian ideal of a union which is perfect only "when all the uniters are isolated."

By its resolution of this basic conflict jazz relates itself intimately with the industrial society out of which it evolved. The problems with which Armstrong and Goodman are concerned have much less to do with the problems of the artist, in the traditional sense, than with those of industrial organization. It is not in traditional art criticism that we will find comparable values expressed, but in passages like this from Frederick Winslow Taylor's *Principles of Scientific Management,* published just seven years before the first jazz recordings were issued:

> The time is fast going by for the great personal or individual achievement of any one man standing alone and without the help of those around him. And the time is coming when all great things will be done by that type of cooperation in which each man performs the function for which he is best suited, each man preserves his own individuality and is supreme in his particular function, and each man at the same time loses none of his originality and proper personal initiative, and yet is controlled by and must work harmoniously with many other men.

In other ways, also, jazz relates itself to the vernacular tradition out of which it came. Like all the patterns which that tradition has created, it is basically a very simple form. Harmonically it is little more than the repetition of four or five extremely simple and rather monotonous chord sequences. Melodically, it consists of the repetition of extremely simple tunes which, however lovely or amusing they may often be, are not subject to elaborate development, as are the themes of western European music. They may be worried and fooled with in hot solos till they are practically dismantled, but they are not thematically developed. Finally, even in its rhythm, where jazz displays so much ingenuity, it is restricted to four-four or two-four time.

As a musical form, then, jazz is so simple as scarcely to be a form at all. The "piece" being played always has, of course, at least an elementary formal pattern—a beginning, middle, and end; but the jazz performance as such usually

does not. It merely starts and then—after an interval which
has probably been determined more by the duration of phono-
graph records than anything else—it stops. But this structural
simplicity accords with the other vernacular characteristics
that jazz displays. The polyrhythmic and syncopated flights
of hot solos and breaks, with their abrupt, impulsive adjust-
ments to ever-changing rhythmic situations, give jazz an extraordinary flexibility; but they could exist only in a simple,
firmly established musical framework. Similarly, it is the
structural simplicity of jazz which makes it, like other vernacular forms and patterns, so suitable for mass participation
and enjoyment and so universally available.

In these terms one can understand Le Corbusier's brilliantly perceptive observation that the skyscrapers of Man-
hattan are "hot jazz in stone and steel." Jazz and the skyscrapers! It is these two, and jazz in a "more advanced" form
than the other, which to one of the world's greatest living
architects and city planners "represent the forces of today."
And both, as we have seen, are climactic achievements of the
vernacular tradition in America. Neither implies anything
resembling the cultivated tradition's negation of or contempt
for the actualities of a civilization founded upon technology
and shaped by democratic political and social institutions. (It
is no mere coincidence that in Nazi Germany and Communist
Russia, and wherever authoritarian regimes have existed, the
men in power have attempted to discourage if they have not
forbidden the performance of jazz.)

Let it be clear that in making these points we are not
implying the aesthetic superiority of jazz over western European music or of Rockefeller Center and the McGraw-Hill
Building over the cathedrals of Chartres and Salisbury. Such

comparative valuations have no place in the context of this book, whether or not they have validity elsewhere. Judged strictly in its own terms, jazz is admittedly limited in its emotional range. Like other vernacular forms, notably journalism and radio serials, it is pretty much restricted to moods of humor, sentimental sadness, and sexual excitement; it is difficult to conceive of a jazz performance which would evoke the moods of tragedy, of awe, or of spiritual exaltation which are found in the masterpieces of western European music. Furthermore, there is some question whether jazz is capable of evolutionary development. To many critics it seems that jazz today is in all essential respects precisely what it was at the moment when it emerged from the New Orleans sporting houses to sweep the country. Others might agree with the present writer that works like George Gershwin's *An American in Paris* and parts of his score for *Porgy and Bess,* and more recent works like Robert McBride's *Quintet for Oboe and Strings,* give evidence of an evolutionary process whereby the vernacular jazz tradition interacts creatively with the cultivated tradition, losing none of the former's vitality and immediate relevance but greatly augmenting its expressive range.

Certainly skyscraper architecture at its best owes more than a little of its success to cultivated influences which have modified its vernacular qualities. But the essential fact is that both of these forms fully acknowledge their vernacular roots. Both are forms of artistic expression which have evolved out of patterns originally devised by people without conscious aesthetic purpose or cultivated preconceptions, in direct, empirical response to the conditions of their everyday environment.

It is clear that these vernacular forms and the others we

have touched upon in this essay do not—by themselves—
yet offer a medium of artistic expression adequate to all our
needs. Forms inherited from an older tradition still must play
an important role if we are not to be aesthetically starved, or
at least undernourished. Opera and poetic drama, for example, may be as moribund as their most candid critics assert,
but there will inevitably be periodic attempts to rejuvenate
them. And such attempts will be made not only because of the
cultural (and social) prestige which attaches to these and
many other heirlooms of the cultivated tradition but also because we cannot yet afford to let them die.

Meanwhile the techniques and forms of the vernacular
are rapidly attaining widespread influence and prestige, and
their popularity throughout the world serves to remind us
once again that it is not their specifically American quality,
in any nationalistic sense, which gives them their fateful
significance. The products of the vernacular in America do,
of course, bear the stamp of the national character, just as the
artistic achievements of other peoples display certain national
characteristics. But these are superficial features. The important thing about the vernacular is that it possesses inherent
qualities of vitality and adaptability, of organic as opposed
to static form, of energy rather than repose, that are particularly appropriate to the civilization which, during the brief
life span of the United States, has transformed the world. By
an accident of historical development it was in America that
this tradition had the greatest freedom to develop its distinctive characteristics. It should, however, temper any undue
nationalistic pride which that fact might induce in us, to remind ourselves that people in other lands have sometimes been
more ready than we to appreciate the human and aesthetic

values of vernacular modes of expression. Foreign movies have, after all, frequently surpassed ours in creative realization of the cinema's potentialities, and European and South American architects sometimes seem to be more alive than our own to the expressive possibilities of vernacular construction.

As a nation we have often been hesitant and apologetic about whatever has been made in America in the vernacular tradition. Perhaps the time has come when more of us are ready to accept the challenge offered to the creative imagination by the techniques and forms which first arose among our own people in our own land.

List of Sources and References

The following chapter-by-chapter list includes A: books and articles quoted or mentioned in the text, arranged alphabetically by author, if the author's name appears in the text, or otherwise by subject; and B: a selection of books and articles which, though not specifically quoted or referred to, were directly useful to the writer and which may be of interest to the reader.

1. ART IN AMERICA

A. Sources quoted or mentioned

Beard, Charles, "Is Western Civilization in Peril?" *Harper's Magazine*, August 1928.

Burke, Kenneth, *Counter-Statement*, New York, 1931.

Fiske, John, *The Beginning of New England*, Boston, 1889.

Hall, James: see John T. Flanagan, *James Hall*, Minneapolis [1941].

Hubbell, Jay B., "The Frontier," *The Reinterpretation of American Literature*, edited by Norman Foerster, New York [1928].

James, Henry, *The American Scene*, New York, 1907.

Longfellow, Henry Wadsworth, *Kavanagh: A Tale*, Boston, 1849.

Lowell, James Russell, *The Bigelow Papers*, 2d Series, Boston, 1867.

———, *A Fable for Critics*, Boston, 1848.

————, "Leaves from My Journal in Italy," *Graham's Magazine*, April, May, and June 1854.

Mackay, Alexander, *The Western World*, 2 vols., Philadelphia, 1849.

Marryat, Captain Frederick, *Diary in America*, 3 vols., London, 1839.

Martineau, Harriet, *Retrospect of Western Travel*, 2 vols., London, 1838.

————, *Society in America*, 3 vols., London, 1837.

Richards, I. A., *Science and Poetry*, New York, 1926.

Sherman, Stuart P., *The Genius of America*, New York, 1923.

Trollope, Frances, *Domestic Manners of the Americans*, 2 vols., London, 1832.

B.   Additional references

Brooks, J. G., *As Others See Us*, New York, 1908.

Burlingame, Roger, *The March of the Iron Men*, New York, 1938.

Kouwenhoven, John A., "Arts in America," *Atlantic Monthly*, August 1941 (the first statement of the general theory which this book explores).

Mumford, Lewis, *The Culture of Cities*, New York, 1938.

————, *The Golden Day: A Study in American Experience and Culture*, New York, 1926.

Nevins, Allan, *American Social History as Recorded by British Travellers*, New York, 1923.

Polanyi, Karl, *The Great Transformation*, New York, 1944.

Rourke, Constance, *The Roots of American Culture and Other Essays*, edited by Van Wyck Brooks, New York [1942].

2.   WHAT IS VERNACULAR?

A.   Sources quoted or mentioned

American watches—comparative tests: Edward Knight, "Clocks and Watches," *Reports of the United States Commissioners to the Paris Universal Exposition, 1878*, Washington, 1880, Vol. IV.

Anderson, William, "Railway Apparatus," *Reports of the United States Commissioners to the Paris Universal Exposition, 1878*, Washington, 1880, Vol. IV.

Arnold, H. L., and Faurote, F. L., *Ford Methods and Ford Shops*, New York, 1915.

Atlantic Monthly, September 1876.

Barnard, Charles, "English and American Locomotives," *Harper's Monthly Magazine*, March 1879.

Bartholdi, Frédéric Auguste: see Robert Stowe Holding, *George H. Corliss of Rhode Island*, The Newcommen Society of England, American Branch, New York, 1945.

Burlingame, Roger, *The March of the Iron Men*, New York, 1938.

Centennial, member of German delegation to: see Siegfried Giedion, "American Development in Design," *New Directions 1939*.

Centennial, typical account: *Souvenir of the Centennial Exhibition*, Hartford, 1877.

Collins plow: see Horace Greeley and Others, *The Great Industries of the United States*, Hartford, 1873, p. 139.

Colt, Samuel: Charles T. Haven and Frank A. Belden, *The History of the Colt Revolver*, New York, 1940; Bernard De Voto, *The Year of Decision*, Boston, 1943, pp. 215–16; and Jack Rohan, *Yankee Arms Maker*, New York [1948].

Cooper, James Fenimore, *Notions of the Americans: Picked up by a Travelling Bachelor* (first published 1828), New York, 1850.

Crystal Palace: see *Great Exhibition, 1851. Official Descriptive and Illustrated Catalogue*, 3 vols., London, 1851.

Durfee, W. F., report on Pratt and Whitney machines in *United States Centennial Commission, Reports and Awards, Group XXI*, Philadelphia, 1877.

Evans, Oliver, *The Young Mill-Wright and Miller's Guide*, 5th ed., Philadelphia, 1826, pp. 201–10, 275–77. See also: Greville and Dorothy Bathe, *Oliver Evans*, Philadelphia, 1935.

Flint, Charles L., "Agriculture in the United States," *Eighty Years Progress of the United States*, New York and Chicago [1861].

Ford, Henry (in collaboration with Samuel Crowther), *My Life and Work*, New York, 1923.

Fritz, John: see F. B. Copley, *Frederick W. Taylor, Father of Scientific Management*, 2 vols., New York, 1923, Vol. 1, p. 110.

Giedion, Siegfried, *Mechanization Takes Command*, New York, 1948.

Hall, James: see John T. Flanagan, *James Hall*, Minneapolis [1941].

Josiah Allen's Wife as a P.A. and P.I.: Samantha at the Centennial [by Marietta Holley], Hartford, 1877.

Lewis, H. L. B.: advertisement reproduced in Edward Hungerford, *From Covered Wagon to Streamliner*, New York [1941].

London *Times*, August 22, 1878.

Mackinnon, Captain, "English and American Ocean Steamers," *Harper's Monthly Magazine*, July 1853.

Manufacturer and Builder, Vol. VIII, No. 6, June 1876.

Martineau, Harriet, *Retrospect of Western Travel*, 2 vols., New York, 1838. (Vol. 2, p. 45.)

Mauritius *Commercial Gazeteer:* see Carl C. Cutler, *Greyhounds of the Sea*, New York [1930].

McHardy, David: *United States Centennial Commission, Reports and Awards, Group XV*, Philadelphia, 1877.

McKay, Donald: see Carl C. Cutler, *Greyhounds of the Sea*, New York [1930].

Monroe, Harriet, *A Poet's Life; Seventy Years in a Changing World*, New York, 1938.

Pendred, Vaughan, *The Railway Locomotive*, New York, 1908.

Porter, William T., "Machines and Machine Tools," *Reports of the United States Commissioners to the Paris Universal Exposition, 1878*, Washington, 1880, Vol. IV.

Randall, G. P.: advertisement in *Vermont Watchman and State Journal*, Montpelier, January 15, 1846.

Richards, John, *Treatise on the Construction and Operation of Woodworking Machinery*, London, 1872.

Roe, Joseph W., "Early American Mechanics—Philadelphia," *American Machinist*, December 17, 1914.

Royal Small Arms factory at Enfield: see Hubbard (below under B).

Scientific American Supplement, No. 19, May 6, 1876.

Sellers, William: see F. B. Copley, *Frederick W. Taylor, Father of Scientific Management*, 2 vols., New York, 1923, Vol. 1, p. 110.

"Shreve, Henry Miller," *Democratic Review*, Vol. XXII, No. CXVI, February 1848.

Steel spade used by member of the American Institute: see *Transactions of the American Institute of the City of New York for the Year 1854*, Albany, 1855, pp. 231–32.

Steers, George: see Carl C. Cutler, *Greyhounds of the Sea*, New York [1930].

Stevenson, David, *Sketch of the Civil Engineering of North America*, London, 1838.

True Guide: *The British Mechanic's and Labourer's Handbook, and True Guide to the United States*, London, 1840.

Willis, Robert, *The Principles of Mechanism*, London, 1841.

Wilson, Joseph M., "The Mechanics and Science of the Centennial Exhibition," *The Masterpieces of the Centennial Exhibition*, 3 vols., Philadelphia [1877].

B. Additional references

Alexander, E. P., *Iron Horses. American Locomotives 1829–1900,* New York [1941].

Art and Industry as Represented in the Exhibition at the Crystal Palace, New York—1853-4, revised and edited by Horace Greeley, New York, 1853.

Bishop, J. L., *A History of American Manufactures from 1608 to 1860,* 3 vols., Philadelphia, 1866.

Butterworth, Benjamin, *The Growth of Industrial Art,* Washington, 1892.

Clark, Arthur H., *The Clipper Ship Era,* New York, 1910.

Clark, Victor S., *History of Manufactures in the United States,* 3 vols., New York, 1929 (especially Vol. 1, Chapters XVI and XIX).

Dorsey, Edward B., *English and American Railroads Compared,* New York, 1887.

Eighty Years Progress of the United States (by various authors), New York and Chicago, 1861.

Galton, Douglas, report to British commission on American railroads, *United States Centennial Commission, Reports and Awards, Group XVIII,* Philadelphia, 1877.

Howe, Henry, *Memoirs of the Most Eminent American Mechanics,* New York, 1844.

Hubbard, Guy, "Development of Machine Tools in New England," *American Machinist,* August 30, 1923, and January 24, 1924.

Hubbel, William Wheeler, "First Eight-Wheel Locomotive," appendix to Charles B. Stuart, *Lives and Works of Civil and Military Engineers of America,* New York, 1871.

Knight, Edward H., *Knight's American Mechanical Dictionary,* New York, 1875.

——, *Knight's New Mechanical Dictionary,* Boston, 1884.

——, "Mechanical Progress," *The First Century of the Republic,* New York, 1876.

Mumford, Lewis, *Technics and Civilization,* New York, 1934.

Riddle, Edward, "Report on the World's Exposition," *Report of the Commissioner of Patents for the Year 1851. Part I. Arts and Manufactures,* Washington, 1852, pp. 347–485.

Roe, Joseph W., *English and American Tool Builders,* New York, 1926.

White, George S., *Memoir of Samuel Slater,* Philadelphia, 1836.

3. TWO TRADITIONS IN CONFLICT

A. Sources quoted or mentioned

Allen, Lewis F., *Rural Architecture. Being a Complete Description of Farm Houses, Cottages, and Out Buildings, etc.*, New York, 1852.

Appleton's Journal, April 10, 1869 (on iron architecture, p. 58).

Balloon frame denounced: S. B. Reed, *House-Plans for Everybody,* New York, 1879, pp. 73–74.

Bancroft, Hubert H., *The Book of the Fair,* 2 vols., Chicago, 1893.

Beecher, Catherine E., and Stowe, Harriet Beecher, *The American Woman's Home,* New York, 1869.

Bode, Wilhelm: see Siegfried Giedion, *Space, Time and Architecture,* Cambridge, Mass., 1941, pp. 285–90.

Bridges, Lyman: see James H. Bowen, "Report upon Buildings, Building Materials, and Methods of Building," *Reports of the United States Commissioners to the Paris Universal Exposition, 1867,* Washington, 1869.

Browne, D. J., "Construction of Farm Cottages," *Sixth Annual Report of the American Institute,* Albany, 1848.

Clarke, Thomas C., "American Iron Bridges," *Scientific American Supplement, No. 32,* August 5, 1876.

Ducker Portable House Co., *Illustrated Catalogue. Ducker Portable Houses,* New York [1888].

Eads bridge: see Steinman and Watson, *Bridges and Their Builders,* New York [1941].

Etzler, John Adolphus, *The Paradise Within the Reach of All Men, Without Labor, by Powers of Nature and Machinery,* Pittsburgh, 1833, pp. 65–67.

Etzler (of England): T. De Witt Talmage, *The Abominations of Modern Society,* New York, 1872.

Ferguson, James, quoted in *Scientific American Supplement, No. 11,* March 11, 1876.

Field, Walker, "A Re-examination into the Invention of the Balloon Frame," *Journal of the American Society of Architectural Historians,* Vol. 2, No. 4, October 1942.

Fowler, Orson S., *A Home for All, or, The Gravel Wall and Octagon Mode of Building* (original ed. 1849), New York, 1854.

Gems of the Centennial Exhibition, New York, 1877.

Giedion, Siegfried, *Space, Time and Architecture*, Cambridge, Mass., 1941.

Great Industries of the United States, The (by Horace Greeley and Others), Hartford, 1873.

Hamlin, Talbot, *Architecture Through the Ages*, New York [1940].

Hunt, Richard Morris, "Architecture," *United States Centennial Commission, Reports and Awards, Group XXVI*, Philadelphia, 1877.

Industrial Chicago, 6 vols., Chicago, 1891–96, Vols. 1 and 2.

Iron fronts: see George W. Howard, *The Monumental City, its past history and present resources*, Baltimore, 1873; *Fifth Annual Review of the Commerce, Manufactures, and the Public and Private Improvements of Chicago, for the Year 1856*, Chicago, The Democratic Press, 1857, pp. 7–8; and *The St. Louis Riverfront. An Exhibition of Architectural Studies*, St. Louis Public Library, 1938.

Kettell, Thomas P., "Buildings and Building Material," *Eighty Years Progress of the United States*, New York and Chicago, 1861.

Klondike. The Chicago Record's Book for Gold Seekers, Boston, 1897.

Lafever, Minard, *The Architectural Instructor*, New York, 1856.

New and Complete American Encyclopaedia; or, Universal Dictionary of Arts and Sciences, The, New York, 1805–11, Vol. 1, p. 504.

Pope, Thomas: see David B. Steinman and Sara Ruth Watson, *Bridges and Their Builders*, New York [1941], pp. 116–17.

Putnam's Magazine, March 1854 ("New York Daguerreotyped").

Reed, S. B., *House-Plans for Everybody*, New York, 1879.

Robinson, Solon, "How to Build a Balloon House," *Transactions of the American Institute of the City of New York for the Year 1854*, Albany, 1855.

Roebling, John A.: quoted in Steinman and Watson, *Bridges and Their Builders*, New York [1941]. See also Hamilton Schuyler, *The Roeblings: A Century of Engineers, Bridge-Builders and Industrialists*, Princeton, 1931.

Ruskin, John, *The Seven Lamps of Architecture* (originally published 1849), New York, 1871.

Skillings, D. N., and Flint, D. B., *Illustrated Catalogue of Portable Sectional Buildings*, Boston and New York [1862].

Stevenson, David, *Sketch of the Civil Engineering of North America*, London, 1838, pp. 192–95.

Sullivan, Louis, *Kindergarten Chats and Other Writings*, New York, 1947.

278 **List of Sources and References**

Sullivan, Louis, to Claude Bragdon: see Claude Bragdon, *More Lives than One*, New York, 1938.

[Thoreau, Henry], "A Mechanical Utopia," *Democratic Review*, November 1843.

Vaux, Calvert, *Villas and Cottages*, New York, 1857.

Wahl, William H., *Building and Engineering* [no place, no date], Arts and Sciences Publishing Co. (Internal evidence indicates a date circa 1889.)

Washington, George, *The Writings of George Washington*, edited by Jared Sparks, Boston, 1838, Vol. IX, p. 115.

Woodward, G. E. and F. W., *Woodward's Country Homes*, New York, 1866.

Woollett, William M., *Old Homes Made New*, New York, 1878.

Wright's Suntop Homes: Henry-Russell Hitchcock, *In the Nature of Materials. The Buildings of Frank Lloyd Wright*, New York, 1942.

B. Additional references

Coolidge, John, *Mill and Mansion, A Study of Architecture and Society in Lowell, Massachusetts, 1820–1865*, New York, 1942.

Hamlin, Talbot, *Greek Revival Architecture in America*, New York, 1944 (especially Appendix A, "The American Development of Greek-Inspired Forms," pp. 339–55).

Jarves, James Jackson, *The Art Idea: Sculpture, Painting, and Architecture in America*, New York, 1864.

Mumford, Lewis, *The Brown Decades*, New York [1931].

Schuyler, Montgomery, *American Architecture*, New York, 1892.

———, "Glimpses of Western Architecture," *Harper's Monthly Magazine*, August 1891.

Tallmadge, Thomas E., *The Story of Architecture in America*, rev. ed., New York [1936].

4. THE PRACTICAL AND THE AESTHETIC

A. Sources quoted or mentioned

Abbey, E. A.: see E. V. Lucas, *Edwin Austin Abbey*, New York, 1921.

Benjamin, S. G. W., "Fifty Years of American Art," *Harper's Monthly Magazine*, October 1879.

————, "Present Tendencies of American Art," *Harper's Monthly Magazine,* March 1879.

Benson, Eugene, "Museums of Art as a Means of Instruction," *Appleton's Journal,* January 15, 1870.

Blake, J. L., *The Family Encyclopedia,* New York, 1834 (article on "Taste").

[Curtis, George W.], "The Editor's Easy Chair," *Harper's Monthly Magazine,* April 1876.

Ellsworth, William H., *A Golden Age of Authors,* Boston, 1919.

Greenough, Horatio, "American Architecture," *Democratic Review,* August 1843 (not identical with chapter on same subject in *The Travels, Observations, etc.,* see below).

————, and Emerson: see *The Letters of Ralph Waldo Emerson,* ed. by Ralph L. Rusk, New York, 1939, Vol. IV, p. 312.

————, *Letters of Horatio Greenough to His Brother Henry Greenough,* edited by Frances B. Greenough, Boston, 1887.

————, "Remarks on American Art," *Democratic Review,* July 1843 (not identical with the material included in *The Travels, Observations, etc.,* see below).

————, *The Travels, Observations, and Experience of a Yankee Stonecutter,* by Horace Bender, New York, 1852.

Harper's Bazaar, July 1, 1876.

Hone, Philip, *The Diary of Philip Hone,* edited by Allan Nevins, New York, 1936.

Howells, William Dean, *Criticism and Fiction,* New York, 1891.

Jarves, James Jackson, *The Art Idea: Sculpture, Painting, and Architecture in America,* New York, 1864.

Jig saw: see "Fret-Sawing and Woodcarving," *Harper's Monthly Magazine,* March 1878.

Johnson, Robert Underwood, *Remembered Yesterdays,* Boston, 1923.

Lathrop, George Parsons, "The Study of Art in Boston," *Harper's Monthly Magazine,* May 1879.

Lourdelet, M., "Industries and Commercial Machinery of the United States," translated from the French and printed in the report of U. S. Consul Frank H. Mason, Marseilles, May 10, 1884, *Reports from the Consuls of the United States,* No. 42, June 1884, Washington, D.C.

Pomological Annex at Centennial: see Thompson Wescott, *Centennial Portfolio,* Philadelphia, 1876, p. 12.

Simonin, L., *A French View of the Grand International Exposition of 1876,* translated from the *Revue des Deux Mondes* by Samuel H. Needles, Philadelphia, 1877.

Smith, Walter, "Industrial Art," *The Masterpieces of the Centennial Exhibition*, Philadelphia [1877], Vol. II.

Tryon, Dwight W.: see Henry C. White, *The Life and Art of Dwight William Tryon*, New York, 1930.

Tuckerman, Henry T., *American Artist Life*, New York, 1870.

B. Additional references

Benjamin, S. G. W., "American Art Since the Centennial," *New Princeton Review*, Vol. IV, 1887.

Clarke, I. E., "Art and Industrial Education," *Education in the United States*, edited by Nicholas Murray Butler, Albany, 1900, Vol. II.

Jarves, James Jackson, *Art Hints*, New York, 1869.

LaFollette, Suzanne, *Art in America*, New York, 1929.

Oppé, A. P., "Art," *Early Victorian England, 1830–1865*, edited by G. M. Young, 2 vols., London, 1934.

5. THE FIGURE IN THE CARPET

A. Sources quoted or mentioned

Downing, Alexander J., *The Architecture of Country Houses . . . with Remarks on Interiors, Furniture, etc.*, New York, 1850.

"Editor's Table," *Harper's Monthly Magazine*, August 1859.

Emerson, Ralph Waldo, "Art," *Essays, First Series*, Boston, 1841.

———, *The Conduct of Life*, Boston, 1860.

Great Industries of the United States, The (by Horace Greeley and Others), Hartford, 1873.

[Holley, Marietta], *Josiah Allen's Wife as a P.A. and P.I.: Samantha at the Centennial*, Hartford, 1877.

Humphreys, Mary Gay, "The Progress of American Decorative Art" (from the London *Art Journal*), *Household Art*, edited by Candace Wheeler, New York, 1893.

Illustrated London News, June 17, 1876.

Nordhoff, Charles, *The Communistic Societies of the United States*, New York, 1875.

Poe, Edgar Allan, "The Philosophy of Furniture," *Burton's Gentleman's Magazine*, May 1840.

Shaker laundry at Canterbury: see J. W. Meader, *The Merrimack River: Its Sources and Tributaries*, Boston, 1869.

[Stephens, Ann S.], *High Life in New York*, Philadelphia, 1854.

Twain, Mark, *Life on the Mississippi*, New York, 1883.

Whitman, Walt, *The Uncollected Poetry and Prose of Walt Whitman*, edited by Emory Holloway, Garden City, 1921, Vol. II, pp. 311–12.

Wyatt, Sir Matthew Digby, *Industrial Arts of the Nineteenth Century*, London, 1853.

B. Additional references

Gilman, Roger, "The Romantic Interior," *Romanticism in America*, edited by George Boas, Baltimore, 1940.

Morse, Florence, "About Furnishings," *Household Art*, edited by Candace Wheeler, New York, 1893.

Robsjohn-Gibbings, T. H., *Good-bye, Mr. Chippendale*, New York, 1944.

Wharton, Edith, and Codman, Ogden, *The Decoration of Houses*, New York, 1897.

6. TO MAKE ALL THINGS NEW

A. Sources quoted or mentioned

Appleton's Journal ("Table Talk"), April 3, 1869.

———, ("Table Talk"), July 10, 1869.

Barnum, P. T., *Struggles and Triumphs*, Buffalo, 1872.

Brown, Herbert Ross, *The Sentimental Novel in America, 1789–1860*, Durham, N.C., 1940.

Brownson, Orestes, "Origin and Ground of Government," *Democratic Review*, August 1843.

Burlesque writer: see Walter Blair, "Burlesques in Nineteenth-Century American Humor," *American Literature*, November 1930.

Byles, Mather, "Bombastic and Grubstreet Style," *American Magazine and Historical Chronicle*, January 1745.

Carlyle, Thomas: see *The Correspondence of Thomas Carlyle and Ralph Waldo Emerson*, 2 vols., Boston, 1888.

Channing, William Ellery, "Honor Due to All Men," *The Works of William E. Channing*, new and complete ed., Boston, 1875.

———, "The Present Age" (1841), Ibid.

———, "Remarks on National Literature," Ibid.

Chase, Dr. A. W., *Dr. Chase's Recipes; or, Information for Everybody* ("Seventy-third edition"), Ann Arbor, Mich., 1876.

Crockett, Davy: see Constance Rourke, *Davy Crockett*, New York, 1934.

Crowe, Pat, *Pat Crowe. His Story, Confession and Reformation*, New York, G. W. Dillingham Co. [1906].

Drake, Daniel, *A Systematic treatise, historical, etiological, and practical, on the principal diseases of the interior valley of North America, etc.*, 2 vols., Cincinnati, 1850.

Drake, Daniel: see Charles D. Drake's introduction to Daniel Drake, *Pioneer Life in Kentucky*, Cincinnati, 1870; Ralph L. Rusk, *The Literature of the Middle Western Frontier*, New York, 1926, Vol. I, pp. 206–07; and Geddes Smith, *Plague on Us*, New York, The Commonwealth Fund, 1943.

Eggleston, Edward, *The Circuit Rider*, New York, 1874.

Emerson, Ralph Waldo, "Art," *Essays*, Boston, 1841.

——, *The Journals*, edited by Edward Waldo Emerson and Waldo Emerson Forbes, 12 vols., Boston, 1909–12.

——, *Representative Men*, Boston, 1850.

Fuller, Margaret: see Ossoli, below.

Garland, Hamlin, *A Son of the Middle Border*, New York, 1917.

Goodrich, S. G., "The Peddler. A Chapter from an Unpublished Romance," *Cyclopaedia of Wit and Humor*, edited by W. E. Burton, 2 vols., New York, 1857.

Great Industries of the United States, The (by Horace Greeley and Others), Hartford, 1873.

Hill, Thomas E., *Hill's Manual of Social and Business Forms* (Thirty-ninth edition), Chicago, 1883.

Howells, William Dean, *Criticism and Fiction*, New York, 1891.

Jemison, Mary: James E. Seaver, *A Narrative of the Life of Mrs. Mary Jemison*, 1824 (and many subsequent editions; see *The Colophon*, Part Seven, 1931).

Kerr, Orpheus C.: see Rourke, Constance, *American Humor*, below.

Lippard, George, *New York: Its Upper Ten and Lower Million*, Cincinnati, 1854.

Longfellow, Henry Wadsworth: see Lawrance Thompson, *Young Longfellow*, New York, 1938.

Lowell, James Russell, "Emerson the Lecturer," *The Complete Writings of James Russell Lowell*, 16 vols., Boston, 1904.

Lutes, Della T., "We Had a Book," *Saturday Review of Literature*, November 27, 1937.

Melville, Herman, "Hawthorne and His Mosses," *Literary World*, August 17, August 24, 1850.

——, *Israel Potter*, New York, 1855.

————, letter to Abraham Lansing, January 2, 1877, in *Family Correspondence of Herman Melville*, edited by V. H. Paltsits, New York Public Library, 1929.

Mencken, H. L., *The American Language*, 4th ed., New York, 1945; and *The American Language. Supplement I*, New York, 1945.

Olson, Charles, *Call Me Ishmael*, New York [1947].

Ossoli, Margaret Fuller, *Woman in the Nineteenth Century and Kindred Papers*, Boston, 1855 (review of *Ellen: or, Forgive and Forget*, pp. 269–75).

Poe, Edgar Allan, letter to Charles Anthon: see Arthur Hobson Quinn, *Edgar Allan Poe*, New York, 1941.

————, review of Hawthorne's *Twice-Told Tales* and *Mosses from an Old Manse*, in *Godey's Lady's Book*, November 1847.

Rourke, Constance, *American Humor*, New York, 1931.

————, "The Shakers," *The Roots of American Culture and Other Essays*, edited by Van Wyck Brooks, New York [1942].

Rusk, Ralph L., *The Literature of the Middle Western Frontier*, 2 vols., New York, 1926.

Schlesinger, Arthur M., Jr., *The Age of Jackson*, Boston, 1945.

Scott, Walter, *The Messiahship, or Great Demonstration, Written for the Union of Christians, etc.*, Cincinnati, 1860.

Scott, Walter: see A. S. Hayden, *Early History of the Disciples in the Western Reserve*, Cincinnati, 1876.

Sedgwick, Catharine Maria, "Our Village Post Office," *The Token*, Boston, 1838.

————, *The Poor Rich Man and the Rich Poor Man*, New York, 1836.

Simms, William Gilmore, "Dedication" (dated September 1856) of *The Wigwam and the Cabin*, 1857.

Sinclair, Upton, "Letters to Editor," *Atlantic Monthly*, October 1946, p. 29.

Turner, Frederick Jackson, *The Frontier in American History*, New York, 1920.

Twain, Mark, *Mark Twain's Letters*, edited by Albert Bigelow Paine, 2 vols., New York, 1917.

Whitman, Walt, "Democratic Vistas," *Complete Prose Works*, Philadelphia, 1892.

————, "Elias Hicks," Ibid.

————, "Specimen Days," Ibid.

Winslow, Ola Elizabeth, "Books for the Lady Reader," *Romanticism in America*, edited by George Boas, Baltimore, 1940.

Yankee Smith's American Broad Grins, No. I, London, R. MacDonald [no date].

B. Additional references

Blair, Walter, *Native American Humor*, New York [1937].

Blegen, Theodore E., *Grass Roots History*, Minneapolis [1947].

Case, Victoria and Robert Ormond, *We Called It Culture. The Story of Chautauqua*, New York, 1948.

De Voto, Bernard, *Mark Twain's America*, Boston, 1932.

Holbrook, Stewart, *Lost Men of American History*, New York, 1946.

Horner, Charles F., *The Life of James Redpath and the Development of the Modern Lyceum*, New York, 1926.

Kittredge, George L., *The Old Farmer and His Almanack*, Boston, 1904.

Matthiessen, F. O., *American Renaissance*, New York [1941].

McLean, J. P., *A Bibliography of Shaker Literature*, Columbus, O., 1905.

Pond, F. E., *Life and Adventures of "Ned Buntline,"* 1919.

7. SEEING IS BELIEVING

A. Sources quoted or mentioned

Alcott, Louisa M., *Little Women*, Boston, 1868.

Art Journal, 1876 ("Paintings at the Centennial Exhibition," pp. 283–85, signed by "S.N.C.").

Benjamin, S. G. W., "Fifty Years of American Art," *Harper's Monthly Magazine*, October 1879.

Burroughs, Alan, *Limners and Likenesses*, New York, 1936.

Eakins, Thomas, "The Differential Action of Certain Muscles Passing More than One Joint," *Proceedings of the Academy of Natural Sciences of Philadelphia*, 1894.

Feininger, Lyonel: see *Lyonel Feininger . . . Marsden Hartley*, Museum of Modern Art [1944].

Goodrich, Lloyd, *Thomas Eakins, His Life and Work*, New York, 1933.

Greenough, Horatio, "American Architecture," *Democratic Review*, August 1843.

Grosz, George: see George Heard Hamilton, "A European Artist's Reaction to the American Scene," New York *Times Book Review*, April 29, 1945.

Hart, Joel Tanner: see *Dictionary of American Biography*.

Homer, Winslow: see William H. Downes, *The Life and Works of Winslow Homer*, Boston, 1911.

Howells, William Dean, "A Sennight at the Centennial," *Atlantic Monthly*, July 1876.

James, William: see Ralph Barton Perry, *The Thought and Character of William James*, Boston, 1935, Vol. I.

Jarves, James Jackson, *The Art Idea*, New York, 1864.

Lipman, Jean, *American Primitive Painting*, New York, 1942.

Mount, William S.: see B. Cowdrey and H. W. Williams, Jr., *William Sidney Mount*, New York, 1944.

Powers, Hiram: see Henry W. Bellows, "Seven Sittings with Powers, the Sculptor," *Appleton's Journal*, June 12, June 19, June 26, July 10, August 7, August 28, and September 11, 1869.

Richardson, Edgar P., *The Way of Western Art, 1776–1914*, Cambridge, Mass., 1939.

Rockwell, Norman: see Arthur L. Guptill, *Norman Rockwell, Illustrator*, New York, 1946.

Rourke, Constance, *Charles Sheeler, Artist in the American Tradition*, New York [1938].

Sheeler, Charles: see Rourke, Constance, above.

Vogel, Hermann Wilhelm, "Photographs at the Centennial Exhibition," *Scientific American Supplement, No. 40*, September 30, 1876.

Whitman, Walt, "Good-bye, My Fancy," *Complete Prose Works*, Philadelphia, 1892.

B. Additional references

History of Ashtabula County, Ohio, Philadelphia, 1878.

Isham, Samuel, *The History of American Painting*, new ed., New York, 1927.

LaFollette, Suzanne, *Art in America*, New York, 1929.

Saint-Gaudens, Homer, *The American Artist and His Times*, New York, 1941.

Taft, Lorado, *The History of American Sculpture*, New York, 1903.

Tuckerman, Henry T., *American Artist Life*, New York, 1870.

8. THE ARTIST'S DILEMMA

A. Sources quoted or mentioned

Hawthorne, Nathaniel, *The American Notebooks*, edited by Randall Stewart, New Haven, 1932.

———, "The Ancestral Footstep," *The Dolliver Romance, Fanshawe, and Septimius Felton,* Boston, 1883.

———, "The Artist of the Beautiful," *Democratic Review,* June 1844 (included in *Mosses from an Old Manse,* 1846).

———, *The Blithedale Romance,* Boston, 1852.

———, *Dr. Grimshawe's Secret,* Boston, 1883.

———, *The English Notebooks,* edited by Randall Stewart, New York, 1941.

———, *The House of the Seven Gables,* Boston, 1851.

———, *The Marble Faun,* Boston, 1860.

———, *Passages from the French and Italian Notebooks,* London, 1871.

———, *The Scarlet Letter,* Boston, 1850.

———, "A Select Party," *Democratic Review,* July 1844 (included in *Mosses from an Old Manse*).

James, Henry, *Hawthorne,* Boston, 1879.

Sedgwick, Catharine Maria, *Letters from Abroad,* 2 vols., New York, 1841.

Whitman, Walt, "A Backward Glance O'er Travel'd Roads," *Leaves of Grass,* Philadelphia, 1891–92.

———, "Democratic Vistas," *Complete Prose Works,* Philadelphia, 1892.

———, "Preface, 1855," Ibid.

———, "Preface, 1876," Ibid.

B. Additional references

Kouwenhoven, John A., "Hawthorne's Notebooks and *Dr. Grimshawe's Secret,*" *American Literature,* January 1934.

9. SPACE AND CHANCE

A. Sources quoted or mentioned

American Research and Development Corporation (a brochure), Boston, January 1, 1947.

Beard, Charles A., "The American Invasion of Europe," *Harper's Magazine,* March 1929.

Bennett, Arnold, *Your United States,* New York, 1913.

Clark, Wallace, "European Manufacturing Plants Slowly Emulating American Methods," *Iron Age,* December 18, 1930.

Cohn, David L., *Combustion on Wheels,* Boston, 1944.

Copley, F. B., *Frederick W. Taylor, Father of Scientific Management*, 2 vols., New York, 1923.

Evans, Bergen, "Auto-intoxication," *Harper's Magazine*, May 1947.

Ford, Henry, *My Life and Work*, New York, 1923.

Grattan, C. Hartley, *The Three Jameses, A Family of Minds*, New York, 1932.

Hawthorne, Nathaniel, *The English Notebooks*, edited by Randall Stewart, New York, 1941.

————, *Our Old Home*, Boston, 1863.

Hirschfeld, C. F.: see *Toward Civilization: A Symposium*, edited by Charles Beard, New York, 1930.

James, Henry, *The American Scene*, New York, 1907.

————, *Hawthorne*, Boston, 1879.

————, *The Letters of Henry James*, edited by Percy Lubbock, 2 vols., New York, 1920.

Kallaher, Mike, "How to Change Layouts Often," *Factory*, March 1943.

Krutch, Joseph Wood, "Still Innocent and Still Abroad," *Harper's Magazine*, April 1931.

Land, Edwin H., "Research by the Business Itself," *The Future of Industrial Research*, Standard Oil Development Co., 1945.

Leaver, Eric W., and Brown, John J., "Machines Without Men," *Fortune*, November 1946.

Mayo, Elton, *The Social Problems of an Industrial Civilization*, Boston, 1945.

Mill and Factory, May 1947 (special issue).

Morse, Richard S.: see National Research Corporation.

Motor World ("Before New York Show Issue"), December 27, 1916.

National Research Corporation: see John A. Kouwenhoven, "An Experiment in Enterprise," *Harper's Magazine*, October 1944.

Neal, Julia, *By Their Fruits. The Story of Shakerism in South Union, Kentucky*, Chapel Hill, N.C., 1947.

Paul, Howard, *Dashes of American Humor*, New York, 1853.

Redlin, A. W., "Handling Materials in an Automatic Frame Plant," *Transactions of the American Society of Mechanical Engineers*, New York, 1930, Vol. 52, Part II.

Roethlisberger, F. J., and Dickson, W. J., *Management and the Worker*, Cambridge, Mass., 1934.

Siegfried, André, *America Comes of Age*, New York, 1927.

Stow flexible shaft: see Charles E. Emery, "Motors, Hydraulic and Pneumatic Apparatus, etc.," *Reports and Awards, Group XX*, United States Centennial Commission, Philadelphia, 1878. For

London *Times* comment see: *Reports of the United States Commissioners to the Paris Universal Exposition, 1878,* Washington, 1880, Vol. I, p. 449.

Taylor, Frederick Winslow, *The Principles of Scientific Management,* New York [1911].

Wells, H. G., *The Future in America,* New York, 1906.

White, Lee Strout (pen name of E. B. White and Richard Lee Strout), "Farewell, My Lovely," *New Yorker,* May 16, 1936.

Wilde, Oscar, *Impressions of America,* edited by Stuart Mason, Sunderland, 1906.

B. Additional references

Bourdet, Claude, "The Battle for Post-war France," *Harper's Magazine,* April 1948.

Bush, Vannevar, *Endless Horizons,* Washington, D.C. [1946].

Economic Development in Selected Countries. Plans, Programmes and Agencies, United Nations, Department of Economic Affairs, Lake Success, October 1947.

Hayes, Samuel P., Jr., "France," *Towards World Prosperity,* edited by Mordecai Ezekiel, New York [1947].

Lloyd, E. M. H., "Modernization of Industry in Britain," *Towards World Prosperity,* edited by Mordecai Ezekiel, New York [1947].

Product Engineering (special issue on "Designs for Material Conservation"), April 1942.

Recent Social Trends in the United States. Report of the President's Research Committee on Social Trends, 2 vols., New York, 1933.

Science and Life in the World (The George Westinghouse Centennial Forum), 3 vols., New York [1946].

Wartime Technological Developments. A Study Made for the Subcommittee on War Mobilization of the Committee on Military Affairs, 79th Congress, 1st Session, Senate Subcommittee Monograph No. 2, May 1945.

10. STONE, STEEL, AND JAZZ

A. Sources quoted or mentioned

Adams, James Truslow, "Our American Upper Class," *Harper's Magazine,* January 1932.

Amman, H. O.: see American Society of Civil Engineers, *George Washington Bridge Across the Hudson River at New York*, Port of New York Authority, 1933, p. 51.

Anderson, Sherwood, *Perhaps Women*, New York, 1931.

[Anonymous], "The Future of America," *Harper's Magazine*, June 1928.

Armstrong, Louis, *Swing That Music*, New York, 1936.

Babbitt, Irving, "The Critic and American Life," *Literary Opinion in America*, edited by Morton Dauwen Zabel, New York, 1937.

Bataille, Georges, "On Hiroshima" (translated by R. Raziel from an article in *Critique*), *politics*, July–August 1947.

Croly, David Goodman, *Glimpses of the Future*, New York, 1888.

Future editor of *Reader's Digest:* Ferguson, Charles W., "High Class," *Harper's Magazine*, March 1932.

Goodman, Benny (and Irving Kolodin), *The Kingdom of Swing*, New York, 1939.

Gropius, Walter: see Siegfried Giedion, *Space, Time and Architecture*, pp. 265–66.

Hamlin, Talbot, "Architecture in America Today," *New Republic*, August 4, 1941.

———, "Farm Security Architecture," *Pencil Points*, November 1941.

Hood, Raymond M.: see "Raymond M. Hood," *Architectural Forum*, February 1935.

Howells, William Dean, *Criticism and Fiction*, New York, 1891.

Kahn, Albert, "Architects of Defense," *Atlantic Monthly*, March 1942.

Knowlton, Don, "The Anatomy of Jazz," *Harper's Magazine*, April 1926.

Le Corbusier, *When the Cathedrals Were White*, translated by F. E. Hyslop, Jr., New York, 1947.

Lewisohn, Ludwig, "Literature and Life," *A Modern Book of Criticism*, edited by Ludwig Lewisohn, Modern Library, New York [n.d.].

Morison, George S., *The New Epoch as Developed by the Manufacture of Power*, Boston, 1903. See also: George Abbot Morison, *George Shattuck Morison, 1842–1903, A Memoir*, Peterborough [N.H.] Historical Society, 1940.

Mumford, Lewis, *Sticks and Stones*, New York, 1924.

Port of New York Authority, *First Progress Report on Hudson River Bridge at New York*, January 1, 1928.

Santayana, George, *Reason in Society*, New York, 1905.

Sargeant, Winthrop, *Jazz: Hot and Hybrid*, new and revised edition, New York, 1946.

Steinman, David B., and Watson, Sara Ruth, *Bridges and Their Builders*, New York [1941].

Sullivan, Louis, "What Is Architecture?" *Kindergarten Chats and Other Writings*, New York, 1947.

Tallmadge, Thomas E., *The Story of American Architecture*, New York, 1927.

Taylor, Frederick Winslow, *The Principles of Scientific Management*, New York, 1911.

Whitman, Walt, "Poetry Today in America—Shakespeare—The Future" (1881), *Complete Prose Works*, Philadelphia, 1892.

B. Additional references

Architectural Forum (special issue, "Design Decade"), October 1940.

Borneman, Ernest, "The Jazz Cult" (Parts I and II), *Harper's Magazine*, February and March 1947.

Gaines, M. C., "Narrative Illustration, The Story of the Comics," *Print, A Quarterly Journal of the Graphic Arts*, Vol. III, No. 2, Summer, 1942.

Harap, Louis, "The Case for Hot Jazz," *Musical Quarterly*, January 1941.

Hobson, Wilder, *American Jazz Music*, New York, 1939.

Jacobs, Lewis, *The Rise of the American Film*, New York [1939], Chapters III and IV.

Johnson, Philip, *Machine Art*, Museum of Modern Art, New York, 1934.

MacDonald, Dwight, "A Theory of Popular Culture," *politics*, February 1944.

Seldes, Gilbert, *The Seven Lively Arts*, New York, 1924.

Smith, Charles Edward, and Others, *The Jazz Record Book*, New York, 1942, pp. 1–125.

Waugh, Colton, *The Comics*, New York, 1947.

Index

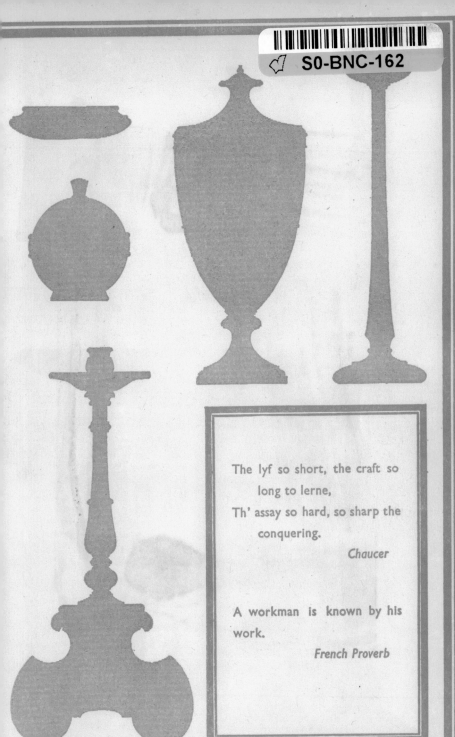

The lyf so short, the craft so
long to lerne,
Th' assay so hard, so sharp the
conquering.

Chaucer

A workman is known by his
work.

French Proverb

THE PRACTICAL
WOOD TURNER

WOODWORKER HANDBOOKS

" Tools do what *you* want them to do
when you know what *they* want to do "

"MY INSTRUCTIONS MEAN JUST WHAT THEY SAY

You may be troubled with tools digging in. Well, if you follow my words carefully, they won't. My aim is to show you how to cut wood as it prefers to be cut."

THE PRACTICAL WOOD TURNER

USE OF GOUGE AND CHISEL
FACE-PLATE TURNING
CHUCKING : PARTING : BORING
SPECIAL WORK, ETC.

BY

F. PAIN

J. B. LIPPINCOTT COMPANY

Philadelphia   New York

FIRST PUBLISHED
IN 1957
REPRINTED
IN 1958

749.123
P

MADE AND PRINTED IN GREAT BRITAIN BY WILLIAM CLOWES AND SONS, LIMITED, LONDON AND BECCLES

CONTENTS

v

INTRODUCTION

THE Worshipful Company of Turners once bought a trumpet for six shillings to blow at their dinners. I am hoping to provide you with a sort of feast on wood-turning, and so please allow me a modest blow on my trumpet first. The aim of this book is to set you thinking on the right lines, so that you *cut wood as it prefers to be cut.* It would be easy to give bare instructions and designs, but it is much better when you know why we do a job in a certain way. It enables you to apply the idea to your own work.

I have been associated with wood-turning for fifty years and have had a business of my own, doing furniture work both antique and modern, builders' requirements up to some fifteen feet long, fancy wood-ware for gift shops, automatic lathe work, and extremely accurate work for instruments. During the last five years or so I have been to exhibitions and schools demonstrating and answering questions, and I've been to a prison too.

Now this fanfare on my trumpet is blown solely to give you confidence that it is a practical man who is trying to help you with advice. I say this in all sincerity. The best way to learn a trade is to compete in quality and price with others, and so I'll now retire and get on with the job until I hear Gabriel blowing *his* trumpet.

Now, whereas you can *scrape* an object to shape without any trouble, good wood-turning runs very close indeed to spoiling the work. If, however, you follow my instructions carefully, you should be able to learn just how it is done. Remember that scraping is not true craftsmanship at all. Should you be like one man I know who throws the job he is doing across the shop if it is difficult, well, throw the tools as well. You see, I get disheartened when I hear a man say, "Oh! he's a blooming expert, I can't do it." Believe me, many "blinking amateurs" do far better work than some "blooming experts". So go forward and enjoy wood-turning, one of those creative arts still left to us, and create things with your own personality written in wood.

My instructions mean just what they say. For instance, they advise you to hold the tools lightly. At exhibitions I often swank, and although I use all the power the motor will give yet hold the tool lightly between two fingers only. You may be troubled with tools digging in. Well, if you follow the words carefully, they won't.

It would be much better to show you personally how to use the tools, but I cannot reach everybody and have therefore to rely on words and sketches.

It would be nice to see the book propped up in front of the lathe, and a scrap piece of wood in the lathe and you trying out the movements (quite a lot would prefer to learn boxing this way). My five years of demonstrating have taught me a lot of what people wish to know. Generally I prefer to teach boys and ladies because they both do what they are told (?), at least when turning. Men will invariably force the tools around, although, believe me, the tools will do the jobs themselves if you only hold them right.

You will find ideas for turning everywhere around you; such things as railings often have nice finishes on them; the jewellers will have some nice shapes for cruet sets or light candlesticks; the antique shops often have some old things which suggest items to make. My men used to say that I saw too much. Once a chalk mark and date was put on the factory wall. It puzzled me, so I asked what it was for. It seems that I remarked that a certain job was perfect, and, as I had done many hundreds of pounds' worth of work for the King's woodcarver, it must have pleased me. Well, constructive criticism always helps, especially when you apply it to your own work.

F. PAIN.

High Wycombe,
1956.

THE PRACTICAL
WOOD TURNER

CHAPTER I : ABOUT LATHES

MACHINERY is often made locally to suit a trade, and a consultation between maker and user results in something that really suits the user. First was the bodger's lathe which revolved back and forth, being pulled in the return stroke by the branch of a tree. This gradually gave way to the wheel lathe which often needed

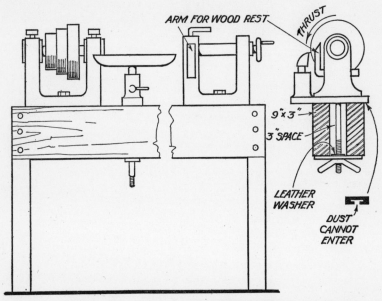

FIG. I. WOOD BED LATHE OF TYPE WIDELY USED IN THE TRADE
The bed is made of B.C. pine bolted to uprights. This drawing is diagrammatic and is intended to show the main lay-out, not to give details.

help in treadling, especially when turning a big job. Then steam came along, and so we had power lathes—one firm made them by hundreds for the local furniture firms. The factory where I worked as a boy had fourteen of them, and they did over six thousand designs of furniture. Electricity succeeded steam, and firms began to make

I

lathes who had not this link with a local trade to tell them just what
was wanted.   Thus it is we now have many lathes which are not as
suitable for wood-turning as they could be.   So many manufacturers
think in terms of metal-turning lathes and design our wood-turning
lathes accordingly.

Wood bed lathe.   The standard practice locally in my time was
to cast the headstock with two lugs $1\frac{1}{2}$ in. wide.   The lathe bed had
a 3-in. space between its beds, so you can see how loose the fit was.
Engineers' lathes would be hopeless with such a lot of play, but it
was no disadvantage to us.   The lathe bed consisted of two pieces
of 9-in. by 3-in. British Columbian pine as shown in Fig. 1.   This is

FIG. 2. 6-in. LATHE HEADSTOCK AND TAILSTOCK, REST, AND PULLEY GEAR.
These are intended to be mounted on a timber bed, being held by a heavy screw and wing nut.
By courtesy Dexter & Co. Ltd., High Wycombe.

soft by nature, and formed a springy bed so that when the tailstock
was tightened up it held the work with a certain springiness between
centres.   This is again the reverse of what engineers aim at in a
lathe bed.

You may well wonder why this springiness is desirable.   Well,
in use the prong or driving chuck enlarges its slot, and the tail-
stock centre bores a little into the other end.   The springiness takes
this up so that we don't have to be continually tightening up the
tail-stock wheel.   In this way the metal bed and small centre height
of the modern lathe go against us.

And here let me say that some great engineers have made the
mistake of thinking that solidity is needed, whereas it is really
springiness that is wanted.   Isambard Kingdom Brunel was a great
engineer (1806-1859) who thought that railway lines ought to be on

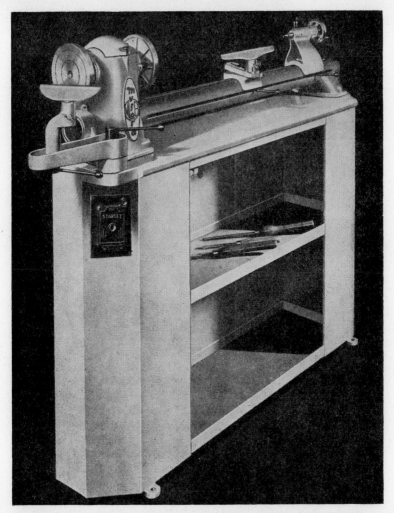

FIG. 3. THE M.L.8 MOTORISED LATHE WITH 8-in. SWING OVER THE BED
Standard distance between centres is 30 in. Longer bed lengths are available. Large diameter work, bowls, etc. can be turned on a face plate at the other side of the headstock as
shown. The lathe is also available without the stand.

By courtesy Myford Engineering Co. Ltd., Nottingham.

a very solid foundation, and so laid large baulks of timber lengthwise along the track bolted to stakes driven into the earth. In the
event this proved too solid in use, and the track is laid on sleepers
to-day in the way you well know. Have you noticed how the
sleepers allow the rail to go up and down as the train goes over them?

Thus it is that I prefer a lathe with a wood bed and a fine solid head with solid bearings to a light lathe with a host of attachments such as steadies, etc., that we cannot use. On the other hand I do realize that the space occupied is important to the man who has only

FIG. 4. THE CORONET MAJOR LATHE WITH 4½-in. CLEARANCE BETWEEN CENTRE AND BED.
For turning large diameter work the headstock can be pivoted round at right angles to the bed, enabling table tops, etc. to be turned.
By courtesy Coronet Tool Co., Derby.

a small workshop, and the all-metal lathe is capable of good work (it must be or the firms making them would go bankrupt).

Bearings. Ball bearings seem ideal as the thrust is rather heavy on a wood-turning lathe, because, owing to the poor centres often fitted, we often have to force them (more anon about these). One trade lathe I know has bearings 4¼ in. long by 2 in. diameter, but of course it would use a lot of power (what a lovely solid job for face-turning it would be). So perhaps ball bearings are all right as we have so little power to play with as a rule. Furthermore if the oil can is not used freely a plain bearing would soon be ruined. In any case we cannot use the large single-phase motor that solid bearings would need from the house supply. As for speed, why waste power unnecessarily? 1,400 r.p.m. is ample in the lathes we have in mind.

The power that a lathe consumes is a very real problem, but we should grumble more if it were missing. For face-turning I could easily use all a 2-h.p. motor could give (a 5-h.p. was fitted to mine). It is usual to fit a 1-h.p. motor for spindle work, which is much lighter on the power consumed.

Centres. In our trade our centres screw in and need no hole right through the headstock to poke them out, as there is a hole across by which they may be unscrewed with a tommy-bar. Taper

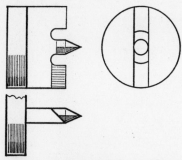

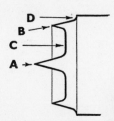

FIG. 5. CORRECT FORM OF FORK CHUCK.
Note that edges of prongs are staggered.

FIG. 6. RING TAIL-STOCK CENTRE.
A. Centre point. B. Ring. C. Flat. D. Shoulder. Both C and D should push against end of wood.

centres often get fixed in, and force has to be used to poke them out —which does the ball races no good.

Just what steel some driving centres are made of is a mystery to me. The prongs bend over inwardly, and it is not good enough. The tail-stock centre pushes only, and ordinary bright bolts turned suitably have proved to be all right, so long as we don't knock our wood sideways between centres to true it. Manufactured centres, however, should stand up to this, as it is the accepted way of turning squares. Fig. 5 shows how a centre should look. Some centres have no space between centre point and fangs, and so long as nothing prevents the fangs from penetrating into the end grain all is well. You could file this away, and also touch up the bevel, which is 45° and flat on the driving side.

In the trade we never stop our lathes in spindle work but put our hand around the wood and ease back the tail-stock. Someone once asked my man if the wood often hits you, and he assured him, "No, generally only once." Still I would not advise you if I thought it dangerous practice, and if your hand is around the work all is well. The reason for not stopping the power is that small A/C motors don't like being started and stopped. If the centre does not come away easily out of the wood, look for a burr on the driving centre, as this is probably the cause. Whenever we have trouble with a tail-stock

FIG. 7. UNION JUBILEE LATHE WITH EITHER 5-in. OR 6-in. HEIGHT OF CENTRE.
Distance between centres can be 30 in., 42 in., or 54 in. Large diameter face plate work is done at the left-hand end.
By courtesy T. S. Harrison & Sons Ltd., Heckmondwike.

centre burning we look at the driving centre first (but then our tail-stock centres are of the correct shape). You may be troubled with a deep groove in the tail-stock centre filling up with charcoal. Well, it should not be there.

Fig. 6 shows a correct ring centre. The flat part pushes the wood on to the driving chuck and is not very deep. The fact that a tail-stock centre pushes cannot be too strongly emphasized, for so many fail here. With a happy pair of centres which don't need continual tightening up we shall enjoy wood-turning.

A special centre we found useful was a long one that went into the hole of a candlestick (which is always bored first). We also had some other special sizes so that when we turned pins or dowels on the work we could make the size of the pins the same as the centre. This saved using callipers.

Rests. Lathe rests get me all hot and cross, for some are just as awkward as they can be. If only lathe manufacturers would draw

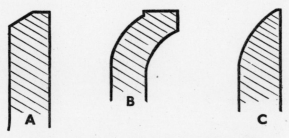

FIG. 8. SECTIONS THROUGH DIFFERENT RESTS.
"I do not like either A or B. That at C is the best shape."

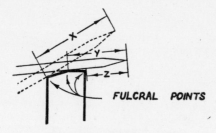

FIG. 9. "SIDE VIEW OF REST WHICH I DO
NOT FAVOUR."
This shows how the tool passes through an abrupt
change as the handle is raised or lowered, owing to
its bearing upon a different point of the rest

a curved line for the top of the rest to show its section, then show a tool with the handle moving up and down as in turning, they would make much better rests. All sorts of things get in the way as we move the tool about, not to mention the shape of the rest itself. A parallel rest is wanted, as we sometimes slide the hand along it. I admit it does not look so nice as a shaped one, but we have them for use.

I know of a very cheap lathe, and one that costs £3,500. Both have perfect rests (I shall one day) and they cost no more to make than poor ones. Some rests have fancy shaped tops, and as we do curves the tool rests on different parts just as a sort of handicap. Fig. 8 shows what I mean.

The ideal rest for spindle work is made of wood. A pin goes into the T rest and stand, and an L bolt (X) holds the other end. Fig. 10 shows clearly the idea. The idea could be worked out to suit the particular lathe. All trade lathes have this form of rest, and it is ideal. They need truing up from time to time as they mark in use,

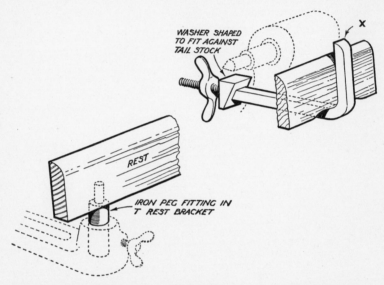

WASHER SHAPED
TO FIT AGAINST
TAIL STOCK

X

REST

IRON PEG FITTING IN
T REST BRACKET

FIG. 10. METAL FITTING USED FOR ATTACHING WOOD REST TO LATHE

so a spokeshave is included among the tools. This marking or notching on the rest is an advantage in repetition work, however. The notches formed by the tools prevent slips and spoilt work. Another advantage is that we can have the rest the length of the work, and this saves having to move it about.

For faceplate work we do use a metal rest, and please see that it is forward enough to be near the work, as when, say, turning a bread board. A rest just above its pin is of little use, for the stand gets in the way.

Drive. Trade lathes have a countershaft with fast and loose pulleys so that the flat belt 2 in. wide can be slid gradually on. This is useful for some work, and I feel that a clutch (which might only raise the motor up) to allow a V belt to slip a bit would be an improvement. Some people might think a lathe with 7- or 8-in. centres could not do small work. Well, one lathe we had did finials for a building which had balls 16 in. in diameter; and also did a pair

FIG. 11. CORRECT HEIGHT FOR COMFORTABLE WORKING.
The centre is about in line with the elbow.

of candlesticks for "The Queen's Doll's House" which went away in a matchbox.

No part of the stand holding the lathe bed ought to be more forward than the edge of the bed itself or it will be in the way of the feet. A useful height is when the elbow with hand up is centre height as in Fig. 11. It avoids bending the back.

Now I've often said, "Listen to an expert's advice then do it your own way", and the late Mr. Middleton of garden fame said,

2—P.W.T.

"People have done exactly the opposite of what I recommend with most excellent results." I often think of expert musicians in church who so complicate the music that we cannot join in. May I very sincerely say that I want to encourage good wood-turning, and help you to enjoy it. My job is not to run down anything, but rather to set everyone thinking clearly about what is wanted.

To my simple mind to have a round bed, then to fit a saddle on to it with a flat surface on top to hold a T-rest stand seems wrong in design, for it could have been flat at the start if only a flat bed had been used. (This does not mean that lathes so fitted are wrong, as other reasons probably governed the design.) The flat top of the bed takes the downward thrust in a more straight forward way as Fig. 1 shows. There is also a lot to be said for a design that does not clog up with dust or polish. Some of us use friction polish in the lathe, and it *will* get on to the lathe bed. Still the lathes sold are capable of good work, so don't go all sorry and sad over this chapter.

FIG. 12. MACHINE FOR TWIST TURNING SHOWING MASTER PATTERN.

It is not practicable to do twist turning in the ordinary simple lathe. This machine has a revolving head (centre) with specially shaped cutters. The wood is passed across this head and revolved spiralwise, being controlled by the master pattern in the tail-stock.

By courtesy of Dexter & Co., Ltd., High Wycombe

FIG. 13. WOLF CUB LATHE POWERED BY AN ELECTRIC DRILL
For small work this gives good results. A small face plate is also available.

By courtesy Wolf Electric Tools Ltd., London.

FIG. 14. UTILITY LATHE DRIVEN BY AN ELECTRIC DRILL
Either between-centre work or small face plate work can be done.

By courtesy Black & Decker Ltd., Harmondsworth.

"CUTTING WOOD AS IT PREFERS TO BE CUT."

One of the secrets of both gouge and chisel turning is to let the bevel of the tool rub the work. If it does this the tool cannot dig in. But don't just take my word for it. Get your tools and try it for yourself.

CHAPTER 2 : YOUR TOOLS—GOUGES

IT does seem to me that to have the right tools and to sharpen them properly is a tremendous help in wood turning. I therefore give straightway what I recommend. Fig. 1 gives the chisels and gouges used for true turning, and Fig. 4 the scraping tools for face plate work and special jobs. I show them here in a group so that you have a good idea of what is wanted, but I discuss them in detail in the chapters dealing with their use.

GOUGES

The local tool merchants in High Wycombe stock the tools in Fig. 1, for they are used in the furniture trade here, but curiously few are in the booklets issued by the British Standards Institution. I once asked a manufacturer what a certain tool was used for. He replied that he did not know, but it was easy to make. I then asked why he did not make deep half-round gouges and was told that they are hard to make.

Well this is a sorry start and things are likely to get worse because fewer wood-turning tools are being used by the trade since automatic machines do the bulk of the work. On the other hand there are many more amateur hand-turners about, men who do wood turning as a relaxation from their normal jobs. Unfortunately the amateur does not know the best shape for tools. There are far too many shallow gouges about, and I suspect that manufacturers make them because they are easy to forge.

Range of gouges. First let us consider the tools, and I turn to the gouges in my own kit (Fig. 1). I've a $\frac{3}{8}$ in., deep, long and strong (A), which I use for rough turning any size of bowl. Then I've a $\frac{3}{8}$ in., long and strong (B), but just a plain half of a circle, not a shallow one. Another useful gouge I have is a $\frac{3}{4}$-in. half-round (C), which is ample for most roughing-out purposes; also a $1\frac{1}{4}$ in. (D), the same, which youngsters enjoy to handle, but which I like for turning the larger legs, etc., used in the furniture trade. A $\frac{1}{4}$-in., rather deep gouge, long and strong (E), for deep hollows; and a $\frac{1}{4}$-in. half-round (F), for simple hollows. The only shallow type of gouge is a $\frac{5}{8}$ in. (G), which is useful for hollows in the feet of chair legs as it is practically the finished shape desired.

The caption says that these tools are used by me, but, alas, so

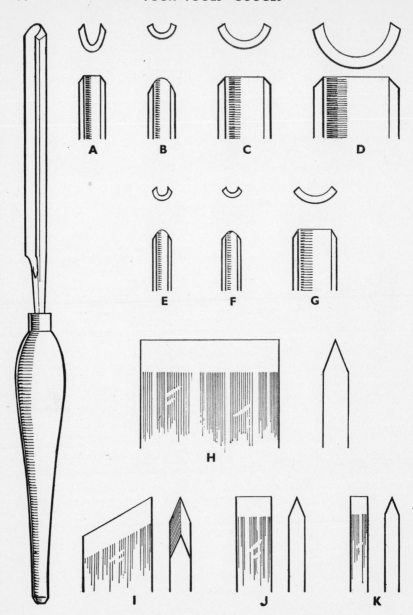

FIG. I. GOUGES AND CHISELS I USE IN TURNING.
A. $\frac{3}{4}$ in.-deep long and strong. B. $\frac{3}{4}$ in. half-round long and strong. C. $\frac{3}{4}$-in. half-round.
D. I$\frac{1}{4}$-in. half-round. E. $\frac{1}{4}$-in. deep, long and strong. F. $\frac{1}{4}$-in. half-round. G. $\frac{1}{2}$-in. shallow.
H. 2-in. square. I. I-in. long-cornered, J. $\frac{1}{2}$-in. square. K. $\frac{1}{4}$-in. square.

many ask for my tools at demonstrations, they seldom are in my tool box for long. Few tool merchants stock them, in fact I know of only one who does. Many years ago you could buy a case containing seventy-five gouges all different, but you cannot to-day. Actually it is not necessary to have so many and I ask manufacturers for just six on your behalf.

Gouges are generally required to remove wood quickly while chisels are for paring a nice surface, but, of course, gouges are necessary to finish off hollows in turning. So let us look at gouges (C) and (D), which I suggest you grind square across as in Fig. 2. You will notice that no matter how you rotate the gouge the cutting edge is the same. Thus the whole of the cutting edge can be used.

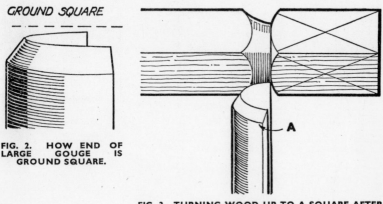

GROUND SQUARE

FIG. 2. HOW END OF LARGE GOUGE IS GROUND SQUARE.

A

FIG. 3. TURNING WOOD UP TO A SQUARE AFTER END OF LATTER HAS BEEN ROUNDED WITH THE CHISEL.

Some gouges are ground to a nose for another purpose, but (C) and (D) are roughing-out gouges intended to turn wood up to about 2 or $2\frac{1}{2}$ in. The larger the diameter of the work the smaller the gouge we use, generally speaking. Of course it depends on the power available (when in business I had 5 h.p.), and the kind of wood and length of work also play their parts.

Using the gouge. Fig. 3 shows, say, a 2-in. square cut down to leave a pummel or square part. The gouge is laid on its side, and I would like you to hold the gouge lightly and do that cut. Notice how bevel (A) tends to move the gouge to the right, for it naturally slides that way. The idea I'm trying to get across is that tools do the job themselves if only they are presented correctly to the job. I've amused many by holding tools very lightly to show the idea

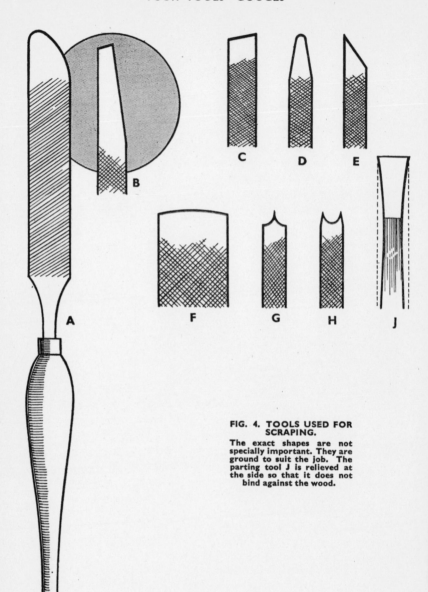

FIG. 4. TOOLS USED FOR SCRAPING.

The exact shapes are not specially important. They are ground to suit the job. The parting tool J is relieved at the side so that it does not bind against the wood.

and to try to stop people forcing them about (you could with force move the tool against its natural tendencies).

Please try out the movements now. If you hold the tool lightly, you will get the feel of it. If you lay the gouge over on the other side, it will tend to move to the left, and this is how I remove the wood, as in a chair leg for instance. Any part of the cutting edge can be used between the pummels; and if you are lazy, you can even make the tool work itself along the leg by moving the handle end a little to the left, or right. I don't know whether lazy is the right word: I find that I do it myself anyway. Fig. 5 shows a cylinder being roughed out with the gouge.

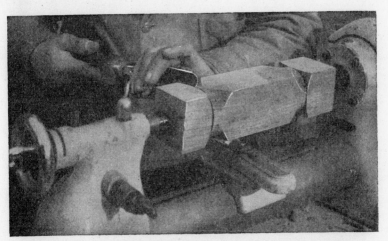

FIG. 5. CYLINDER WITH SQUARES AT THE ENDS BEING TURNED.
The ends of the squares are cut in with the chisel (see page 111) and the half-round gouge used between. See also Fig. 3.

Some may ask, "What is the correct height for the rest?" Well, just what suits you is correct so long as the bevel of the tool rubs the work. The comfortable height of centres seems to be your elbow when your hand is on the shoulder as you stand upright (see page 9). If the lathe is too low, you may find a higher rest a help. Many lathes are made for school use and are too low for adults. It is easy to raise it up and is well worth making the alteration.

Many of you will have a shallow gouge, and it will take a broad shaving rather than a rope-like one. It will tend to lift the work out of the lathe if it is a springy job, and in any case it won't remove wood so easily and will need holding more carefully. A chisel can remove wide shavings, but a curved wide shaving has considerable strength.

ROUGHING DOWN WITH THE LARGE GOUGE.
I always grind this gouge square with no point or nose (see D, Fig. I, page 14). This enables every part of the edge to be used since it can be rotated.

It will force the tool down whereas a flat shaving just bends. So these shallow gouges tend to dig in if used for heavy cuts.

You may understand better about curved shavings by thinking of those flexible steel rules that will stand straight out because they are curved in section. That is the reason why for springy work or large diameter work we use a smaller size of gouge. The shallow wide gouges are used for hand-turned brush handles and of course cannot turn a hollow smaller than their own radius. A small radius gouge used for the same job could show ribs.

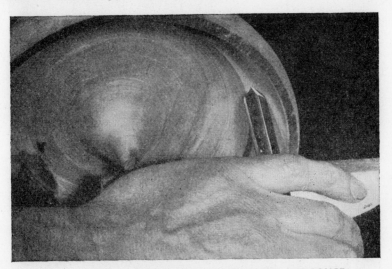

FIG. 6. TURNING THE INSIDE OF A BOWL WITH THE GOUGE.
The end of the gouge is ground square (A, Fig. 1, page 14), and the bevel at about 45°
The bevel must rub the whole time.
By courtesy E. Barrs, Myford Engineering Co. Ltd.

Gouges are made *ordinary* and *long and strong* (often labelled L and S only). It is the section of these roughing-out gouges that gives them their strength. The ordinary kind is all right for normal work. The L and S would be used for large diameter table legs because the cutting edge may have to project a long way from the rest when turning hollows.

L and S gouge. Let us have a look at (A) Fig. 1, which is a $\frac{3}{8}$-in. deep L and S, a favourite of mine for bowl turning. (E) is the same but smaller and would be ideal for hardwood, say, turning oak bowls from some old church timber. (A) is ground square across when used for bowl turning or face plate work, and if I could write in three dimensions I could show why more easily. However,

I will try by a photograph.   Fig. 6 shows the tool well inside a bowl, and you can see that if the gouge were ground to a nose it would not take the heavy cut the turner is taking.   It would be ground away just where it is wanted, for the side of gouge is cutting and the bevel at the centre is resting on the wood.

This bevel resting on the work prevents that dig-in which worries so many people.   The handle end of the tool is held well down,

FIG. 7. GOUGE IS TURNED OVER ON SIDE WHEN TURNING OUTSIDE OF BOWL.
Note how bevel rubs. Compare with Fig. 8.

and so presents the cutting edge at a favourable angle to cut.   Note, however, that the gouge is ground at at least 45°.   Any lower angle than this will cause digging in because the bevel will be unable to rub on the wood owing to the angle at which it must be presented. I am grateful for permission to use this photograph as it is the best I've seen to show this principle.

Fig. 7 shows me holding the gouge on the outside of a bowl, and Fig. 8 illustrates the complete movement.   Quite frequently, however, it is the side of the gouge rather than its middle that does

most of the work.   That is the reason I like a deep L and S gouge
for this kind of work; the large diameter can be a strain on the tool.
Fig. 8 shows how the movement of the handle end of the gouge
governs the shape of the work.   You can try this principle on both
inside and outside of the bowl.   Perhaps you can see that if you
move the gouge from A to B it cuts deeper into the wood, and so we
vary the shape by this movement.   A correctly ground tool tends

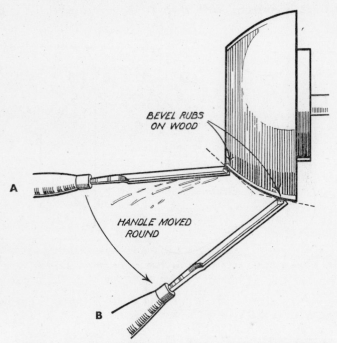

FIG. 8.   PLAN VIEW SHOWING OUTSIDE OF BOWL BEING TURNED.
Note how the handle is swung round to enable the bevel to follow the curve.

to keep against the wood by the action of its shaving, and would dig
in bodily if the bevel did not rub and so prevent it.

Letting the bevel rub.   To learn more about this tool try to
turn the wood without the bevel rubbing the work and let the centre
of the tool cut.   It may dig in or shudder and you can only maintain
an even cut by using force.   This is the very thing I wish you to
avoid, for it is impossible to feel the tool working if you hold it
tightly.   When I'm swanking I just hold the end of the tool handle
between two fingers and take off heavy cuts, even slowing up the

motor.   The rope-like shavings run down the hollow of the gouge
which shows that you are *cutting wood as it prefers to be cut.*

My swanking demonstrations are to give you confidence in turning,
as those who can feel the tool working get so much pleasure from it.
A blind man I taught does it for a living now, and says that he enjoys
it so much that he will turn in his grave.   If I can show you how
to get such pleasure, I shall be indeed humbly grateful.

Bevel of tool.   The bevels of my tools are shorter than many
people think is correct.   Well, there is no correct bevel but if too

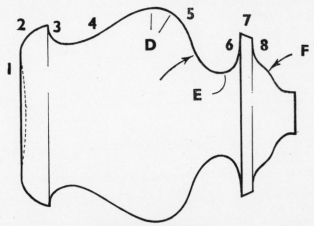

FIG. 9. DESIGN FOR TABLE LAMP IN THE FORM OF A CHINESE VASE
It measures about 5 in. in diameter.

long they don't seem to retain for long their sharpness.   Furthermore you cannot use a gouge with a long bevel inside a bowl.   A
friend of mine who has the "Freedom of the City of London" for
his hand-turning seems to use the bevels that I do and so do trades-
men generally, so it is probably right, but by all means try out other
bevels.   (B) and (F), Fig. 1, could have a longer bevel and be ground
to a nose rather than square across, for they are for turning hollows.
If a gouge is rather wide for the hollow we wish to turn, it is ground
more pointed.

Ming vase table lamp.   Now if you break the minute hand off
the clock and put it in front of you and fix a nice chunk of wood in
the lathe, we will try to follow what a gouge can do.   The Westminster Abbey clock would do as that has only an hour hand, but
it will help to follow how to twist the gouge in turning shapes.
Fig. 10 shows the idea.   The gouge is how you would see it when

using it—that is, you are standing behind it with the handle next to you.   The clock times given refer only to how the gouge is twisted, not to other movements such as the handle end up or down and sideways.   We will use the $\frac{3}{8}$-in. half-round L and S gouge only, but any gouge you have will work the same in principle, so don't hold up the job because you have not one (very few people have).

There are two ways of rounding our square, one by moving it along the rest, which is the usual way of doing it; but for some unknown reason I prefer to tilt the gouge to 2 o'clock with handle well to right, and keep lifting the handle.   It may well be owing to the fact that many lathes I work won't swing a large block and I have to start with the T rest stand at the end of the work.   So now we have a round block of wood, and you can try out the movements which refer to the final cut rather than those just removing wood.   Fig. 9 shows the shape to be turned.

Detail No. 2 is done with the gouge at 12 o'clock *always starting at*

FIG. 10. DIAGRAM SHOWING GOUGE POSITION AS SEEN BY USER.

the largest diameter.   Then, twisting the gouge to 9.30 as you move handle to right, gradually lift it, which of course moves the cutting edge downwards.   The centre of the gouge does the cutting and bevel underneath rubs the work.   For a larger curve than that shown the gouge could slide along the rest to the left slightly; in fact quite large balls can be turned this way.   I suggest that you refer to these movements in what you wish to do, rather than copy the whole design (unless you wish to, of course).

Detail 3 is started with gouge at 1 o'clock and handle to right. When in a little way the gouge is twisted to 2.30 and the handle moved over to the right so that the bevel is square to the work.   We would like to start with the gouge at 2.30 and the bevel square to the centre line of the work, but until we were in a little way the bevel could not rub and the gouge might slip into the wood and spoil the shape.   But you could try holding the tool more firmly just for the start and see whether you manage starting the curve at 2.30 rather than 1 o'clock.

You will notice if we use a gouge with too obtuse an angle for the bevel we have to move the handle too far over, and that is why we use different angles for gouges used in spindle turning than for face plate work. We gradually lift the handle and twist the gouge to 12 as we move the handle to left. For an inside curve as that shown the tool does not slide along the rest, but ends square to the work and at 12 o'clock, but for larger curves it could slide to the right a bit so that it ends as above.

Detail 4 is done with the gouge at 2, sliding it along the rest as we lift the handle. It is a case of sliding it and lifting handle in a co-ordinated movement to follow the desired outline. A chisel would be better, but more skill is required on large diameter stuff, and this is a safer way of doing it. The gouge is square to work, that is handle neither to left or right and you could twist the gouge to 12 o'clock at bottom of hollow but that's not important in long hollows. Detail 5 starts with gouge at 12 o'clock, gradually twisting it to 2.15 and sliding it along the rest to right a little.

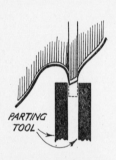

PARTING TOOL

FIG. II. PARTING TOOL USED EACH SIDE OF LIP PROJECTION.

This brings us to the arrow. You may note that so far it is just the same as detail 2 only larger and the other way round. The tool is twisted gradually to 12 o'clock as we lift the handle, and the cut ends at the bottom of hollow. You will notice that just twisting the gouge from 2.15 to 12 o'clock makes the tool do the shape itself; the bevel pushes it round the curve, so to speak.

Cutting detail 6 and 8 could slip and remove 7 entirely for until we have a surface to rest the bevel of the gouge on it has no support, so if you fear that you will slip up just push in a parting tool or ¼-in.

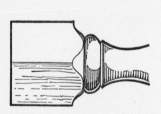

FIG. 12. OGEE FINISH TO PUMMEL

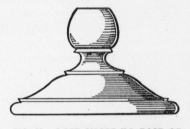

FIG. 13. OGEE SHAPE TO BASE OF STANDARD.

chisel as in Fig. 11. The bevel of the tool will then rest against the surface. Only go a short way in for the cuts will not leave a clean cut surface Detail 7 removes the roughness later. If you do this detail note that 6 starts at 9.30, and detail 8 at 2.30.   If you do not use the parting tool, detail 6 starts with the gouge at 11 and the handle to the left.   Gradually twist the handle to 9.30 and lift the handle, then twist the tool to the end at 12 at the bottom of the hollow. This is similar to detail 3 but the other way round.

Detail 8 is started with the handle to the right and gouge at 1.

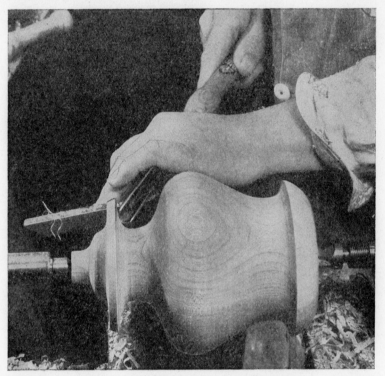

FIG. 14. TURNING NECK OF MING VASE
The gouge is taken in from the larger to the smaller diameter, and the bevel rubs the whole time.

Roll the gouge over to 2.30 and move the handle more to the right so that the bevel is square to the centre line of the work.   Lift the handle too, at the same time, bringing us to arrow (F).   We must now move the handle to the left a little which will move the tool more to the right because of the bevel rubbing the work.   The rest acts as a fulcrum and we twist the tool to 1.30, moving the handle to the left a little more and gradually twisting the gouge to 2.30.

Now we slide the tool along the rest to the right, and, as we lift

3—P.W.T.

the handle more we twist the gouge to 12.30. This makes the tool do a nice hollow all by itself; you only move and twist the tool. This rather involved procedure might be better followed if you think of the point of the gouge doing the work and twist it accordingly. A similar shape is often used on table legs and table lamps as in Figs. 12 and 13, so it is a process well worth learning.

Detail 7 is simple. With gouge at 1.30 we move the handle to the left which shifts the cutting edge to the right. It does not slide

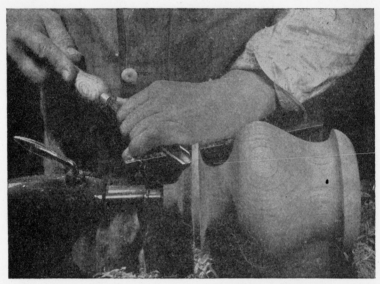

FIG. 15. HOW "LID" OF VASE IS TURNED WITH GOUGE.
As before, work from the larger to the smaller diameter.

along the rest, but only swivels, and, as we do it, we lift the handle a little. For detail 1 the tool is held at 10 with the handle well to left so that the bevel is practically at right angles with the work. You just lift the handle, and when you hear the chuck being turned as well you have gone too far. To make a nice clean bottom reverse the wood in the chuck and do it with point of the long-cornered chisel. It may be of interest to know that something like this design is in the British Museum and is Chinese of the Ming Period.

May I draw your attention to hollow at E as drawn. The design shows it as a lid on a pot so F must be smaller than E. The shoulder D gives it character and is important. The whole job takes two or three minutes to turn from the square, and if you take longer you are slower than I am. Elm is an easy wood to turn. I've been several times at exhibitions doing them, but it takes much longer to explain than to turn. Fig. 14 shows how much sideways the tool moves. When you try it make sure that you move the handle of the tool about, up and down as well as sideways. Don't use a very thin gouge or it will snap, or, if you do, at least avoid heavy cuts. Above all, don't say you cannot do it, for I've taught a blind man and he sells these lamps. His secret is that he feels the tools working; mine is that I prayed to be shown how to help him.

Here is a true story. The blind man wrote a letter to the Editor of the *Woodworker* and I was asked to answer it. It so happened that I was at a London store, and in my prayers I wished that I could show him. He turned up next day at the store from the wilds of Yorkshire. He only goes to London once a year, and he certainly did not know that I was going to be in London!

An example. My idea in describing movements when doing the vase in Fig. 9 is that you can choose from its details just what you want to do. It includes quite a lot of features used in the other turnings. It may well be that a chip on the rest will make a curve uneven and you wish to just take a little off; or maybe the co-ordinated movement of both hands on the tool do not quite produce what you have in mind. Well, present the gouge with the heel of the bevel rubbing the work and ease the hands up or possibly sideways a little so that it can cut and you can true up the curve without fear of a dig in. Sometimes a long curve on, say, a floor standard shows ribs when the chisel is used. A gouge may help if used instead, though it will not be quite so smooth as a chiselled surface.

The more beautiful the wood the more twisted the grain. Those who use a hand plane know that some woods cannot be planed either way. It has to be scraped. We could scrape it in turning, too, but a gouge is often better as it cuts through the fibres, whereas a chisel might just lift them out.

The movement of the gouge governs the shape but a $\frac{5}{8}$-in. shallow (G, Fig. 1) nicely fits the hollow of the toe of cabriole legs and also the toe and hollows in a twist leg before it is twisted. It does not lift the work as the hollows are near the centres of the lathe.

Cabriole leg. The best cabriole legs are shaped by hand, but you can make an inexpensive type entirely on the lathe. I deal with it more fully on page 101, but I give it here briefly as it exemplifies the use of the gouge. First we turn it as in Fig. 16, the wood running true between centres and the square left at one end. Now the foot end is put out of centre towards one corner of the leg for a square stool or table, and to one side if for a round stool or coffee table. The extent to which it is moved out of centre is half-way between true centre and the outside. The top end is put out of centre the other way so that the leg runs true where the round meets the square. Fig. 17 shows the idea.

The $\frac{5}{8}$-in. shallow gouge would be useful to do the toe with as it

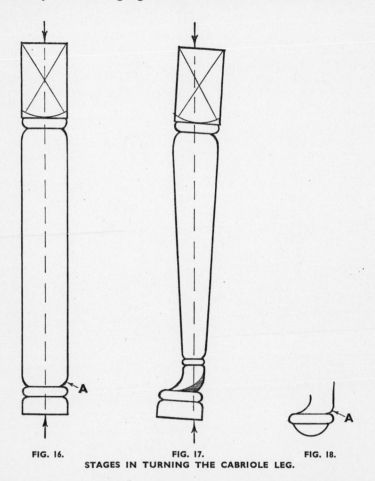

FIG. 16.   FIG. 17.   FIG. 18.

STAGES IN TURNING THE CABRIOLE LEG.

is not a continuous cut and with a smaller gouge you might get an uneven curve. The gouge is presented at 10.30 with the handle to the left and as you lift the handle twist it to 12. You may feel nervous that you may spoil it as it is not a continuous cut so hold the tool a bit more tightly and see that bevel is rubbing as you do it. Quite probably it will rub too much and you will see ribs where the tool starts each cut and wood has pushed it over. You ought also to feel it knocking.

The bead is not essential; in fact it weakens the leg. It only remains to re-chuck the leg to make it run true again and finish the toe as in Fig. 18. This makes it slide nicely on the carpet and also makes the toe not so liable to break off. The curve shown by the arrow can be much longer. It varies the look of the finished toe, and I suggest you vary it to see just how you like it.

Letting the bevel rub. Often I'm asked whether it is safe to use a gouge so high up on the work (Fig. 15) instead of holding it level to avoid digging in. It is absolutely a safe way of working

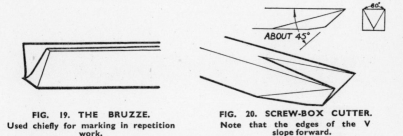

FIG. 19. THE BRUZZE.
Used chiefly for marking in repetition work.

FIG. 20. SCREW-BOX CUTTER.
Note that the edges of the V slope forward.

providing you let the bevel rub the work, but if the bevel is dubbed when sharpening and the tool has to have the handle lifted to enable it to cut then you will have trouble.

It would be as well for an instructor to show this principle with the work still and peep between bevel and work. If you start with the heel only on the work then lift handle to make it cut all is well. Care should be always taken, too, that the tool is on the rest before it touches the revolving work. In eagerness to work well on top of the work it may quite easily not touch. It is interesting to try it out though the tool may break or go through the window.

Bruzze. A buzz or bruzze is a tool that you need not buy. It is a V tool for marking the work where details come. We use it in repetition work but they are made so weak and generally lop-sided too that they are not much use. If you have one here are a few hints. When you sharpen it a little point is formed as in Fig. 19 caused by the slight hollow at the bottom of the V groove. If it is used on a metal rest it will probably slip sideways rather than go straight forward, so move it one way as you turn with it. This action is caused by one side cutting better than the other or by collisions of the two shavings (this can break it too).

In repetition work we hold it level and push it where grooves are worn in wooden rest.   For turning a pin at the end we tilt it on its side and this cuts the joint cleanly and does the pin as well.   A traveller said that we in High Wycombe were his only customers to-day for them, but some sets of tools include one.

There is a cutter very similar, Fig. 20, which is used in boxes for cutting external threads and cuts very cleanly indeed.   It must be sharpened as shown or it will not work.   The action is that the wood is forced towards the centre as it is being cut rather than lifted up. Perhaps you can understand it better if you realize that the top of the groove in the thread is cut before the bottom.   If the bottom were first the top of the groove would break away or lift off in a large chip.

Well you can take Westminster Abbey clock back now, and if you got into trouble breaking the minute hand off yours at home, I'm sorry for I have only tried to help.

FIG. 21. TURNING MAIN BODY OF THE VASE.
As a matter of interest you may like to know that I reckon to finish one of these from the rough square in 2 minutes.

CHAPTER 3 : USING THE CHISEL

MANY people think that a wood-turning lathe must go at a terrific speed, yet I know a pole lathe turner who completes a Windsor chair leg in 1 minute 20 seconds, complete with beads and

FIG. I.   HOW LONG SLENDER WORK IS SUPPORTED.
Note how the left-hand thumb rests on the chisel, the fingers being taken right round beneath the wood.

hollows, his speed being five revolutions forwards and backwards per movement of his leg as he works the treadle. The art of wood-turning is in paring off long, wide shavings with a chisel, or rope-like ones with a gouge, not a lot of dusty ones. We certainly do use speed, but the aim of this chapter is to show the mastery of wood-turning chisels, and speed will not help us to learn that.

Sharpening the chisel. Let us first sharpen the chisel. I deal with this fully in Chapter 5, but we can't do any turning until it is

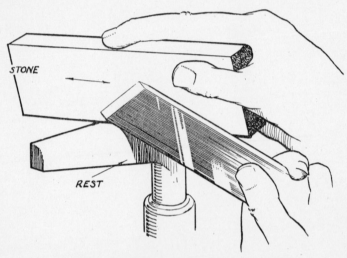

FIG. 2. SHARPENING CHISELS ON OILSTONE.
Note that the chisel is held on its side and remains stationary, the oilstone or oilstone slip being rubbed back and forth.

sharp. If it is new it will have a curved bevel (which is a mystery to me, as in the trade we use just a plain bevel on each side). There are two sorts you may buy; ordinary, and "long and strong" which is stouter in section. They range from $\frac{1}{8}$ in. to 4 in. wide. I suggest $\frac{1}{4}$-in. L and S, and $\frac{1}{2}$ in. either kind, $1\frac{1}{2}$-in. L and S, and a 2-in. ordinary. (If you want a 4 in. one, and can use it well, you can be excused from reading any more of this book.)

To grind the chisel an ordinary carborundum wheel mounted in the lathe is often used and is quite satisfactory, although a wet grindstone is preferred by many craftsmen. The thing to aim at is a nice even bevel, and if you can steady the handle against your body as you grind it is most helpful. My electric grinder is low and I steady the handle against my leg, taking care not to burn the steel.

I think the main trouble with carborundum wheels is that we use just what we come by (honestly I hope); yet before me is a book of 150 pages by the Carborundum people on grinding. If our wheel is too coarse it will be a job to get a good edge as, of course, it is what is left that cuts, not what we grind away. If the wheel glazes easily it is probably too hard, and the harder the steel the softer the stone to use. For carbide tools, which are extremely hard, the correct wheel is "Green Grit," which is quite friable and you can break pieces out of the wheel quite easily. I mention this about wheels as it is the reverse of what you might think. Still, carbide tools are not used for wood-turning. We use carbon steel which, when in the form of a file, is harder than high speed steel.

The oilstone. A lot of oil-stoning is not necessary, but please note that it is an *oil*-stone. If we do not use oil it will get clogged up and only burnish the tools (perhaps you go best well oiled?). Some like a little paraffin in the oil, and as long as we avoid thick, gummy oils all will be well. "Washita" stones were what we used, but like the "Arkansas" (which is an extremely good stone) they come from Oklahoma, U.S.A., and may be hard to come by. The manufactured ones we can get easily do not seem to give such a lasting edge, and my theory is this.

You will understand it better if you think how glass is cut by just a scratch with a diamond, yet the glass is fractured right through. I think there can be minute splits in the hard surface of steel, caused by too coarse a grinding wheel, or some sorts of oilstones. The idea is rather borne out by an oilstone in a rosewood case my father gave me. It was nothing more than Welsh slate, but it was the best stone I have ever had for getting a really fine edge. Now, Welsh slate is in layers. It is not a sandstone, so probably it did not score the steel so much as cut it. Slates vary in their capacity to cut, but mine was first rate.

When using an oilstone the oil should go black. My Dutch hone, which cost £5, soon makes the oil dark, which shows that it is cutting. The reason I mention it is that some of you may experiment with odd pieces of stone, and the speed with which the oil discolours is a sign of cutting. One of my men used a hard flooring tile from a church, and found it most excellent, and for four generations there was no Scottish blood in his veins to my knowledge. An 8 in. by 2 in. by 1 in. is the best size to use. The tool is held stationary, and *oilstone moved*. The tool rests against something, often on the tailstock, and gradually the stone wears a flat on the tail-stock where it rubs. This practice is not to be recommended, but is how we do it, as it is just a handy height. Fig. 2 shows the operation. If the chisel is held on its edge as shown, it is easy to see whether the stone lies flat against the bevel.

The side of the oilstone is used for gouges, and it soon develops a hollow, an advantage in use. For chisels the wide, flat surface is used. This should be flat and true and when necessary it should be corrected by rubbing on a floor stone, or letting the sander in the factory true it up for you when the garnet paper is worn out. If you true a natural stone on a carborundum wheel it does not cut for some time, and a light is seen where it rubs as you do it. Still, I have often done it, and made a slip for a gouge out of a larger piece of oilstone.

We will put our oilstones carefully into a cigar box to keep the shavings, etc., from them, and give the chisels we have sharpened a

FIG. 3. USEFUL STROP FOR FINISHING OFF THE EDGE.
It is of leather glued to wood and dressed with oil.

rub on the piece of leather we have on a piece of wood as a strop. This strop is shown in Fig. 3. The rounded edges (they can vary) are handy for stropping the insides of gouges. If you did not have a box of cigars at Christmas, well I am sorry, but stones are best put somewhere away from dust; they can break or chip if dropped. If you wish to see whether your chisel is sharp, trail your thumb-nail along the edge and you will notice an even bite which is hard to describe, but I am sure you will get to know it if you wish to.

We do *not* oilstone tools to a shorter bevel than we grind them as is done with some plane irons and firmer chisels. I measured the angle on my own chisel and found it to be in the region of 43° as shown in Fig. 4.   If your thumb-nail detects a gash (a sore place, I call it) along the edge you may be sure that it will mark the wood when in use.   Another point is that if you turn wood which has been sandpapered this will put plenty of sore places on the tool edge, so do not sandpaper work until you have finished turning it.

Action of the chisel.   First you should understand clearly how a chisel works.   A chopper will help you better to grasp what I am trying to describe.   You will notice when you chop up the firewood for the wife, that, after the edge has touched the wood, the sides of the chopper do the work; the cutting edge may not be doing anything

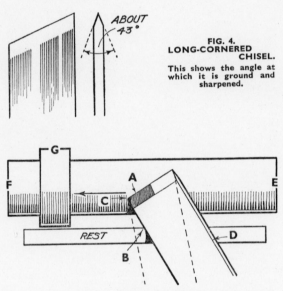

ABOUT 43°

FIG. 4.
LONG-CORNERED CHISEL.

This shows the angle at which it is ground and sharpened.

FIG. 5.   POSITION OF CHISEL FROM ABOVE WHEN TURN-
ING CYLINDRICAL SHAPE.

at all.   Now if you could force the chopper down at an angle to the line of cut, the chip would be bent or broken away, and the cutting edge would be rubbing hard against the wood all the time (if we could force the chopper down at all).   This very principle explains why some wood-turners lose the cutting edge of their tools and say that the steel is of no use, for in turning the tools can be held so that the edge does most of the work.   One test of a turner is the straightness of the shavings that come off.   In using a chisel they should be like flat pieces of ribbon.

Practical work. We will start work now. The wood has been turned round with a gouge, and we will just chisel along so that the shaving comes off in one long ribbon. Fig. 5 shows better than

FIG. 6. FINISHING CYLINDER WITH THE CHISEL.
When the long-cornered chisel is used only the half near the heel is used. See also Fig. 5.

words just how the tool is held. At my works we once had a shaving fifty feet long. You may not learn it as quickly as a boy I once saw at an Exhibition. When I asked him if he would like a lesson in turning he replied, "No, thank you, teacher taught me all about

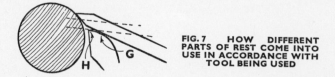

FIG. 7   HOW   DIFFERENT PARTS OF REST COME INTO USE IN ACCORDANCE WITH TOOL BEING USED

turning last week." Still I am anxious that you should enjoy the sense of achievement that comes when you master the action of wood-turning tools.

It is not important where your hands are; if some other way suits

you well, do it that way.   It is how the tool is placed that matters
as that is what does the work; you only guide it.   As I am ambidextrous I reverse hands, and hold the tools either side of my body (my
body is large and it saves moving it), but many do not and get on

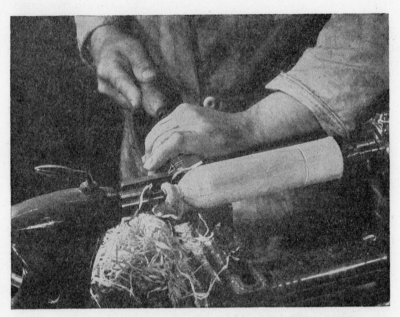

FIG. 8. ROUNDING OVER END OF CYLINDER WITH CHISEL.
Again only the heel portion is used.   Note that in both this and the operation in Fig. 6 the
bevel must rub on the wood.

just as well.   Fig. 5 shows a chisel which has been ground square
and one (dotted lines) ground "long cornered."   If you have two I
suggest a 2-in. wide chisel ground square across, and a 1½-in. one
ground long cornered.   If only one, the latter is the better as you
will see later on.

The cutting edge touches the wood at just the same angle as Fig. 5
shows.   You may have bought all of the chisel, but you must use
only part of it for this job.   If you want to learn quickly, just try
using the part that is not shaded.   The chisel will stab the work,
and, if a part of your hand is between the right-hand side (in sketch)
of the chisel and the rest, you will get a nasty nip, because this side
of the chisel is lifted up from the rest.   The part of the tool which
should do the work is the cutting edge at (A) or any part shown
shaded.   If too near (C), however, a feather of a shaving may form

at the left-hand corner to the side of the tool, and prevent the chisel from sliding along in the direction of the arrow. Sometimes it saves a ripple or a lot of twisted ribs on the work if we let (C) just cause a little feather of a shaving. This applies only to slender work.

The bevel of the tool is touching work that has been turned round previously. This is why you cannot start work at (E). Try it, and learn what happens. To turn (E) you face the tool the other way. The wood itself forms a sort of rest for the tool and the latter only touches the rest at (B). If your rest is uneven, this will prevent the tool from sliding nicely along, and the only thing I can think of is to put it right.

Now in the trade we prefer and use wooden rests for long jobs. Metal T rests are used for face turning or short work of large diameter. The rest becomes marked by small gouges, or by the chisel in doing various shapes, etc. If we do a lot of one pattern, quite pronounced grooves form in the wooden rest. These, however, do not in practice hinder the chisel from sliding along smoothly as Fig. 7 will explain. The part of the rest marked (G) is used for the chisel as we have to point the chisel more to the top of the work than we do with other tools which use the part marked (H). These notches that form are in fact a help as they prevent tools skidding about, and is why we prefer wood for rests for turning, say, chair legs.

In Fig. 5 is a projecting detail marked (G). It may be only a bead, but we obviously cannot get the chisel edge at (A) cutting without the corner (C) bumping into this detail. We only have to ease the tool forward gradually so that (C) only is cutting. There may be a snag, however. The splitting action of the chisel may remove some of the bead in front of the cutting edge. If the wood is of that nature the thing to do is to cut the fibres with the point of a long-cornered chisel before turning the cylindrical part. This will end the shaving where we want it to end.

Long work between centres. Fig. 1 shows how I use my hands to steady long cylindrical work (not that a sample of long work is shown in the lathe). The chisel is moving to my right, towards the tail-stock, and my hand is around the work with the thumb on top of the chisel. Fig. 9 shows the idea more clearly. The handle of the tool is touching my side, and I can twist it so that it cuts. If it were flat on the rest it would not cut at all; if lifted too much it would cut a taper; or it might—Oh, darn well try yourself and find out what happens! As the bevel does not rub the work anything might occur, and that is just how you will learn. Your mistakes will teach you much more than success. The whole idea of putting your hand

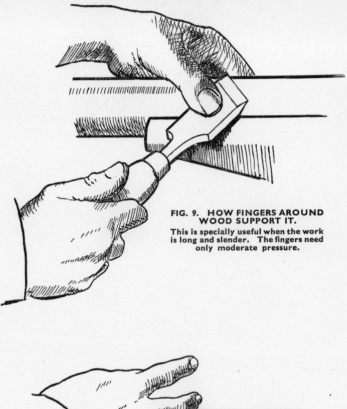

FIG. 9. HOW FINGERS AROUND WOOD SUPPORT IT.
This is specially useful when the work is long and slender. The fingers need only moderate pressure.

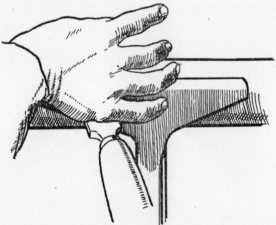

FIG. 10. FINGERS USED TO DEFLECT CHIPS.
This is useful if you find that you are put off by chips flying into your face.

around the work is to steady it—it seldom wears through to the bone. In fact it is quite harmless and is a good thing to learn to do.

Another way of holding the chisel is with the thumb beneath and the fingers curled over the top. Fig. 10 shows how the fingers can be opened up to form a shield to prevent chips from flying into the face.

Avoiding ribs in turning. It may well be some ribs will appear in long work. These appear as a sort of rough spiral. Well, try giving the tool more angle, that is, in Fig. 1 move the handle more to the left. It will lessen the width of shaving. Also try having just a little whisker of shaving by using the near corner of the tool a little. A steady is described in chapter 6 that will help a lot.

Ribs are caused on work by the wood bending away from the tool, then trying to come round and climb on top of the tool. It cannot do this and so ribs form. The steadies supplied by many lathe manu-

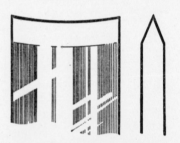

FIG. 11. BODGER'S CHISEL.
Ground to a hollow shape to give a longer cutting edge.

facturers are suitable for metal turning, but useless for wood turning, as we want a sort of elastic bias, or the work slightly bent to prevent this ribbing effect. For much turning the hand around the work is ample, however. We are not likely to hold the hand there until it burns, though a steady can burn the work if we do not take care.

My 2-in. chisel with its handle is 20 in. long, and to turn as in Fig. 5 I find my right hand is on the end of the handle at my side, and my left hand over the top of the chisel with the meaty part of the hand (which is on the other side of my hand to where I notice my thumb is) bearing against the rest. The fingers are curled round the chisel, and so can twist it to the right angle for turning. We always turn from larger to smaller diameter. If the chisel is lifted at (D), it takes more off the work, and that is how we govern those long curves in say a floor standard. Do not let your finger get between the chisel at (D) and the rest, unless you want to have a nip, for you certainly will if by chance you let the shaving come from the right hand side of the chisel.

In Fig. 8 the chisel is being used to round over the end of a cylinder. Exactly the same movement is followed, the bevel of the tool rubbing the work all the time.

To chisel towards the right I suggest you move your body to the left, and use your hands just the same. It seems a little less natural, but to change hands may cause you never to quite master the movement unless you do a lot of turning.

You have to be so careful in describing turning. I once said to a man, "Change the tool round", and he caught hold of the chisel blade and held the handle on the rest asking what he should do next!

The bodger's chisel. The bodgers of Buckinghamshire who

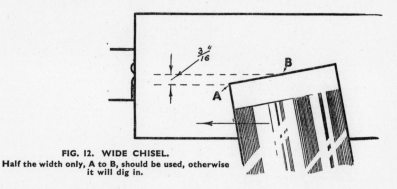

FIG. 12. WIDE CHISEL.
Half the width only, A to B, should be used, otherwise it will dig in.

turn chair parts in the beech woods use a pole lathe, and one I know uses a chisel 2 in. wide as shown in Fig. 11. He grinds it to a hollow curve as this gives it a longer cutting edge on curved work such as the bulbous part of a leg or on the underframing of chairs. The shavings he removes are $1\frac{1}{2}$ in. or so wide, and, when you consider that his power is only his own foot pulling down on a piece of string tied to the branch of a tree above, it is not bad going.

Now I don't advise you to grind your chisel so, except as an experiment, as it causes it to dig in more easily, but if you are going to use a Bodger's lathe (which is another name for a pole lathe) you will find it an advantage because of its slow speed of five revolutions for one push of the treadle. He has told me it is lovely in the woods at 4 a.m., but I should have thought the second line of "It's nice to get up in the morning" would have applied.

Wide chisels. Now I like wide chisels, 2 in. or more across, but they are expensive and not to be found in many tool shops. So let

4—P.W.T.

us have a few thoughts on wide chisels (thinking is not harmful, although some seem to manage without it). As I'm often at Exhibitions I bring mine out. It is 2 in. wide and 20 in. long, including its split handle, and I swank by taking off shavings, and have been photographed with shavings right across the stand. If any of my former workmen were around, however, I would not do it as it is so simple to use. One man at the works brought off a shaving 50 ft. long.

I will try to show you why a 2-in. chisel is useful to have, and why, although it is all yours, you must use only half of its width, (A) to (B) in Fig. 12. Please don't take my word for it, but try it and see what

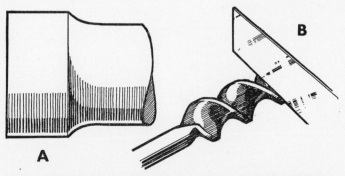

FIG. 13. (A) CURVED SHOULDER CUT WITH STRAIGHT CHISEL.
(B) SHOWING HOW STRAIGHT-EDGE LIES FLAT ON TWIST BIT.

happens. You can, of course, turn it over and use the other part of chisel to the right, but the sketch shows the tool moving to the left.

So we have an inch of cutting edge at an angle, and the shaving can come off anywhere in that inch. This position is maintained by keeping the tool at the same projection from the rest, letting the meaty part of the hand rub the rest as we slide the tool along.

You may understand the point I am trying to explain better if you realize that this 1 in. of cutting edge has only $\frac{3}{16}$ in. play forward or backward before you are in trouble. The dotted lines in Fig. 12 help to explain the point. You have to maintain this position of the tool against the cut, as of course the wood tends to force the tool towards you. You can increase the safe distance by twisting the tool to a greater angle as seen from above, but it does not give so clean a cut.

Straight lines on curves. It is an interesting point (although of no practical value) that the wood is of curved shape where being turned although the chisel is straight, as in Fig. 13 (A). The greater

the angle at which it is held the more the wood is curved.   A straight-
edge will touch the entire curve of a Jennings bit if held across it at
an angle as shown in Fig. 13 (B).   Thus we have the curious feature
that a straight edge can form a curve.   However, all this is getting
hypothetical rather than practical.

You will realize that a narrow chisel has to be kept more in the
correct place than a wide one, and that is why the latter is easier to
use; also, being heavier, it damps out vibration and is easier to hold
too.   Everything is in its favour except the price, availability, and

FIG. 14.   CHISEL USED WITH SCRAPING ACTION
The cutting edge is worn away rapidly.

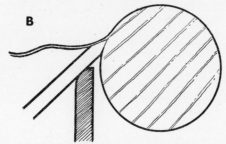

FIG. 15.   CORRECT METHOD OF USING THE CHISEL.
Long shavings are removed resulting in a cleaner finish.
The cutting edge lasts much longer.

the fact that it needs room to work on, but it is worth having if you
are serious.

Some books advise you to use a plane to turn with.   Well, the
principle is all right, but I see no advantage, and have never used one.
Barbers use a cut-throat razor for their enjoyment, whereas we use
safety razors and mowing machines, so let's be professional in turning and use the naked blade of steel, and get a lovely clean cut.

You may have such a curly grained piece of wood that the chisel just splinters up the wood in the same way that a hand plane will. A gouge may solve your difficulty. This cuts through the fibres of the wood in a different way from a chisel, and you will better see this point if you cut a curve as in Fig. 13 (A) with the chisel and then cut one with the gouge. The chisel tends to lift the fibres whereas a gouge cuts through them. Try it for yourself. Words are not so good as actions to find out what happens.

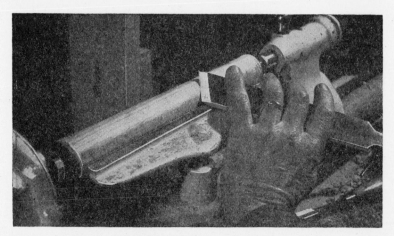

FIG. 16. ENLARGED VIEW OF HOW CHISEL IS HELD

A gouge would scarcely be suitable to shave with as it would cause grooves in the face, and fibres stand up on mine anyhow. So our gouge will leave grooves, but these are better than pieces being splintered out on troublesome wood.

Letting the bevel rub. In all chisel work the bevel must rub the work just as I explained for the gouge. It prevents the tool from digging in. There is more in it than that, however. Fig. 14 shows the chisel used with a scraping action and it is clear that the wood acts as a sort of grindstone and takes off the edge quickly. When used in the proper way as in Fig. 15 the chisel cuts the wood and the shavings pare off sweetly on top. Used in this way the cutting edge will last a lot longer.

CHAPTER 4 : SCRAPING

AFTER having told you so often about cutting wood as it prefers to be cut, I now have to speak about wood as it does not mind being cut, to wit, scraping it. Let me say at once, however, that it is not good practice for spindle turning, that is, work between centres, although it is for face turning. One of my friends has several tons of ebony, boxwood, and rosewood, for he is an exotic wood merchant, and much of this will be turned by scraper tools, because it does not mind such treatment. To me it is a far less interesting way of turning. Ordinary spindle turning demands movement of tools in

FIG. I. INK POT IN IMITATION OF BELL.
This is a good example of work which must be scraped in parts

three directions, whereas in this scraping action the tool moves rather in one plane only.

The great advantage is that fine detail work can be easily done without much skill, but only suitable wood should be treated in this way. One school for instructors advocates scraping cuts for safety reasons. Well, if my advice is followed there is no danger at all in learning

45

to turn properly. I wonder whether girls are taught to cook in the refrigerator to save burning themselves?

Where scraping is essential. Now, I turned a number of ink-pots from some old oak beams from a belfry and I had to scrape parts of them. Fig. 1 shows the design, and you just cannot turn parts of it any other way. First I turned it with a gouge to the general shape of the bell, then with a sharp-pointed tool cut each side of the little beads (see A, Fig. 1). A file was ground just a little narrower than the space between the beads, and it was left just as it was from the grinding wheel with a slight burr on it. This removed the wood and did not damage the beads. As it was

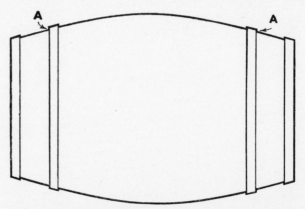

FIG. 2. SMALL BARREL WHICH NEEDS SCRAPING TO FINISH CLEANLY.
After the general shape has been turned with gouge and chisel the corners of the bands need to be scraped, especially at (A).

narrower a slight sideways movement for the final cut removed any lines the rough edge might have left on the surface of the work.

The inside was hollowed out with a scraper tool because end grain wood works nicely this way. It is much easier to cut a true hole if the tool rests flat on the rest. The tool tries to bob up and down a bit, so you rest your elbow on the tail-stock, and all is well. The lid was fitted and was turned as a solid job between centres. Some had hand-carved tops or cannons such as old bells have. Modern bells are bolted to a flat surface on the headstock, which is much more mechanical, but not so nice to look at.

Barrels are another job where a scraper tool is necessary, for a chisel to cut corner (A, Fig. 2) cleanly it must touch the wood. Can a chisel cut at all if it does not touch the wood, you may well say!

Now, if you have followed previous chapters you will have seen that the leading corner and to about half way along the cutting edge only must be allowed to cut; also that we must always cut from larger diameter to smaller. So to turn corner (A) we must either cut like sharpening a pencil the wrong way from the point end, or let the trailing corner do it, and then it will dig in nicely! So here again a scraping tool helps us.   Some barrels are turned with grooves for bands, but this does not look so well.

If the wood is not of a fibrous nature you can turn it all right by first using the chisel to cut to one corner, then turning it over to cut to the other.   Great skill will be needed to make the line of barrel follow through nicely, and it would certainly look bad if it did not do so.   You will gain most help from these notes if you try out the ways wood prefers to be cut, and also see how the tool digs in.

I have advised my daughter, who is going to Africa, to watch and see whether the top or bottom jaw moves in an alligator and crocodile, for I think they work a different way, but she says, "I'll just run when I see one."   Perhaps it does not matter, but the way wood wants to be cut and how to prevent tools digging in, does matter to a wood turner.   Sometimes a piece of turning seems nice but has a little corner that wants removing, and you feel that you may spoil it by using the chisel again.   This is a real fear as it is difficult to take just a little off with the chisel, especially if it is none too sharp. Well, we do just lay the chisel flat on the rest and scrape with it for safety's sake, but don't get into the bad habit of scraping the wood to shape when it can be properly turned.

Angle of scraping tool.   I was explaining to some choir-boy friends how unhygienic it is to kiss young ladies.   "Yes, I know, for Daphne smacked my face," said one, "but she kissed it better." Well, scraper tools can do the same, and a blind man who came to me broke a heavy file in three pieces and cut himself just because he would not let it trail a little.   He was told several times how dangerous it was to point it upwards, but simply would do it his way.

The blind man whom I taught has turned six sackfuls of bowls, and writes that he does it nicely using the gouge for the insides. His worry is that his polishing is not good enough, though he sells them.   I mention all this both as a warning and as an encouragement (I honestly believe kissing is all right—in fact, my wife of blessed memory sometimes made me late for work because of it).

Some are worried about the height of the rest in face-plate turning and spindle turning.   Well, it does not matter, but see that the tool slopes down a little when scraping.   Then when it cuts it goes away from the work, and it won't smack your face.   The idea is shown in Fig. 3. In spindle turning, of course, the bevel of the tool rests on the work, and that prevents it from digging in, which is a different principle.

Fine work. Now, such things as tiny knobs for miniature cabinets, pegs for violins, and so on are often done in boxwood, and here small scraping tools are ideal. It is advisable to oilstone these tools, as a burr is not wanted, but oilstone the bevel last. A hard marble-like stone is needed. Arkansas is ideal, but is an awful price. Still, for serious fine work I do think it worth acquiring one. Why not let a friend know when your birthday is?

The skill in turning these small items is in knowing how much pressure to apply, for a hollow in the neck of a knob would require

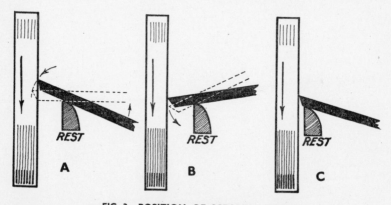

FIG. 3. POSITION OF SCRAPING TOOL.
(A) shows how tool is liable to dig in if caught in wood. At (B) the tool runs away from the wood if it catches in. Although the tool slopes up at (C) the rest is close to the work and there is no great leverage.

more than that needed in just rounding a bead. So here is another case of handling tools gently rather than using brute force.

Practice cuts. Now as you wait at the dinner-table just draw in ink on the tablecloth a few simple designs, then grip, say, a knife and pretend that the edge of the table is the rest. (With the choir-boy in mind, however, perhaps it would be better not to use ink for hygienic reasons.) Your left hand can hold the blade with the thumb underneath (which I find most natural), and with your right hand just move the handle about to follow the design. What I want you to discover is how you can push the blade forward, compressing the parts of your left hand against the table edge. You will find for larger curves it is better to grip between the fingers, but let part of the hand near the wrist-watch touch the table edge. It is a controlled movement that we are trying to get, and this action of one hand against the rest, while the other moves the tool about is ideal for this sort of face turning.

The pair of rosewood candlesticks (Fig. 4) were done in this way circa A.D. 1908, but carved by the boy next door. They are not given as an example of good design, but I'm proud of them as I was a youngster then. The central part is a copy of a silver cup you can win by sailing your yacht round the Isle of Wight. It is a good thing to keep your eyes open for nice combinations of curves, and it will surprise you in the way it will broaden your outlook on what to turn.   When in business I always looked in antique shops, some of which had old stuff in them, and in those days people intro- duced such work into the job, whereas modern stuff is designed so that it can easily be sanded smooth in a machine.

Those who have to turn large diameter work will find scraping tools a help —I'm thinking of pattern makers in particular. Their trouble is that the shape must be true to a template, and it is often built up with wood which has the grain in various directions.

FIG. 4. CANDLESTICK IN ROSEWOOD TURNED MANY YEARS AGO.

Scraping tools. Some people like to buy ready-made tools. I've a set myself made specially for brass finishers, as shown in Fig. 5. Files are quite all right, however, or, for very small work, pieces of band-saw blade.   You certainly will find yourself using just two or three and find the movement of the hands provide all the curves you need. Should your aspirations rise to making a set of chessmen, I do suggest that you grind tools to suit the main curves, and just push them in. Then all will be alike.

For some woods such as elm you can use the scraper direct from the grinding wheel. Other woods need the tool to be finished off on the oilstone. In all cases the top serrations of the file are ground away first, and the edge ground to the required shape *afterwards*.

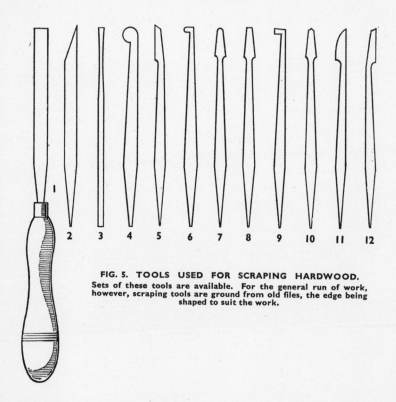

FIG. 5. TOOLS USED FOR SCRAPING HARDWOOD.
Sets of these tools are available. For the general run of work, however, scraping tools are ground from old files, the edge being shaped to suit the work.

Sometimes you get a better result using a scraping tool finished with a ticketer. This turns up the edge just as a cabinet maker's scraper is sharpened. The method of sharpening is described on page 61.

Incidentally the inside of a bowl is always finished with the scraper (see page 86). It is a help to grind several files to various shapes to suit the curvature of the bowl.

CHAPTER 5 : SHARPENING TURNING TOOLS

"IT is not what you grind away that counts, but what you leave", might be a good slogan for this chapter. Boys will quite happily make the sparks fly when grinding a knife and then blame the steel as being of no use because the blade bends and won't take an edge. A wiser boy might ask me to sharpen it, whereupon I would ask him what he wished to cut.

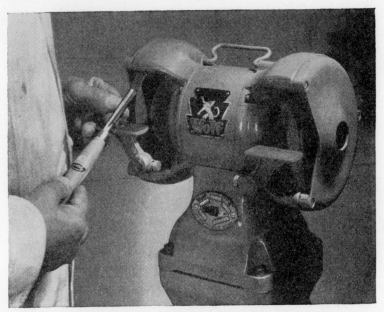

FIG. I.   GRINDING A GOUGE ON A DRY GRINDING WHEEL.
Be careful to avoid burning the edge.

How tools cut. Now for a moment let us consider cutting edges. I know that we don't use knives, etc. in wood turning but it will help in understanding the problem if we think also of the other tools. A bread knife has a notched edge and cuts bread well, but if used on cheese it would certainly not cut cleanly at all. In the first case we have a sawing action whereas the cheese needs more of a cutting action. We don't use a saw when doing wood turning, I can hear you say, but consider, what is the difference? It is chiefly that in turning it is that the wood is moving, not the tool. The action is partly cutting as we cut cheese and partly sliding along as in cutting bread.

Let us now sharpen my lady's scissors. We file or grind them, not oilstone them. The reason is that we want the fibres of cotton to catch in the slight roughness caused by the grinding wheel or file and not slide away and avoid being cut.

If the above has set you thinking it will do no harm but the problem is not quite so simple as it first seems. The turning tools you buy *will not be ground as they should be.* The gouge will have too long a bevel and the chisels a curved bevel. Don't ask me why. It is one of those curious conventions. Every new turning chisel I have seen has had a curved bevel; yet no practical turner ever uses it so. A flat bevel is always used. I mention this because you might well think that you could not go wrong if you retained the rounded bevel.

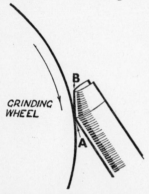

FIG. 2   GRINDING GOUGE.
The heel bears against the wheel first.

Grinding. Fig. 1 shows how I grind a gouge. I am standing quite firmly with the wheel at a height that suits me. My right hand is against my side and can rotate the gouge while my other hand steadies itself on the rest and forms a place for gouge to rest in. I should grip a chisel and slide it across the surface of the wheel, but neither hand moves about much. Thus a nice even bevel results. Some might prefer to have the rest at an angle but I find that this way suits me best.

I start to grind as in Fig. 2. The cutting edge is away from the wheel and is not spoilt. I then raise the handle until I feel the bevel nicely resting on the wheel. You can also see the sparks coming down the top surface of the tool whereas before they mostly passed beneath. Little pressure is used and no harm is done such as burning the edge, although some old craftsmen might prefer a sandstone wheel which is just an ordinary grindstone running in water. When using this pressure *is* needed. It seems to me so wet and mucky, however, that only boys and comedians would appreciate it.

I can hear the old craftsman saying "the edge will stay longer if ground on a grindstone" and this is true. Consider a diamond glass cutter. A split will go right through the glass but only a scratch shows on the surface. Well, it may be that your fast-cutting corundum wheel has caused a lot of scratches in your tool and that these are deeper than is apparent from the appearance. Still your humble servant avoids grinding to the extreme cutting edge which is oilstoned only, not ground.

Grinding wheels are certainly made in a large variety for special jobs, coarse and fine; also hard and soft bonding. My bandsawyer once sawed a stone in half, yet it was the proper wheel for sharpening some wide machine plane irons. Some are for use with a cooling liquid or they will burn the steel, so don't use any old wheel and then condemn grinding wheels as useless for the purpose.

Oilstones. Let us think about oilstones now. My father gave me a stone in a rosewood case, and it was a wonderful stone for giving a fine edge. On asking what it was, he told me "Welsh slate". Now if he had called it a fine argillaceous rock of the Cambrian period containing small colourless mica in size 6,000 to the inch I should have been more impressed. Its layer formation might have explained why it cuts rather than scores the surface. When I was in North Wales I saw mountains made of it, and they are probably there now, but it varies immensely, and I do think someone ought to make tests in different places to find a sort that does sharpen tools. Marble too is often worth experiment.

A barber once sold me a Dutch hone. It shows a black smear in the oil when used indicating that steel is being removed, yet it is so smooth that it could scarcely scratch. It is similar to Arkansas stone which comes from U.S.A. Another good stone is the Washita which is a bit coarser and most suitable for our use. It is difficult to buy washita stones to-day in Britain. All this is perhaps rather ideal; most of you will use a manufactured stone. If you do, use the fine grade.

Oilstoning a chisel. More important than the kind of stone is how you use it. The way I describe is for *wood turners* not carpenters or cabinet makers. The aim is not to shorten the bevel nor dub it over because in turning it has to rub the work. If we make a little short oilstone bevel such as that in an ordinary woodworking chisel we must lift the handle end of the tool to make it cut, but as only a short bevel is rubbing the work it digs in. You can use force and make it stay where you want it to, but it is so much nicer to turn properly and let the tools just do it themselves.

Once when I was swanking at an exhibition (confession is good for the soul) I said "you only have to move the tools about and they do the work themselves." "Yes, for you, but not for us", said a man, and a chorus of six said "So say all of us".   Well it seems each one had sharpened his tools with the oilstone on the bench, moving the tool along it, and I believe that was the trouble.   In the trade we generally run the oilstone along the top of the tail-stock, the tool resting against the tightening bolt that stands up as in Fig. 3.   Of course it spoils the look of it so why not fix up a post or find a place that suits the job?

We want a place to slide the oilstone (preferably 8 in. × 2 in. ×

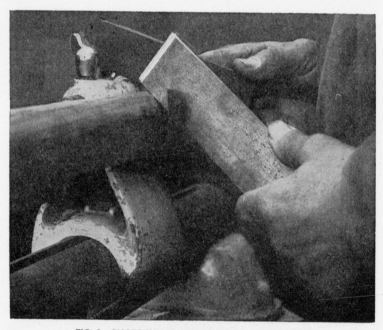

FIG. 3.   SHARPENING CHISEL WITH OILSTONE.
The chisel is supported on its side and is held stationary.   The oilstone is held flat against the bevel and rubbed back and forth.

1 in.) which is at a natural height to suit us, and a place to rest the chisel against.   We slide the oilstone backwards and forwards in a straight line with just a little oil on it, but rubbing it on the back part of the bevel away from the cutting edge.   Then as we get going nicely we can move the chisel so that the oilstone rests nicely flat on the bevel, and the little oil shows clearly what we are doing.   Too much oil would be inclined to hide the tool.   Later we can feel how the oilstone is and then we need not look so much.

The chief trouble in sharpening turning tools is to remove the burr caused by the grinding wheel, and that is why I don't grind quite to the edge if I can help it.   A coarse oilstone also puts a burr on (sometimes we can use this to advantage).

Testing.   Let us now see how to test the edge with the fingers. As you progress you will know when tools need sharpening.   At the works where we would turn 2 gross of chair legs a day, probably four or five tools would be used and they would be ground once a

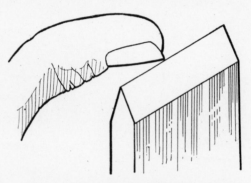

FIG. 4.   DETECTING KEEN EDGE ON CHISEL.
The finger- or thumb-nail is drawn along the edge.

day.   Some work of course might call for more frequent grinding, whereas for some beech jobs they might last for days.   In a large shop where they had fourteen lathes it was quite usual for one grind on a wet sandstone or grindstone to last the day, and this on bone dry wood.

I mention this because a lot of unnecessary grinding takes place because people *won't cut wood as it prefers to be cut*.   If you merely scrape the edge is lost in no time.   I mentioned earlier about a saw action in cutting.   Well, oak can make an edge sore or rough, and if we turned beech afterwards it would show scratches on the work. But this sore edge or one with a bite in it is ideal for cutting cleanly through the fibres of oak.   Fig. 4 shows how to detect this bite. So I don't advocate too much oilstoning and as long as no burr exists all is well.   In fact we sometimes don't oilstone at all for turning oak.   When beech and oak jobs are to be turned the beech one is done first.   So for beech, and of course similar woods a nice smooth edge is wanted and the finger-nail can detect it.   It is surprising how a small notch, quite undetected by eyesight, can cause a mark on beech.

A chisel used to turn a slight hollow as in Fig. 5 needs the corner of the bevel removed or it will score the work. Only the corner is removed. It is not ground away up to the point. It is used only for a slight hollow as a chisel does these much more cleanly than a gouge would.

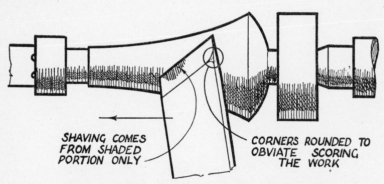

SHAVING COMES
FROM SHADED
PORTION ONLY

CORNERS ROUNDED TO
OBVIATE SCORING
THE WORK

FIG. 5. TURNING SHALLOW HOLLOW WITH CHISEL.
Unless the corner is removed it bears on the wood and scores an unsightly mark.

Grinding a gouge. Gouges are certainly ground in all sorts of ways. One of my men ground his obliquely (see Fig. 6) so that he was opposite the work with the tool held slightly sideways. So if you see some tools ground not as stated here, well don't worry; it takes all sorts to make a world. Let us consider our ¾-in. or 1-in. roughing-out gouge. It is ground square across as in Fig. 7, and it

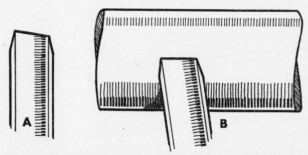

FIG. 6. GOUGE GROUND AT ANGLE FOR ROUGHING OUT.

needs its corners left projecting as much as the rest of the edge. Fig. 1 shows exactly how I would grind it, just twisting the handle and resting the end as shown, giving a nice even true bevel. If you have a small L and S gouge, say $\frac{3}{8}$ in. for face plate or bowl work that too is ground square across (see Chapter 8 for why).

But spindle work demands a different end to the gouge (except in the roughing-out gouge) and a lot depends on whether we wish to do hollows nearly the size of gouge or larger hollows. Briefly, if the gouge seems too large for the hollow make it more pointed. This makes a smaller length of cutting edge but is not so troublesome to use. Fig. 8 shows clearly just how to grind them, but be sure when grinding that you are looking at the actual cutting edge, not a burr of steel which when oilstoned away leaves the tool quite another shape. Men in the trade like a lathe with a wood bed, and the usual thing is to jab the tool into it to push this false edge or burr away.

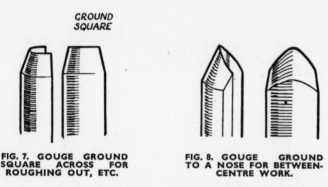

FIG. 7. GOUGE GROUND SQUARE ACROSS FOR ROUGHING OUT, ETC.

FIG. 8. GOUGE GROUND TO A NOSE FOR BETWEEN-CENTRE WORK.

You cannot do this with a metal lathe bed, but you can push the tool into any block of wood.

With continuous use a series of hollows is worn into the edge of the oilstone and these are helpful. Be careful not to round over the bevel. The inside is not so important and the only difficulty is to remove the burr cleanly. The gouge is rested on the tail-stock or post, and the oilstone rubbed up and down with a bit more pressure on the cutting edge as in Fig. 9. You can if you like just hold the gouge in the hand and move the oilstone up and down. Gouges are not so fussy as chisels, but the bevel rubs on the work just the same.

The buzz or bruzze needs both sides balanced in grinding and this is quite a test in grinding. The tool is not essential, however. There should be a little point at the bottom of the V because of the small hollow in the tool. This seems to help the tool in working. Fig. 10 shows better than words just what to look for. These tools always seem too light in section and break off occasionally which must be good for the tool trade (or is it?). They make them lop-sided

5—P.W.T.

too, and I don't think anyone is keen on them, but for repetition work in the furniture trade they have their uses (or used to have before automatics began to do repetition work).

Scraping tools. We will now consider scraping tools made out of files, and let me say at once we use them as they are without altering the temper, for all thick files are softer inside and are ideal.

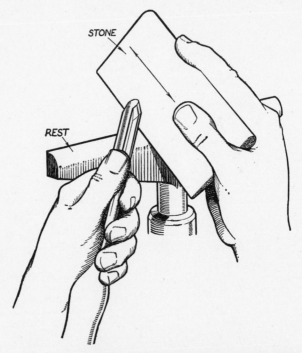

FIG. 9. SHARPENING THE GOUGE AGAINST THE REST.
The gouge is held stationary against the rest and the stone moved across it. The gouge is gradually revolved so that all parts of the edge are sharpened. The bevel is kept flat.

They are not liable to snap off if you use thick ones. The bevel is not important but it is certainly not acute—in fact it could be nearly square across. The side view, E, Fig. 12 shows it. This would absorb heat from the cutting edge and also give it better support. There is no need for a long bevel in any case. The bevel does not rub the work as the paring cut of a chisel would do. I find the shape (C) is nice for bowl turning, etc., but the scrapers can be ground to suit the job in hand. A set of tools used for brass turning is shown on page 50, and might please those who want to do small scraper work in the lathe in such nice woods as box or ebony. These tools are used just as we buy them, and I suggest that the only burr needed is that caused by the oilstone, so oilstone the bevel *after* rubbing the face.

By trailing your thumb across the surface of the tool as in Fig. 11 you can feel this little burr catching your skin, but for bowl turning in elm or oak we need a larger and coarser burr such as that caused by the grinding wheel.

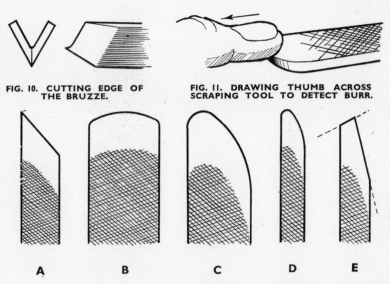

FIG. 10. CUTTING EDGE OF THE BRUZZE.

FIG. 11. DRAWING THUMB ACROSS SCRAPING TOOL TO DETECT BURR.

A   B   C   D   E

FIG. 12. SCRAPING TOOLS GROUND TO VARYING SHAPES FROM OLD FILES. The shape is made to suit the work in hand. Note how the top is ground off at a slight angle.

Grinding. I hold the file which I'm grinding in much the same way as in Fig. 1, but at a much less bevel, and for sides of curves I push it up higher on the wheel as Fig. 13 shows. The same result could be got by moving the end in a circle or arc, but it is more involved in the movement required than laying the tool over a little and pushing it up on the wheel.

Just a word of warning on grinding anything held freely in the hand as I am doing in Fig. 1. To grind an ordinary chisel or gouge with a bevel is all right but grinding a tool nearly square across could cause a dig into the wheel and give trouble. In any case it would chatter and kick if pressed too heavily. So perhaps you would prefer to have the tool supported on the rest or the little flat platform provided on grinding machines.

The burr is caused by the wheel and is probably the result of the sparks burning themselves back on to the edge. So we grind the bevel last and that is all there is to it. You can grind it for too long a period, however, so that instead of a neat burr you have quite a mess on the top of the tool and this won't cut. Just once round on the wheel seems right for the final grind. Stroke your finger off the edge to detect it, and learn just what is best for the job in hand.

Use of the ticketer. Beech, sycamore, and similar woods do not require such a coarse burr as elm, oak, and some mahogany, etc.

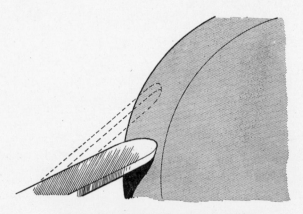

FIG. 13. GRINDING FILE ON THE WHEEL.

and here we want a "ticketed" edge such as cabinet-makers have on their scrapers. We first oilstone the edge with the finest stone so that there is no burr and we test it with the fingers. A "bite" when you run the finger-nail along the edge is desirable. Now with a ticketer, which may be any ¼-in. dead hard steel rod, we bend the edge over. First we rub the ticketer on top of the tool with heavy pressure, then on the bevel with pressure rather on edge, as in Fig. 14. You should have a smooth edge, but some steel won't ticket and some ticketers are not hard or smooth enough.

I once carried out a test on forty-eight steels for a steel-maker to find the best to use for a tool to be ticketed. The best was from Swedish iron turned into steel and used very soft indeed. The action of ticketing it seemed to harden the edge, and it bent up easily. It is a subject needing research. A German maker and

French maker of hand scrapers may come to the mind of an older craftsman.

It's a mystery what makes good scraper steel. In many ways steel is a mystery in any case. In my tool box is a thick file sawed through with a soft steel bandsaw with no teeth on it, like sawing a file in two using the back of a hand saw. Friction saws run very fast indeed and pressure is needed, but it is the hard file that suffers not the soft saw blade! Now cast steel or carbon steel as used in

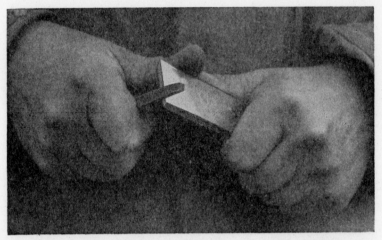

FIG. 14. TURNING EDGE OF SCRAPING TOOL WITH TICKETER.
A hard steel rod is used to turn the edge similarly to that of a cabinet-maker's scraper.

razors is harder than high speed steel, but engineers don't use cast steel tools so much because high speed steel is so much better for retaining its edge. There are qualities in steel besides hardness, and one maker of cold chisels claims that it can be forced through two and a half inches of mild steel, and when blunt can be filed sharp again.

This is mentioned because I've been told we are behind the times and we ought to use tipped tools which have an extremely hard insert of carbide in them. These tools quite happily turn the hard scale of cast iron off at good speed, but their cutting edge is weak if made thin and easily breaks, and that would be like turning with tools made of glass which would be hard but brittle.

In plain English if your tools won't keep sharp they are probably all right, but you are holding them at work wrongly or running the lathe far too fast *without removing any wood*, and just wearing them away. To temper them harder would not help much—in fact the edge might break away. Often a heavier cut enables a tool to keep sharp longer, for the pressure and hard rubbing is further back than the extreme cutting edge, but don't try it when shaving.

Just a final word; the sparks from a grinding wheel can burn themselves into glasses so stand sideways to avoid them if they are liable to come near. Of course they are harmful to the eyeballs too. A piece of glass held in the stream of sparks will show clearly afterwards as you can feel them in the glass if you pass the hand across.

LARGE PATTERN BEING TURNED ON A SMALL LATHE.
The machine is the Coronet Major, and a special pulley has been incorporated to reduce the r.p.m. to a rate suitable for the work.

By courtesy of the Coronet Tool Co.

CHAPTER 6 : PRONG CHUCKS, CENTRES, STEADIES

A FURNITURE manufacturer once told me he always kept "Ginger" wild because he did more work that way. Well, centres in a wood-turning lathe that will not drive, or are always burning, can make one wild, and throwing the wood across the shop does not help very much. So let us have a few thoughts on what is required of these centres, for, of the large number of lathes I have come across in fifty years of turning, only one lathe manufacturer sends out the centres as we use them in High Wycombe.

Prong chuck. It is obvious that the purpose of the prong chuck is to rotate the wood. It seems unnecessary to mention it, but so many gradually wear and develop faults that prevent them from doing their work. When a prong chuck fails to be satisfactory the usual plan is to sharpen its fangs. This makes its central point relatively

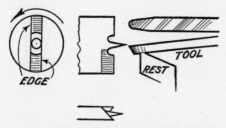

FIG. 1. THREE VIEWS OF PRONG CHUCK, SHOWING HOW IT CAN BE TRUED WITH A FILE GROUND TO A SPECIAL SHAPE.

longer, and if too long or fat it will prevent the chuck from penetrating the wood, because the fangs cannot reach without undue strain being put on the lathe by screwing up the tail-stock centre extra hard. This centre then starts to make the wood burn and we blame it, whereas the blame should be on the other end.

When a centre is always burning look first to the chuck end to see what is wrong. There are three main faults we may find: the point is too long or fat; the space between the point and fangs needs filing away; or the fangs are too blunt. The first fault can be cured by putting the T rest near to it, and turning it with the end of a file suitably ground for the job as in Fig. 1. It is advisable to run the lathe not too fast. The cutting edge of the file is as shown, not as when we turn wood. The tool is moved forward at centre height as in the sketch which is a side view of the job. The shape of the tool is a small radius to suit the hollow which is between the point and fangs.

This brings us to the second fault, that of the space between point and fangs needing to be filed away (if we cannot manage to turn it away when we are touching up the point). Some chucks have no space and so long as nothing prevents the point and fangs from penetrating wood it is all right. Most people give the fangs far too sharp a bevel, or even put a bevel both sides. Some makes of chuck are such poor stuff they bend backwards in use; and some turners

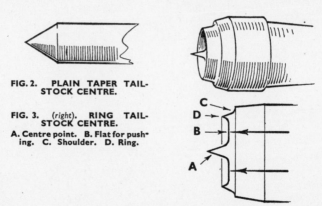

FIG. 2.   PLAIN   TAPER   TAIL-
           STOCK CENTRE.

FIG. 3.   (right).   RING   TAIL-
           STOCK CENTRE.
A. Centre point.   B. Flat for pushing.   C. Shoulder.   D. Ring.

catch their tools on them in use. Aim at making the driving face flat, and the trailing angle at about 45°.

In the trade the lathe is seldom stopped. Instead the tail-stock centre is eased back and the hand put around the wood which should stop. This is a good policy as small A/C motors do not like a lot of stopping and starting. If the wood hangs on the chuck end and perhaps flies out when tail-stock centre is eased back look for a burred or bent fang. The remedy is obvious. So if your lathe will not easily give up driving the work when you slacken the back centre do not get nervous. Try to find out why. If you keep your hand round the work no harm will come to you.

Tail-stock centre. Let us now consider the tail-stock centre. We use two types; a plain taper of 60° such as engineers use, best for heavy work such as 10-in. squares in hard oak (Fig. 2), and the ring centre (Fig. 3). The home craftsman will find the latter the more suitable. It is here where some manufacturers slip up, for they do not realize that the job of this centre is to *push*. They remove the very part of centre that could push. A taper point in use works its way into the end grain; so will a ring, and we have to give the tail-stock wheel another turn. Often we give it too much, so straining the lathe and causing the centre to start burning. Fig. 3 shows a good ring centre. The flat part between point and ring can push the wood against the prong chuck and will not penetrate nor burn.

Fig. 3 is enlarged to show the idea more clearly. A diameter of $\frac{1}{4}$ in. to $\frac{5}{8}$ in. would be the two limits probably for general use. Now (A) is the point and does not project too much from the ring. It would depend on the wood to be turned generally speaking. The softer the wood the longer it should be for centering purposes. The part (B) pushes and when it has pushed and still more pressure is

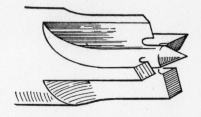

FIG. 4. FOUR-PRONGED CHUCK.

applied part (C) can push as well. Note that (C) is not cone shaped but is flat. (D) is the ring and has no sharp corners to start burning or to collect dust, and is not very pronounced. I have made many of these centres from set-screws. Ordinary mild steel is just good enough if you do not hammer hard wood true. These seem to wear very smooth. If we had a lot of $\frac{5}{8}$-in. pins to turn we would use a $\frac{5}{8}$-in. diameter centre. Cutting pins to size is then easy. This may seem a lot of bother about lathe centres, but a happy pair of centres will help you to enjoy wood turning. No set sizes are given as lathes vary; also the work we do.

Trade lathe centres screw in, either $\frac{5}{8}$ in. or $\frac{3}{4}$ in. and I prefer this type of centre for wood-turning lathes rather than the tapered kind. The reason is that one can unscrew a centre without hurting the bearings, and a hollow mandrel is of little use in wood-turning lathes. A four-prong chuck is useful for chair legs and similar work (see Fig. 4), and a wide two-prong chuck, called a chisel chuck, is best for turning back feet of chairs. A small chisel chuck is best for small lathes as four-prongs need more pressure from the tail-stock to make them drive. Some woods easily split if a faulty chisel chuck is used.   The driving edges should not radiate from the centre as both fangs would be in one line.   Also it is important not to have the bevel too acute so that the chuck has a splitting action.

One last word to help when you have a lot of pins to turn to one size.   You can have a tail-stock centre made to the same diameter and you have only to chisel to that size.   It avoids the unnecessary

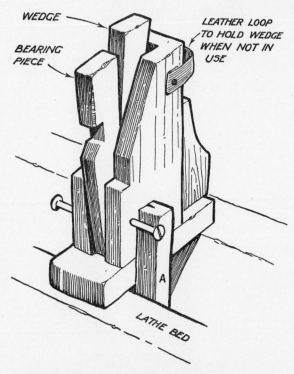

WEDGE

LEATHER LOOP
TO HOLD WEDGE
WHEN NOT IN
USE

BEARING
PIECE

A

LATHE BED

FIG. 5. BACK STEADY USED ON AN OLD LATHE.
This apparently crude device is most effective in use.   It is sketched
from an old lathe in the Museum at High Wycombe, Bucks.

use of callipers.   It is a good thing to have a drill, and a centre the same size.   In practice only a few sizes are needed.

Wood steadies.   Early wood-turning for chairs was done in the forest itself on a pole or bodger's lathe around the High Wycombe district, and one is still at work there (or was when I was writing this).   In the town a treadle wheel lathe could frequently be found in a little shed at the end of the garden even within a few years back. It was hard work to treadle all day, however, and so sometimes others helped. Then steam power came, driving long lengths of shafting which worked various machines, and the chips and shavings fed the furnace, so we had cheap power. The electric motor of to-day works on a different principle, and shaving disposal is a

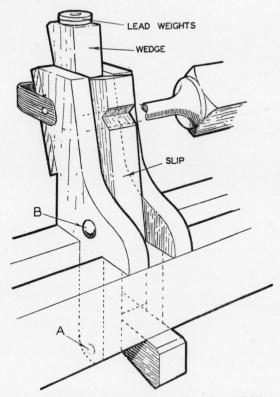

FIG. 6. SIMPLE YET EFFECTIVE STEADY FOR WOOD
The great advantage of this is that it maintains a constant light pressure. At the same time it is positive in that it resists thrust. Furthermore it automatically takes up to the reduced size of the wood when the latter is turned right opposite it.

problem, but of course electricity is handy and eliminates shafting, etc. To start or stop a machine a belt was slid along from a fixed pulley to a loose pulley, an ideal system for wood-turning lathes. The modern push-button control is all right for some jobs, but it would be impossible to turn the back legs of chairs in this way as in some jobs we want a gradual start.

The old-time lathe. When you bought a lathe you had a countershaft with a three-speed cone at one end, and two pulleys about 10 in. diameter to take a 2-in. belt, one fixed to the shaft, and the other free to rotate. You bought a built-up wooden pulley to fix on to the shaft to give you the speed you wanted. The lathe had a heavy head-stock which you could only just lift, and had a central bolt hanging down. There was a tail-stock nearly as heavy, and a T rest stand, both with long bolts, and these had flat bars of iron as nuts to save using spanners.

The T rest was a casting with at least a 1-in. diameter pin, and was used for face turning work only, as in those days only chairs were made. It had a 5-h.p. motor and 10-in. centres, and if you wanted to do large diameter discs you just packed some wood under the head-stock. I could turn large table tops for letting lino in for teashop tables (far better than eating on the floor lino). The lathe beds were two pieces of British Columbian pine, and you had them planed up on the machine, and a piece sideways formed the stand at the end. Mine took 15 ft. between centres, and was used for turning newels which reached to the upstairs landings from the ground floor. We see these old lathes in local factories being made redundant by the changing design of furniture, the automatic lathe doing the mass production stuff.

Steady. But let us now study the steady which was wanted chiefly for back legs and armchair legs. One is shown in Fig. 5 and is in the High Wycombe museum. These steadies were very crudely made. Wood-turners are notoriously bad at making things. In fact, if no wood-turning was needed, they would have to go plank-stacking in the timber-yard. A few lathe manufacturers do make steadies, and although they are ideal for metal, they are of little use for wood. A steady for metal has to retain the work solidly against the thrust of the tool, and metal does not bend one way more than the other as wood does. I've yet to see metal burn as wood can.

So for wood we require a gentle thrust to counteract its tendency to bend more easily one way than the other (this is often the start of chatter in wood turning). We want a simple means of relieving this thrust when the wood starts burning; and it must have enough clearance so that a square can revolve before the wood is turned round. It must not be fussy as to size, for when we reduce the wood opposite the steady, it must adjust itself. Then, as only a few jobs require a steady, it must be easily removed from the lathe.

The wood-turner needing a steady would ask the timber-yard foreman for a chunk of throw-out wood. This he would ponder over, and at a suitable moment ask the band sawyer to saw out something as in Fig. 6. There always seemed to be a box of old bolts, and one was fitted at (A) and another (probably ½ in.) with a wing nut on at (B). A chair-maker was enlisted to screw a block of wood on the back, and it was tried several times in the lathe to see whether the wood could revolve with it in place, and whether it would come out with the rest still in. The slip with a notch in it was pivoted at (B), and the width of wedge tried out by experiment.

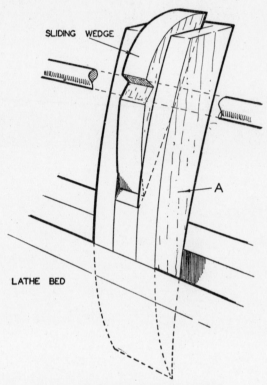

SLIDING WEDGE

A

LATHE BED

FIG. 7. SIMPLE ALTERNATIVE STEADY.
Although not so effective as the steady in Fig. 6, this has its uses for some jobs.

In the end, with the co-operation of the whole factory except the polishing shop, the job was done, a fine museum piece of work, which gladdened the heart, for it worked (that was the only reason it was made). It would help us if manufacturers would give us a start and provide the main part to fit on to the lathe bed, which is invariably round, and less handy than the two oblong sections of wood to fit it to.

Why the steady works. Let us see why it is so good. Fig. 6 shows a wedge against the underside of the lathe bed, pressing against the bolt, so forming a simple way of holding the steady firmly, yet easily removed by a biff. The wedge can be easily removed, and is to hand at the back of the steady when needed. The wood slip fits the work, and needs no special fitting. Its crudeness in no way hinders its use. If the wood becomes hot a rub with some candle-

FIG. 8.   SIMPLE WOOD STEADY MADE FOR MYFORD LATHE.
The idea could be adapted to suit any make of lathe. (A) is the wedge which tends to drop down by gravity and keep the slip (B) up to the work. The slip is pivoted at (C).

grease will cure it. Should the work require more thrust, it can be given by nailing lead on to the wedge; or a rubber band can be passed over the top of the wedge and down beneath.

One man I know has a screw which grips the wedge. He pushes the wedge down and tightens the screw which holds it there. A wing nut exerts enough pressure to prevent the slip from rising or falling, but allows it to swivel by action of the wedge. Some use a wood screw, but the principle is all you need worry about. If you draw a square at centre height at your lathe bed, you can work one out for your lathe. The wedge can be quite wide as when it is withdrawn the slip goes further back out of the way. If you wish to do long stuff it is an ideal steady, and well worth making.

Alternative steady. If your lathe has twin beds you can make a simpler one which helps to steady the work, but is not as good. Still it has its uses as it can be quickly slipped into the bed where it is needed. Fig. 7 shows its principle. Part (A) slides down and so forces the slip against the work, but it does not prevent the work from moving up and down.

Perhaps you want a still simpler steady. Well, a wedge inserted between the rest and the work helps to do some jobs, but it burns easily as it has only a line contact.

Preliminary rounding. These steadies must have the work round, and back legs can be tiresome to turn round. You lightly put your hand round the revolving back leg, and, with a $\frac{3}{8}$-in. gouge, turn the part where the steady is to come. For an extremely difficult job you can rasp it round first. The hand is around the work, not so much as a steady, but to catch the job if it flies out. Remember that we are thinking of long, springy items, or they would not require a steady. If you find that it wears through to the bone, or if you can smell burning pork, try another way. Still, to put your hand around the work is helpful and safe.

CHAPTER 7 : CHUCKING JOBS

SHALL we have a few thoughts on chucking your job? A simple way of holding a bowl on a face plate is to fix it with wood screws. If a piece of baize is fixed on the bottom afterwards it hides the holes. Now, if my mother's only son had made the face plate its

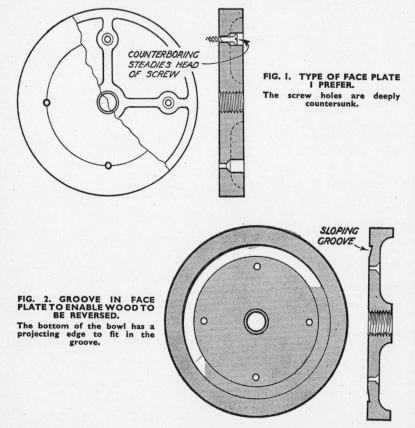

COUNTERBORING
STEADIES HEAD
OF SCREW

**FIG. I. TYPE OF FACE PLATE
I PREFER.**
The screw holes are deeply
countersunk.

SLOPING
GROOVE

**FIG. 2. GROOVE IN FACE
PLATE TO ENABLE WOOD TO
BE REVERSED.**
The bottom of the bowl has a
projecting edge to fit in the
groove.

holes would have been made to hold a definite screw size and be deeply countersunk. The screw would remain square to the wood, because its head would fit the hole (see Fig. 1). We like short, fat screws so that we can turn the bowl thin without the screws passing right through. I lay the baize on the bottom of the bowl, and rub the corner of the bottom of the bowl with a piece of chalk. The size can be seen quite easily.

A bowl. The block of wood to form a bowl has its outer side turned true to enable the inside to be hollowed out. I have a blind friend who turns a lot of bowls, and he leaves a short pin about ¾ in. diameter on the bottom and this fits into a hole in a disc of wood. In his case this disc is fixed to the face plate proper with four wing nuts and ordinary screws hold the bowl to the disc. This short pin he removes later with a plane which is held in his vice, and he drags the bowl across it. There is no reason why you could not leave a pin and let it go into the face plate. If the face plate stands out from

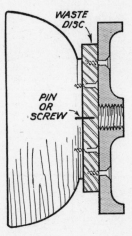

FIG. 3. WASTE DISC WITH CENTRE PIN TO SIMPLIFY REVERSING.
The outside is turned first and a little hole made in centre. When the wood is reversed this hole fits over the pin.

the nose of the mandrel you could turn a shallow depression there for most likely it is threaded and so not truly circular.

One method I adopted for this reversing business was to turn a sloping groove in the face plate as in Fig. 2. When I turned the bottom of the bowl I made the edge project to catch in it. There is the added advantage that, should the bowl warp, this edge could be trued up on a sheet of glasspaper resting on a flat surface.

It may well be that you prefer your bowl fixed to a disc of wood (as the blind man does) and you could put a pin in this disc which would centralize the bowl, for the little hole required would be cut while turning the bottom of the bowl (see Fig. 3).

When fixing wood to the face plate if a screw seems to pull it out of truth, I ignore that screw and try another, and do this screw last.

6—P.W.T.

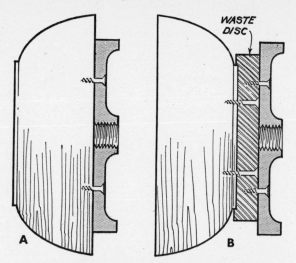

FIG. 4. ARRANGEMENT FOR REVERSING WOOD.
After turning outside as at (A) a waste block is fixed to the face plate. A recess is turned in this to receive the base of the bowl. If the face plate has a double set of holes the second set of screws can pass right through the disc into the bowl.

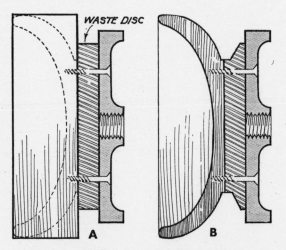

FIG. 5. TURNING WITH SINGLE CHUCKING.
Both inside and outside are turned in one operation.

It is the grain of the wood that makes the screws wander; they will find the soft spots.

Quite often a 6-in. face plate is the correct size for the bottom of the bowl, and so you can just watch that these agree. Another method is that in Fig. 4. You fix the wood to the face plate and turn the outside as at (A) the screws being near the middle where the wood is turned away later. It is removed from the face plate and a waste block screwed to the latter as at (B). A recess is turned in the waste block *exactly* to the size of the bottom of the bowl as shown, and the latter held in it with screws. Many face plates have a double set of holes, and clearance holes are bored right through the waste block to enable screws to pass through into the bowl.

Alternative chucking. Yet another plan is to turn the whole

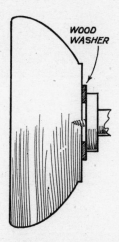

FIG. 6. SCREW CHUCK USED TO HOLD BOWL.
The washer is advisable as it ensures that the wood beds solidly.

WOOD WASHER

bowl from one side in a single operation as in Fig. 5. The waste block has clearance holes and the fixing screws pass through both it and the face plate into the wood for the bowl. This method is handy when the wood you have is green and has to dry out. You fix the wood as at (A), rough turn it to a generous oversize, and leave to dry out for as long as possible. If you do a lot of bowls you can leave them for months. They will probably twist and shrink across the grain, and that is why you leave the wood of ample thickness. You then re-chuck as at (B) and complete the turning.

In this method you have to turn away the waste block to an extent, but this does not matter. It is also necessary when you re-chuck the wood to plane the bottom flat as it is almost sure to have twisted slightly in the drying-out process.

Those who want the best work will want no screw holes, etc., and they can glue a bottom of waste wood on the bowl and put the screws into that. It is split off when finished. As an alternative you can follow the method in Fig. 4, except that the bowl is glued into the recess with newspaper between instead of being screwed. It holds strongly for turning, but is easily prised away afterwards.

Screw chuck. Whichever way you use make sure that the bowl is firm and does not rock owing to an uneven surface as this is

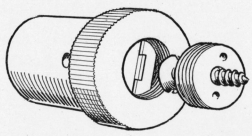

FIG. 7. SPECIAL SCREW POINT CHUCK FOR CORONET LATHE.
An ordinary wood screw is used. This avoids the fault so many screw chucks have, that of screw point breaking off.

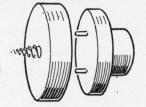

FIG. 8. SCREW POINT CHUCK MADE IN TWO PARTS.

asking for trouble. It is a good idea also to see that the rest is firm. A good central screw chuck of 3 in. diameter as in Fig. 6 can hold a 10-in. bowl easily—I have done many hundreds on one. Be sure to note how fat and short the screw is, however. A fat screw can swell the wood around it, so either use a thin ply washer between the wood and chuck face, or remove the swollen part and put the block of wood on again, testing to see that it is free from any tendency to rock. The thin washer is the better method if the wood is inclined to be a trouble to unscrew.

This is a useful chuck for turning wheels on, such as are used on toys and tea trollies, etc. as the work can be easily reversed. It is an advantage if the chuck is in two parts as in Fig. 8 as then we can use the backplate as a small face plate. We could make special discs to hold say a pot lid with a much smaller screw.

The ideal is to thread the backplate and then we have a chuck for holding egg-cups, or cruet sets absolutely rigidly with no fear of accidents such as catching the fingers on the jaws of a three-jaw chuck or the wood flying out. This chuck as shown in Fig. 9 is really the answer for school use, and could be made in the engineering department as it is only simple turning and screw cutting. It is shown in

FIG. 9. CHUCK TO HOLD WOOD FOR EGG-CUPS, ETC.
A sectional view of the chuck is given on page 92.

section in Fig. 3, page 92. I have made twenty using 26 threads per inch which could, of course, be varied. I left the bevel rough so that the wood caught in the ring and twisted it tighter. I made a bar as in Fig. 4, page 92, to undo it. I have never used it, but boys might need it.

A disc of ply as Fig. 10 might help to centralize wood on the face plate, and variations to suit your needs can be thought of. We found a disc as in Fig. 11 useful to mark the bases of floor standard or smoker's companions where the three feet came.

The holes in egg-cups are turned first, unless the chuck in Fig. 9 is used. If your lathe is true you can fix a nose piece on your screw chuck as in Fig. 12. This will drive the egg-cup block nicely between centres. The advantage of doing it this way round is that you remove the centre mark as you part the bottom off. A disadvantage is that the block might slip on the nose piece. Perhaps chalking it will help, but we put in a gramophone needle as shown. It was not seen on the finished job. You could turn half an egg and run this on the tail-stock centre as in Fig. 13. It ought to be flush with the top of the hole in the block or it will twist out.

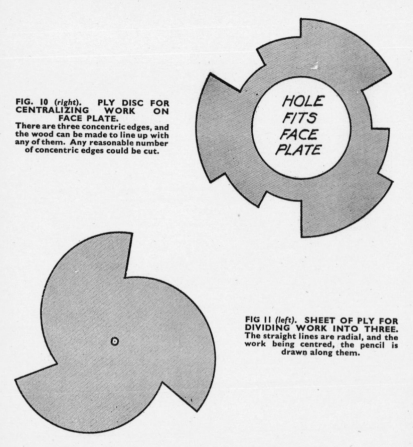

FIG. 10 (right). PLY DISC FOR CENTRALIZING WORK ON FACE PLATE.
There are three concentric edges, and the wood can be made to line up with any of them. Any reasonable number of concentric edges could be cut.

HOLE FITS FACE PLATE

FIG 11 (left). SHEET OF PLY FOR DIVIDING WORK INTO THREE. The straight lines are radial, and the work being centred, the pencil is drawn along them.

Serviette rings. These are held on a tapered mandrel as in Fig. 14. This can be chalked to give a grip, and if you leave it rough it will help to drive the ring better. You might like to use wood with the heart in it for rings as this would show a nice grain. I have done a few from an apple tree branch from my orchard. The hole must be made before it starts to split, even if it has to be trued up again after seasoning.

Fig. 15 shows a useful chuck for holding round blocks of wood when boring the holes for egg-cups or serviette rings. It can be made from a faulty piece of wood and there is no need to bore the hole smooth (which is easy). The same idea of pushing wood into a hole can be used for discs for bread-boards if care is taken not to make your cuts too heavy. If it does fly out you will not be in line of rotation and it will only be a window gone. It does save screw

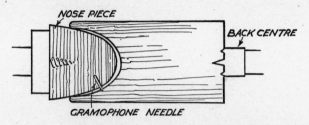

FIG. 12. NOSE PIECE ON SCREW CHUCK FOR EGG-CUPS.

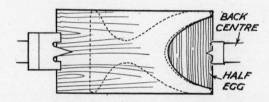

FIG. 13. ALTERNATIVE WITH NOSE ON BACK CENTRE.

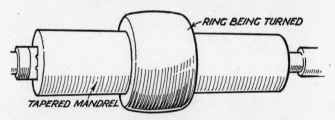

FIG. 14. TAPERED MANDREL TO HOLD SERVIETTE RINGS.

holes in the bottom of the bread-board. My men have done fancy lids, bases, and bread-boards this way, sometimes trapping a piece of garnet cloth in to give added grip.

If you wish to make the idea more complicated a tapered pin as in Fig. 16 is effective. Be sure to put in as shown as then the wood

tends to tighten itself when turned.   You might like to cut a groove
in the wood for this to engage in.   Note the direction of the grain
of the wood to prevent the tapered pin from splitting it.

Back legs of chairs.   Fig. 17 shows how the back legs of chairs
are held.   The more the pressure between centres the tighter the
wedge grips.   If balanced nicely quite a good speed can be used if

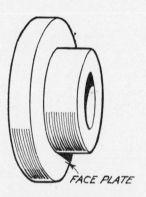

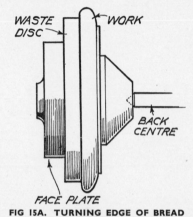

FIG. 15. SIMPLE CHUCK FOR SMALL ROUND BLOCKS.
The wood makes a friction fit in the hole.

FIG 15A. TURNING EDGE OF BREAD BOARD.
The work is held by friction between the waste disc and the cone-shaped block on the back centre.

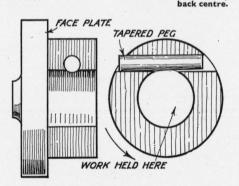

FIG. 16. CHUCK TO HOLD SMALL ROUND BLOCKS.
It is in wood screwed to face plate. Note direction of grain.

you are not nervous.   A visitor at my works asked, "Do they often
hit you?" and my foreman replied, "No, generally just once".   The
precautions to prevent that "once" are to chalk the wood and wedge
to prevent it from slipping about.   We have used so much chalk in

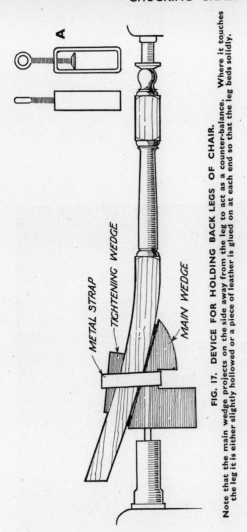

METAL STRAP

TIGHTENING WEDGE

MAIN WEDGE

A

FIG. 17. DEVICE FOR HOLDING BACK LEGS OF CHAIR.

Note that the main wedge projects on the side away from the leg to act as a counter-balance. Where it touches the leg it is either slightly hollowed or a piece of leather is glued on at each end so that the leg beds solidly.

High Wycombe that it's in a valley now. You can either hollow the wedge or put on pieces of thin leather as in Fig. 17 so that the ends of the driving wedge do press hard on the work. The link or strap can have a screw in as at (A) or a wedge driven in as shown in Fig. 17, but it must tighten when end pressure is put on, so it should be at a slight angle.

The main wedge is as far up the back leg as possible to shorten the distance between centres. The length of the driving centre and design of the bearings govern this. This main wedge is either loaded with lead or made much larger so that it balances the job. If held lightly between centres you can detect whether it is out of balance by the heavy part going down. Large numbers of back legs have been done in this way, but now a patent lathe is made with an extended bearing to hold the back leg at seat level, enabling them to be done at top speed.

CHAPTER 8 : TURNING BOWLS

AS an example let us take a small bowl of about 6 in. diameter by 3 in. deep, useful for nuts or sweets, but probably used for the oddments one accumulates in a home. A simple chuck with a central screw would be ample to hold it in the lathe, but do see that the disc is firm as the screw tends to swell the wood round the hole, causing the disc to rock. This is a cause of chatter, and can be obviated

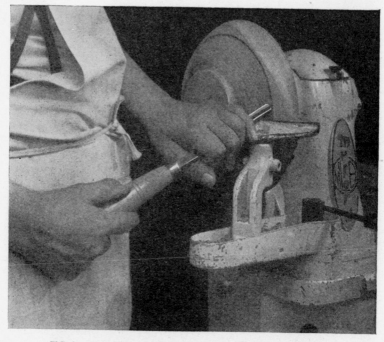

FIG. I. TURNING OUTSIDE OF BOWL WITH ⅜-in. GOUGE.
To see the movement of the gouge turn to Figs. 3 and 4, page 84.

by the use of a ply disc as in Fig. 2, or by just removing the swelling round the hole.

Alternatively the disc can be fixed to the face plate with screws (see page 73).

The gouge. The outside and bottom of the bowl are done first, using a gouge. Mine is $\frac{3}{8}$ in. measured across the inside of the hollow, and is ample to take all the power a $\frac{1}{2}$-h.p. motor can give. It is a "long and strong" type of deep pattern, but this is hard to get, and expensive, and you can get on quite well without it. The term "long and strong" is a trade term for a stouter section tool than normal, and you will see why I suggest its use later on. An illustration of it appears on page 14.

Speed. "What speed do I need?" is often asked. About 1,000 r.p.m. or a speed slower than the usual speed of $\frac{1}{2}$-h.p. motors (which is about 1,400) is satisfactory. However, aim at a heavy cut at slow speed, rather than a high speed at which the tool merely brings off dust, and loses its edge. The rigidity of the lathe and its rest governs speed quite a lot.

Another question I am always asked is, "What height should the

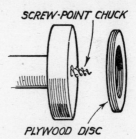

FIG. 2. DEVICE TO PREVENT WOOD FROM ROCKING ON THE SCREW-POINT CHUCK.

SCREW-POINT CHUCK

PLYWOOD DISC

rest be?" This does not matter much, and if you follow the instructions you will find out what suits you. Some of us are upright, some bent; lathes vary; people have their own preference in holding tools; and some like to stand with the face near to see what is happening, others well up and away from the shavings.

Cutting action of gouge. Now the following I lay great stress on. To get it right is the whole art of turning. It is "cutting wood as it prefers to be cut." When I am swanking at a demonstration, I get the tool correct, and hold the handle between two fingers, taking off long rope-like shavings that run down the hollow of the gouge. The tool does not dig in, and can use all the power with no effort on my part. If you find you have to hold the tool tightly you are probably holding it at a wrong angle to the work, so do please try to find out this straightway.

Get a cup or basin and your gouge (if anyone thinks you crackers, well don't worry; I have been so for years). Hold your basin as

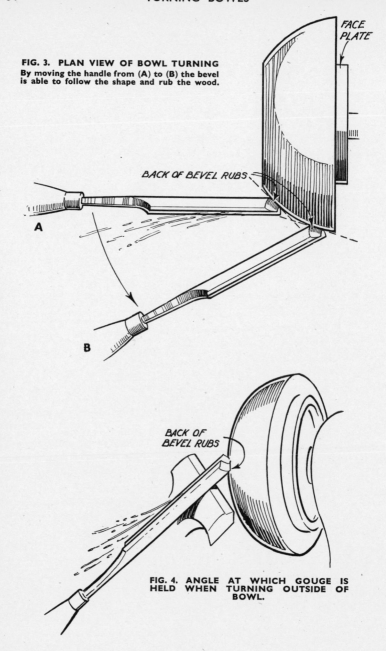

FACE PLATE

FIG. 3. PLAN VIEW OF BOWL TURNING
By moving the handle from (A) to (B) the bevel is able to follow the shape and rub the wood.

BACK OF BEVEL RUBS

A

B

BACK OF BEVEL RUBS

FIG. 4. ANGLE AT WHICH GOUGE IS HELD WHEN TURNING OUTSIDE OF BOWL.

though you were turning it and hold your gouge slightly on its side, but with its short ground bevel rubbing the cup. Fig. 3 will help you to see what I mean. Move the tool from (A) to (B), and you will notice that the end of the handle moves through quite a distance. You govern the shape of the bowl by how you move the end of the handle. Perhaps you can picture yourself taking a heavier or lighter cut by adjusting the bevel to the work.

The tool points upwards as in Figs. 1 and 4, and you will see now the most suitable height of rest for you. Possibly the lathe bed may get in the way, but you will find you can get over this trouble in practice.

Sharpening angle of gouge. Now gouges for face plate turning are best ground square across and at the angle shown in Fig. 5 (about 45°), not as you buy them, which is far too long a bevel (don't

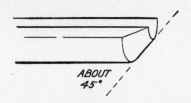

ABOUT
45°

FIG. 5. SHARPENING ANGLE OF GOUGE.

ask me why they do it). You may think that the corners will dig in, but in practice they do not. I suggest that you hold the gouge to the cup again. If your gouge has too long a bevel it has to be pointed upwards at such an angle that it is not possible to use the rubbing effect of its bevel to avoid its digging into the work.

Also, if the tool is ground to a nose point instead of straight across, you will notice that the cutting edge recedes from the work just where you want it to cut, which is from the centre of the gouge to one side.

The bottom of the bowl must be finished as it is not possible to work on it again. It should be slightly hollow. One other point; before you take it from the lathe make a little centre hole to go on to the chuck when it is reversed. If, however, you are using the face plate rather than the screw point chuck this is unnecessary.

I have drawn the shape I like in Fig. 6, but it is a free country so you can do your own design. Between you and me, however, a shape that is not drawn with compasses does not show up if it is not nicely true. If you doubt this try turning a ball.

Hollowing. The block is now on the chuck for hollowing out,

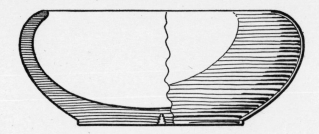

FIG. 6. ATTRACTIVE SHAPE FOR BOWL.

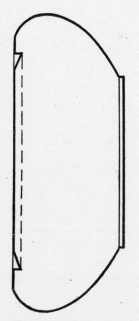

FIG. 7. PRELIMINARY NICK
MADE WITH SCRAPING TOOL
BEFORE GOUGE IS USED FOR
INSIDE OF BOWL.

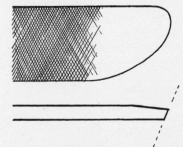

FIG. 8. SCRAPING TOOL MADE
FROM OLD FILE.

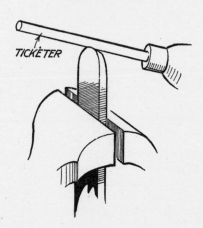

TICKETER

FIG. 9. TURNING EDGE OF SCRAP-
ING TOOL WITH TICKETER.

nice and firm owing to the slightly hollow surface.   In the case of
face plate fixing remember to use short screws; otherwise they will
project through the bottom of the bowl and leave unsightly marks,
to say nothing of knocking the edge off the turning tool.   First
make a groove near the edge of the bowl as in Fig. 7.   This is to
prevent the gouge from sliding across as it is started.   It is formed
by using the chisel flat on the rest.   You cannot have the bevel of the
tool rubbing until it has something to rub on, and this groove
provides a rubbing surface for it.

The same principle is employed in using the gouge inside as
described in turning the outside; keep the bevel rubbing.   If in your
design there is a flat part at the bottom of the bowl, hold the tool
near the rest and slide your hand along.   Fig. 6, page 19 is a view
of the bowl from above showing how the gouge is used with its bevel
rubbing.

Scraping rather than cutting.   I now describe a tool which
calls for entirely different treatment, so do not apply the same
methods as those just described.

Many like this tool as it has no funny ways, and requires little
skill in its use.   However, it needs skill in getting a good edge on it,
and in finding suitable steel.   A file is generally all right, but not
so satisfactory as an old mortise chisel.   Fig. 8 shows how to grind
it.   Note that the curve as shown is more useful than if it is just a
half-round.   The side view shows the angle at which it is ground.
Note that the top surface is ground well away as the middle of the
file is softer and better for use.

There are two ways of sharpening it after grinding to shape.   One
way is simply to give it a *few* rubs with a coarse stone on the bevel
to leave a burr on the face or top surface.   For some woods it can
be used direct from the grindstone, in which case the edge is always
ground *after* the top serrations have been ground away.   This kind
of sharpening is best for elm, oak, and poor mahogany as the burr
grips the fibres, and removes them.   For walnut, beech, or similar
woods an edge put on with a ticketer is better as this cuts it cleanly.
As a comparison think of a bread knife with its notches cutting bread,
and a ham knife cutting slices of ham.   (I won't suggest that you
cut up the ham now as we must get on with our bowl.)

To those not familiar with a "ticketer", it is only a hard steel
rod.   The tool is first given a fine edge with an oil stone.   Mine is
a hone as used by barbers and cost £5, but any fine stone is satisfactory.   The ticketer is rubbed across the top face of the tool with
pressure at the edge rather, evenly all over.   Then two or three rubs
on the bevel, again towards the edge, will put a good edge on the

tool as shown in Fig. 9. Cabinet-makers use the ticketer when sharpening a scraper for cleaning up veneers, etc. The turned-up edge for turning is similar.

Hunting for steel and experimenting on sharpening these scraping tools can be most interesting. Many turners prefer them entirely for face turning as they cut the parts of work which are against the grain better then gouges do. Of course, we never finish off with a gouge—unless we wish work to be entirely hand-turned. The

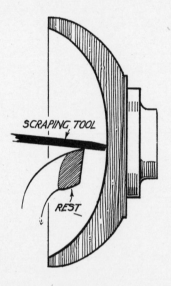

SCRAPING TOOL

REST

FIG. 10. FINISHING INSIDE OF BOWL WITH SCRAPING TOOL. When the grain runs across as here only fine cuts should be made, specially for final cuts.

scraper tool points slightly downwards from the rest, which is about centre height, see Fig. 10. If you point it upwards it will dig in badly and may break the tool. Try to take a shaving off rather than just let the tool rub the work as the edge soon goes off if it only rubs the work.

There is little more to add in using these tools, but to get the "feel" of them try the rest a little away from the work, and you will feel a nice bite when the sharpening angle of tool is right and the angle you are holding it is correct. When you have mastered it, long ribbons of shavings will go over your head, and you will get the thrill of craftsmanship.

To finish off the surface should be glasspapered. The thin edge especially is best done with glasspaper; fibres are inclined to break out if turned. Let the paper trail in the direction of rotation or it may double your fingers back. Too high a speed will burn them, too, so I do urge you not to rely on glasspaper to do the job of turning. Rather try to turn your bowl cleanly. It always seems to look much better if turned without a lot of papering. Few woods need no glasspapering, however; the smoother the surface the better the polish.

Wet wood. Sometimes you will have wood for turning which is not dry. As wood for bowls is invariably thick it takes a long time to dry out naturally. In this case the best plan is to rough turn the wood whilst it is wet, and then set it aside for as long as possible to dry before finishing it off. The hollowing-out speeds up the drying considerably. When you come to finish it off you will probably find

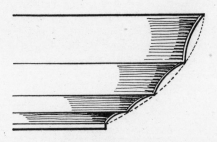

FIG. 11. HOW BOWL WITH HOLLOWS FOLLOWS
SWEEPING CURVE.

that it has become oval and most likely twisted. Run a plane over the bottom to level it before re-chucking it. It is of course necessary to leave the bowl very full in size when rough turning, as otherwise there will not be enough wood left for the finished shape.

In Fig. 11 is a bowl design with a series of shallow hollows on the outside. Note, however, that the general line of the bowl follows a sweeping curve as shown by the dotted line. Pencil lines are marked on the revolving bowl at the ridges, and the hollows formed with a rounded scraping tool.

Incidentally in any bowl in which the grain runs across there will be two places in which the grain is liable to tear out (the idea is shown clearly in Fig. 8, page 146). The remedy is to keep the scraping tool sharp and remove only fine finishing cuts. In this way all roughness can be taken out.

Small flexible hand scrapers shaped with a curved end are extremely useful for troublesome places. They are used with the work still (not revolving).

7—P.W.T.

THE purpose of this chapter is not so much to give designs as to discuss the problems involved in their turning and to see how to overcome them. When you have a number of similar items to turn you soon learn to devise methods of doing the work well and quickly.

EGG-CUPS

Holding the wood. Now from long experience I am sure that it is advisable to bore the hole first, or, at least, only to round the blocks before finishing the outside. The holding of the blocks firm in the lathe is really the trouble, as turning the hollow involves rather a wide cut. You may have a three-jaw chuck such as engineers use, and if you turn a little rim on the end of the block to catch in the little hollow in the corner of the jaws, they will be held quite firmly. In fact using this method I recently turned a large hole 12 in. long in a piece of cherry to hold a scroll to present to Her Majesty the Queen. A three-jaw chuck is not often found in a wood-

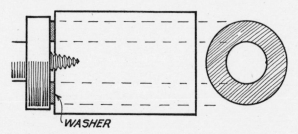

FIG. I. SCREW CHUCK WITH WASHER FOR EGG-CUP.

turner's kit, however, as its jaws can injure you. In any case it soon becomes clogged with dust, so do not shout up the chimney for one at Christmas.

Some hold the block on the screw chuck, and, as egg-cups are turned in a close-grained wood, it is often successful. Be sure they do not rock, however. The trouble is that screws do not hold well in end grain wood, so rather than screw up too tight put a washer behind the block as in Fig. 1. This will also avoid rocking. A

90

better way is to bore a hole in a thick piece of wood fixed to the face-plate to take the blocks after they have been rounded to size. Do not bore the hole too smooth (this should be easy), and take care that the blocks fit, especially at the front end, or they will come out. The blocks are driven into the hole, and either an oblique hole or a hole in the middle, if your lathe mandrel is hollow, will enable you to poke them out with a rod when finished.

A useful form of screw chuck in which an ordinary wood screw is used is shown on page 76. The weakest part of a screw chuck is that the screw is liable to snap off with continued use. Any size of ordinary countersunk screw within the limits of the chuck can be used.

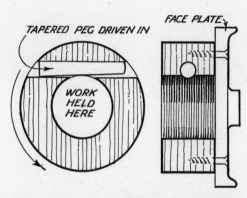

FIG. 2. DEVICE FOR HOLDING WOOD WHEN TURNING.

Wood chuck. If you delight in and enjoy making something complicated, a taper pin driven in as in Fig. 2 holds the work firmly, and is on the same principle as the fixing of bicycle pedal cranks. It is advisable to use a large-diameter block so that the pin does not protrude, and note that the pin goes in away from you when the hole is above centre. This is because the wood will tend to pull it in more as you turn. The hole is across the grain, or you might split the block. If you are still not satisfied turn a little groove in the egg-cup block where the taper pin goes.

Special chuck. I have left the best way of holding blocks until the last, but it requires an engineer's lathe to make it (see Fig. 3). It is described because many schools have a metal lathe, and some wood turners have friends. One advantage is that there is no need for great accuracy in rounding the blocks, and although a bevelled part is left on the block this bevel need not be continuous if the size does not allow it.   Another good point is that there are no dangerous projections; the whole thing is quite smooth, so school teachers will sleep better at night.   The whole of the egg-cup can be turned, inside and out, but it does waste a short piece in the chuck.   The many chucks I have made have 26 threads per inch, and I mention this because it has proved satisfactory in use.   A fine thread holds tighter than a coarse one.   If you are worried about undoing it, a tool as Fig. 4 will grip it well, though I have found the one I made not wanted.   Still the idea may help in removing things, say, from a screw chuck that have got too tight to remove with the hands alone.

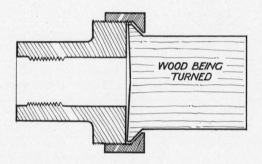

FIG. 3.   METAL CHUCK TO HOLD WOOD FOR EGG-CUP.
A photograph of a chuck of this type appears on page 77.

WOOD BEING TURNED

IRON OR STRONG WOOD LEVER

ROLLER CAUGHT IN LOOP OF BELT

WORK TO BE UNDONE

FIG. 4.   DEVICE TO UNDO WORK TIGHTLY HELD IN SCREW CHUCK.

STRONG LEATHER BELT

The wood is roughly turned to the required shape between centres first.

Hollowing out.   Our wood ought to be held firmly now by one of the methods, so we will hollow it out, a quite simple matter. A turner was giving a demonstration and used a special rest fitted with a handle.   This was placed on the rest proper, and used to support the tool which was held in the other hand.   But at his works he did not do it that way.   You do not need anything so elaborate. A scraper tool, made from an old file a little smaller profile than an egg is what you require; that shown in Fig. 5 would be ideal as we are dealing with close-grained wood.

I would like you to follow closely the following as it is quite possible to rake out the wood and leave a poor finish if you do not understand the principle. Now it is a fact that a gentleman once gave me a first-class lathe for saying "Don't turn the taper on that leg from the small diameter end; you would not sharpen a pencil that way." The idea is so simple that it seems silly to mention it, but in fact this very principle of cutting wood the way a pencil is sharpened is extremely important. *"Cutting wood as it prefers to be cut"* I call it, and in spindle turning it means always cutting from larger diameter to smaller.

To get the same effect in our hole in the egg-cup we must start in the middle at the bottom, and work outwards. I think that is clear.

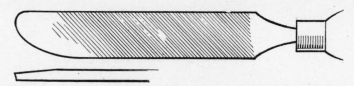

FIG. 5. SCRAPING TOOL MADE FROM OLD FILE.

In sharpening a pencil we probably hold the knife at an angle so that it slices rather than cuts squarely across. A paring cut is much nicer, and the same effect is got by holding the chisel at an angle in spindle work. To get this paring action in our hole we must point the tool upwards so that the point of the tool is higher, or we can lift the right-hand side of the tool from the rest which has a similar effect. If you do this you will get a cleaner cut.

It may be that your lathe is rather light and chatters. Well it helps if the right-hand side of the cutter rubs the work as it comes up. The idea is shown in Fig. 6. In fact many tools use this action for doing long holes 6 ft. long and 3 in. diameter in textile rollers and holes in ships' metal shafts, so it may help you in some of your turning problems. Many use a small gouge for doing this hollow in egg-cups, but its cutting action is wrong as we ought to start at the bottom and come out. Try it, and you may succeed as it is a nice piece of work, but it requires skill, and for that reason I say "Try it".

Egg-cups are usually done in sets, and a drill helps some people to get them all the same depth. I am thinking of a large drill held in tail-stock chuck, and just a pencil mark on it as in Fig. 7. The drill

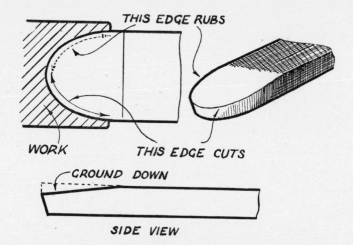

FIG. 6. HOLLOWING TOOL FOR INSIDE OF EGG-CUP.

An old file makes an excellent tool for this work. In use one edge cuts while the other rubs. Note that the upper face is ground down in order to use the file's soft centre.

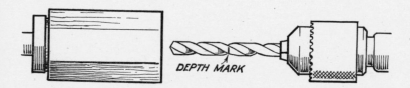

FIG. 7. PRELIMINARY HOLE BEING DRILLED.

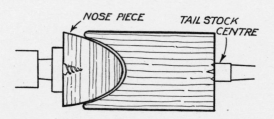

FIG. 8. WOOD HELD ON HALF-EGG ATTACHED TO NOSE PIECE.

is stationary, and the mark lasts quite a time in showing how deep to bore the hole. The diameter of the hole can be checked with dividers, taking care that the point bears on the rest near to you before you let it touch the work (see Fig. 9). Generally we prefer a pencil mark and a piece of card or ply, as dividers are liable to shift. If you must have a template for the shape of the hole, well do so, but it is quite unnecessary. If you use an actual egg as the lathe is going, please let me know how you get on, but do not send the results.

While we are doing the hole it is helpful to do the top, either square across or with a small radius according to the design. With just a rub of paper we then finish our hole.

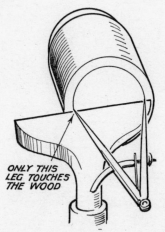

FIG. 9.   HOW END OF WOOD IS MARKED   WITH   DIVIDERS   TO SHOW EXTENT OF HOLLOW.

ONLY THIS LEG TOUCHES THE WOOD

Turning the outside. Now we will mount the block to finish off the outside, and if your lathe runs truly, that is the two centres are in line, I recommend that you turn a nose piece fixed on your screw chuck, like half an egg only longer. Your hole will fix on that, and the tail-stock centre will push against the bottom of the egg-cup as in Fig. 8. Thus it will be easy to cut the bottom of the egg-cup cleanly down. If you are worried by the half-egg of wood not driving the work, rub a little chalk on it. At the factory we put a little nail in it, and filed it to a point. It may be of interest to you that our ring centre in the tail-stock for turning egg-cups was less than $\frac{1}{4}$ in. diameter and so did not absorb much power.

If your lathe is not quite true, turn half an egg or less so that it fits the hole in the block and is about flush with top of the egg-cup. You must make it a nice fit. If too long it will not be firm when you start turning. Let this half-egg run on the tail-stock centre, and oil it well to prevent it from burning on the centre. Sometimes chalking will stop it moving about in its hole.

Designs. Now comes the great moment when we turn it to our own design, and I am sure your first attempts will be quite exclusive. Please do not think I am disparaging your work as many amateurs

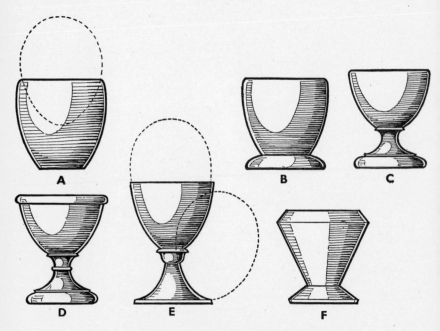

FIG. 10. SIX DESIGNS FOR EGG-CUPS.
A stand with recesses to hold egg-cups could also be turned.

do extremely fine work, and I am trying to help. Someone once said "there should be nothing in a design without a reason for it". Well (A) Fig. 10 suits that all right, and, as we always steady an egg-cup in use, it would be quite satisfactory. It is similar to a *Virol* jar which was designed by a famous man, but a foot will help to make it more steady so (B) will provide that. Tradition seems to want a small neck such as those on china cups and wine glasses, so here is health to (C). For some reason necks always look best thin, and then we find we must put something round them to make them larger. So we will copy the architect when he wants to make a pillar look fatter (D).

Art students are fond of designing around imaginary circles, and

can create a cat, or bird using circles and ovals to start off with.
Using a couple of eggs (E) is the result. Some may see a modern
look in (F), though the artist may well say that it is hopeless to ask
a hen to lay an egg to suit it. Incidentally straight lines in turning
are best if curved a little (if you know what I mean); concave to give

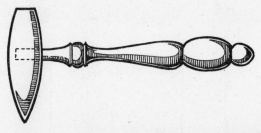

FIG. 11. MINIATURE MALLET FOR CRACKING EGGS.
These are quite unnecessary but they make a turning job.

a lighter look and convex to give a heavier look. A long parallel
spindle is inclined to look hollow. We could go on with these
designs indefinitely but it does seem that the simpler designs look
best. Of course, if you like your eggs fried you won't need a design
for our egg-cup at all.

Mallets. Mallets are a luxury at the table. Although their use
is to break the egg with, other means are just as effective. But
perhaps a little game of table croquet or golf will liven the meal up.
I have only drawn one (Fig. 11), but I think it is worth while in a
happy household to have some.

SERVIETTE RINGS

The same system of holding the wood for doing the hole in our
egg-cups is used except, of course, that we bore a plain hole. Fig. 12
gives several designs. It is good practice to see how cleanly we can
bore this hole by holding the tool so that it pares the wood out. If
we hold it level the fibres of wood will tend to be raked out, and the
tool tends to chatter as well. To do the outside of the ring we
just drive it on to a slightly tapered piece of wood held between
centres, and chalk it should it tend to slip (Fig. 13).

You may have some wood perhaps with the heart in it, and normally it would split as it dries if turned into, say, a leg. It is quite all
right for serviette rings providing that it is not split already. If it is
green wood (unseasoned) bore it out, and leave it for a time. Wood

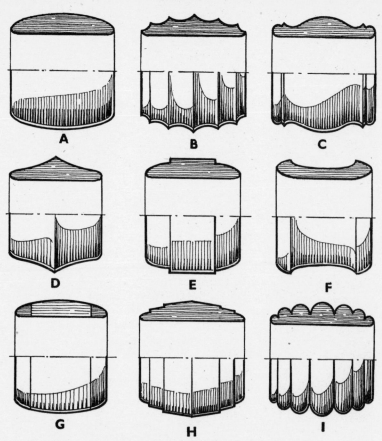

FIG. 12.   DESIGNS FOR SERVIETTE RINGS IN PART SECTION.

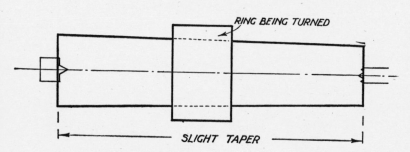

FIG. 13.   WOOD FOR SERVIETTE RINGS HELD ON TAPERED PIECE.

turned this way has a nice grain which we cannot have in other articles because it will split. There is a famous college near Windsor that complained that my serviette rings were not thick enough, for in throwing them about at the table they break. Well they evidently have their use, but on this score I am in favour of mallets as well.

FIG. 14. SET OF RINGS BUILT UP IN TWO WOODS.
These rings were turned by E. C. Elstree-Wilson to whom we are indebted for this photograph.

There is just one point in boring the hole in the mallet and similar jobs. The drill will wander unless you bore it across the layers of grain (which is best) or with them. There are I know bits such as the *Forstner* which bore nicely in any direction, but are not often found, so if you put a little point on your twist drill when you grind it you won't have so much trouble in drilling wood true.

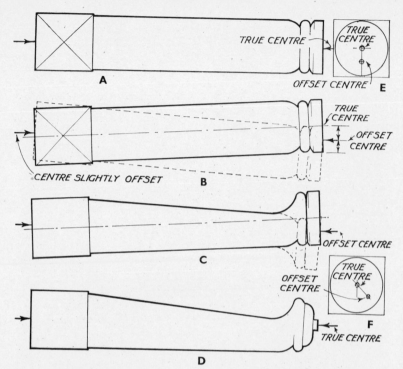

FIG. 15.   A. Both ends at true centre, and wood turned to a cylinder except the square.   B. Wood offset at tailstock midway between true centre and edge of wood. Headstock end slightly offset other way.   C. Wood turned down to taper in line with "cone" (see Fig. 16). D. Wood back at true centre and toe turned.   E. Direction of offsetting for round table. F. Direction of offsetting for square stool.

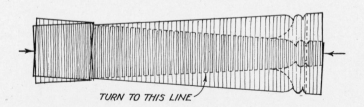

FIG. 16. HOW "CONE" APPEARS ON REVOLVING WOOD.
The wood is turned down to the dotted line including the hollow at the foot.

CABRIOLE LEG

We come now to a leg much in favour for stools, and easy to do. Its top part ought to be shaped by hand, but we are wood turners. You can, of course, do it all complete with corner pieces, and only turn the toe, which is very helpful.   Incidentally we earned 12s. an hour doing these toes at 1½d. each, but there was never enough of them.   The first thing is to turn the leg as in Fig. 15A, and then to put it out of truth (B) about half way between the true centre and the

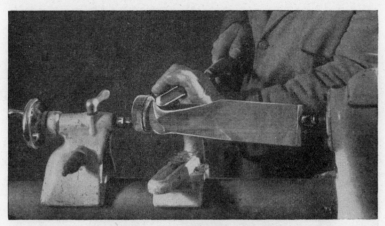

FIG. 17. PHOTOGRAPH OF CABRIOLE LEG BEING TURNED.
This shows how the wood is offset at the centres.

outside edge.   For round stools or coffee tables it is out of true towards one side (E), but for square stools towards a corner (F).   If we did it to a corner in a round stool it would appear to be marching round.   It shows a finer sense of observation if we make the grain of the wood follow the leg.   Few squares of wood have the grain running straight down them.   Fig. 17 shows the work in the lathe.

As the wood revolves we can see the bead; also the outline of a cone. The latter appears solid, whilst the rest can be partly seen through as it revolves as shown in Fig. 16.   With a large gouge we turn away the leg to the cone just avoiding touching the bead.   The gouge is not twisted as is usual in using gouges, but if you use a small gouge twist it as you do hollows in a normal way.   The gouge is $\frac{3}{4}$ in. ground squarely across, and so the shavings come off from different parts as we move it round the hollow, taking care we just let the bevel rub in the hollow.   The gouge is right for sliding down the leg, too, but is followed by a fine cut with the chisel.

The little bead at the ankle on page 28 is not usual; in fact it weakens the leg, but it looks nice. The top of the leg has to be knocked true so as to have full diameter near the bead. Glasspaper

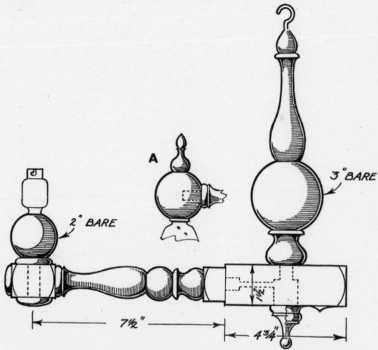

FIG. 18. DESIGN FOR PENDANT WITH EITHER THREE OR FOUR ARMS.
If the hanging type of lamp and shade is preferred the detail at A can be followed.

is a useful stuff for turners, although I have not used it for many years. It will soften the unevenness caused where true centre meets out of centre at the top of the leg. (In High Wycombe we use partly worn garnet cloth and paper from the furniture firms.) Now we set the leg to run on its true centre and round the bottom of the leg (Fig. 15D). This prevents weakness in the toe; it also is nicer to move about on carpets, etc.

BALLS

The pendant in Fig. 18 is given, not so much as a design, but because it exemplifies some interesting work in turning, notably in ball turning.

Turning balls. All sorts of things in art are repeated, music especially, and it does seem to show a pattern. In this design it is a ball, or rather ten of them. The finer points to remember in the design are that balls are best done *round*. It is quite an art, and makes you feel proud when you have done one. (Quite honestly I do too, but I usually used to avoid them when I was an employer.)

To make a good job of turning balls, calliper the diameter of the wood as turned, and measure along the same length. Cut down, using either a ¼-in. chisel or the corner of the long cornered chisel. We have now the diameter and length right as in Fig. 19.

In large balls use the small gouge. Other balls are best done

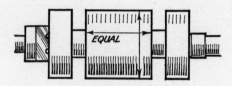

FIG. 19. PRELIMINARY STAGE IN TURNING A BALL.

using a ½-in. chisel ground square across, but any size *would* do it. The gouge, say ⅜-in. half-round, is started square to the work, with the underneath bevel touching as at (A), Fig. 20. The rest is not too near. The handle moves to left and the cutting edge goes to the right (B and C). It does not slide along the rest as it does this right-hand half of the ball. The handle is also lifted in a circular motion as Fig. 20 shows. Note how the tool swivels on the rest, and is twisted too as it goes over. The height of the rest does not matter; just suit yourself, but if too near the work it makes the movement too severe to control. The underneath bevel rubs the work and does not dig in if you observe this rule. Generally turners do not work on top of the work enough. The gouge will not do a clean corner, but this is easy to correct with the point of the long-cornered chisel.

For smaller balls I suggested a chisel ground square across, and the reason is that it avoids having two goes at it. The heel of the long-cornered chisel is best for doing gentle curves, but the point for when you get more round the curve. Therefore you have to twist the chisel over in doing a ball, but if you use one ground square across the job is done in one movement. The difficulty is the start on top of the ball, but if you use the right-hand corner of the tool and rest the bevel of the chisel on top of the wood (which means keeping the handle end low) all will be well. The handle is to the left which gives the tool a paring action same as a long-cornered chisel would do.

The above is for the right-hand half of the ball, and you can easily follow it for the other half. The handle is moved in a rising circular movement, and it is this that governs the shape of the ball. You can take it from me that wood-turners detest ball designs, but feel proud when they do them nicely, which is true craftsmanship. There is far more joy in mastering something difficult than dodging

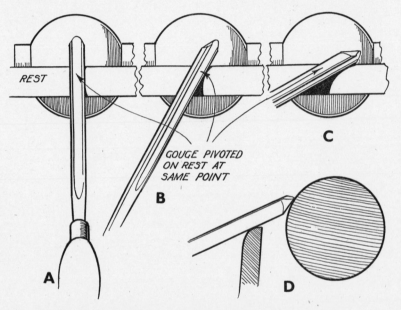

FIG. 20. HOW BALL IS TURNED USING THE ⅜-in. GOUGE

Start the cut as at A, and, pivoting the gouge on the rest, move handle to the left as at B and C, twisting the gouge over on to its side. D is a side view.

round it and introducing something else, so get some scrap wood, and try doing a few balls as practice.

Angle of tools. The fault of many wood-turners is that they hold the tools far too tightly and try to force them around, whereas a gentle touch is much more likely to produce good work. The angle at which a tool is held is well worth a careful study. If correct the tool will not dig in, and you will enjoy a thrill that only the true craftsman can have. If the job, whatever it is, need not be done well, need it be done at all? I would like you to think on this point as too many never strive for perfection. They themselves suffer, and never enjoy the thrill of successful accomplishment that could be theirs.

It is odd that I am explaining how to do a ball as I generally recommend avoiding curves that can be done with compasses, but a ball is the only shape that looks the same from all angles. Now the upright part in Fig. 18 has not quite the same outline as the arms, because we look at it from a low angle. It therefore has the neck longer, and thinner as shown.

Centre boss. The central boss can be square, or round having four or three arms, just as you like. It is $4\frac{3}{4}$ in. across and, as it has to be mounted on the face plate to recess it for the wires, you may as well turn it as shown.

Holes. The holes and pins can be a headache when it comes to

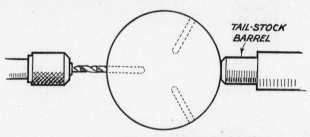

FIG. 21. HOW HOLES IN THE BALL ARE DRILLED.
The centre is removed from the tailstock.

fixing it all up, and care taken here is well repaid. The holes are best done first as the drill governs their size and this in turn governs the pin size. We used Russell Jennings bits just the same as cabinet-makers use. Ask for "dowel" bits as they are shorter. They are also made for machine use with a parallel shank if you like, but we used to cut off the square from the hand-brace type.

We mark where the holes are to go in our central boss, then with a $\frac{1}{8}$ in. or just over ordinary twist drill bore the holes. In the square design we use the tail-stock centre to push the wood against the drill held in the chuck. For the round boss which has three holes we take the centre out and let the tail-stock barrel push the wood as in Fig. 21. If you wish you can, when in a little way, let the wood rotate on the drill. If the rest is near you can see if the hole is going towards the centre of the boss by noting how near each side is to the rest. We just let the wood spin, and if out we push the wood with a bias to correct the error (it can break the drill). The

8—P.W.T.

trouble is that wood can be bored truly with the grain or across it, but with three radial holes we just cannot do it, so sometimes you must bore the holes and allow for the drill to wander in the bias you put so that the hole is really where you want it.

Useful template. If you are likely to want several things with three holes in them such as bases, etc., which would always stay level (whereas four feet might not) it is a good plan to make a template as shown in Fig. 22. Ours had an inch hole in it, and we just

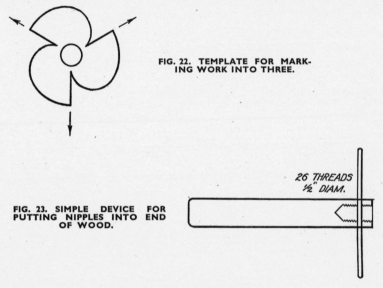

FIG. 22. TEMPLATE FOR MARK-ING WORK INTO THREE.

FIG. 23. SIMPLE DEVICE FOR PUTTING NIPPLES INTO END OF WOOD.

26 THREADS
½" DIAM.

laid it on the wood and drew lines where the arrows are. It proved very useful.

Sizes of holes. We now have $\frac{1}{8}$-in. holes in our boss. The point of the bit will follow these holes, but we have to push the blocks using the tail-stock as before. You can remove the thread on the point of bit. We left ours on, but don't try to bore holes without the pilot hole if you do leave the thread on centre of the bit. It will only pull into the wood. The correct point is a pyramid for fast rotating machine bits. The sizes of holes we used were: central one for column $\frac{3}{4}$ in., but we threaded that one; $\frac{3}{4}$ in. plain hole for arms; $\frac{5}{8}$ in. for lamp ball which had $\frac{1}{4}$ in. hole for wire, but $\frac{5}{16}$ in. for the brass nipple in its top. These nipples have $\frac{3}{8}$ in. coarse Whit. thread which screws nicely into a $\frac{5}{16}$ in. hole. The lamp holder is $\frac{1}{2}$ in. by 26 threads same as $\frac{1}{2}$ in. brass thread, but other sorts of nipples are available.   The hole for wire in arms was $\frac{5}{16}$ in. and also in column, but this also had a nipple.   A hook was screwed on here to hang it up by.   Some of these hooks have the screw in them. Their use does give that professional look to the job.

In some houses the electric bulbs are too near the ceiling.   They can hang down instead of being on top.   In this case the arm can end in a pin, say $\frac{5}{8}$ in., and go into a ball as in Fig. 18 (A).   We did the holes in the arms in rather a dangerous way.   First we drilled a $\frac{5}{16}$ in. hole using a drill in the lathe and pushed the wood on to it. When in a little way we let the wood revolve and could then easily centralize it if out.   We had now a hole which was, we hoped, in the right direction and we put a special shell auger in the lathe, letting it stick out about $8\frac{1}{2}$ in. so that it just met the hole drilled across end of arm.   The dangerous part was that it could come out in the neck, so we avoided putting our fingers there.   These shell augers will drill long true holes when the wood revolves and the augur is stationary, but it is hardly worthwhile to do it for these arms.

The cross hole in the arm for the lamp holder is bored $\frac{1}{8}$ in., then the $\frac{5}{8}$ in. dowel bit, Russell Jennings pattern, is put in the chuck of the lathe and the tail-stock, with no centre in it, brought to bear against it.   The hole is bored from both sides to save splitting out the wood.   If your bit has been sharpened badly (by someone else), that is, if the fangs have been sharpened from outside, it will split the arms.

Special device for nipples.   Now, if you are going to do electric woodware in a serious way you soon find nipples for lamp holders can be troublesome to screw in, and get all cockeyed.   So I suggest you get an old brass lamp holder or anything with a $\frac{1}{2}$ in. brass thread (26 threads per inch) in it, and make a tool, fixing it into a suitable handle.   I've made quite a lot of them for my friends as in Fig. 23, and, like me, it's darned simple but it works.   You screw the nipple into it, then screw the nipple into the wood.   You can see how true you are doing that by looking at the handle.   The handle is now unscrewed from the nipple, but, by the way of things in this world, out comes the nipple from the wood.   In fact, however, it does not do so for the pin is pulled out of the tool and so the thread is quite free in the tool.   The cross handle helps you to twist the tool easily. It is well worth making if you propose to do much in this line.

Our factory had a lot of various special things and we knew where to find them.   As you accumulate them I do suggest drawers, boxes, etc., to keep them in for shavings do hide things so easily in a turning shop.

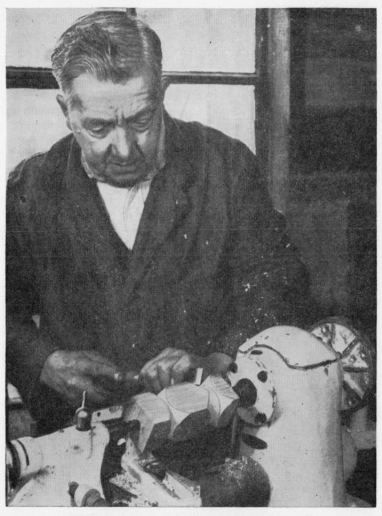

CUTTING CURVED SHOULDER WITH THE CHISEL.
This shows the second cut being made after the waste has been cleared away.

CHAPTER 10 : CUTTING DOWN SQUARES, TURNING PINS, PARTING, HOLLOWS

I NOW describe the use of the $1\frac{1}{2}$-in. long-cornered chisel in cutting down squares or pummels such as in chair legs.

Cutting down squares. Nearly all legs which are used in tables, stands, chairs, and stools have them. The square of wood from which the leg is turned is left untouched locally to enable mortises or dowel holes to be cut. It is easy enough to turn the wood between the squares with gouge and chisel. The problem is in finishing up to the square. Sometimes the finish is straight across as at A, Fig. 1. In other cases it is rounded or of serpentine shape (B and C).

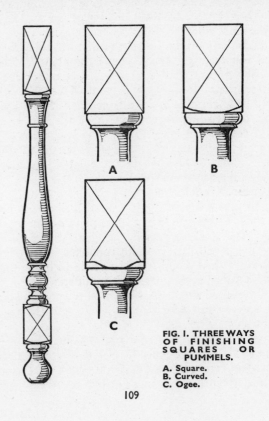

FIG. 1. THREE WAYS OF FINISHING SQUARES OR PUMMELS.

A. Square.
B. Curved.
C. Ogee.

Only one end is described as the other end is cut in the same way, but the other way round.   Fig. 2 shows what we are trying to do. In turning we mark a cross on the parts of the wood to be left square. We first hold the long-cornered chisel over the work on its edge, and, as we lift the handle, down goes the point of the chisel into the square.   It is shown away from the wood in Fig. 3 for clearness. We have a part of the square cut away in triangular shavings as shown. The handle of the tool is held to the left so that bevel (A) is in line with the cut across the work.   If the tool were held square to the work it would rub at an obtuse angle.   The bevel of the tool (B) which is underneath rubs the work and prevents digging in.   As the tool penetrates we tip part (C) over to right a little, as the shavings might get larger than we can manage.   We go in until we get a continuous line round the work.   Note that we *lift the handle* end, not push it in.

The next operation is to point the tool where the curve starts, and split pieces off as we lift the handle up the same as we did before. The bevel (D, Fig. 5) rubs the curved part, so we start with the handle to the right and the tool tilted over as shown.   As we lift the handle end it is moved to the left so that we end with the tool on its edge and square to the work.   Only the point of the tool does any work.   We do not remove shavings, but rather cut the wood with splitting action.   If our wood is too hard we make a second cut. We can do a little curve or quite a large one.   Should your design be as in Fig. 6, cut square across, we have the handle end of the chisel over to left so that bevel (E) lies flat against the square to be left on the work, and take just a little off as our first dig in leaves it rather sore.   If your tools are sharp and you hold the tool as shown, it will not chip the corners off, but leave a clean job.

Turning pins.   Stools are often made with turned legs having pins which fit into holes in the top.   I describe here how to turn these pins.   First bore a hole in a spare piece of wood using the bit you propose to use.   Drills vary in size, generally because they have been badly sharpened.   It is quite usual for a man buying, say, $\frac{3}{8}$-in. dowels in High Wycombe to take a hole with him to show what size of $\frac{3}{8}$ in. he wants, as they are made in different sizes.   The wood must be well seasoned and dry or else the pins will soon become loose. This being so we must take care we don't split the corners off in doing our pins.

We use our long-cornered chisel just as though we were going to turn a pummel; that is the point of the chisel does the work.   The action of the tool is that it cuts through the fibres of the wood before it removes the wood as a shaving as in Fig. 8.   Please don't read on

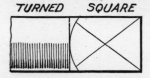

FIG. 2. SHOULDER OF SQUARE WHICH HAS TO BE FINISHED IN A CURVE.

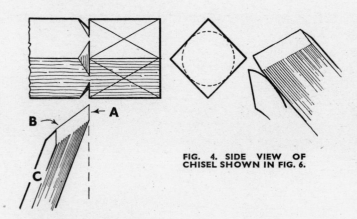

FIG. 4. SIDE VIEW OF CHISEL SHOWN IN FIG. 6.

FIG. 3. FIRST STAGE OF REMOVING WASTE IN CUTTING THE SHOULDER

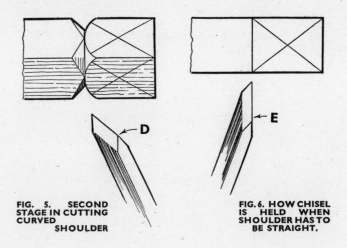

FIG. 5. SECOND STAGE IN CUTTING CURVED SHOULDER

FIG. 6. HOW CHISEL IS HELD WHEN SHOULDER HAS TO BE STRAIGHT.

unless you quite understand what is meant, for this principle is important in many turning operations, and in many other ways of working wood too. The pin is at the tail-stock end, and the long-cornered chisel is held with the handle down, and to right a little with it to 1.30 o'clock. The handle end is raised and triangular shavings come off.

There is no need to go further than the corners of the square once

FIG. 7. CLOSE-UP VIEW OF OPERATION SHOWN ON PAGE 108.
Here as in all other chisel and gouge work the bevel of the tool rubs the wood. Unless it does this a dig-in is almost inevitable. The first cut removes the wood on the turned side (see Fig. 3). The second cut shown here starts at the outer point of the curve, and as the curve is followed the handle is raised.

the cut is continuous. It is very easy to cut wood out of square by this method, and this would form a bad joint. It is still the best way to do it, however, because it does not break away the corners; in fact even dead wood (which you should not use) can be cleanly cut down.

We now pick up our $\frac{1}{2}$-in. chisel (if we have one, of course), though any square-across chisel will do, and use it as in Fig. 9. By lifting the handle end, down goes the cutting edge and a long ribbon of wood comes off. If we have a back centre turned to the size of the drill we use, the chisel goes down until it rests on it, otherwise we must use callipers. There is an arm fitted to a chisel which slides under the pin when it is to size, but this means that the chisel must be pushed forward, which is not cutting wood as it prefers to be cut. If you study Fig. 10 (first position) you will note that the wood is rubbing *across* the cutting edge and so blunting it, and no nice long shaving is coming off. In Fig. 9 you have easy control of the tool as its lower bevel is supported by rubbing on the work as well as on the rest; whereas in Fig. 10 the work is pulling the chisel

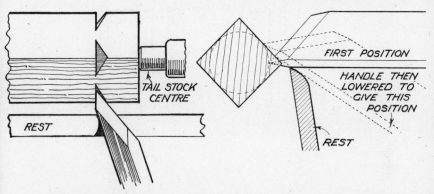

FIG. 8. USING THE LONG-CORNERED CHISEL WHEN CUTTING THE SHOULDERS OF A PIN.

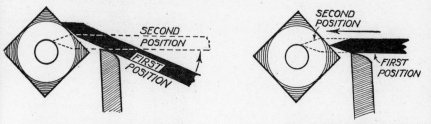

FIG. 9. CUTTING THE PIN ITSELF USING THE ¼ IN. SQUARE CHISEL.

FIG. 10. LESS SATISFACTORY METHOD IN WHICH CHISEL SCRAPES.

down, and if the rest has to be well back from the work this can be a real difficulty. It makes the tool chatter and, if it breaks the tool, you as well.

The best calliper to use is a slot cut in a stout piece of iron about ¼ in. thick as in Fig. 11. You force it over the pin when nearly to size, and it bruises or nearly burns the pin to size (or shows that you have gone too far). Just a touch with chisel over the rest of the pin clears it to size. We have used this system for many years. The iron bears on the rest, and is eased on to the pin as it might pull itself down and twist the pin off. Remember that it is all done with the wood revolving. It is well worth making for the pin sizes you use.

You may well think this a lot of fuss about a simple job. Well pins are not so good as tenons for joints, but they are needed for some jobs, and in commercial work are often a necessity.

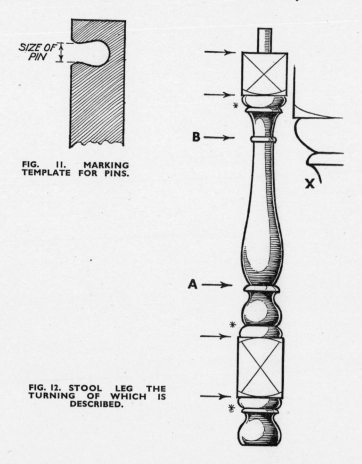

SIZE OF PIN

FIG. 11. MARKING TEMPLATE FOR PINS.

B →

X

A →

FIG. 12. STOOL LEG THE TURNING OF WHICH IS DESCRIBED.

Sets of legs. Now years ago I counted my children and did four legs for each with four over, and made some delightful stools. I mention it here because they are a good example of the work I am talking about. Sixteen legs had to be all alike as in Fig. 12. The pin at the top had to go into an oblong ash seat 1 in. thick. The four rails to fit in the bottom pummels had pins turned on them. The first leg was turned to my liking and the wooden rest marked at positions shown by the arrows. This is how we do lots of work all alike in wood turning, and gradually the rest becomes marked by the tools.

Sometimes we use a carpenter's pencil and put a line on the wood, say, where the pummel is wanted. There is no need to mark all four sides of the wood, but it is best to use a square as it shows up much more clearly as the wood revolves if the line is square across the work. When a lot of work has to be marked we mark a pair of legs and lay a dozen or so between them. In some work it is best to put crosses on the pummels, as the pin might be turned into a foot in an unguarded moment.

Using the gouge. We have cut our leg down and rounded it, removing wood with the gouge to something like the general outline of the leg. Generally speaking, a gouge is the tool to remove wood and a chisel to pare it smooth with. Someone told me recently that the easy way I remove wood looks like murder. It is not clear just what was meant, but if you gently push someone over a cliff (please don't) he will do the rest himself. Well, if you hold the gouge to one side it will work itself along. In many turning jobs the tools do the job themselves; you just set the angle of cut. Blind men have a fine sense of touch and a St. Dunstan's man did a good job of turning recently, so I do urge you to try to find out the angles the tools work on and not to force or hold them too tightly. Just gently ease them about.

Our leg is roughed out and we cut little grooves with the corner of the long-cornered chisel at arrow (A, Fig. 12) and either side of arrow (B) which is a bead, and near the squares where the asterisks are. Some people put so many lines to guide them and use so many callipers that they cannot trust themselves to use their own eyes to guide them, so such beads, etc., are not marked. With our $\frac{1}{4}$-in. chisel we do the beads. I'm in favour of the shape as shown in Fig. 12 (X), as curves that cannot be done with a compass always seem better. These details give that individualistic appearance of your own work. The half beads are also done with the $\frac{1}{4}$-in. chisel and are that shape instead of being parallel so as not to reduce too much the hollow nearby.

Beads. If you are not good at turning beads just practise on a spare piece of wood, but don't develop the habit of using force or just scrape them to shape. If you persistently slip stop the lathe and peep underneath the tool and find out whether the tool is rubbing. The instructions are these: see that your chisel has an even bevel, not as you buy it. Hold its cutting edge on top of the wood

so that it cannot cut, that is with the handle end low. Now turn
the left-hand side of the bead. Move the handle slightly to the
right and let the left-hand corner of the tool be in the middle of the
bead, the cutting edge level to start with. Then, making the
corner of tool do the work, raise the handle in a circular movement
until the cutting edge is vertical. The lower side of bevel rubs all
the way round, and the shape and size of bead is governed by the
movement of the handle.

The other side of the bead is, of course, obvious but, as you become
more skilful, less movement seems necessary, just as riding a bicycle
which still must lean over in turning a corner. I could ride no
hands, but cannot do turning no hands yet. On page 104 I describe
the turning of larger beads with the gouge.

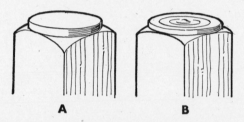

A   **B**

FIG. 13. WAYS OF FINISHING THE TOPS OF
SQUARE LEGS.

The $\frac{1}{2}$-in. chisel is best for the toe and larger curves, where
exactly the same principle applies. The long curve is best done with
the long-cornered chisel, and when near the little bead just push it
forward so that the heel of the chisel cleans the corner out. The
curve above the little bead is done with the gouge on its side at
9 o'clock, or our $\frac{1}{4}$-in. chisel could just clean the corner out. The
small hollows such as in the foot are simple small gouge work. We
gouge down from the large diameter to the bottom on one side and
then on the other. The middle of the gouge (cutting edge, of course)
does the work so that it is twisted in use from its side to lying level
or at 12 o'clock in bottom of hollow. These gouges are ground a
little to a point, but roughing-out gouges are square across.

Decorative cuts. Now if I told you pennies would cost you
half-penny each you would think me crackers, yet that is the standard
charge (my billheads had on them "Longest twisting experience in
the trade"). Of course, there is a catch in it, and I am referring
to the top of a leg which often has a turned patera on it. Craftsmen
know that wood shrinks, and make allowance for it. Side rails of

stools, etc., are not exempt from this law, and it is always towards the heart (I've gone the other way) except in a very few cases which need not concern us. So to save the leg standing proud at the corners we turn a little design on it, and then it does not matter. The simplest is a penny (A, Fig. 13), but a much nicer one is similar to draught-board checkers (B). This is done with a small gouge on its side, and $\frac{1}{4}$-in. chisel for the members. It is partly a scraping action as we are working on end grain.

The simplest stool of all to make is a milking stool, but do make it strong as so much relies on the fit of the legs in the seat. The seat can be turned with a slight hollow in the top and a groove round its edge. A nice scraper cut is ideal as little wood has to be removed. If the wood chatters owing to its hardness, or because the lathe is light, use a narrow cut. To avoid grooves when using narrow tools for face-turning set the rest parallel with the work and let the hand holding the tool slide along the rest. (Just a note to lathe manufacturers; we would like our rests parallel with no pieces sticking out as we slide our hands along them just as your slide rest goes along the lathe bed.) In fixing our stool legs we can drive them through the top and wedge them, cleaning all off flush with a scraper, or just make a good fit into a blind hole.

PARTING

The use of the parting tool can be most interesting. Amateurs find that they want to use it often, but the trade more often uses a circular saw which can part two thousand or so pieces an hour. It is entirely mechanical and far from interesting, though for joints a saw is ideal, since the uneven surface is excellent for glue.

Using the $\frac{1}{4}$-in. chisel. Let us take an actual example. First I tighten up the tail-stock to force the wood well on to the driving centre, and then ease it back a bit. The reason is that when the tool is nearly through the wood will collapse because of end pressure. Consequently I don't tighten the tail-stock more than is necessary to drive the work. It could be eased back just before final cut if you like. The $\frac{1}{4}$-in. chisel is not just pushed in, but rather the handle is raised. Fig. 14 shows how in this way the bevel of the tool rests on top of the work, holding it down as it is being cut. The tool will keep sharp much longer, too, since the wood is being cut as it prefers to be cut.

You will have noticed that a $\frac{1}{4}$-in. chisel has been mentioned, not a parting tool. That is because I want to show that a parallel tool is all right for parting with. If you have a proper parting tool which is relieved as in Fig. 15 by all means use it, but even so it is still good practice to do the following.   Just put your left hand around the work and ease it towards you, especially when nearly through.   This opens the slot, as in Fig. 16, and prevents the wood from binding on the sides of the tool.   Some use leather in the hand, but I don't recommend it unless you are thin-skinned.

Parting with the long-cornered chisel.   You will notice that

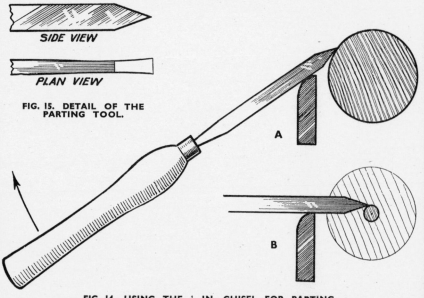

SIDE VIEW

PLAN VIEW

FIG. 15.   DETAIL OF THE PARTING TOOL.

A

B

FIG. 14.   USING THE ¼ IN. CHISEL FOR PARTING.
Note that the bevel rests upon the wood as at (A).   By raising the handle as at
(B) the bevel still rests upon the wood.

the surface of the cut is rather sore as the fibres have been broken off, and not cut through.   There will also be the centre which breaks off as the wood collapses.   This may be an advantage in a joint to be glued, but if these things matter you can do a much cleaner job by using the long-cornered chisel.   It will use more wood to work in nicely and require more skill, but who is afraid to learn?   It is more difficult to describe too, but I'll try.   There are two quite distinctly different cuts involved, and when you have understood that it will help immensely to understand the principle involved.

The first cut makes shavings.   In the case of a square they are triangular in shape, but quite definitely shavings.   The handle end is lifted up as the cut is deepened (in the same manner as for the

¼-in. chisel), but is slightly to the left, too, as in Fig. 17.   This is to
avoid the corner of the chisel rubbing the work as in Fig. 19.   The
point end of the chisel is used and it is laid at an angle with the lower
bevel rubbing the wood.   If the shaving gets too wide to control the
tool is tilted to a more vertical bevel so that the edge near the point
does the work.   The result of this cut is as in Fig. 17, but the surface
is still sore as the fibres of wood are broken off.

Now we come to the second cut, and this does not remove a
shaving so much as a fuzzy little ring of fibres.   The point only of

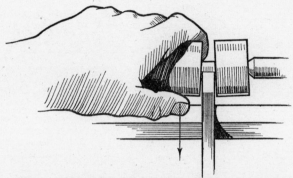

FIG. 16.   PLAN VIEW OF PARTING WITH ¼ IN. CHISEL.
By pressing the work towards you (shown in exaggeration) any tendency for the chisel to bind is avoided.

the tool does the work.   The bevel of the tool is lying against the
finished end and as we raise the handle end of the tool up, the point
goes down, just making a fine cut, and cutting cleanly from the part
we want left.   There seems to be a sort of satirical remark here, and
I'll let you find out what it is, for good turning methods run very
close to spoiling the job.   Fig. 18 shows the position of the chisel
as seen from above when making this second cut.

If you get the bevel wrong, or take too much, or have a slight burr
on the point of the tool it will slip and spoil the job.   Note I said
"burr".   Well, you can burn the point in grinding and so that the
steel is soft and easily bends.   Then again, as much cutting down
is near the tail-stock centre, you may have just bumped into it, and
caused a little burr.   If you have watched me carefully at work,
and I was anxious not to slip, my finger would just feel the point
to see whether it was burred over.   Sometimes tools fall down and
it is invariably the point that catches it.

We have now one end nicely cut down and when you see the
principle involved you can apply it to the other side of the cut.

Briefly the first cut removes wood in shavings, and the second cut pares a little off the part we want left. Figs. 20 and 21 show the two operations photographically.

There is still the very centre of the job to be parted, and a sudden break through might tear a little bit out. It is therefore advisable

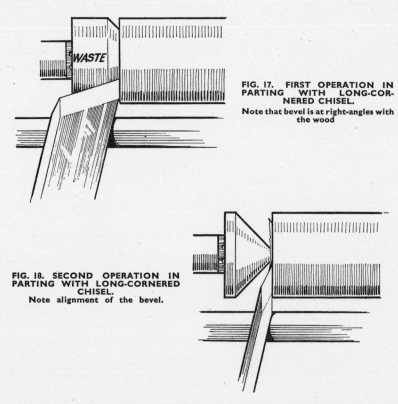

FIG. 17.   FIRST OPERATION IN PARTING   WITH   LONG-CORNERED CHISEL.
Note that bevel is at right-angles with the wood

FIG. 18.   SECOND   OPERATION   IN PARTING WITH LONG-CORNERED CHISEL.
Note alignment of the bevel.

to make the final cut away from the finished surface and pare it off afterwards.

Specially ground parting tool. It may well be that this is too tedious and possibly you have a lot of discs to part cleanly off and don't want to use too much wood in the cut. An excellent idea is to groove your parting tool as in Fig. 22. The corners will cut through the fibres before the wood is removed just as in the case of a cross-cut saw. I've often told people to try to keep a sharp corner on their grinding wheels as this is just where you need it.

When I demonstrate I often turn little candlesticks and I turn a candle down to about $\frac{1}{8}$ in. diameter in the wood, and then boldly part off the square at the base.   The secret here is a bold, steady cut, for if you take too fine a shaving the wood just bends away, bounces forward, and vibration sets up.   Don't be too bold, however.   You can often damp out vibration or chatter in turning by increasing the cut, but experience alone will teach just what you can do.   Besides a bold cut I see that the parting tool is sharp on both corners and that the bevel is rubbing on the work so as to avoid lifting the latter.

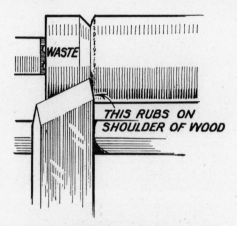

FIG. 19.   INCORRECT WAY OF USING LONG-CORNERED CHISEL.
The corner of the bevel rubs and cannot give a square shoulder.

A miniature sundial has a thin top about $\frac{1}{16}$ in. thick and is left the full size of the square.   For this it is essential to have a sharp long-cornered chisel and to do exactly as described earlier, using the two types of cutting, shavings, and ring of fibres.   The secret of not knocking this thin square to pieces, however, is to not let the bevel of the tool rub it hard and break it.   To the onlooker it looks just the same as when I cut down, but the tool knows that I'm keeping it away from exerting pressure on the work.

When you hold a lady's hand many subtle pressures may go on quite unknown to others—my dear wife and I used to play guessing tunes in this way as we went along.   You may ask what has this to do with turning.   Well, my friends, the fact is that a gentle touch so that you can feel the tool cutting is much better than force.   If the tool digs in, it is being held at the wrong angle.   I do so stress this because I've seen the joy many get in mastering the art, whilst

9—P.W.T.

others simply will not hold the turning tools gently and feel them cutting, but rather force them about.

Please don't misunderstand me. I'm not advocating treating the wood gently, and taking off meagre shavings, for those who have seen me working know the reverse. "It's just murder to watch you and see how wood suffers," was a remark a large manufacturer of lathes said. But I feel the wood enjoys it, as my aim is to *cut the wood as it prefers to be cut*, and it must be much nicer to be murdered by someone enjoying it, than one who is afraid to do it, although I'm not speaking from experience—yet.

Turning a hollow. This frequently occurs in spindle work, and a common error is to use the gouge as in Fig. 23 with a scraping

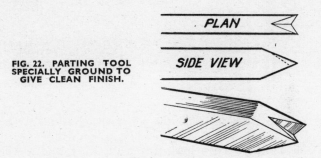

FIG. 22. PARTING TOOL SPECIALLY GROUND TO GIVE CLEAN FINISH.

action. It removes only dust and it leaves a ragged edge. In softwood the whole thing would be rough.

The proper way is to start with the handle well down, and the tool on its side with the handle over to the left when doing the right side of the hollow as at (A), Fig. 24. The handle end is raised, and the side of the gouge, with the bevel rubbing work, reduces the work. At the same time the gouge is twisted so that it is flat on its back when the centre of the hollow is reached (see A and B).

This twisting of the gouge makes it do the hollow itself as the bevel rubs against the work all the time. Of course you have to watch the curve of the hollow being generated, and that is where practice in twisting the tool about comes in. When I do this work I govern the thickness of shaving by how I lift the handle end, and continue the curve by how I twist the handle. The tool cannot dig

FIG. 20. (*top left*) **PARTING WITH LONG-CORNERED CHISEL.**
This is the first stage in which the bulk of the work is done. The chisel leans over at an angle.

FIG. 21. (*bottom left*) **SECOND STAGE IN PARTING.**
Here the bevel of the chisel is square to the work and only a thin shaving removed.

in because the bevel prevents it by rubbing the work. It keeps sharp longer because the whole of the cutting edge is used, not the point only; also because the wood does not move across the cutting edge but in line with it. Thus the shavings slide down the hollow.

A little experiment on a spare piece of wood may help you to

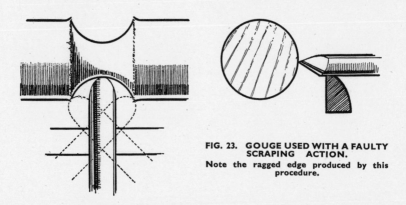

FIG. 23.   GOUGE USED WITH A FAULTY
SCRAPING   ACTION.
Note   the   ragged   edge   produced   by   this
procedure.

understand how the tools do the job themselves. Take a small gouge, $\frac{1}{4}$ in. or $\frac{3}{8}$ in. with a nice deep hollow, and hold it very lightly on its side a little. Then push it into the work, and it will itself slide to right or left, and the bevel will rub the work and do it. When I demonstrate this I hold the handle between two fingers, and place just one on top of the gouge near the rest to steady the tool. You can try twisting the handle too.

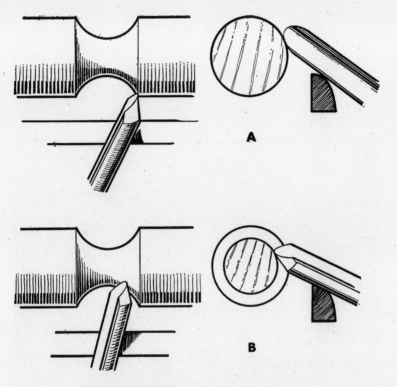

FIG. 24. CORRECT USE OF THE GOUGE.

The gouge is held on its side at the start and is twisted until by the time it has reached the centre of the hollow it is on its back. Note that the bevel is made to rub the work during the entire operation.

FIG. 25. METHOD OF STARTING THE CUT WHEN AN EXTRA DEEP HOLLOW IS REQUIRED.

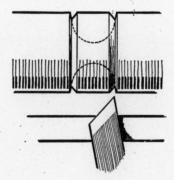

FIG. 26. TURNING END OF CYLINDER TO ROUNDED CURVE.

CHAPTER 11 : BORING HOLES

THE patron saint of wood-turning, St. Catherine of Alexandria, cannot help us much as history cannot prove that she ever lived (only that she died). We must share her with wheelwrights and mechanics for she is their patron saint too, but I feel sure you won't mind. I do not think she has been modernized so knows nothing about floor standards.

We are thinking about floor standards, and these do demand a high standard of workmanship and have their own problems too, such as boring long holes. Wood also is a problem (as apparently it was in 1417 A.D. when some wood-turners and clog-makers got into trouble for using wood good enough for arrows).

Boring long holes. Now the following is the quickest and best way of boring long holes that I know of. A judge, some prisoners, several ladies, and lots of boys have been successful at their first

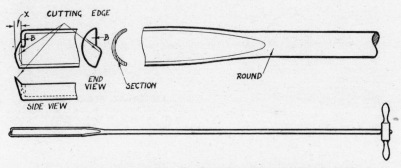

FIG. 1. DETAIL OF BORING AUGER FOR LAMP STANDARDS, ETC.
Distance **X** gives thickness of cut. The rubbing portion B prevents the tool from digging in.

attempt. One boy at an exhibition does it blindfolded. The above is mentioned to give you confidence, and to knock the idea on the head that boring long holes is a difficult job. Incidentally, the boy at the exhibition put a bottle of pop under the bench. When he had bored the hole he went to it and held it up saying, "Now I know why I was blindfolded." You see the level had gone down quite a bit.

The boys put five holes down a 1¼-in. square 30 in. long, and three down a broom-stick, so it must be easy to bore one hole.

Auger and attachment. A special auger and attachment are needed, but if a school has a metal turning lathe it can be a joint operation. The auger is rather special, being made by a firm which

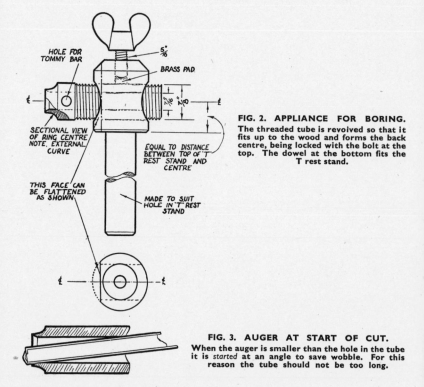

FIG. 2. APPLIANCE FOR BORING.
The threaded tube is revolved so that it fits up to the wood and forms the back centre, being locked with the bolt at the top. The dowel at the bottom fits the T rest stand.

FIG. 3. AUGER AT START OF CUT.
When the auger is smaller than the hole in the tube it is *started* at an angle to save wobble. For this reason the tube should not be too long.

delights in awkward drills, etc., but its cost is only 9s. or so. Fig. 1 explains itself, and so long as the wood can revolve about 1,000 revolutions a minute all is well. The attachment, Fig. 2, is not intended to guide the auger, but rather to keep the wood up to the driving chuck. It has a hole for the auger to do its job. In some proprietary attachments, however, the hole in the tube is made to suit the size of boring auger being used. In this case it is essential that the tube is in perfect alignment with the work. For a simple job wood will do for the attachment with a tube fitted. Even a short piece of gas-pipe will do for the tube centre. The augers

sold sometimes have the parrot's nose end (see Fig. 9). These cut
cleaner holes than those square across, but can wander as the point
finds softer grain, so I advocate and always use the kind in Fig. 1.
Large holes 3 in. diameter and 6 ft. long are best done with the parrot
nose auger as this cuts a cleaner hole—short holes too if clean holes
are essential. Large holes are needed for textile rollers, and if you
want a bit 10 in. in diameter with a cart-wheel on the end to rotate it
for boring wooden water pipes I know of one.

The boring operation. The wood is revolving and we gently

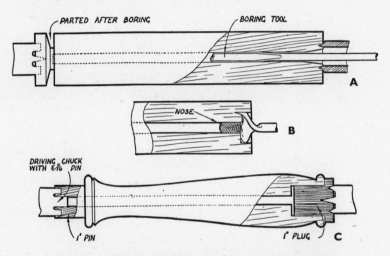

FIG. 4. STAGES IN BORING AND TURNING THE SHAFT.
A shows the boring operation. B gives the method of counter-boring with plug on nose
of bit. C is the 1 in. plug which fits in the back centre. Note also the special driving chuck.

push our auger slightly sideways into the hole of the attachment.
This is to prevent it from getting a wobble as it has no point. So we
steady it as in Fig. 3, and for this reason don't have the hole in the
attachment too long. The auger is held in one hand, and we don't
let it clog too much. It is necessary to withdraw it from time to
time. If you run the work too fast it will warm up, but don't go
too slow either—about 1,000 r.p.m. seems best. At one school a
boy looked through while another blew all the dust into his eye; they
were so eager to see through it. (Note to instructors. Don't tell
boys about blow-pipes with poisoned arrows, or pea-shooters. It
holds up production.)

Counter-boring. So the wood has a hole down it now, as at (A),
Fig. 4, and one end probably has to fit on to another piece, so we need

to counter-bore our $\frac{5}{16}$ in. or $\frac{7}{16}$ in. hole out to 1 in. diameter. This must be done carefully, and I suggest that you buy a 1 in. bit (other sizes are made) and fit a nose-piece on it as at Fig. 4 (B). Use either the chuck in your lathe, pushing the wood on to it, the bit revolving, or do it with hand brace. These bits cost about 2s. 10d., but one made for a machine costs 8s. 6d. or so, and is no better for the purpose. This type of counter-bore is suggested because the nose-piece will guide it to follow the hole already bored, and it has no part to catch into the sides of the hole after the cutting edge such as a long twist drill would have.

So our hole is true to size and parallel. It is an easy matter to turn a pin on the part to go into this hole, but don't hurry fitting it, as a sloppy fit is nothing to be proud of and will cause trouble.

To hold the work whilst this and the rest of the turning is done you can make a plug to fit the 1-in. hole and this run on the centre as at (C), Fig. 4. For the other end I once made a driving chuck with a $\frac{5}{16}$-in. pin on it to go into the hole as at (C), but never used it, so you can please yourself as it depends on your chuck diameter a bit, but undoubtedly a chuck with a pin to fit the hole is best.

Some of you may wish to screw the parts together. Well, thousands of gift standards were made that had a thread cut in them, but it powders away in use, and one man who did it is in a lunatic asylum, so be warned. If you must screw them, brass fittings are sold to fix on to the ends of the wood, but you have to recess the wood to take them. In any case screws don't hold well in end grain. When I fit parts together I try to match the grain. This, too, is against using these fittings.

Design. Whilst we are talking

FIG. 5. TYPICAL LAMP STANDARD.

about lamp standards we may as well briefly discuss the general work as well. The simpler the design the better it looks. You will find if you look around you that many beautiful things are quite plain except for some detail that holds your attention. The plain part is always nicely finished, however, showing up the grain of the material. A plain square tapered nicely and veneered with some beautiful wood is a joy to the maker, while a fussily turned column can be a worry. Turned details all the way up never look well. You can often copy the turning of the legs of a chair or table in the bottom half of a floor standard, the top half being a long gentle curve with an interesting detail to hold the lamp holder as in Fig. 5.

These long curves can be more trouble than a lot of hollows and beads, etc., as the line must be a nice gentle one. If you measure it as you go along all will be well. You will need a steady, and the best is that described on page 68. I can honestly say that I've never seen any other type used successfully in the furniture trade during the past fifty years. Some use lead weights on the wedge, some elastic, and some a screw to hold the wedge a little, but the principle is *right*. My living to-day is metal turning, and I am fully acquainted with the type of steady the engineer uses, but for wood it is not suitable. Floor standards are usually 5 ft. tall and so call for two 30 in. lengths of turning. A steady is a great help (though we can just manage without one).

I feel sorry for those who have to keep pushing the rest along the bed to turn another part. We always have a wooden rest long enough to do the whole job at once. If I say much more about lathe manufacturers, however, they won't like me, but it is obvious that a long, continuous flat curve needs a long rest so that the chisel can be taken along in an unbroken movement.

Base. Our base can be 12 in. or more diameter and it calls for a different treatment in design. The outline of the column is seen, but the reflections of light show the design of the base. There is another point. We often want the base to look thicker than it really is (this applies to bread-boards too). A few years back we used coffin boards to turn into bread-boards, and by Act of Parliament these were reduced from 1 in. to ¾ in. thick, but they looked nice as the shape made them look thicker. The section was quite simple (Fig. 6). It showed a broad surface at the outside and again the eye noted the inner bump, while the little sharp, hollow curve was not noticed unduly. Design is a subtle thing indeed, and often we can bring out more beauty by using a simple device. All true art uses skill, whether it be music, painting, or designing, to emphasize some point, and the result is much more interesting than plain mechanical curves.

So far we have the bottom part of the standard like the furniture it is to go with, and a nice heavy-looking base has been used. Straight lines always seem wrong mixed up with curves, yet much modern furniture is all straight lines.   If you do turn straight parts they always look better if slightly curved (? ?).

The joint in the column where it joins the base needs special treatment for it will show up the smallest difference in size, or any

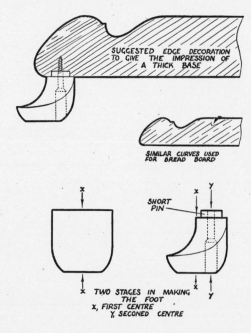

SUGGESTED EDGE DECORATION TO GIVE THE IMPRESSION OF A THICK BASE

SIMILAR CURVES USED FOR BREAD BOARD

FIG. 6. SECTION THROUGH BASE.

Also the special foot made with two centres.   This is provided with a short pin which gives exact positioning, and a counter-bored screw is driven through it to the base.

SHORT PIN

TWO STAGES IN MAKING THE FOOT
X, FIRST CENTRE
Y, SECONED CENTRE

other inaccuracy.   For this reason it is advisable to turn a bead at these places and so hide any error.

At the base three toes are preferable as they always stand level. On the other hand four feet spread over a greater area and so help more in preventing the standard from falling over, so you can make your own choice.

To give our feet a wider area we can turn them on two centres, first as in Fig. 6 (left), then as at (right).   It is easy indeed to do and they peep out from under the base so to speak.   We found, however, that they were inclined to become loose as the pressure was not even.

We found that an ordinary screw was more satisfactory than a pin, so we used a short ¾ in. diameter pin with a screw running up its middle. This made a good strong fixing.

Larger holes. "A bung-hole without a barrel" won ten shillings in a competition to describe "nothing". It was sent in by one of my men, and his wife thought it very silly, but made a fuss of him when the money came. Well, in this chapter we are just thinking of holes. In wood-turning we soon find the need to bore a hole, although the local need for worm-holes in antique work has died out.

Let us now think of a really large hole such as that in a circular picture frame, or the front of a loudspeaker in a radio cabinet. In these the wood is mounted on the faceplate of the lathe. The chief troubles are springiness (unless the lathe is very solid), failing to cut cleanly, not to mention the liability to split right across.

Marking out. We will mark the size with pencil as the wood

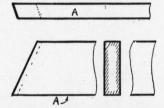

FIG. 7. SIDE VIEW AND PLAN OF FILE USED FOR BORING LARGE HOLES.

revolves. If you must use dividers just touch the side nearest to you with the point of the dividers on the rest, the other point against the far side of the circle you are scratching. Do not press against the revolving wood too hard or it certainly will catch in. You could set the dividers to half the size of the finished hole and put one point in the middle, which is easily seen as the work revolves. Personally, I much prefer to use a pencil and rule, as dividers do often catch in the revolving work.

Tool to use. An old file ground as Fig. 7 is needed, and please note that if the required holes are large only the end is bevelled, not either side. The tool is used practically level, just above centre height, and is simply pushed straight into the work. The bevel of the tool as seen from above keeps it against the finished hole, and as the side of the tool cannot cut it does not enlarge the hole, but keeps it parallel if the tool is square to the work. Should the tool be forced down it is also forced away from the wood into the scrap centre piece so the work is all right. That is why the sides of the tool have no (or very little) bevel.

The grain of the wood is cut cleanly through, and the bevel is still cutting the waste wood as it goes through so that the tool does not fall through suddenly owing to, say, a springy job. If the tool were ground square across it would go through suddenly and might catch us out. It certainly would not cut the fibres or grain so cleanly as a point would.

We could hold the work on a central screw in the waste centre piece or in other ways, according to the job. It would probably be

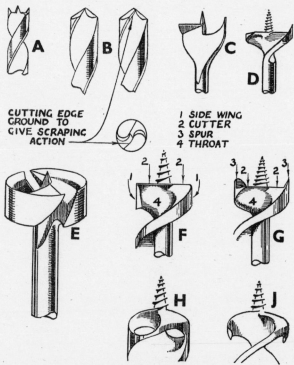

CUTTING EDGE
GROUND TO
GIVE SCRAPING
ACTION

1 SIDE WING
2 CUTTER
3 SPUR
4 THROAT

FIG. 8. TYPES OF DRILLS AND BITS USED IN BORING.
A. Specially ground drill for wood. B. Drills ground for brass. C. Simple centre bit. D. Special pattern centre bit. E. Forstner bit. F and G. Parts of bit: 1, side wing, 2, cutter, 3, spur, 4, throat, G. is the Jennings pattern bit. H. Solid nose bit. J. Gedge pattern bit.

a help to rest the elbow on the tail-stock to save the tool handle from moving about. The same tool would help to bore out, say, cigarette boxes or powder boxes for "My Lady's" dressing-table.

You will find that deep holes have a way of becoming smaller the deeper you go, and it is necessary to see that the tool is presented square to the work to avoid it.   The side of the tool could have a *little* bevel on it so that it just cuts the sides cleanly.   It might well be a piece of oak you are working, and you find that the tool rakes out the fibres a bit when you are boring along the grain.   Should you be troubled with long fibres coming out and spoiling the surface, make a final cut with the handle lowered slightly, and it will help. In the case of a cigarette box a disc could be turned to fit the hole and it could be finished off between centres as though it were a solid job.

Candlesticks.   Early candlesticks did not have holes, but spikes. We do not use them to-day, however, so we will think of candlesticks with sockets.   It is possible to buy candles from $\frac{3}{8}$ in. up to 2 in. diameter in over one hundred different sizes from stock.   Much larger ones are also made—in fact, one special one is thirty-six feet tall—rather awkward in a house.   It was lit in the Abbey where Queen Elizabeth was crowned and was an Easter candle to tell and remind us of the glorious message of Eastertide.   The various sizes available are mentioned because it does seem nice to break away from the ordinary size; it is much more interesting and distinctive looking.

If any of you have tried to bore a candlestick after it has been turned you will have found that the drill just will not go where you want it to.   You may also find that the thin neck is just not strong enough to take the strain of boring the hole, and something goes bust.   The remedy is simple; bore the hole first, and let the centre run in it.   If your centre is not long enough, at least start the drill. When we did that at the works it was a great improvement.   It was one of those things that did not dawn on us for a few years, and perhaps it has not on others.   We used a twist drill sharpened as at (A), Fig. 8.   The drill revolved in the lathe and the work was pushed by the tail-stock centre, being held from rotating by the hand.

You will find that drills, augers, twist bits, etc., which are parallel, or nearly so, have a habit of getting out of control if the work is allowed to move sideways at the end.   The sides of the drill catch the sides of the hole and wrench it out of your hand.   So, although you might be strong enough to push the wood, it is advisable to use the tail-stock centre to steady the end.   You must keep the wood against the centre as you bring it back, too, or at least pull it back carefully.   In these matters I do advise you to see just what happens, as some drills are more prone to this than others, and by their faults ye shall know them.

Kinds of drills.   I've two catalogues of about 120 pages with different drills on each page, so you see there is a large range to choose from.   I go to a lot of trouble to find out the best, though, of course, I have not come across every sort in my work.   (Not many of you want a 3-in. bit 6 ft. long, or one costing £25.)

A drill will bore fairly truly across the grain—that is like boring towards centre of tree.   We come to a hard layer of grain, then a soft layer, and the drill keeps fairly true.   We can also drill truly with the grain.   So now picture, say, a cross with a central ball across which we wish to drill a hole.   If we drill parallel with the grain or across it all will be well.   Just to see clearly what a drill does, you could get a round piece of wood like a broomstick and drill holes across it.   You will see how most drills wander.

In, say, a disc to hold three lights we must drill at an angle to the grain, of course, and I have found that the Jennings pattern bit is good, the dowel type (which is short) being the best.   First, however, we bored with a $\frac{1}{8}$-in. twist drill, and the centre of the bit followed that hole.   Of course, we could have fixed the job into a drilling machine, and had a stiff twist drill which would go where it was forced to, but this is not the way for amateurs.

Sharpening bits.   I think it would be helpful here to quote from the makers, Messrs. Ridgway (who only sell to shops) the instructions on sharpening (I've their permission to quote them).

"Generally speaking, bits are sharpened more often than necessary, and the life of many is considerably shortened by incorrect filing.   Carefully examine a bit before sharpening, and when filing endeavour to keep to the original shape.   Keep the balance of the nose of a bit.   Each side should do the same amount of work and to ensure this always file both sides equally.   Use a smooth file, and file lightly with the object of removing only as little metal as is necessary.

"*Sharpening the side wings.*   Rest the bit on the bench with the screw lead down.   Work with the file passing through the throat of the bit.   Never file the side wings on the outside, or the clearance will be spoilt.

"*Sharpening the cutters.*   Hold the bit in the same way as you would to sharpen the side wings, and file the cutting edges on the underside only, i.e. with the file working through the throat of the bit.   It is essential that the cutters should be at the same level so that they cut chips of equal thickness.

"*Sharpening the spurs.*   Hold the bit, nose uppermost, with its twist firmly against the edge of the bench.   File the inside of the spur.   Never file the outside, as this reduces the clearance, and causes binding and clogging when boring. Never attempt to sharpen a bit by grinding."

Well, the above is the maker's advice, and I agree very much with it.

Clean holes. I think a few thoughts on boring clean holes may help here, and let us start with the Jennings type. The spurs cut through the fibres before the cutters remove the wood, and this is an ideal state of affairs. The screw is either in a small hole already bored, or it is made into a brad point (like a pyramid) so that it does not pull in. These last remarks are for the bit when used in the lathe; we want the screw if we are using the bit in a hand-brace.

Now there is another way of cutting a clean hole, and that is using a curved nose. Fig. 9 shows a spoon bit of the type at (K). It was widely used in the chair trade at one time. The bench was low, about 12 in. from the floor, and three wooden pins stood up,

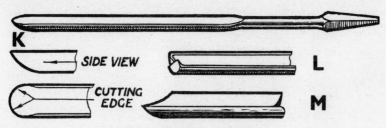

FIG. 9. BITS FOR SMALL HOLES.
K. Spoon bit with enlarged views below at left. L. Special auger for deep holes. M.
Parrot nose bit.

as in Fig. 10. A wedge held the legs to be bored. Since a part of a spoon bit rubs, it was always dipped into a box of grease before each hole was bored. The bit is rather a job to start as it has no point, and it is turned both ways with quite a pressure on the hand-brace. The workman wore a curved piece of wood on his chest so as to spread the strain a bit. It did bore a clean hole because of its curved nose.

Parrot-nosed bits (M), Fig. 9, Gedge's pattern (J), Fig. 8, solid nose with holes in it (H), Fig. 8, and others have a similar principle, and if you think you will see why the sides of the hole are nice and smooth. This Gedge's or solid-nose pattern bit is good to bore a hole at an angle; in fact, when the screw is in a little way you can carefully move the bit over, as there is no spur as in a Jennings type to catch into the work.

Principle of the drill. It may be as well to consider why drills, etc. are made as they are, as if you sharpen them wrongly you will have trouble. You will notice there is a part of the drill rubbing the work and preventing it from pulling in. A twist drill is ground at its nose at about the angle of its feed and it is a mistake to bevel it too much. The square-nosed bit I advocate for boring long holes —three down a broomstick blindfolded—has a part of the auger to rub on the opposite side of the cutter (L), Fig. 9. A Jennings (G), Fig. 8 and similar bits have the cutter at an angle so that it is prevented from pulling in. The makers say, don't alter it, so keep your files off it and try to see just which part of the drill prevents this pulling-in effect, or you may not enjoy boring holes.

Twist drills for boring wood are ground as at (A), Fig. 8, using the corner of the wheel. In the furniture trade they have a $\frac{3}{8}$ in.

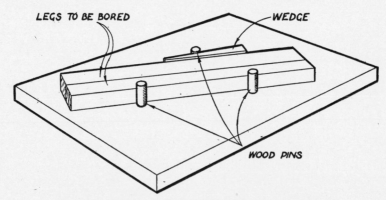

LEGS TO BE BORED   WEDGE

WOOD PINS

FIG. 10. HOW CHAIR PARTS ARE HELD WHEN BORING.

diameter thread on them to screw into the drilling machine. This is because a bunch of drills for boring holes for dowels is used together and there is no room for a chuck. When the drills become too short they are discarded. Some are left-handed to suit the machine, and so you have a left-handed drill.

Twist drills are meant for metal, of course. For iron they are all right as sold, but if you find it hard work, just a little touch on the wheel as at (B), Fig. 8, does help immensely. I always try to keep a corner on my grinding wheel for this purpose. Now brass ought to have a straight twist drill—no, I mean a straight-fluted drill with no twist. Personally, however, I find a twist drill better, but altered as at (B), Fig. 8. It is only a trifle, not enough to get to the relieved part, or it will be hard going. If you don't do it the drill pulls through and becomes seized. An oilstone could alter the drill, and is well worth doing if you drill brass.

Some bits must involve complicated methods of manufacture. I am thinking of a Forstner bit (E), Fig. 8, which will bore cleanly a flat-bottomed hole. It will also bore at any angle, and even bore half a hole. You could use it on your table and cut hollows out on the edge. Overlapping holes, too, can be bored and the direction of the grain does not affect it. It is an expensive bit, however, as it is so awkward to make. They are made up to 2 in. diameter.

I've hardly touched on drills, but do hope those I've mentioned may help you to understand those you come across. Special jobs need special drills; some are for wet wood and generally cut one side only; some are for heavy work where clean cutting is not necessary. If you use one having a screw point in the lathe or drilling machine do either bore a small hole first so that screw does not pull in, or alter it to a brad point. Of course, if your lathe goes slowly, all is well, but few do. Many of you probably only want to bore a few holes, and hand-drills are much cheaper than machine bits, so that may help save £ s. d. I used them for years. I sawed off the square that goes into the brace and used them in my drilling machine.

The makers are trying to popularize a short drill, like a Jennings at the end, but having only half a turn of twist (D), (Fig. 8). It seems a good idea as a long twist part is not always wanted. They are to take the place of the carpenter's centre bit (C), Fig. 8, which needs pushing. During the war I bored holes for those walkie-talkie sets, and got some out of truth. They were about 8 ft. long, and I enquired what error I was allowed and was told 3/1,000 in. I asked the man how he tested them and he replied that he had good eyesight. Well! I do believe in accuracy in holes, but to put 8 holes in 8 ft. accurately to that error is fairly good going (if we did?). Well, I hope you have not been bored, and will be able to bung holes in wood.

HOW TO FEEL COMFORTABLE

IT is difficult to do good work if you do not feel comfortable, and you certainly will not enjoy your hobby if you are working in a strained position. Here I hope to show you how you can enjoy wood turning more comfortably.

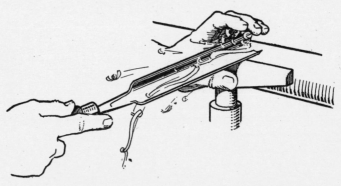

FIG. I. PREVENTING CHIPS FROM FLYING INTO THE FACE.
By cupping the fingers over the tool the chips can be deflected.

Dust. Let us first consider the eyes. The chief worry from our point of view is dust, or rather chips of wood. Professional turners do not wear protective glasses; they cup their hands over the flying chips or direct them elsewhere than into their face as in Fig. 1. In my experience people find it a job to do this, possibly because they want to see the tool cutting whereas the professional turner looks on the outline of the job more and feels the tool doing its job.

If you do not wear glasses, perhaps a pair of goggles will help to give you confidence against the chips entering your eyes (Fig. 2). There is no need for special ones as I have never heard of chips breaking the glasses.

Now, all the people I know have the habit of breathing and so you can take in dust. The fact is, however, that there ought to be little dust if you cut the wood cleanly. When glasspapering you cannot help it, except by seeing where it goes and dodging it. So far as I know it is nothing much to worry about—not like the dreaded disease miners and masons can get. I suppose it is not exactly good for you (certain fancy woods can give you a cold in de nose) but, my friends, do not worry about it. Just keep on breathing. Personally I have grown fat on it.

Satin wood and a few other species can cause little pimples on the skin of some people, but little of the wood is about now. Twenty per cent, used to be added to wages when it was worked, but few people were affected by it. Dust can cause dermatitis of the skin to some people, but it is comparatively rare and is similar to that which bakers get, and is hardly worth even thinking about.

Dress. Your neck may well catch the shavings, and your bedroom floor will tell the tale when you undress (not to mention feeling the chips working themselves down or getting stuck half way down). The fourteen turners we had always had a carpenter's apron on and by a knot made it tight under the chin. It is better than a smock dust coat. For myself I wore a scarf and some declared it was never tight enough. Anyhow, my lady of the house will welcome less chips about, and on this score remember that the turn-ups of trousers can bring home the chips. There are some lady turners and they solve the problem quite happily.

FIG. 2. SOME MAY PREFER TO USE GOGGLES.

Height. When you stand upright and put your hand to your shoulder, the elbow is just a happy height for the centre line of the lathe (see page 9). Most likely yours is too low (many are) and you have to bend over, getting the dust in your face and developing backache too. The remedy seems obvious, and you may wonder why manufacturers make their lathes so low. The answer one gave me was that so many of their lathes go to schools. It seems a fair answer, but we hardly go on using our children's push-bikes so let us have a lathe to suit our height and avoid backache —let gardening provide that.

Hands. Somewhere I have read that one should not let the left hand know what the right one is doing, but it could hardly have been a talk about turning. The two hands work in harmony. The following is written chiefly for right-handed people and I hope that left-handed people will see what I am getting at and apply the idea to themselves. For my part I am ambidextrous (besides being other things, as I am told). The actual movement the tools require for the various operations is dealt with elsewhere, and these remarks concern the way the hands can do it. Some teachers lay down hard-

and-fast rules, but I think the fact is that we all work out ways which suit us.

Broadly speaking it does not matter a lot. The way most professional turners work is that the right hand holds the end of the handle in an easy way so that he can twist it on its axis or raise and lower it. We are thinking now of spindle work such as a chair leg. The left hand has the thumb under the tool, and four fingers above in an arch to trap the shavings from flying into the face as in Fig. 3. There is a meaty part of the hand opposite the thumb and this rubs comfortably along a wooden rest, which is (or should be) parallel.

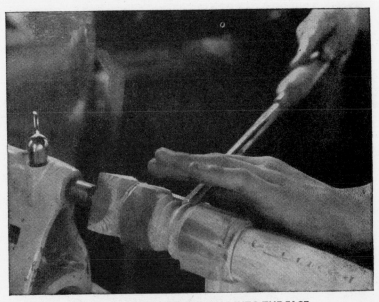

FIG. 3. AVOIDING CHIPS FLYING INTO THE FACE
Some people find it distressing to have a stream of chips flying into the face. Arching the fingers over the tool prevents this.

Manufacturers invariably sell metal rests and often make them a fancy shape, whereas we just want a simple parallel one. Wood is nicer to feel in any case. Some metal rests are the right shape although they taper at the ends. If your hand holding the tool slides along parallel with the work, all is well. Should your rest be wrong perhaps a file will help matters—but why should they be made wrong?

Tapered work. We have been thinking so far of the hand

moving along the rest as, say, for a rolling-pin. Let us now consider taper or shaped work. Here the tool must go forward, for we always work from the larger diameter to the smaller. So you can picture the meaty part of the left hand against the rest with the tool held between thumb and fingers and eased towards the work without loosing the steadying anchor on the rest. What I'm trying to say is that we don't advance the tool by first having the hand away from the rest so losing the steadying effect. Rather we manipulate the hand without shifting it from the rest.

Some chisels, especially wide ones, have to be kept at a certain

FIG. 4. HOW LONG TAPERED WORK IS TURNED.
Keep the left hand on the rest and ease the tool forward, the grip being maintained without shifting the position of the hand on the rest.

angle. They don't lie flat on the rest. The thumb underneath with the fingers on top and perhaps curled around the chisel will help nicely here. Fig. 4 shows the method well. The weight of the hand has a good effect in holding the tool down, sometimes damping out vibrations. When we turn long, slender work our right-hand fingers can curl round the work with the thumb only on the chisel to hold it down as in Fig. 5. This is a nice way of steadying the work and is quite safe. It is often a help against ribbing, and you don't really wear through to the bone. You stand with the left side of the body nearer to the lathe, just sideways a little.

Face plate work. In face-turning work, say the inside of a bowl, the flat scraping tools lie flat on the rest with the cutting edge pointing slightly downwards. The right hand holds the end of the tool. The grain of the wood does sometimes tend to make the tool wobble up and down, but it can easily be checked by resting the elbow on the tail-stock, which is not in use. We wish to push this tool evenly into the work and we can anchor the palm of the hand on the end of the rest. By closing the hand we can bring the tool along the rest, the thumb not being used. One word of warning. You can be so occupied in thought about the tool that the hand rubs the bowl and this is not nice.

Some find the shavings sting them as they fly off and gloves might

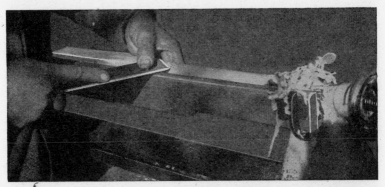

FIG. 5. CHISELLING A LONG CYLINDER, FINGERS AROUND WORK.
This is a specially useful method for long slender work. It is a great help in avoiding ribbing.

help here, but do take care that they don't get caught in revolving parts. A coat sleeve caught on a shaft coupling at my works caused a man to lose an arm. Admittedly that was using big power but I say again be careful if you use gloves. Should you find that you get on better by gripping the tool with the fingers underneath and the thumb on top, well it's a free country, but you cannot check the shavings as they fly off—but then you may not want to. For small intricate work this is quite a good way to control the tool, and you can still hold the fingers against the rest to govern the feed.

Elsewhere I've written, don't hold the tools tightly. There is no need to make your muscles tense in wood turning and so tire yourself. My aim in developing a light touch is that the tools convey to you how they are getting on. You feel it and know when all is well or that a chatter has been set up requiring an alteration of tool angle somewhere. The tools do all the work and you have only to just move them about (although there does seem to be an art in it somewhere). If you have to use brute force to move the tools about your methods are wrong.

Lighting. Bad lighting can worry you. In a new factory we went modern and had tubular lights fitted, but the men asked for the old system back again, just electric bulbs in shades to prevent the light from falling on their eyes. A window in front of you is ideal and no skylight. Perhaps when you have been driving your

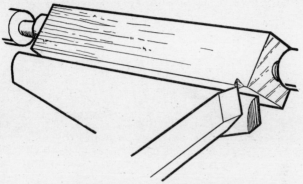

FIG. 6. CENTERING WOOD AT TAILSTOCK END.
The wood is centred as near as possible by eye, the wood revolved, and a nick made with chisel at the end.

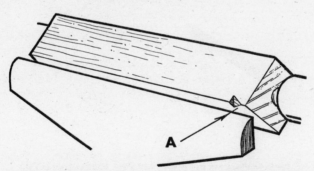

FIG. 7. HOW NICK REVEALS WHETHER WOOD IS CENTRED.
If only one corner is nicked as at (A), or if one corner is nicked more than the others, give the wood a knock with the chisel in the direction shown by the arrow.

car at night-time you have noticed how the headlights have shown up the unevenness of the road. This is just where tubular lights fail, for we wish to see the undulations of the shapes and the older type of light shows this better.

Centering. It is often recommended that you mark the ends of the wood to find the centre of the square but you will find it seldom runs true this way as the point wanders to a soft part of the grain. I do not recommend this way except for squares of over 3 in. diameter. The trade way is to put the wood between centres as true as you can guess it, with the back centre only slightly screwed up, and just nick the corner as it revolves as in Fig. 6. We then hold the wood still, and give this corner a biff with the chisel (for we certainly have no time to pick up anything else) as in Fig. 7 and

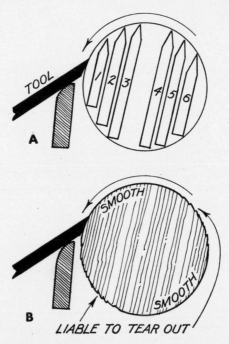

FIG. 8. LIABILITY OF GRAIN TO SPLIT.

(A) shows imaginary pencils on a face plate, tool being used at the edge. Pencils 5 and 6 are liable to break away. The actual wood is shown at (B) and the tendency of the corresponding parts to split is shown.

tighten the back centre. We never stop the lathe, but probably it would be better if you do. Certainly this method soon finds fault with a bad pair of centres, but then why have them wrong?

If your centre bends in use tell the makers about it. I've been instrumental in improving some, but why some lathes are fitted with such poor centres beats me. I've purposely bent some. You must excuse my remarking about centres, but I am sure that many have no idea how a nice happy pair of centres give joy in their use, and save excessive pressure on the bearings too.

Face plate work. As many of my followers are not in the wood line I am putting in this next bit to help them understand wood better. I've shown in Fig. 8 a disc of wood on a face plate and pictured it at (A) as a lot of pencils, as I feel some may understand this better. Only the pointed ends are referred to in the text. One of my slogans is "*cutting wood as it prefers to be cut,*" and pencil No. 1 is ideally placed. whereas No. 6 is like trying to sharpen a pencil from the point inwards. It is clear, then, that we cannot apply our slogan in this case, so we must see what we can do about it.

The tool is shown on the edge of the disc in Fig. 8 (B), but in Fig. 9 the tool is at the face of the disc. It is something like laying our pencils on the table and forcing a chisel down across the grain. This is not such a nice way to cut wood, but splits won't occur, such as in pencil No. 6 in Fig. 8. Thus it is an improvement to work across the disc rather than on the edge.

Now Fig. 9 shows a square piece which we wish to turn round (when in business we often had similar jobs as it saved sawing). The end view shows the tool, and please note we are aiming at just turning a round disc, which could be a toy wheel, egg stand, bread board, or base of table lamp when finished. The tool shown is a flat scraper tool, and part (A) is doing all the work, and this is on the waste wood. The point of the tool is just cutting across the fibres of grain (which is really our trouble) and these fibres are held by the disc proper at one side, and by the waste piece of wood at the other.

If we were to work on the edge of the wood the tool could easily split the grain off, and it could be dangerous. By working from the face, however, we are not in line and when the waste flies off it only goes through the window. If your finished disc must have a good edge, either reverse the wood on the face plate, or go slowly, as it could break away a bit on going through.

From the above you will see that it is often desirable to work from the face rather than the edge in face-turning, and also to have the tool flat. In this way the grain of the wood is held from both sides, and so is cut across without splitting. A properly sharpened cross-cut saw uses the same principle. The point of each tooth cuts cleanly, and the wood is removed as sawdust by a bevel.

Unseasoned elm. Now recently it was my birthday, and it was so successful that I think I'll have another one soon, as so many boxes of sweets came. Well, some humbugs in a tin seem hygroscopic; that is, they like moisture (one of my men liked moisture too, but not water); and some wood, notably elm, is the same. We have to use heat to dry it out, though steam is used in the trade. On its own it just remains wet and goes rotten with fungus. It can be as much as half water by weight, yet elm, by its short grain and the fact that it does not split easily, is a good face-turning wood. Wood

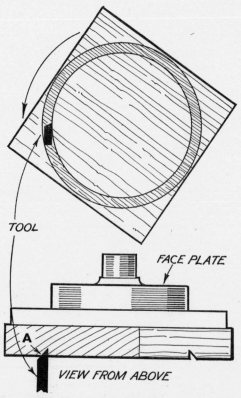

TOOL

FACE PLATE

A

VIEW FROM ABOVE

FIG. 9. TOOL USED FROM FACE RATHER THAN EDGE.
The tool is used with a scraping action, the cut at (A) being on the waste wood.

is best shaped to nearly the finished size, then seasoned and finished off. This, in the case of the elm, prevents fungus from starting, avoids surface splits, and allows for all sorts of warping and internal stresses. In its fresh state we can turn it easily. A 10-in. disc can shrink ⅝ in. or so, and lose half its weight in drying. When in business and roughing out elm bowls the sap was flung out by centrifugal force, and ran down the walls.

I think we can say with such a variety of wood to choose from and with such a lot of troubles it is heir to, wood can be extremely interesting. Each wood seems to have good and bad points, but so much wood in England has in the past been like Topsy in Uncle Tom's Cabin; it just growed. No doubt we do get unsuitable wood. English oak will easily split except where grown on boggy soil, whereas Austrian and Polish oak is ideal for carving or for turning bowls, and is very mellow. American oak is different again.

Ring shakes. In this one year's ring does not join on to the previous year's, and turned work can split lengthwise down that year in a way that will quite surprise you. Altogether, wood is a complex material, prone to all sorts of troubles, and our designs and work must allow for it. Some woods become quite brittle and short in the grain with age (mahogany does), and in this state can be weak for such purposes as legs, etc. Oak seems to improve with age, both in colour and working, but dead wood is of no use to turners, and some drying methods can cause this.

Some of my friends find that about six weeks in a warm airing cupboard is right for elm, but you can observe this for yourself better than I can advise, as conditions vary so.

POLISHING IN THE LATHE

(continued from page 163)

rather hard and not too wide an area, moving it slowly from one part of the bowl to the other as the lathe revolves, a sort of burnishing action of *once only*. If you start too soon, you just wipe it off; if too late, you have to bear too hard on to the work and burnt ribs of stuff result, but when you have found the knack it is extremely easy to get a quick shine. We sometimes used a pullover both on cellulose and shellac polish, and the action is that it softens the surface and by gentle holding of the rag smooths the surface better. The trouble when using a lathe for polishing is that you want eight or more in a row so that the work has time to harden a bit.

One last thought. A boy finished off with water may be far better to look at than someone done in a special beauty creation. So first a good surface, then a thin clear polish that does not hide the beauty.

In rather a famous church I noticed that the font cover, which was very elaborate, was covered with thick varnish. It was to strengthen it I was told. Personally I believe I've got to that stage when varnish is needed; I wish I was a boy.

CHAPTER 13 : DECORATIVE TURNERY

THIS is the name often given to turned items which are inlaid or built in various ways. The work is done almost entirely in the lathe, though for some operations the tool revolves and the work is pushed up to it. Some extremely attractive work can be made in this way, an example being given in Fig. 1. The main part of the bowl is of oak relieved with sycamore, with inlays of cocus and tulip

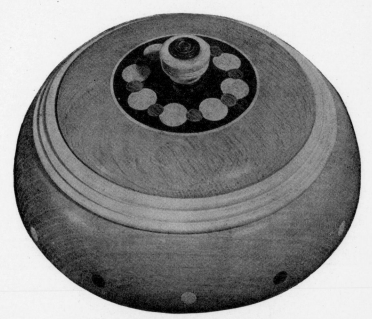

FIG. 1. ATTRACTIVE OAK BOWL AND LID WITH HARDWOOD INLAYS.
The entire work including the inlays can be done on the lathe.

wood. The whole process is carried out on the lathe. It makes a delightful bowl, extremely rich in appearance, and is excellent practice in careful, accurate turning.

As a good deal of work is put into the bowl it is well worth while to make sure that the timber is of first quality, sound, nicely figured, and seasoned. It would be annoying later to have trouble due to

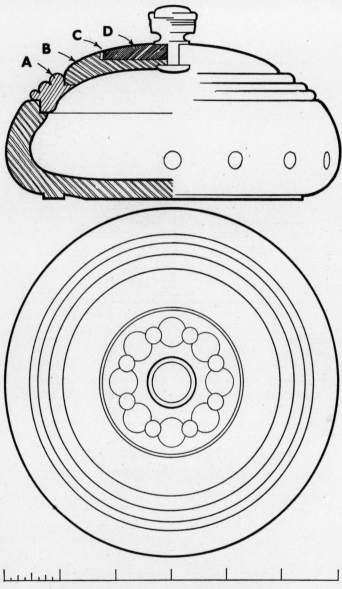

FIG. 2. ELEVATION IN PART SECTION AND PLAN.
A. Sycamore.   B. Oak.   C. Sycamore.   D. Cocus.

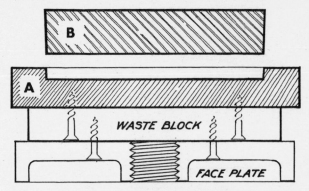

FIG. 3. FIRST STAGE, OAK PIECE (B) BEING LET INTO RECESS
TURNED IN SYCAMORE (A).

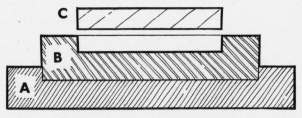

FIG. 4. SYCAMORE INLAY (C) RECESSED INTO OAK (B).

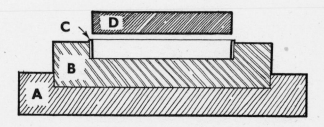

FIG. 5. COCUS DISC (D) RECESSED INTO SYCAMORE (C).

movement. Since the majority of the work is put into the lid it is advisable to make this first and turn the bowl to it.

Lid. From Fig. 2 it will be seen that the lid consists of a ring of sycamore (A) beaded in section with a main oak portion (B) let into it. Within this again is a ring of sycamore (C) encircling a cocus portion (D), this being inlaid with inlays of sycamore and tulip.

Begin by turning the oak piece (B). Fix a waste piece of hardwood to the face plate with screws, turn its face true, and glue the oak to it with a piece of newspaper interposed. Turn the oak to the finished size with the edges *very* slightly tapered towards the side to be glued. Lever away from the waste and clean off the paper.

Now prepare the sycamore (A), cutting out a disc of ¾-in. stuff to finish 5¼ in. diameter. Fix it to a piece of waste hardwood with screws driven through the latter as in Fig. 3. Put the screws well

FIG. 6. SPECIAL
SCRAPING TOOL
FOR   TURNING
SMALL   BEADS.

in from the edge in positions where they will be removed when the inside is turned later. Fix the waste to the face plate with screws. Once again the waste piece must be trued up beforehand by turning it before fixing the sycamore. Turn the latter slightly full in size and form a recess in it as at (A), Fig. 3 to receive the oak (B). The edges of the recess should be at a slight angle to align with those of the oak, but the latter must bed right down. The simplest way is to turn the recess slightly small and gradually enlarge it to take the oak, constantly trying the latter in position for size. Leave the sycamore in position on the face plate.

Glue in the oak, and when dry turn a recess to receive the sycamore (C) as in Fig. 4. Once again glue in and, when set, turn a further recess to receive the cocus disc (D), Fig. 5. The sycamore ring can be a bare $\frac{1}{16}$ in. wide. Both (C) and (D) are turned on the screw chuck. Glue in (D), and the whole is then ready for turning to the finished shape. Turn to the main curve first, and nick in where the sycamore separates from the oak. It is advisable to use scraping tools throughout. A special tool can be ground to form the beads as in Fig. 6.

All the inlaid circles in Fig. 2 are centred on a common circle.

To ensure their being correct turn a scratch (no more) in the correct position. The large inlays are put in first, and their centres are best marked by stepping around the scratched ring with dividers. It is advisable to prick the final marks deeply. Place a centre bit with round shank in the lathe, using the drill chuck or self-centering chuck. Hold the work by hand so that its surface is as near as possible square with the bit. It is a help to bring up the back centre to steady and position the work. Bore each hole about ⅛ in. deep.

The inlays can be turned in a row between centres as in Fig. 7. Note that the grain runs crosswise. Separate them and glue them into their holes so that they stand proud. When dry turn down level and bore the holes for the smaller inlays. Glue in as before, and turn finally to the finished shape. Also bore the centre hole for the handle. Note that in the entire process the work has not been

FIG. 7. TURNING IN-LAY.
Note direction of grain.

removed from the face plate. Parts (C) and (D) can be turned on the screw chuck, or held in any other convenient way.

To turn the inside to shape fix a waste piece to the face plate, and turn a recess in it to take the lid. The curve need not align closely, but there should be an accurate fit at the edge. Fix with a bolt passed through the centre hole. Turn down to shape, leaving a "pillar" at the middle. Finally turn in a recess to receive the hiding button. When the bolt is removed the pillar can be snapped off, levelled, and the button glued in.

Bowl. This calls for no special instructions. The best way is to fix the wood with the top against the face plate and turn the base with its rim and recess for the leather facing. It is removed, and a waste block screwed to the face plate. A recess is turned in this to take the rim (accurate fit), and the bowl glued in with waste paper interposed so that it can be levered away later. This enables the sides and the inside to be turned. The dots are bored and inlaid similarly to those of the lid.

Built-up bowl. Another popular form of decorative bowl in which a number of small pieces of wood are glued together is that shown in Fig. 8. The segments are assembled in layers and these glued together. An almost unlimited variety of designs is possible.

The way in which the parts are assembled is the chief factor in the resulting pattern. That shown in Fig. 8 is one of the simplest. There are three rings, each of twelve pieces mitred together. In the assembling of the rings the joints are staggered, so that the pieces lie above each other brick fashion. One advantage of the method is that it enables oddments of wood to be used up.

In the bowl in Fig. 8 only two different kinds of wood are used.

FIG. 8. BUILT-UP BOWL SHOWING THE "BRICKS"
This is a simple pattern with three layers, each of twelve "bricks." More elaborate designs could be worked out on the same principle.

Any number could be employed, each ring having its own particular woods, or they could be distributed generally. One important point is to avoid using woods of widely varying hardness, as this may cause difficulty in the turning owing to the tool pressing more into the soft woods than the hard ones. Apart from this the choice is unlimited. It is always an advantage to have an even number of pieces to each ring for a reason that will appear later.

Setting out. To enable the sizes and angles to be ascertained a full-size drawing such as that in Fig. 9 is needed. In this particular instance there are twelve pieces to each ring, but this could be increased for a larger bowl. The section will reveal the width required for the blocks to enable the shape to be worked. Be

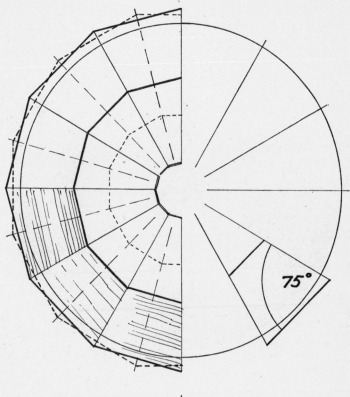

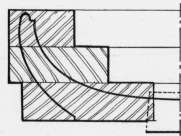

FIG. 9. PLAN AND SECTIONAL ELEVATION.

It is advisable to set out these in full size so that the sizes of the layers can be ascertained.

generous in this, because it is difficult to centre the bowl exactly and a little latitude is a safeguard.

Cutting the blocks. Assuming that you are using twelve blocks per ring the ends of all pieces will be cut off at 75°. If you have a circular saw the cutting is simple. It is merely a matter of setting the mitre gauge to the required angle and cutting one end of all the pieces. A stop is then attached to the table, the wood pressed up to

FIG. 10. THE GLUED-UP ASSEMBLY READY FOR TURNING.
Each layer is glued up independently and the surfaces levelled. All three are then put together.

it, and the cut made. If you are making a number of bowls, and are using strip material, you have only to reverse the wood after each cut, press it up to the stop, and repeat the process. The angle is the same, of course. If a fairly small-toothed saw is used, or if a planer saw is used, the parts can be glued up without further attention, though it is obviously necessary for the angle to be accurately set.

In the case of handwork a mitre box will have to be used, this having kerfs specially sawn in it at the required angle. When strip material is being used one end of all the strips is sawn first. A piece of wood with one end sawn to the required angle to form a stop is nailed to the bottom of the box as in Fig. 11 (A). The wood is held up to this and a cut made at the kerf. After removing the required block the strip is turned over, pushed up to the stop, and the process

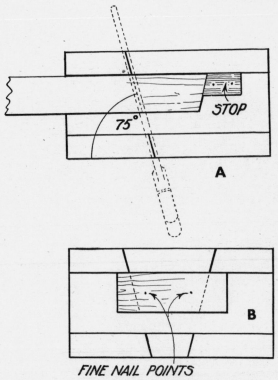

FIG. 11. SAWING MITRES OF BLOCKS BY HAND.
For strip mitreing follow method (A). When small oddments
are being used follow method (B).

repeated. In this way a single kerf in the box enables all the cuts to be made.

When oddments of wood are used all the pieces are brought to the same width first, and the method at (B), Fig. 11, followed. The kerfs are positioned so that their distance apart gives the required length. When the parts for the lower ring of the bowl (which are shorter) are being sawn a parallel packing piece can be placed at the back of the box. If the wood shows any tendency to move, a couple of nails can be partly driven into the bottom of the box, nipped off short, and the projections filed to a sharp point.

For a really good job the ends of the pieces should be trimmed on the mitre shooting board as in Fig. 12. Little more than a single shaving is needed.

Assembling. Each ring is glued up independently on a flat board with paper beneath to prevent it from sticking. The parts are rubbed together, and the simplest way is to assemble each ring

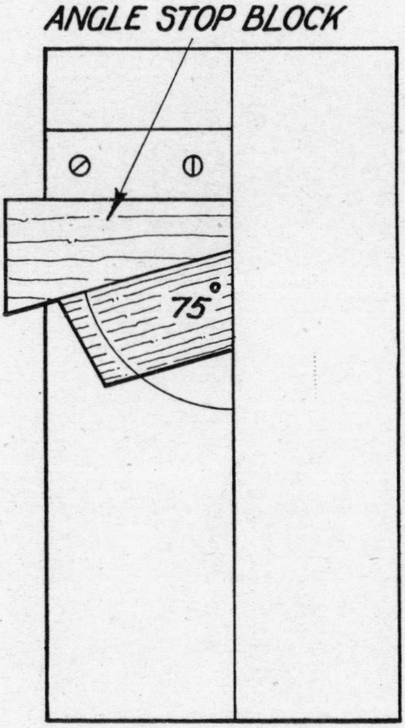

ANGLE STOP BLOCK

FIG. 12. SHOOTING BOARD FOR
TRIMMING MITRES.
The angle stop block is tapered to give a reading of 75° (or whatever angle is needed).

75°

in two halves.   When the glue has set, each half ring is placed on the shooting board and the joints trimmed as in Fig. 13.   Since the rear of the plane bears on the other end of the half ring the joint is bound to be true.   This is much simpler than attempting to glue the whole in one operation, since it is always awkward to trim and insert the last piece.   The slightest inaccuracy in the mitres can throw the whole thing out.   This is the reason why an even number of pieces is an advantage.

When all three rings are together the surfaces are trued up with the plane and glued together, cramps being used.   To prevent the parts from floating out of position on the wet glue a few positioning nails can be tapped in as in Fig. 14.   Fig. 10 shows the completed assembly.

Turning.   The outside is turned first, and the work can be mounted on the face plate and held with screws as at (A), Fig. 15. The bulk of the waste can be removed with a small gouge, but scrap-

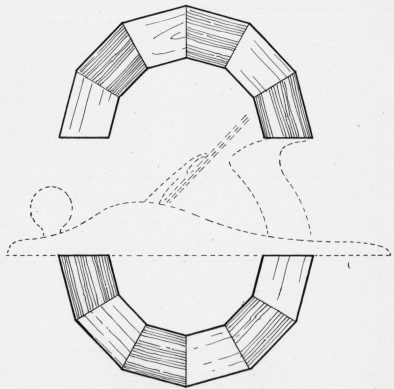

FIG. 13. HOW LAYERS ARE ASSEMBLED IN HALVES.
This enables the last mitres to be trimmed easily with the plane.

ing tools ground from old files are needed to finish off.   Since one half of each block will be turned against the grain a fine cut is essential for finishing.   Most woods can be scraped with the tool straight from the grinding wheel.   The burr set up when the edge is ground helps the cut.   Other woods may need the finer edge given by oilstoning; in other cases it is an advantage to actually turn up an edge much as a cabinet scraper is sharpened.   Turn the whole thing to shape, then go over again taking fine cuts only.

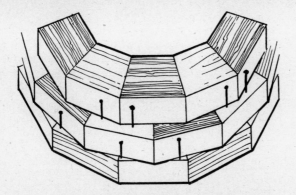

FIG. 14. NAILS USED TO POSITION LAYERS WHEN ASSEMBLING.

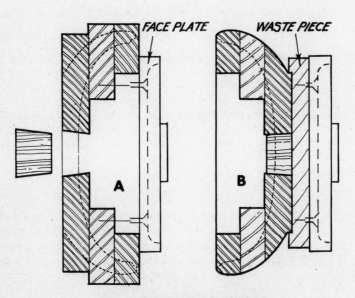

FACE PLATE   *WASTE PIECE*

A

B

FIG. 15. TWO STAGES IN TURNING

The outside is turned first and a bottom plug inserted as at (A). To complete the inside turn a recess in a waste piece to take the base as at (B).

The hole at the bottom is turned to a regular circle and is slightly tapered (Fig. 15, A). A block is turned independently to fit it and glued in. Make sure that it is a close fit inside as it is here that the joint shows. Level this when dry and remove from the face plate.

To turn the inside a waste piece is attached to the face plate with screws and a recess turned in it to take the bottom rim of the bowl as in Fig. 15 (B). It is glued in with newspaper interposed to enable it to be removed easily later. Turn with scraping tools as before and finish with glasspaper. If the lathe has reversible drive it is an advantage in taking out any slight roughness left by the tool in working against the grain. The bowl can be finished with the special french polish made for the lathe applied whilst work revolves slowly. A certain knack is necessary for this since it is essential to know when to stop. It is burnished with saliva from the mouth applied with a pad. Alternatively wax polish can be used. A useful compromise is to lightly body the bowl with french polish and finish with wax.

CHAPTER 14 : POLISHING

POLISHING is a beauty treatment, and intended to bring out the beauty *already there*; to enhance the grain so that we can enjoy a marvel of the Creator as shown in wood. It is needed, too, for protection, to encase the object in a transparent film that will handle nicely and also to seal the grain against changes in the air, for wood is liable to swell, shrink, warp, and so on.

Let us consider a bowl on the lathe needing this beauty treatment. You have of course turned it beautifully, no ribs or sore places, and hand scraped those troublesome parts, and used glasspaper to get a nice clean surface. Now (with boys at least) beauty treatment starts with water. It raises the grain, and we can lightly glasspaper it afterwards or use a hand scraper to get it smooth again (use a scrubbing brush on boys). It may well be that this only presses the grain down again, so a coat of shellac polish to set the fibres will help to make them firm against this glasspapering or hand scraping. If you wish to stain the work, this would rather upset matters, but for more instructions in this consult *Staining and Polishing*, a companion handbook.

My aim so far is to have a clean open-grained surface (if the wood has any) so that boiled linseed oil or olive oil, if it is a salad bowl, can penetrate. You can use furniture creams or beeswax and turpentine, for the purpose is to give "life" to the wood and to seal the grain too. Some woods are so close-grained that this does not happen; box, for instance, may well be left alone, with just a coat of polish for clean handling.

French polish. I'm old fashioned and like ordinary french polish afterwards or for a final coat to seal in what we have used first. You must not run the lathe too long, or too fast, as it will burn the surface and cause ribs of dirty polish which will need to be cleaned off. The heat generated will also force the first coats to go further into the grain, and give the work a hungry look.

It may well be you would like a filled surface. A light papering after you have put the first coat of oil, or wax on, will do that for the dust forms a filler. There are several friction polishes on the market, and we used one at the works for cheap jobs. You just brush it on, and when nearly dry hold a cloth on rather firmly to burnish it as the work revolves.

Wax. Carnauba wax is one that can be obtained in various coloured chunks from dark brown to light. At one handicraft exhibition I saw some lovely turned work finished off in this alone, but I did wonder if the glossy surface would stand up well to use. It is a very hard wax, and when you cut it with a knife it fractures rather like a stone. My opinion is that used sparingly on hard close-grained wood it gives a marvellous finish, but if put on too thick would chip off. So it does seem that something to soften it is desirable, and is probably the trade secret of some of the polishes we can buy. Beeswax takes a lot of beating, and I put the paste inside a cloth and hold it onto the revolving work. This does not waste much, and the heat generated helps to force it into the grain It can leave the surface a bit grubby but a light use of shellac polish would alter that.

Cellulose. So far I have not mentioned cellulose, although at one time I used twenty-five gallons a week. Handles were dipped into a tank of it and withdrawn in five minutes or so by a young lady. The job was to turn a handle one revolution in five minutes and this lifted a board with handles hanging down from the tank. Now this is all mentioned because some jobs can be dipped into a container and withdrawn, but the trouble is that the outside surface forms a skin and the liquid slips down underneath forming lumps, but it is a process used for some turned work.

I have seen cellulose used too most successfully on elm bowls. You just brush plenty on of clear cellulose, and then at the right moment run the lathe at a medium speed. You hold a cloth on

(continued on page 149)

INDEX